CONTENTS

ILLUSTRATIONS

The illustrations are from the British Library copy of Jacques Callot, *Balli de Sfessania*, published by C. Allard, Amsterdam, 1690.

OXFORD WORLD'S CLASSICS

THE GOLDEN POT
AND OTHER TALES

ERNST THEODOR WILHELM HOFFMANN (1776–1822) was born in Königsberg, the birthplace also of Kant and Herder. He studied law and held several administrative posts in the Prussian civil service. His enthusiasm for music, which led him to replace the name 'Wilhelm' with 'Amadeus' in honour of Mozart, also encouraged him to attempt a career as an orchestral conductor and composer for the theatre in Bamberg, where he became assistant to the director of the theatre. After a spell as conductor in Dresden, where he composed his opera *Undine*, he found himself obliged to re-enter the civil service as a judge in Berlin. He died in 1822 of liver disease, degeneration of the spinal marrow, and paralysis.

Hoffmann turned seriously to fiction, as a way of supplementing a scanty and irregular income, in 1814. In that year he wrote *The Golden Pot*, which both he and posterity recognized as his masterpiece, and began the Gothic thriller *The Devil's Elixirs*. There followed another novel, *Life and Opinions of Murr the Cat*, and a large number of stories. These include tales of terror and the supernatural, of which *The Sandman* is the most famous example, and elaborate and humorous fairy-tales, such as *Princess Brambilla* and *Master Flea*. Many other tales attest Hoffmann's skill at psychological exploration within a realistic setting: these are represented here by *My Cousin's Corner Window*. Of all the German Romantics he is the writer whose reputation among the general reading public has endured most strongly.

RITCHIE ROBERTSON is Reader in German at Oxford University and a Fellow of St John's College. He has published *Kafka: Judaism, Politics, and Literature* (OUP, 1985), *Heine* (1988), *The 'Jewish Question' in German Literature, 1749–1939* (OUP, 1999) and edited *The German–Jewish Dialogue* for Oxford World's Classics.

OXFORD WORLD'S CLASSICS

*For over 100 years Oxford World's Classics have brought
readers closer to the world's great literature. Now with over 700
titles—from the 4,000-year-old myths of Mesopotamia to the
twentieth century's greatest novels—the series makes available
lesser-known as well as celebrated writing.*

*The pocket-sized hardbacks of the early years contained
introductions by Virginia Woolf, T. S. Eliot, Graham Greene,
and other literary figures which enriched the experience of reading.
Today the series is recognized for its fine scholarship and
reliability in texts that span world literature, drama and poetry,
religion, philosophy and politics. Each edition includes perceptive
commentary and essential background information to meet the
changing needs of readers.*

OXFORD WORLD'S CLASSICS

E. T. A. HOFFMANN

The Golden Pot
and Other Tales

Translated with an Introduction and Notes by
RITCHIE ROBERTSON

OXFORD
UNIVERSITY PRESS

OXFORD
UNIVERSITY PRESS

Great Clarendon Street, Oxford OX2 6DP

Oxford University Press is a department of the University of Oxford.
It furthers the University's objective of excellence in research, scholarship,
and education by publishing worldwide in

Oxford New York

Athens Auckland Bangkok Bogotá Buenos Aires Calcutta
Cape Town Chennai Dar es Salaam Delhi Florence Hong Kong Istanbul
Karachi Kuala Lumpur Madrid Melbourne Mexico City Mumbai
Nairobi Paris São Paulo Singapore Taipei Tokyo Toronto Warsaw

with associated companies in Berlin Ibadan

Oxford is a registered trade mark of Oxford University Press
in the UK and in certain other countries

Published in the United States
by Oxford University Press Inc., New York

First published as a World's Classics paperback 1992
Reissued as an Oxford World's Classics paperback 2000
Reissued 2008

British Library Cataloguing in Publication Data

Data available

Library of Congress Cataloging in Publication Data

Hoffmann, E. T. A. (Ernest Theodor Amadeus), 1776–1822.
The golden pot, and other tales / E. T. A. Hoffmann;
translated and edited by Ritchie Robertson.
(Oxford world's classics)
Includes bibliographical references.
1. Hoffmann, E. T. A. (Ernest Theodor Amadeus), 1776–1822.
Translations, English. I. Robertson, Ritchie. II. Title. III. Series.
PT2361.E4R634 1992 833'.6—dc20 91–583

ISBN 978–0–19–955247–4

1

Printed in Great Britain by
Clays Ltd, St Ives plc

INTRODUCTION

IN the account of German Romanticism he wrote for the French
public in the 1830s, Heinrich Heine informed his readers:
'Hoffmann is now not at all in fashion in Germany, but he used
to be. In his time he was much read, but only by people whose
nerves were too strong or too weak to be affected by gentle
chords.' Heine further indicates Hoffmann's contemporary
reputation by depicting him chiefly as an author of horror
stories, whose works are 'a hideous shriek of terror in twenty
volumes'. Poetic souls, Heine continues, had less time for
Hoffmann than for the arch-Romantic Novalis.

But in all honesty [*Heine concludes*] Hoffmann was much more important
than Novalis as a poet. For the latter, with his idealistic figures, is always
floating in the blue air, while Hoffmann, with all his bizarre grotesques,
still always keeps a firm grip on earthly reality. As the giant Antaeus
remained unconquerably strong when he kept one foot on Mother Earth,
and lost his power as soon as Hercules raised him aloft: so the poet, too,
is strong and powerful so long as he does not leave the firm ground of
reality, and he becomes impotent as soon as he floats around rhapsodically
in the blue air.[1]

The stories I have chosen for this collection include only one
horror story, *The Sandman*. My aim has been to illustrate a
different side of Hoffmann's genius by concentrating on his
fairy-tales. The three longest tales in this volume, *The Golden
Pot*, *Princess Brambilla*, and *Master Flea*, are all tales of the
supernatural; but, despite some alarming incidents, they are
humorous, not blood-curdling. The humour comes from the
incongruity of supernatural beings at large in an ostentatiously
everyday world. The subtitle of *The Golden Pot*, 'A Modern
Fairy-Tale', could also apply to the others. All are set in
Hoffmann's own times: *The Golden Pot* in contemporary Dresden, *Master Flea* in Frankfurt, and *Princess Brambilla* in Rome
at an indeterminate period, suggesting the late eighteenth

---

[1] H. Heine, *Die Romantische Schule*, in *Sämtliche Schriften*, ed. Klaus Briegleb, 6
vols. (Munich, 1968–76), iii. 440–1.

century. As Heine said, Hoffmann's fantasies are firmly anchored in reality; and this separates him from the first generation of German Romantics, represented by Novalis, who were attracted by the idealism of Fichte and its claims for the creative authority of the mind. 'We dream of journeys through the universe,' Novalis wrote; 'is not the universe in us? We do not know the depths of our mind. The mysterious path leads inwards. Eternity with its worlds, the past and future are in us or nowhere'.[2] Although Hoffmann's undoubted admiration for Novalis has left many traces in his writings, he transfers the emphasis from the inner to the outer world. In these tales, however, the interplay of inner and outer realities is more complicated than Heine acknowledges, and the status of each is continually called into question.

The relations of reality and fantasy are different in each tale, and my selection is intended to disclose a development in Hoffmann's treatment of this theme. *The Golden Pot* (1814) ends with the triumph of the imagination: its hero takes up his abode in Atlantis, the world of poetry. *The Sandman*, which was written almost two years later, is a negative counterpart in which the hero's imagination propels him into madness and suicide. *Princess Brambilla* (1820) uses the familiar image of the theatre in a highly unfamiliar way to complicate the relations between reality and fantasy and to recommend the acceptance of everyday reality, however modest. *Master Flea* (written in the winter of 1821–2) concludes with a more decided rejection of fantasy: the hero finds happiness in a domestic idyll that anticipates the cosier side of Dickens. *My Cousin's Corner Window* treats this theme differently: it is a wholly realistic tale with no supernatural admixture; the imagination of the crippled poet, the 'cousin' of the title, is applied to the day-to-day life he sees below his windows in the centre of Berlin. It is one of Hoffmann's last stories: he sent the fair copy to his publisher on 14 April 1822, three months before his death.

This transfer of emphasis from fantasy to everyday reality may be called, in terms of German literary history, a development from Romanticism to Biedermeier. The Romantics dreamt of changing the very nature of human existence: 'Our life is not a dream,' said Novalis, 'but it can and perhaps will become one.'[3] The dominant tendency among Biedermeier writers, those who wrote in the period 1815–48, is to reject such aspirations and to settle for the modest possibilities of happiness available in one's immediate world. This may sound rather tame; but Friedrich Sengle, whose massive *Biedermeierzeit* is perhaps the masterpiece of post-war German literary scholarship, has shown that in the major writers of the time this process of adjustment involves heroic efforts to sustain a self and a world threatened by conflict and fragmentation. In this perspective, conservative writers like Grillparzer or Mörike turn out to have much in common with their radical contemporaries Heine and Büchner. It is no disparagement, therefore, to see the later Hoffmann as a Biedermeier writer.[4]

In much of Hoffmann's fiction, the relation between reality and the imagination follows what he calls the Serapiontic principle. When living in Berlin, Hoffmann belonged to an informal circle called the Serapion Brethren, because it was founded on 14 November 1818, the feast-day of St Serapion. In 1819–21 he published four series of stories under the general title *The Serapion Brethren*, in which the stories are related and discussed by members of the circle. Early in the first volume one member recounts his meeting with Count P., who was living as a hermit in a wood near Bamberg and claimed to be none other than St Serapion, an early Christian martyr. 'Serapion' further claimed that he was in the Egyptian desert, and that the towers of Bamberg, visible in the distance, were those of Alexandria. When challenged, he asserted that the mind held absolute supremacy over the organs of perception, implying that if the two differed the mind must always be right. The Brethren conclude that 'Serapion' possessed a true poetic imagination, but went astray in assigning absolute authority to the visions of his inner world:

[3] Ibid. 461.

[4] Friedrich Sengle, *Biedermeierzeit*, 3 vols. (Stuttgart, 1971–80). The term 'Biedermeier' is applied to 19th-cent. English literature in Mario Praz, *The Hero in Eclipse in Victorian Fiction*, tr. Angus Davidson (London, 1956), and more generally by Virgil Nemoianu, *The Taming of Romanticism: European Literature and the Age of Biedermeier* (Cambridge, Mass., 1984).

Poor Serapion, your madness consisted only in the fact that some hostile
star deprived you of the awareness of the duality by which our entire
earthly existence is governed. There does exist an inner world, and so does
the spiritual power of beholding it in full clarity, in the supreme brilliance
of active life; but it is our earthly birthright that the external world in
which we are lodged serves as the lever that sets that power in motion.
Inner phenomena are absorbed into the circle formed around us by external
phenomena, and which our minds can only transcend in dark, mysterious
intuitions that never become distinct images.[5]

'Serapion' did not realize that we cannot behold the reality
transcending the empirical world; we can at most apprehend it
faintly. The imagination, a power within us, has to be activated
by the external world; and what it shows us is our external
reality, but with a clarity that comes from within. The Serapion
Brethren resolve to exploit this duality in setting their stories
in the external world while endowing them with a vividness
that comes from the faculty of inner vision; and this duality is
Hoffmann's Serapiontic principle.

This principle raises the unanswerable question of where to
draw the boundary between inner and outer reality. The uncertainty of the boundary pervades Hoffmann's stories. We are
constantly in doubt about the limits of reality. Is Lindhorst in
The Golden Pot an archivist or an elemental spirit? When he
suddenly vanishes at the end of the Fourth Vigil, does he really
fly away in the form of a kite? Is the old woman an earth-spirit,
a nursemaid, or a mangel-wurzel, or all three? We need not
answer these questions; what Hoffmann's stories invite us to do
is to accept and enjoy their perpetual bewildering interplay of
reality and imagination. They correspond to Tzvetan Todorov's
definition of fantastic literature, in which 'the text must oblige
the reader to consider the world of the characters as a world of
living persons and to hesitate between a natural and a supernatural explanation of the events described'.[6]

[5] E. T. A. Hoffmann, *Die Serapions-Brüder* (Munich, 1963), 54.
[6] *The Fantastic: A Structural Approach to a Literary Genre*, tr. Richard Howard
(Ithaca, NY, 1975), 33.

The Golden Pot

Underlying the action of *The Golden Pot* we can see a familiar fairy-tale plot. A young man must win the girl he loves by passing a test set by her father. The test is the copying of manuscripts which Anselmus undertakes for Archivist Lindhorst, in order to prove his fitness to marry Serpentina. Moreover, the hero is caught up in a conflict between good and evil powers (the Archivist versus the apple-woman), and his test consists not only in faultless calligraphy but in maintaining his loyalty to the good. For Anselmus, loyalty consists in believing in the supernatural reality represented by the green snakes, something quite incongruous with the mundane world of Dresden and the Paulmann family. And yet the worldly Veronica resorts to magic in order to win Anselmus as a husband. Influenced by her and the apple-woman, Anselmus lapses into temporary disbelief in the supernatural: he enters the Archivist's house in a prosaic frame of mind, in which the talking birds seem to be mere chattering sparrows, and in which he is no longer capable of copying properly, makes a blot on the original, and is punished by confinement in a crystal bottle. His fellow-prisoners resemble the hermit Serapion in having abandoned the duality of the inner and outer worlds: they believe that they are leading lives of pleasure in Dresden, and ridicule Anselmus for pointing out that they are in fact enclosed in bottles.

The fairy-tale plot visible beneath these ramifications owes much to Hoffmann's experience in the theatre between 1808 and 1816. One of the many operas he conducted was Mozart's *The Magic Flute*, in which Tamino is obliged to survive tests in order to be united with Pamina. The tests are imposed on him by Sarastro, who as a wise old man resembles Lindhorst, and who also has a female antagonist, the Queen of the Night. When finally vanquished, the Queen of the Night and her attendants sink into the ground: like the apple-woman, they are associated not only with night but with the base earthy realm. Tamino, like Anselmus, has to learn—in his case, that the Queen of the Night is evil and that Sarastro embodies goodness and wisdom; unlike Anselmus he passes all his tests. Other models include Hensler's romantic opera *The Lady from the Danube* (1798), in which the hero is torn between his earthly bride and an affectionate water-nixie, who eventually seduces him on his wedding-day; her emergence from the Danube recalls the appearance of the snakes beneath the surface of the Elbe, and Anselmus's comparison of them to Sirens. Finally, we must not forget Hoffmann's own opera *Undine*, composed in Dresden, and taken from the famous story by his friend Fouqué; it concerns a water-nixie who gains an immortal soul by winning the love of human being.[7]

In his modern fairy-tale Hoffmann juxtaposed fantasy and reality. He intended it to be 'fairy-like and wondrous, but stepping boldly into ordinary everyday life.'[8] *The Golden Pot* is set in an ordinary German town, inhabited by unimaginative bureaucrats and Philistines (a word derived from German student slang, denoting the unbelieving enemies of the chosen people, the town as opposed to the gown). However, we need to qualify this antithesis. Although the hero is a student, the Philistine characters, even Sub-Rector Paulmann and Registrary Heerbrand, are not portrayed with hostility. Though prosaic, they are kindly, generous, and convivial; Sub-Rector Paulmann composes music, and Veronica sings it. They will never enter Atlantis, but they approach poetic inspiration when intoxicated by punch. And Veronica does enter the world of magic, though she withdraws in time and devotes herself to the pleasure of being a Counsellor's lady.

Moreover, the 'reality' of the Dresden setting is itself a wishful fantasy. Hoffmann's Dresden, where *The Golden Pot* was written between November 1813 and February 1814, was not the peaceful city of the story. Saxony was the setting for the final campaign between Napoleonic France and Prussia, the latter supported by Russia and (from August 1813) by Austria. When Hoffmann reached Dresden in April 1813, the city and its surroundings were swarming with troops. On 8 May he

---

[7] On *Undine* see *E. T. A. Hoffmann's Musical Writings*, tr. Martyn Clarke, ed. David Charlton (Cambridge, 1989), 184–5.

[8] Letter to Kunz, 19 Aug. 1813, in Hoffmann, *Briefwechsel*, i. 408.

witnessed Napoleon's entry into Dresden. Russian troops were still occupying the far bank of the Elbe. Bullets and shells were exchanged; Hoffmann himself was grazed by a bullet. On 26 August Napoleon gained a victory just outside Dresden. Hoffmann visited the corpse-strewn battlefield and described it in his 'Vision on the Battlefield of Dresden'. The French held Dresden until they capitulated to the Prussian besiegers on 11 November, subjecting the inhabitants to famine and disease. Bodies were piled on carts. 'To see Frenchmen dying miserably in the street was quite commonplace', Hoffmann recalled.[9] The pleasure-gardens around the city were ravaged, the trees lining the avenues (like that leading to Linke's Restaurant) were chopped down. Not for nothing is Anselmus denied entry to 'Linke's paradise'. The 'reality' of *The Golden Pot* is itself an inaccessible paradise.

The 'real' events of *The Golden Pot* are entwined with a supernatural world populated by elemental spirits. Although his daughters appear as snakes, we should not imagine the salamander Lindhorst as a kind of lizard. When he appears as a salamander he is clearly a majestic figure. He is one of the elemental spirits described in the book by the Abbé Villars de Montfaucon, *Le Comte de Gabalis ou Entretiens des sciences secrètes* (Paris, 1670), best known to the anglophone reader for having provided Pope with the mythological apparatus of *The Rape of the Lock*. According to this account, the element of fire is inhabited by salamanders, air by sylphs, water by nymphs, and earth by gnomes. Serpentina has something both nymph-like and sylph-like about her. Her father the salamander, however, presides over the action of *The Golden Pot*, just as fire pervades the story's texture as the symbol of passion and of creation.[10]

The 'reality' of Dresden is also set against an elaborate and, on first reading, rather obscure myth.[11] The first phase in the

---

[9] *Briefwechsel*, i. 418.

[10] This association of fire and water has been named 'the Hoffmann complex': see Gastón Bachelard, *The Psychoanalysis of Fire*, tr. Alan C. M. Ross (London, 1987), ch. 6.

[11] Hoffmann's main source was G. H. Schubert, *Ansichten von der Nachtseite der Naturwissenschaften* (Dresden, 1808), where 'Atlantis' is the name given to man's original state of harmony with nature.

myth is recounted by Lindhorst. In the beginning, the world arises from water at the behest of the spirit. But even the natural world contains a restless, creative principle, represented by the black hill, which, when touched by the sun's rays, produces a fiery lily. The lily, as the perfection of nature, desires an existence higher than mere nature can afford, and hence falls in love with the youth Phosphorus, the spiritual principle of light. The union of nature with spirit results in the lily's death. In her *Liebestod*, however, she gives birth to a new being—thought, or consciousness, which cannot find a home in the world and roams through infinite space. It is captured by the black dragon, which, being akin to the mineral world, symbolizes the lower, sensual aspect of nature. The lily is reborn, but is now estranged both from her spiritual goal (Phosphorus) and from her former unity with nature: consciousness torments her and destroys the surrounding natural world. This represents the human condition: we are cut off from the past, now that we are alienated by consciousness from primeval harmony with nature; but we are also cut off from the future, since we are still dependent on our senses and thus alienated from the ultimate spiritual goal towards which we are striving. This twofold alienation is overcome by the victory of Phosphorus, the higher spiritual principle, over the dragon, the lower sensual principle. The lily is freed, *not* from thought, but from her twofold state of alienation. Nature and spirit are reunited in love. This, however, is not the intuitive union with which the myth began; the audible homage of nature's exultant chorus hints that the participants in this unity are now self-aware. Thus the myth is dialectical. Instead of moving in a circle from original unity to its restoration, it moves in a spiral from original unity to the recreation of that unity on a higher plane, enhanced by consciousness.

This basic narrative is twice repeated. On the second occasion the protagonist is the salamander who assumes the guise of Archivist Lindhorst. On the third occasion it is Anselmus himself. Lindhorst's story is recounted by Serpentina in the Eighth Vigil. Like Phosphorus in the original myth, he falls in love, but finds that the consummation of his love destroys his beloved, the green snake; in despair he ravages the garden.

Although the salamander is permitted reunion with the green snake, he is condemned to estrangement from Atlantis, and although he remembers his primal state, he must share the estrangement of mankind 'in that unhappy time when the degenerate race of men will no longer understand the language of nature'. An essential stage in his escape from alienation is his combat with the old woman who, born of a union between a feather from the black dragon's wing and a mangel-wurzel, belongs to the base, sensual side of nature.

Anselmus, the protagonist in the third cycle, possesses a faint intuitive recollection of man's primal harmony with nature, in the form of a child-like poetic spirit which makes him clumsy and inept in the everyday world. His imagination enables him to love Serpentina and to copy the Archivist's Oriental manuscripts, which are themselves the story of the salamander and the green snake. The increasing ease with which he copies them shows that he is developing as a poet: for poetry is, in a sense, only copying, the rewriting of a primal myth. Like Phosphorus and Lindhorst, however, Anselmus is tempted and falls. His punishment, confinement in the crystal glass, is also a loss of vision; but on being freed and united with Serpentina, he receives a symbol of higher vision, the golden pot. The pot, made by the benevolent earth-spirit, is a material object, though of a noble metal. In its reflection, as in the Archivist's ring, Anselmus perceives the snake with whom he is in love. It reveals the hidden reality inaccessible to the conventionally minded. Its counterpart and parody is the metal mirror made by the apple-woman, which shows Veronica the object of her desire—Anselmus.

What, finally, was the winged being that was born of the union between the salamander and the green snake? If the first *Liebestod* gave birth to thought (*der Gedanke*), this is more than thought: it is insight (*Erkenntnis*), an active, dynamic awareness of the harmony of being. This confirms that Hoffmann's myth moves in the appropriately serpentine fashion of a spiral. Anselmus's story continues and amplifies that of Phosphorus. At the end, a fiery lily grows from the golden pot, symbolizing the insight into the harmony of nature which Anselmus has attained. Moreover, the Hoffmann-like narrator implicitly shows the reader how to continue the spiral. Anselmus's happiness, according to this narrator, is nothing other than 'life in poetry'. By writing about him, the narrator participates in that life; and we can do so too by reading the story in the proper spirit of imaginative receptiveness. Thus the spiral coils on, out of Hoffmann's text and into the consciousness of the reader.

The Sandman

It has often been pointed out that *The Sandman*, written in November 1815 and revised in the following months, is a mirror-image of *The Golden Pot*. Everything that in *The Golden Pot* was enchanting and desirable is here distorted into its opposite. The story again centres on a young man with a poetic temperament, placed between two women, one of whom belongs firmly to the everyday world while the other is unfamiliar and alluring. The latter, Olimpia, is presented as the daughter of the scientist Professor Spalanzani, a 'wise old man' figure corresponding to Archivist Lindhorst. Nathanael recalls Anselmus when he justifies his infatuation with Olimpia by saying: 'It is only to the poetic soul that a similarly organized soul reveals itself!' Yet Olimpia, as everyone else suspects, is an automaton: Nathanael's supposedly poetic character blinds him to the mechanical quality of her behaviour, yet leads him to call his sweetheart Clara, when she criticizes his poetry, 'You accursed lifeless automaton!' The narrator, however, has already vouched for Clara's child-like imagination, tender heart, and sharp, discriminating mind; it almost seems as though her poetic sensibility is superior to Nathanael's.

Nathanael's obsession with Olimpia is based on Hoffmann's reading of contemporary psychiatric literature: it conforms closely to what was then called an *idée fixe*. But Hoffmann goes beyond his sources in entering into the sufferer's mind, involving the reader in uncertainty about the borders of reality, and opening up explanatory avenues which were to be explored, over a century later, by Freud in his essay *The Uncanny* (1919).

Freud begins by questioning one commentator's claim that the uncanny effect of the story results from the reader's uncertainty whether Olimpia is a human being or an automaton. The reader, Freud rightly points out, is in no doubt that Olimpia is a machine. Instead, Freud draws attention to the prominence of the Sandman, the fairy-tale being who tears out children's eyes. The child Nathanael identifies this figure with his father's associate, the odious lawyer Coppelius, who threatens Nathanael's own eyes when the latter is caught spying on the two of them. The fear of losing one's eyes, Freud asserts, is a substitute for the fear of castration:

Why [*Freud asks rhetorically*] does Hoffmann bring the anxiety about eyes into such intimate connection with the father's death? And why does the Sand-Man always appear as a disturber of love? He separates the unfortunate Nathaniel [*sic*] from his betrothed and from her brother, his best friend; he destroys the second object of his love, Olympia [*sic*], the lovely doll; and he drives him into suicide at the moment when he has won back his Clara and is about to be happily united to her. Elements in the story like these, and many others, seem arbitrary and meaningless so long as we deny all connection between fears about the eye and castration; but they become intelligible as soon as we replace the Sand-Man by the dreaded father at whose hands castration is expected.[12]

In a long footnote Freud takes this interpretation further, arguing that Nathanael's ambivalence splits his father-imago into the good father (the one who intercedes for the child, and is later killed) and the bad father (Coppelius). Later this splitting produces Spalanzani (Olimpia's 'father', who brings her and Nathanael together) and Coppola (who carries her off). The identity of Coppelius and Coppola can be in no doubt, for Nathanael recognizes the voice of Coppelius coming from Spalanzani's study, in which he discovers Spalanzani and Coppola fighting over Olimpia; and Spalanzani refers to his associate as Coppelius. This scene is a repetition of the earlier one in Nathanael's father's study. The two are linked by the fact that Coppelius then treated Nathanael like a doll, dislocating his limbs and replacing them in their sockets, while now Olimpia, Nathanael's sweetheart, is revealed to be a doll. Olimpia and Nathanael are further linked by Spalanzani's otherwise unintelligible statement that Coppelius stole Nathanael's eyes—the

---

[12] *The Standard Edition of the Complete Psychological Works of Sigmund Freud*, ed. James Strachey, 24 vols. (London, 1953–74), xvii. 231–2.

bloodstained eyes lying on the study floor—to insert them in Olimpia's face. This enables Freud to conclude that Olimpia and Nathanael are really identical: 'Olympia is, as it were, a dissociated complex of Nathaniel's which confronts him as a person, and Nathaniel's enslavement to this complex is expressed in his senseless obsessive love for Olympia.'[13] The real object of Nathanael's love, according to Freud, is his father; his fixation on his father renders him incapable of loving a woman, and capable only of narcissistic love for what is really part of himself.

Subsequent commentary on *The Sandman* has also been a commentary on Freud's interpretation. Literary critics have noted how cavalierly Freud treats the form of the story. In retelling it, he ignores the fact that Hoffmann begins with a series of letters and then pauses to consider other possible ways of starting. But, as John M. Ellis has pointed out, the three possible openings imply different relations between the supernatural and the everyday.[14] The fairy-tale beginning, 'Once upon a time . . .', would imply a mythic world in which the Sandman's existence was quite straightforward. The opening 'In the small provincial town of S. there lived . . .' would introduce a realist narrative in which the Sandman, and the mysterious behaviour ascribed to Coppelius, could only be illusory. To plunge *medias in res* and begin '"Go to the Devil!" cried the student Nathanael' would suggest that the narrator was more involved with his subject-matter and closer to the characters' emotions. Instead, Hoffmann's narrator first presents three letters which themselves adopt irreconcilable views regarding the nature of reality. The first expresses Nathanael's conviction that Coppola is Coppelius, continuing to persecute him in a new guise; in the second, Clara dismisses this with prosaic common sense, explaining away the childhood scene as alchemical experiments, and assuring Nathanael that uncanny figures can have no power over him unless he permits it. Yet she does acknowledge the existence of dark forces, while failing even to mention the

---

[13] *Standard Editions of ... Sigmund Freud*, ed. Strachey, 232.

[14] J. M. Ellis, 'Clara, Nathanael, and the Narrator: Interpreting Hoffmann's *Der Sandmann*', *German Quarterly*, 54 (1981), 1–18.

extraordinary incident of Coppelius unscrewing the child's limbs. Finally Nathanael declares himself converted to Clara's standpoint. Thereupon the narrator himself intervenes with character sketches of Clara and Nathanael; much of his account, however, is ascribed to other sources, some of which consider Clara prosaic, while others recognize her fine qualities. He does not unequivocally underwrite Clara's viewpoint.

Hoffmann does not, then, give us any authoritative account of what really happened, but only, in his much-quoted phrase, 'a dim reflection in a dull mirror' conveying 'the strangeness of reality'. From the materials provided, we can construct a narrative in which Coppelius and Nathanael's father together try to make an automaton; after the explosion and the death of his collaborator, Coppelius flees the town, to reappear much later disguised as a Piedmontese barometer-seller and in league with the physicist Spalanzani; after twenty years of work they have now devised the perfect automaton and are trying it out on Nathanael. In keeping with this conspiracy theory, we may suppose that Coppelius is responsible for the fire which obliges Nathanael to move to a room opposite Olimpia's so that he falls under her spell. But this is a long way from the reassuringly rational explanations provided by earlier writers of Gothic thrillers, like Mrs Radcliffe in *The Mysteries of Udolpho*. This conspiracy may well seem as incredible to us as it does to Clara. Besides, it does not explain away the apparently magical properties of the spyglass which Nathanael buys from Coppola. Despite Freud, then, the sinister effect of *The Sandman* does indeed depend on intellectual uncertainty, and thus conforms to Todorov's definition of the fantastic quoted above. The uncertainty concerns the status of the conspiracy against Nathanael. Although it sounds like a paranoid fantasy, there is considerable though not conclusive evidence that it is really taking place. Its existence and its non-existence are equally incredible.

Freud misses other meanings generated by the text. Most strangely, he overlooks how much the experiments Nathanael spies on resemble a primal scene in which the child becomes aware of the parents' sexual relationship. A drawing of the incident by Hoffmann shows an aggressively masculine Coppelius towering over the bowed figure of Nathanael's father, who is clad in a feminine-looking robe. These two men are making a child by mechanical means. By peeping at them through the curtains, Nathanael initiates the motif of surreptitious looking which runs through the story: he peers at Olimpia, of whom he has a sideways view, and later goes mad when he looks sideways through the spyglass at Clara. An extension of Freud's reading might take this motif as the indirect expression of a sexual curiosity which the father-figure Coppelius both forbids (by threatening to tear Nathanael's eyes out) and encourages (by selling him the spyglass). Even in his daytime appearances Coppelius embodies the prohibitive functions of the father, as when he prevents the children from consuming the cake and wine which their 'real', ineffectually kindly father intends as a treat for them.

Coppelius represents other forms of authority besides the paternal. As an advocate and associate of Professor Spalanzani he belongs to the professional world. In opposition to the protective figures of Nathanael's mother and the maternal Clara, Coppelius embodies those menacing systems of authority that lie outside the shelter of the home. It is not only love, but family happiness in general, that Coppelius repeatedly destroys. Moreover, he represents historical forces. With his 'ash-grey coat of old-fashioned cut', his buckled shoes, and his wig and pigtail, he resembles a figure from the *ancien régime* which was then re-establishing itself after the fall of Napoleon. In his person, history intervenes repressively in 'private' life, frustrating plans like Clara's and Nathanael's marriage which seem to promise hope for the future. Then again, Coppelius and Spalanzani represent the scientific attempt to usurp supreme authority by rivalling the Creator. In making a simulacrum of humanity they are playing God, like Mary Shelley's Frankenstein and H. G. Wells's Dr Moreau. When Coppelius dislocates and replaces Nathanael's joints, he is obliged to conclude: 'The Old Man knew what he was doing!'

At the end of the story Clara finds a 'quiet domestic happiness' beyond the reach of Coppelius. But the closing idyll does not ring true, because, as the story makes clear, the threats to family happiness lie within the family: the Sandman exists in a nursery tale, even before his real-life counterpart, Coppelius,

intervenes in the family to sow dissension between Nathanael's parents and bring about his father's death. Behind the tale of the Sandman there lie sinister forces which Clara tries to ignore, yet even she is sufficiently under Coppelius's spell to be unable to let well alone. After her reconciliation with Nathanael, it is she who spoils their contentment by mentioning Coppelius and thus reminding Nathanael of his poem; it is she who suggests ascending the tower (which overshadows the market-place as Coppelius overshadowed Nathanael's home life), and who, by drawing attention to the 'grey bush' (recalling Coppelius's 'bushy grey eyebrows'), provokes the catastrophe. As for Nathanael, his poetic powers enable him to discern these forces, but not to master them. The narrator tells us that the poems he writes under their influence are very boring; but the terrifying narrative he reads to Clara is not one of these. Instead of boring her, it appals her, and she urges him to throw it in the fire. There is authorial irony here, for in describing how Coppelius destroys the love between Nathanael and Clara, the tale sounds very like *The Sandman* itself. It is characteristic of Romantic writers to distance themselves ironically from their own narratives. The story of Anselmus is only an episode in the myth recounted in *The Golden Pot*; and a version of *The Sandman* is almost thrown into the fire within the pages of *The Sandman*.

Princess Brambilla

This may well be Hoffmann's most bewildering tale. Its 'real' setting, the Roman Carnival, is almost as exotic as the interwoven myth of Urdar. Although he had never been to Rome, Hoffmann gained extensive information about it from travel books and above all from Goethe's essay on the Roman Carnival. The Carnival setting is appropriate to a story dealing with confusion of identity. Carnival is traditionally a festival in which the social order is temporarily suspended, identities are disguised behind masks, and irreverent joking is permitted. Masks and disguises are also essential to the *commedia dell'arte*, the improvised plays performed in Italy by professional entertainers from the sixteenth to the eighteenth centuries. The standard *commedia* characters include Harlequin (Arlecchino), the jester who wears a costume of many-coloured patches and a black mask; the coquettish servant-maid Colombine; Brighella, a ruffianly and cunning servant; Pantaloon, the old man in love, who is always deceived; the talkative and ineffectual Doctor; Truffaldino, an alternative to Harlequin, whose name comes from *truffare*, 'to cheat'; the boastful and cowardly Captain; and Pulcinella, a comic figure originating in Naples, and an ancestor of the English Punch.[15] In the 1750s the Venetian lawyer and playwright Carlo Goldoni tried to reform the *commedia* by making the masks into realistic characters with moral messages. In opposing these reforms, Carlo Gozzi, an impoverished aristocrat who loved dramatic traditions, gained the enmity not only of Goldoni but of the tragedian Pietro Chiari, a version of whom appears in Hoffmann's story. Gozzi's first *fiaba* or fairy-play, *The Love of Three Oranges*, concerns a prince who has been reduced to melancholy by bad poetry (an allusion to Chiari's) and is cured when the *commedia* character Truffaldino makes him laugh.[16] From this source Hoffmann borrowed the motif of laughter as a sign of psychic health in *Princess Brambilla*.

Hoffmann invoked further models by subtitling *Princess Brambilla* 'a capriccio after Jacques Callot'. He had already paid homage to the French draughtsman Callot (1592–1635) by calling an earlier collection of stories (including *The Golden Pot*) *Fantasiestücke in Callots Manier* ('Fantasy-Pieces in the Manner of Callot'). His definition of Callot's manner resembles the Serapiontic principle:

Could not a poet or writer to whom the figures of ordinary life appear in his inward romantic spiritual realm, and who portrays them in the light

[15] See Allardyce Nicoll, *The World of Harlequin* (Cambridge, 1963).

[16] Although he is now remembered mainly for inspiring some modern operas (Prokofiev's *The Love of Three Oranges*, Puccini's *Turandot*, and Henze's *King Stag*), Gozzi's dramas had a great vogue in Germany. Several were performed at the Weimar court theatre, including Schiller's adaptation of *Turandot* (1802), and their influence is evident in Tieck's comedies and traceable later in Grillparzer's *Der Traum ein Leben* and Büchner's *Leonce und Lena*. Serpentina in *The Golden Pot* owes her name and character to the heroine of Gozzi's *The Serpent Lady*. See Hedwig Rusack, *Gozzi in Germany* (New York, 1930); and for Hoffmann's own remarks on Gozzi, *Hoffmann's Musical Writings* (see n. 7), 197–200.

that there plays round them as though in strange and curious finery, at least excuse himself by referring to this master and say that he was trying to work in the manner of Callot? [17]

For his forty-fourth birthday, on 24 January 1820, Hoffmann was given a set of Callot drawings, the *Balli di Sfessania*, depicting figures from the *commedia dell'arte*. Eight of these inspired scenes in *Brambilla*, and are reproduced in most editions. The term 'capriccio' is also borrowed from Callot, who used it to mean a series of loosely linked drawings, such as his *Capricci di varie figure* (1617). The term was also current in music to describe a series of improvisations, and was used by literary critics to indicate the freedom assumed by the humorous writer.

Since the 'reality' of *Princess Brambilla* is the theatre, this story seems the reverse of *The Golden Pot*. Giglio Fava is an actor instead of a Philistine, and in Chapter 1 he comes straight from the theatre where he has been playing the role of Prince Taer in Gozzi's *The Blue Monster*. He recounts a dream in which a beautiful Princess declared her love for him; this earns him a scolding from his girl-friend Giacinta, but she has just been lamenting her poverty and wishing she were wealthy enough to wear the magnificent dress which she is sewing for an unknown customer. Both hero and heroine, then, are obsessed by romantic dreams. Soon their vivid imagination leads them to confuse fantasy with reality. The fact that the magnificent dress turns out to fit Giacinta perfectly leads her to fancy that she is the Princess Brambilla for whom it is destined. Giglio fails to distinguish his real self from the character he impersonates: earlier that day, we learn, he was 'looking somewhat like Prince Taer and feeling exactly like him'. He is said to invite the admiration of the audience and to ignore his fellow-actors, and to be as vain as a young cockerel. In short, he misuses his imagination. Instead of allowing his real self to be absorbed into his role, he uses his role to nourish his own egotism.

In the course of the story, Giglio and Giacinta are cured of his vanity by having their identities doubled. Their fantasy-selves split off and assume independent existence as Princess

[17] E. T. A. Hoffmann, *Fantasie- und Nachtstücke* (Munich, 1960), 13.

Brambilla and her lover Prince Cornelio Chiapperi. This process, stage-managed by Celionati with supernatural aid, also
provides Giglio with a lesson in acting. Near the beginning of
the story his style of acting is described as pompous and declam-
atory, with extravagant stylized gestures. His self-regarding
vanity has to give way to a loss of self: only by being absorbed
into his role will he be truly himself and also a true actor. He
seems to have made some progress by Chapter 4, when he
returns to Giacinta's flat and finds her sewing. She talks mysteriously of her impending marriage to a prince, and Giglio
replies that he is about to marry Princess Brambilla. Yet their
conversation sounds very like a game, especially when Giacinta
says that her husband's kingdom lies near Bergamo (the proven-
ance of some *commedia* characters), and both agree that their
kingdoms had better be transferred to Frascati, a convenient
distance from Rome. Even earlier, Giglio's tragic ranting has
been accompanied by self-mockery as well as by good-natured
gibing from Giacinta. It almost seems that the learning process
is already over, and that Giglio and Giacinta are now able to
use their fantasies as material for a game, while remaining
firmly anchored in reality.

However, Giglio at least has to undergo still deeper self-
estrangement. Like Anselmus, he is tempted and falls. His temp-
ter is the appalling tragic playwright, the Abbate Chiari, who
persuades him to distrust Celionati. In what Hoffmann ironically calls the 'pleasant low-water period, when the human
spirit rejoices in perfect sobriety' (that is, a state of prosaic,
unimaginative common sense, perfectly compatible with admiration for the Abbate's wooden tragedies), Giglio relapses into
his former vanity, dressing up as a prince and boldly entering
the Pistoia Palace in search of Princess Brambilla. Instead of
finding her, however, he is caught and put in a cage as a
'feather-brain' (Hoffmann's word, *Gelbschnabel*, means a fledge-
ling bird and also a simpleton), an episode corresponding to
Anselmus's imprisonment in the bottle. This does not cure his
vanity, however: indeed, Celionati encourages his conviction
that he is Prince Cornelio Chiapperi, and that Princess Brambilla has foisted Giacinta upon him so that she herself may
pursue the wretched actor Giglio Fava. That evening sees the

encounter between Giglio's two selves: the Pantaloon-Brighella mask that he assumed earlier, and the mask with silk breeches and pink stockings that he wore in Chapter 1. The combatants display affection as well as antagonism—after all, they are the same person—but in the end Giglio is killed and his corpse removed amid the merriment of the populace. Later we learn that Giglio was only made of cardboard, that his health was ruined by over-indulgence in Chiari's indigestible tragedies (literary junk food, so to speak), and that in any case his acting was worthless. We learn this from an unnamed young man of mild manners, who describes himself as Prince Cornelio Chiapperi. This of course is Giglio; but not the old, vain, shallow Giglio. He has killed his former self, and assumed the identity of the Assyrian prince; but this new and always fragile identity represents the transition to a new version of his self as Giglio Fava.

Once this transition is complete, the story of Giglio and Giacinta converges with the myth of Urdar which has accompanied their narrative ever since Chapter 3. This likewise falls into two phases, each dealing with estrangement and its overcoming. The tale of King Ophioch and Queen Liris, like the myth in *The Golden Pot*, concerns man's estrangement from an original harmony with nature. Reunion is achieved, on a higher plane, when Ophioch and Liris awake from sleep and look into the well of Urdar. There they behold their world turned upside-down and thus transformed into 'a magnificent new world full of life and joy'. They burst into joyful laughter. As the Magus Hermod cryptically explains, man can overcome his estrangement from nature by perceiving himself and his surroundings in the mirror of art. And one particular kind of art is referred to: comedy, in which, as in the waters of Urdar, the world is reflected upside-down, reversed, topsy-turvy. The story presents Hoffmann's conception of humour, later spelt out by Reinhold, one of the German artists who form Celionati's audience in the Caffè Greco. German humour, according to Reinhold, is the expression of the underlying principle of irony. Its surface extravagances arise from this deep-seated principle, just as ripples in a stream are produced by a concealed rock. He claims that the grotesque features of Italian comedy, on the other hand, are indulged for their own sake, and provide at most an occasional and distorted reflection of the principle of irony. *Princess Brambilla* as a whole may be called a synthesis of both traditions, combining the inventive theatricality of Italian masks with the profundity of German humour.

The second phase of the myth concerns the deeper estrangement that sets in after the deaths of Ophioch and Liris. The over-rational inhabitants of Urdar, now dominated by philosophers (an allusion to the Enlightenment), cannot understand the language of Princess Mystilis, who represents poetry. Misled by an impostor, Princess Mystilis is reduced to a china doll, and the court ladies are set to making lace in which a gaudy bird is to be caught. Here the legend intersects with the story of Giglio; for he in his princely outfit is the gaudy bird to be entrapped in the net. However, when Giglio's transformation is complete, he and Giacinta attain self-knowledge as Ophioch and Liris had originally done. Transported to Urdar, they look into the lake and know themselves for the first time. They laugh and embrace, and Mystilis, now a queen, is reborn from the lotus as a kind of giantess, her feet planted in the maternal soil and her head in the sky, representing the triumph of poetry.

The story ends with Giglio and Giacinta enjoying both self-knowledge and domestic happiness. As a corrective to Giglio's former vanity, Giacinta has now been promoted from seamstress to actress, and the two act in such harmony that they can improvise for long periods without Giglio, at least, noticing. They are also more prosperous than before, thanks to Celionati, now revealed as Prince Bastianello di Pistoia. The well of Urdar, he explains, corresponds to the theatre: both are mirrors which reflect reality more truly than any mere empirical representation. They reflect the true humour with which Giglio and Giacinta are endowed.

Master Flea

Master Flea begins and ends in a manner that calls to mind Dickens's *Christmas Books*. Peregrinus Tyss, a lonely bachelor, is in the habit of buying large numbers of toys and, with the help of his old nurse Aline, staging a distribution of presents on Christmas Eve, in which he plays the role of a child. After this he gives the toys to the children of a poor family. Unable to overcome the trauma of his parents' death, Peregrinus uses his child-like imagination to prolong his childhood. The story deals with his transition to adulthood under the guidance not of Aline but of Master Flea. As in *The Sandman*, Hoffmann questions the central Romantic tenet of the supreme value of the imagination. Nathanael's imagination was a source of revelations too terrifying to live with. Peregrinus's imagination seems to have a merely escapist function.

Hoffmann's doubts about the imagination find expression in the two antitheses on which *Master Flea* is based. One is the antithesis between the Romantic vision of nature and the mechanistic approach of eighteenth-century science. The other is between Romantic passion and married love. Hoffmann affirms the Romantic view of nature but distances himself from Romantic conceptions of passion.

The Romantic view of nature appears in the myth which, though less prominently than in *The Golden Pot* or *Princess Brambilla*, is interwoven with the story's 'real' events. Its setting is the magical region of Famagusta and Samarkand (quite unconnected with the actual places bearing these names), in which nature and humankind retain their original harmony, forming 'a colourful medley of flowers assuming human shape, and human beings that melted into the earth and then gleamed forth as stones and metals'; this resembles the paradisal state imagined by Novalis in *Die Lehrlinge zu Sais* ('The Apprentices at Sais'), a fable expressing the Romantic doctrine of nature which Hoffmann read avidly. Such a view of nature is contrasted with the scientific efforts of Leuwenhoek and Swammerdamm. These two characters have historical prototypes, but in this story they simply typify an anti-Romantic approach to the study of nature. Like the analytic investigator ('Scheidekünstler') denounced by Novalis in *Die Lehrlinge zu Sais*, they regard nature without love or reverence as a mere mechanism. 'You sought to explore nature,' Peregrinus tells them, 'but had no inkling of the significance of her innermost being.' They resemble Professor Spalanzani in *The Sandman*, who tries to rival nature by constructing an automaton which, however, lacks a soul.

Dörtje, for her part, at times resembles Olimpia. Peregrinus notices that she has an unnaturally fixed and rigid look in her eyes. She has to be kept artificially youthful by periodic bites from Master Flea; without them she will shrink into an old woman. This gives rise to a struggle for the possession of Master Flea which sustains much of the action. It also points to a narrative strand which Hoffmann has not followed through: originally there was to be a link between Dörtje and Aline, Peregrinus's withered housekeeper; perhaps, in fact, they would turn out to be the same person, before and after the flea-bite; and Aline would also be linked in some way with the opera *Aline, Queen of Golconda* (1803) by Henri Montan Berton, which Hoffmann produced in Bamberg in 1808. The exotic Golconda might have been linked with India, for Peregrinus and George Pepusch first met in Madras.

Unlike the naturalists, Peregrinus in his mythic identity as King Sekakis has the power of giving life, thanks to the magic carbuncle he wears on his chest. But its effects on him are different from its effects on Dörtje and George. It restores his capacity to love and unites him with Rosie. In the other couple, however, it inspires a Romantic passion. The flowering cactus corresponding to George blooms once and then dies; Dörtje, as a tulip, dies with him. This Romantic *Liebestod*, in which yearning is satisfied in an experience of passionate intensity combining love and death, is juxtaposed to the marriage of Peregrinus and Rosie, which is a way of living and transmitting life. And Peregrinus firmly rejects supernatural power by deciding not to use the magic lens, the counterpart to Anselmus's mirrorlike golden pot, Coppola's fateful spyglass, and the well of Urdar.

This story also expresses Hoffmann's anger with certain abuses of justice in which he was reluctantly involved. The Congress of Vienna, meeting in 1815 after the final defeat of Napoleon, had agreed on measures to preserve Europe from any further upheavals. Prince Metternich, the Austrian Foreign Minister, devised the system of security that was to keep Europe quiet until the abortive revolutions of 1848. One immediate problem was to control those people who had been rendered politically conscious by the Prussian war of liberation against the French. Liberalism and nationalism were both considered hostile to the present social order, and both were widespread among students. They were asserted at the festival held in October 1817 at the Wartburg (the castle where Luther had translated the Bible into German) to celebrate both the defeat of the French at the battle of Leipzig and the tercentenary of the Reformation. The dangers of student politics seemed confirmed two years later when the reactionary playwright and diplomat Kotzebue was assassinated by the student revolutionary Karl Sand. A police campaign was mounted against 'demagogues', as supposed radicals were known.[18] The King of Prussia instituted a commission to investigate secret societies of a subversive nature; Hoffmann, as a respected official in the administration of criminal justice, was one of its members. Those arrested included the leading nationalist Friedrich Ludwig Jahn, who, on his release, lodged a complaint on the grounds of unlawful arrest. Hoffmann took Jahn's side against his superior, von Kamptz, the director of the police ministry. While Hoffmann had no sympathy with would-be revolutionaries, he thought it wrong to prosecute people for their views rather than their actions, and insisted, in a courageous document addressed to von Kamptz, on the necessity for justice to be strictly impartial without regard for persons. He was nevertheless compelled by an order of the King to dismiss Jahn's complaint.

Unable to combat these abuses of justice, Hoffmann attacked them in the Knarrpanti episode of *Master Flea*. Knarrpanti's twisted reasoning resembles that practised by von Kamptz; the very name combines suggestions of 'Kamptz' and 'Narr' ('fool'); and the incident in which Knarrpanti regards as highly suspicious the entry in Peregrinus's diary, 'Today I only killed time', is taken from an incident in which von Kamptz underlined in red the word 'mordfaul' ('bone idle') in a student's diary, as though it were a confession of murder ('Mord'). Hoffmann wrote the Knarrpanti episode in December 1821, but within a

[18] For the historical context, see Michael Hughes, *Nationalism and Society: Germany 1800–1945* (London, 1988), ch. 4.

few weeks he got cold feet, and in a letter of 19 January 1822 he instructed his publisher to remove two particularly dangerous passages. By then, however, it was too late. Having heard rumours about Hoffmann's literary plans, von Kamptz had already sent an agent to interrogate Hoffmann's publisher and confiscate the manuscript. The publisher handed over all relevant documents, including Hoffmann's letter, which, with its reference to passages requiring excision, naturally provided strong evidence of his polemical intentions. Hoffmann was now in serious trouble. He was also gravely ill, and hence unable to appear for interrogation. He did, however, compose a lengthy and disingenuous apologia in which he denied any intention of alluding to von Kamptz's activities and tried to justify the Knarrpanti episode as integral to the narrative: it was a well-established comic device to bring a hero into a situation incongruous with his character; the charge of abduction against Peregrinus Tyss served this purpose, but required that Tyss should be confronted with an unintelligent and persistent adversary, whose intrigues could be exposed by means of Master Flea's magic eyeglass. This apologia did not convince Hoffmann's antagonists, and may not convince us, but it certainly shows that his legal mind lost none of its sharpness when applied to literary criticism. *Master Flea* was published with the offending passages removed; they were not found until 1906. Proceedings against Hoffmann continued, and were only brought to an end by his death on 25 June 1822.

My Cousin's Corner Window

Here, as in *The Sandman*, we have a narrator whom we cannot altogether trust, though instead of an anonymous voice it is now a fictional character. He is something of a Philistine, who enjoys his cousin's stories but professes not to understand them, and treats his cousin's literary tastes somewhat condescendingly. Nevertheless, we owe to the narrator the comparison between his cousin and the French humorist Scarron (1610–60) who was paralysed for the last twenty years of his life; Hoffmann had compared himself to Scarron when laid low by an attack of rheumatism.[19] This comparison also lets Hoffmann define his and Scarron's humour by contrast with the 'wit' customary in France, and testifies to Hoffmann's increasing need to see himself in a literary tradition: his apologia written in the *Master Flea* affair lists a number of predecessors in German satire.

The cousin, unable to put his ideas down on paper, has developed the 'art of looking'. Since his window overlooks the market-place in the centre of Berlin, he can amuse himself for long periods in watching the shoppers and speculating about their lives and characters. For most of the story he instructs the narrator in this art. It requires a thorough knowledge of contemporary customs and a sharp eye for the telling detail: dancing shoes worn in the market, for example, can reveal a whole personality. The anglophone reader may be reminded of Sherlock Holmes and Dr Watson; and the resemblance is not accidental. The social observer and the detective practise a similar form of knowledge: one which consists in scrutinizing the object, getting to know it in intimate detail, and learning to draw far-reaching conclusions from clues invisible to the uninitiated. The historian Carlo Ginzburg has recently described this as a 'divinatory' form of knowledge; he has traced it back to the activity of the hunter, who learns to read the tracks of animals, and contrasted it with the activity of the physical scientist, for whom the object of his knowledge is abstract, quantifiable, and indefinitely repeatable. The doctor who 'reads' symptoms, the art connoisseur who attributes paintings, the detective, and the literary critic are all practising a form of knowledge which cannot be reduced to rules but must be passed on by oral instruction—as the narrator here is instructed by his cousin.[20]

There is a wide gulf between this connoisseurship of everyday life and the grandiose visions of natural harmony enjoyed by Anselmus and Peregrinus. But there is also a resemblance. The cousin's attention is turned outwards, towards the bustle in the market-place; but, still true to the Serapiontic principle, he

---

[19] Hoffmann, *Briefwechsel*, i. 458. He probably had in mind the story by K. F. Kretschmann, *Scarron am Fenster*, publ. in the *Taschenbuch zum geselligen Vergnügen* (1798–9), which evidently provided a model for this one.

[20] Carlo Ginzburg, 'Clues: Roots of an Evidential Paradigm', in his *Myths, Emblems, Clues*, tr. John and Anne C. Tedeschi (London, 1990), 96–125.

SELECT BIBLIOGRAPHY

The literature on Hoffmann in English is still rather scanty and uneven, compared to that on many other German authors. A list of anglophone criticism must therefore omit much of the most important work on Hoffmann.

The responses to Hoffmann by two nineteenth-century readers, Thomas Carlyle and Sir Walter Scott, deserve mention for their historical interest. Although Carlyle translated *The Golden Pot*, along with stories by other German Romantics (Tieck, Fouqué, and Jean Paul), he was surprisingly grudging in his assessment of Hoffmann, calling him a 'caricature-painter', interested only in 'extravagant and ludicrous distortions' of human behaviour ('E. T. W. Hoffmann', *German Romance*, ii (Centenary Edition of Carlyle's Works, 22; London, 1898), 19). Carlyle showed more appreciation, however, than did Scott in the essay first published as 'On the Supernatural in Fictitious Composition; and particularly on the Works of Ernest Theodore Wilhelm Hoffman [*sic*]', in the *Foreign Quarterly Review*, 1 (July and November 1827), 60–98 (republished in *The Miscellaneous Works of Sir Walter Scott, Bart* (Edinburgh, 1870), xviii. 270–332). Here Scott launched an attack against 'the FANTASTIC mode of writing,—in which the most wild and unbounded license is given to an irregular fancy, and all species of combination, however ludicrous, or however shocking, are attempted and executed without scruple' (p. 290). He particularly deplores *The Sandman*. After summarizing it, he concedes: 'This wild and absurd story is in some measure redeemed by the character of Clara, whose firmness, plain good sense and frank affection are placed in agreeable contrast with the wild imagination, fanciful apprehensions, and extravagant affection of her crazy-pated admirer' (p. 330). These essays by Carlyle and Scott are important documents in the history of taste, for while both deplore the Romantic side of Hoffmann, Scott at least acknowledges those elements in his work which I have called Biedermeier, and which appealed to the preferences that came to be labelled

Victorian. Had Scott known Hoffmann's work better, however, he would have seen that the transition from Romanticism to Biedermeier is accomplished in the stories themselves.

In more recent times, many people outside Germany have associated Hoffmann first with Offenbach's opera *The Tales of Hoffmann* (1881), and this is acknowledged in the title of the first major English-language study of Hoffmann, Harvey W. Hewett-Thayer's *Hoffmann, Author of the Tales* (Princeton, NJ, 1948). It can still be recommended as a storehouse of information, particularly biographical, though the critical discussion of the stories is not very probing. A much briefer, indeed slighter, introduction is Ronald Taylor's *Hoffmann* (London, 1963), which emphasizes Hoffmann's musical interests. Horst Daemmrich, *The Shattered Self: E. T. A. Hoffmann's Tragic Vision* (Detroit, 1973), is a more thorough and systematic introduction. The essay by John Reddick in Alex Natan (ed.), *German Men of Letters*, v (London, 1969), is superior to all these, however, in its sophisticated and perceptive critical approach to Hoffmann.

The most substantial recent study of Hoffmann in English is the study by James McGlathery, *Mysticism and Sexuality: E. T. A. Hoffmann*, 2 vols. (Frankfurt, 1981 and 1985). The first volume, *Hoffmann and his Sources*, not only surveys Hoffmann's career as writer and composer and his reception by readers and critics, but is packed with useful information, much of it not otherwise available in English, about Hoffmann's literary sources. The author's industry has given him an impressive command of primary and secondary sources. Unfortunately his second volume, *Interpretations of the Tales*, is a disappointment. McGlathery is anxious to interpret as many of the tales as possible as being about the panic felt by bachelors at the prospect of marriage. In pursuit of this *idée fixe* he tramples ruthlessly through Hoffmann's ironic subtleties. Although his psychoanalytic framework is rudimentary, McGlathery uses it to reduce the stories to case-histories and to generate interpretations which, despite occasional insights, are mostly mechanical, predictable, and implausible.

Kenneth Negus, *E. T. A. Hoffmann's Other World: The Romantic Author and his 'New Mythology'* (Philadelphia, 1965), deals with the relation between myth and 'reality' in several of the stories included here, though his readings are not as penetrating as the best German-language work. Yvonne J. K. Holbeche, *Optical Motifs in the Works of E. T. A. Hoffmann* (Göppingen, 1975), is a useful survey, though her discussions of individual stories are insufficiently analytic. Robert Currie, *Genius: An Ideology in Literature* (London, 1974), has a chapter on the artist–Philistine conflict in Hoffmann, who is suggestively compared to Kierkegaard, Wyndham Lewis, Kafka, and others.

Hoffmann's extensive writings on music and the theatre are now available in an admirable translation by Martyn Clarke, with a learned introduction and notes by David Charlton: *E. T. A. Hoffmann's Musical Writings: Kreisleriana, The Poet and the Composer, Music Criticism* (Cambridge, 1989). This largely supersedes the translations of a smaller number of texts offered by R. Murray Schafer in *E. T. A. Hoffmann and Music* (Toronto, 1975), though Schafer's introductions may still be useful for readers unfamiliar with German culture. Hoffmann's musical interests are interpreted by Pauline Watts, *Music: The Medium of the Metaphysical in E. T. A. Hoffmann* (Amsterdam, 1972).

Among critics of *The Golden Pot*, John Reddick, 'E. T. A. Hoffmann's *Der goldne Topf* and its "durchgehaltene Ironie" ', *Modern Language Review*, 71 (1976), 577–94, defines the story's 'ironic perspectivism' by pointing out that the relation of myth and 'reality' remains ambiguous throughout. L. C. Nygaard, 'Anselmus as Amanuensis: The Motif of Copying in Hoffmann's *Der goldne Topf*', *Seminar*, 19 (1983), 79–104, is narrower in scope. Maria M. Tatar, 'Mesmerism, Madness and Death in E. T. A. Hoffmann's *Der goldne Topf*', *Studies in Romanticism*, 14 (1975), 365–89, relates *The Golden Pot* to Romantic science; some of this material is incorporated into the Hoffmann chapter of her important book *Spellbound: Studies on Mesmerism and Literature* (Princeton, NJ, 1978).

Of the stories in this book, *The Sandman* has received by far the most attention, partly because of the famous interpretation in Freud's essay *The 'Uncanny'*. There are two outstanding articles in English. Freud's interpretation is discussed by S. S. Prawer, 'Hoffmann's Uncanny Guest: A Reading of *Der Sandmann*', *German Life and Letters*, 18 (1965), 297–308, pointing out many aspects of the story which Freud overlooked. John M.

Ellis, 'Clara, Nathanael and the Narrator: Interpreting Hoffmann's *Der Sandmann'*, *German Quarterly*, 54 (1981), 1–18, shows how essential the narrative perspective (and the various possible beginnings which the narrator considers but rejects) must be to the assessment of the characters and their conflicting values.

For post-Freudian readings, see Samuel Weber, 'The Sideshow, or: Remarks on a Canny Moment', *Modern Language Notes*, 88 (1973), 1102–33; Neil Hertz, 'Freud and the Sandman', in J. V. Harari (ed.), *Textual Strategies: Perspectives in Post-Structuralist Criticism* (Ithaca, NY, 1979), 296–321; Françoise Meltzer, 'The Uncanny Rendered Canny: Freud's Blind Spot in Reading Hoffmann's *Sandman'*, in Sander L. Gilman (ed.), *Introducing Psychoanalytic Theory* (New York, 1982), 218–39; Lee B. Jennings, 'Blood of the Android: A Post-Freudian Perspective on Hoffmann's *Sandmann'*, *Seminar*, 22 (1986), 95–111; Malcolm V. Jones, '*Der Sandmann* and 'the Uncanny': A Sketch for an Alternative Approach', *Paragraph*, 7 (1986), 77–101. Another psychoanalytic approach is by Ursula Mahlendorf, 'E. T. A. Hoffmann's *Der Sandmann*: The Fictional Psychobiography of a Romantic Poet', *American Imago*, 32 (1975), 217–39. Some of these approaches are surveyed by Elizabeth Wright in *Psychoanalytic Criticism* (London, 1984).

An earlier book by Elizabeth Wright, *E. T. A. Hoffmann and the Rhetoric of Terror: Aspects of Language Used for the Evocation of Fear* (London, 1978), has a section on the style of *The Sandman*, while Susan Brantly, 'A Thermographic Reading of E. T. A. Hoffmann's *Der Sandmann'*, *German Quarterly*, 55 (1982), 324–35, examines images of heat and light. Maria M. Tatar, 'E. T. A. Hoffmann's *Der Sandmann*: Reflection and Romantic Irony', *Modern Language Notes*, 95 (1980), 585–608, relates the story to Romantic poetics.

All readers of *Princess Brambilla* have reason to be grateful for the learned edition by M. M. Raraty in Blackwell's German Texts (Oxford, 1972), with a forty-page introduction. Helga Slessarev, 'E. T. A. Hoffmann's *Prinzessin Brambilla*: A Romanticist's Contribution to the Aesthetic Education of Man', *Studies in Romanticism*, 9 (1970), 147–60, draws interesting analogies between Giglio's education and the social theories of German classicism, particularly Schiller. *Master Flea* has been almost ignored by anglophone critics, except for the re-examination of the Knarrpanti episode by Marko Pavlyshyn, 'Word as Act: The Debate on E. T. A. Hoffmann's *Meister Floh*', *Seminar*, 17 (1981), 196–204. On *My Cousin's Corner Window* there is an ingenious article by Roger F. Cook, 'Reader Response and Authorial Strategies: E. T. A. Hoffmann's View from *Des Vetters Eckfenster*', *German Studies Review*, 12 (1989), 421–35; this also brings one up to date with critical discussion in German.

On the wider literary and historical context of German Romanticism, see especially James J. Sheehan, *German History 1770–1866* (Oxford, 1989); H. G. Schenk, *The Mind of the European Romantics* (London, 1966); Siegbert Prawer (ed.), *The Romantic Period in Germany* (London, 1970), which fruitfully discusses the different genres of Romantic writing; Glyn Tegai Hughes, *Romantic German Literature* (London, 1979), a concise and witty introduction with an admirable scholarly bibliography; and Theodore Ziolkowski, *German Romanticism and its Institutions* (Princeton, NJ, 1990).

A CHRONOLOGY OF
E. T. A. HOFFMANN

1776   (24 Jan.) Ernst Theodor Wilhelm Hoffmann born at Königs-
        berg in East Prussia (at present Kaliningrad in the USSR). His
        father, Christoph Ludwig Hoffmann, is a lawyer, married to
        Louisa Albertina Doerffer, who comes from an old-established
        Königsberg family. Hoffmann replaced 'Wilhelm' with
        'Amadeus' in 1804, in homage to Mozart.

1778   Hoffmann's parents are divorced. His mother returns with the
        child to her family home.

1792   Hoffmann begins the study of law at the University of
        Königsberg.

1795   Graduates and begins legal practice, first in Königsberg, then
        in Glogau in Silesia (1796–8), then in Berlin (1798–1800).

1798   Becomes engaged to his cousin Minna Doerffer.

1800   Appointed to the court at Posen in Prussian Poland (now
        Poznań).

1802   Breaks off his engagement to Minna Doerffer and marries
        Michalina Rorer (26 July). As punishment for drawing and
        distributing caricatures of eminent citizens of Posen,
        Hoffmann is transferred to the small town of Płock.

1804   Transferred to Warsaw.

1805   Birth of the Hoffmanns' daughter Cäcilie, who dies in 1807.

1806   (19 Dec.) Having defeated the Prussian army at the battle of
        Jena, Napoleon occupies Prussian Poland and enters Warsaw.
        Prussian officials who refuse to swear loyalty to their new
        rulers are dismissed; Hoffmann is among them.

1807   Hoffmann sends his wife to her relatives in Posen and himself
        moves to Berlin. Tries to begin a musical career.

1808   Appointed orchestra conductor in Bamberg.

1810   Becomes assistant director of the Bamberg theatre, as well as
        composer and set-designer.

1811   Falls passionately but platonically in love with Julia Marc, to
        whom he gives music lessons. In December 1812 Julia (then

aged 16) marries a banker and moves to Hamburg.

1813   Moves to Dresden as orchestra conductor.

1814   Publishes his first collections of stories, *Fantasiestücke in Callots Manier* ('Fantasy-Pieces in the Manner of Callot'): the first two volumes appear at Easter, the third, including *The Golden Pot*, in the autumn, and the fourth the following year.
          Falls out with his employer, leaves the theatre, and takes up an appointment at the supreme court in Berlin.

1815   Publishes the first volume of his novel *The Devil's Elixirs* (*Die Elixiere des Teufels*); the second appears the following year.

1816   Publishes *The Sandman* in the first volume of a collection of stories entitled *Nachtstücke* (*Night-Pieces*); the second volume follows in 1817.
          His opera *Undine*, based on a Romantic fairy-tale by Fouqué, is produced with success.

1819   Appointed to a committee investigating supposedly subversive activities; its methods are satirized in the Knarrpanti episode of *Master Flea*.
          Begins publishing the collection of stories *The Serapion Brethren*; further volumes follow in 1820 and 1821.

1820   Publishes *Princess Brambilla* and the first part of the novel *Lebens-Ansichten des Katers Murr* (*Life and Opinions of Murr the Cat*); part 2 follows in 1822.

1822   Falls seriously ill. The manuscript of *Master Flea* is confiscated and disciplinary proceedings instituted because of the Knarrpanti episode. Hoffmann defends himself from his sick-bed.
          Master Flea is published without the Knarrpanti episode.
          My Cousin's Corner Window is written and published.
          (25 June) Hoffmann dies.

TRANSLATOR'S NOTE

German names and titles have been discreetly anglicized whenever possible: thus 'Veronika' becomes 'Veronica', 'Schlossgasse' becomes 'Castle Lane', and so on. 'Thaler' has been preferred to 'dollar' for a silver coin, however, since 'dollar' would have sounded incongruously American. The frequent title 'Counsellor' denotes a rank in the civil service, not membership of a municipal or other council. 'Hofrat' has been translated in *The Golden Pot* simply as 'Counsellor', but in *Master Flea* as 'Aulic Counsellor', in order to retain the suggestion of Knarrpanti's pomposity. Paulmann in *The Golden Pot* is a deputy headmaster, and his title 'Konrektor' has been rendered as 'Sub-Rector', which can be placed before a surname and is licensed by the use of 'Rector' to mean 'headmaster'. 'Registrator' (registrar, an official who deals with incoming documents) has been translated, for the sake of euphony, by the less common form 'Registrary'.

mysterious words had given the ridiculous incident a certain
tragic quality, so that, although they had paid no attention to
Anselmus before, they now followed him with looks of sympathy. On account of the young man's comely face, rendered
still more expressive by the heat of his suppressed anger, and
his sturdy build, the womenfolk forgave him his clumsiness, as
well as his completely unfashionable outfit. The cut of his
bluish-grey tailcoat suggested that the tailor who made it had
known the modern style only from hearsay, and his well-
preserved black satin breeches gave him a rather schoolmasterly
appearance which was entirely at odds with his gait and posture.

By the time Anselmus was approaching the end of the avenue
leading to Linke's Restaurant* he was almost out of breath. He
was obliged to slacken his pace, but he scarcely dared to raise
his eyes, for he could still see the apples and cakes dancing all
round him, and a friendly glance from some passing girl seemed
only the reflection of the malicious laughter at the Black Gate.
In this manner he reached the entrance to Linke's Restaurant;
groups of people in their best clothes were thronging into it.
The sound of wind instruments could be heard from within,
and the crowd of merry-makers was growing noisier by the
minute. Poor Anselmus was close to tears, for Ascension Day
had always been a special occasion in his family; he too had
wanted to share the delights of Linke's paradise and even indulge himself in half a cup of coffee with rum and a bottle of
strong beer, and in order to make a night of it he had brought
more money with him than was proper or prudent. And now
his misadventure in knocking over the basket of apples had cost
him all the money on his person. Coffee, strong beer, music, the
sight of girls in their finery, in a word, all the pleasures he had
dreamt of, were now beyond his reach. He crept slowly past the
entrance and finally went down the road leading to the River
Elbe, which happened to be completely deserted. Under an
elder-tree which grew out of the wall he found an inviting patch
of grass, where he sat down and filled a pipe with the health-
tobacco which his friend Sub-Rector Paulmann had given him.

Directly in front of Anselmus the golden yellow waves of the
beautiful River Elbe rippled and murmured, while beyond it
the magnificent city of Dresden stretched its gleaming spires

boldly and proudly into the translucent expanse of the sky which hung over the flowery meadows and fresh green forests, and the jagged peaks half-hidden by twilight announced the far land of Bohemia. But Anselmus scowled to himself as he blew clouds of smoke into the air, and at last he gave vent to his annoyance with the following words.

'It's true enough, I was born to suffer all the vexation and misery imaginable! Never mind that I've never been chosen King in the Twelfth-Night revels* that I always guess wrong at odds or evens, that my toast always falls on the buttered side; but isn't it a terrible fate that after defying Satan by becoming a student, I must always be a complete duffer?* Do I ever put on a new coat without promptly spilling candle-grease on it or having a cursed hole torn in it by a projecting nail? Do I ever bid good morning to a Counsellor or a lady without throwing my hat away, or slipping on the polished floor and falling flat on my face? Didn't every market-day in Halle cost me three or four pence for pottery that I had broken, because the Devil made me march straight ahead, without looking where I was going, like a lemming? Have I ever once turned up in time for a lecture, or any other appointment? What use was it to leave home half an hour early, for as soon as I was standing on the doorstep with the knocker in my hand, Satan would empty a wash-tub over my head or make me collide with someone who was just leaving, so that I got involved in endless arguments and missed the whole occasion! Oh, where have you gone, you blissful dreams of future happiness, when I was conceited enough to fancy that here I might even rise to the rank of Private Secretary! But my evil star has turned my best-disposed patrons against me. When I was recommended to the Privy Councillor, I knew he could not abide close-cropped hair; the hairdresser, with great difficulty, fastened a little pigtail to the back of my head, but the first time I bowed the wretched string broke, and a jolly pug-dog which had been sniffing round me brought the pigtail triumphantly in its mouth to the Privy Councillor. Pursuing it in alarm, I knocked over the table where he had been taking his working breakfast, so that cups, plates, ink-well, and sand-box fell clattering to the ground, and a stream of hot chocolate and ink flowed over the report he had

just composed. "Are you off your head, sir?" roared the infuriated Privy Councillor as he thrust me out of the door.

'What use is the position as copyist that Sub-Rector Paulmann says I might get? My evil star, which pursues me everywhere, is sure to prevent it! Just take what happened today!
I wanted to celebrate Ascension Day with the best of good
cheer, and not count the cost. I could have called proudly to the
waiter, like any other guest in Linke's Restaurant, "A bottle of
strong beer—your very best, please!" I could have sat there till
late at night, close to some group of beautiful girls in magnificent finery. I'm sure I'd have plucked up courage and become
a different person altogether; so much so, in fact, that if one of
the girls had said, "I wonder what time it is?" or "What music
are they playing?" I'd have leapt to my feet with graceful ease
and without knocking over my glass or stumbling against my
seat; I'd have stepped forward one-and-a-half paces, bowing
respectfully, and said, "Permit me to be of service to you,
Mademoiselle, it is the overture from *The Woman from the Danube*"* or "It's almost six o'clock." Could anybody in the world
have taken that amiss? Of course not! The girls would have
looked at one another with mischievous smiles, as always happens when I pluck up enough courage to show that I can
converse with ladies in an easy, man-of-the-world tone. But
then Satan makes me run into the accursed apple-basket, and
now I must smoke my health-tobacco all by myself . . . '.

Here Anselmus's self-communings were interrupted by a
strange rushing, swishing sound which started in the grass just
beside him but soon slid up into the branches and foliage of the
elder-tree arching over his head. At one moment it sounded as
though the evening breeze were shaking the leaves; at another
moment it sounded like birds billing and cooing in the
branches, playfully fluttering their little wings. Then a whispering and lisping began, and the flowers seemed to tinkle like
tiny crystal bells. As Anselmus listened more and more intently,
the whispering and lisping and tinkling somehow turned into
faint words, trailing away on the breeze:

'Through the trees, through the leaves, through the swelling
blossoms, we slip and slide and slither—sisters, little sisters,
slither through the shimmering sunshine—up and down—the

evening sun shoots its beams, the evening breeze breathes and stirs the leaves—the dew descends—the blossoms are singing— let's raise our voices, and sing with the blossoms and the breeze—soon stars will be shining—we must descend— through the trees, through the leaves, slip and slither, little sisters.'

And so it went on, bewilderingly. 'It's only the breeze,' thought Anselmus, 'though this evening it almost seems to be uttering intelligible words.' But at that moment a trio of crystal bells seemed to peal out above his head; he looked up and saw three little snakes, gleaming in green and gold, coiled round the branches and stretching their heads towards the evening sun. Then the whispering words began again, and the snakes slithered caressingly up and down through the leaves and branches, and their rapid movements made it seem as through the elder-tree were scattering a thousand sparkling emeralds amid its dark foliage. 'It's the sunshine reflected in the leaves', thought Anselmus, but then the bells rang out once more, and he saw the snakes stretching their necks down to him. An electric shock seemed to penetrate his entire body, he trembled inwardly; he stared upwards, and saw a pair of magnificent dark-blue eyes looking at him with inexpressible yearning, so that a mixture of supreme happiness and intense pain, which he had never felt before, made his heart almost burst. And as he continued, full of burning desire, to gaze into those lovely eyes, the crystal bells pealed out louder in delightful notes, and the sparkling emeralds descended and enfolded him, flickering around him in innumerable tiny flames and shimmering gold threads. The elder-tree stirred and spoke: 'You lay in my shade, surrounded by my fragrance, but you did not understand me. The fragrance is my language, when it is kindled by love.' The wind swept past, saying: 'I stroked your temples, but you did not understand me; the breeze is my language, when it is kindled by love.' Rays of sunshine broke through the clouds, and their burning light seemed to say: 'I poured my blazing gold upon you, but you did not understand me; the blaze is my language, when it is kindled by love.'

And as Anselmus gazed ever more deeply into those magnificent eyes, his yearning grew more intense, his desire more ardent. Then everything around him began to stir, as though waking into joyful life. The flowers cast their fragrance upon him like the wondrous singing of a thousand flute-like voices, and the echo of their song was borne away to far lands by the passing sunset clouds. But as the last ray of sunlight vanished behind the mountains, and twilight covered the landscape with its veil, a deep harsh voice seemed to call from far away: 'Hey, hey! What's all the whispering and muttering over there? Hey! Who's searching for the sunshine behind the mountains? You've sung and sunned yourselves quite enough—hey, through the bushes and the grass, through the grass and the river! Hey! Come down here—come do-own he-e-ere!'

Thus the voice died away like the rumbling of distant thunder, but the crystal bells ended in a jangling discord. All was silent, and Anselmus saw the three gleaming, shimmering snakes gliding through the grass towards the river; with a swishing, rushing sound they plunged into the Elbe, and as they vanished into its waves a crackling green flame shot up and flew obliquely towards the town, fizzling out as it went.

SECOND VIGIL

How the student Anselmus was thought to be drunk and mad. Crossing the Elbe. Graun's bravura aria. Conradi's liqueur and the bronze apple-woman.

'That gentleman doesn't seem to be right in the head!' said a worthy townswoman, returning from a stroll with her family. She stopped, folded her arms, and watched the crazy antics of the student Anselmus. For the latter was embracing the trunk of the elder-tree and calling over and over again into the branches and foliage: 'Oh, gleam and shine just once more, you beautiful golden snakes, let me hear your little bell-like voices just one more time! Give me one more look, you lovely blue eyes, just one more, or else I must die in agony and ardent yearning!' And as he said this he heaved the most lamentable sighs and groans, and shook the tree in his ardour and impatience. But the only answer it gave was a low, unintelligible rustling of its leaves, which really seemed to mock Anselmus's agony.

'That gentleman doesn't seem to be right in the head', said the townswoman, and Anselmus felt as though he had been shaken out of a deep dream or wakened suddenly by being drenched with ice-cold water. Perceiving his surroundings again for the first time, he wondered at the strange phantom which had impishly made him talk out loud to himself. After gazing at the townswoman in dismay, he finally seized his hat, which had fallen to the ground, and was on the point of hurrying away. Meanwhile her husband had arrived on the scene, with a child in his arms, and after laying the child on the grass he had been leaning on his stick and watching and listening to Anselmus in amazement. He now picked up the pipe and tobacco-pouch which the student had dropped, handed them to him, and said: 'Don't kick up such a din in the dark, sir, and don't make a nuisance of yourself if there's nothing wrong with you except that you've had a drop too much! Now go home quietly and take a nap!'

Anselmus was deeply ashamed and gave a miserable groan. 'There, there,' continued the good citizen, 'don't worry, sir, it can happen to the best of us, and when you're enjoying yourself on Ascension Day you can easily drink more than is good for you, even if you're a gentleman of the cloth—I suppose you're studying for the ministry, sir. But if you don't mind, sir, I'll just fill my pipe with your tobacco, because mine has run out.'

When the good citizen said this, Anselmus was already on the point of putting his pipe and tobacco-pouch in his pocket; but now the man cleaned his pipe slowly and deliberately, and began filling it equally slowly. Several girls who had joined the group were talking with the woman in low voices and giggling as they looked at Anselmus. For his part, he felt as though he were standing on sharp thorns and red-hot pins. No sooner had he got his pipe and tobacco-pouch back than he took to his heels. All the wonders he had seen had vanished from his memory, and he remembered only that he had talked all sorts of nonsense out loud under the elder-tree. This memory was made yet more dreadful by his lifelong aversion to people who talk to themselves. His headmaster used to say that Satan was speaking through their mouths, and Anselmus firmly believed this. It was unbearable to think that he had been mistaken for a divinity student who had got drunk on Ascension Day. He was about to turn into the avenue of poplars near Kosel's Garden, when a voice called to him from behind.

'Anselmus! My dear fellow! In heaven's name, where are you off to in such a tearing hurry!' Anselmus stood stock still, convinced that a new misfortune was about to befall him. Again the voice was heard.

'Anselmus, my dear fellow, do come back, we're waiting here beside the river!'

Only now did Anselmus realize that it was his friend Sub-Rector Paulmann who was calling to him. He went back to the Elbe and found the Sub-Rector with his two daughters, as well as Registrary Heerbrand, on the point of getting into a rowing-boat. The Sub-Rector invited the student to cross the Elbe with him and then to spend the evening in his house in the suburb of Pirna. Anselmus accepted gladly, thinking this would enable him to escape the evil destiny that was dogging his steps. It so happened that, as they crossed the river, a display of fireworks was released from Anton's Garden on the opposite bank. The rockets shot up, hissing and spluttering, and the glittering stars flew apart in mid-air, scattering countless crackling flames and rays all round them. Anselmus was sitting, deep in thought, beside the boatman at the oars, when he suddenly noticed the sparkling, crackling flames reflected in the water, and fancied that the little golden snakes were swimming through the waves. All the strange things he had seen under the elder-tree returned vividly into his mind, and once again he felt the inexpressible yearning, the ardent desire, which had made his heart quake with convulsions of agonizing delight.

'Oh, have you returned, you golden snakes? Sing, please sing! Your song will bring back those lovely dark-blue eyes! Are you really beneath the waves?'

As he uttered these cries, the student Anselmus lunged forward as though to fling himself out of the rowing-boat into the waves. 'Are you crazy, sir?' exclaimed the boatman, catching him by his coat-tails. The girls sitting beside him shrieked with terror and took refuge on the other side of the boat; Registrary Heerbrand whispered something to the Sub-Rector, of whose reply Anselmus could catch only the words: 'these fits—never noticed before?' Thereupon Sub-Rector Paulmann also rose; assuming a certain grave and solemn expression befitting his official rank, he sat down beside Anselmus, took him by the hand and said: 'Are you all right, my dear fellow?'

Anselmus was close to fainting, for a wild conflict had arisen within him, which he was trying vainly to control. He could now see quite plainly that what he had taken for the sparkling of the golden snakes was only the reflection of the firework display in Anton's Garden; yet his heart was convulsed by a new and unknown emotion, of which he himself could not tell whether it was joy or pain, and every time the boatman thrust the oars into the water, making its ripples splash and bubble as though in anger, Anselmus heard amid the tumult a stealthy whispering and lisping: 'Anselmus! Anselmus! Don't you see us always swimming ahead of you? Our little sister will be sure to gaze at you again—believe—believe—believe in us.' And he thought he could see three fiery green lines in the reflected light. But as he gazed wistfully into the water, hoping that the lovely eyes would look out of the waves, he perceived quite clearly that the fiery gleam only came from the lighted windows of the nearby houses. He sat in silence, inwardly struggling with himself; but Sub-Rector Paulmann repeated more insistently: 'Are you all right, my dear fellow?'

The student replied in a despondent tone: 'Oh, my dear Sub-Rector, if you only knew what remarkable dreams I've just had while wide awake, with my eyes open, under an elder-tree at the wall of Linke's garden, you wouldn't take it amiss that I am so absent-minded, as it were . . .'

'Come now, my dear fellow,' interrupted the Sub-Rector, 'I always took you for a thoroughly respectable young man, but to dream while wide awake, and then suddenly to try to jump into the water—I'm sorry, but nobody would do that except a madman or a fool!'

The student Anselmus was feeling quite downcast by his friend's harsh words, when Paulmann's eldest daughter Veronica, a very pretty, blooming girl of sixteen, said: 'But, father, Mr Anselmus must have met with something remarkable, and perhaps he just imagines that he was awake, when in reality he fell asleep under the elder-tree and had all sorts of foolish fancies which he is still thinking about.'

'Moreover, my dear young lady, and my worthy friend,' put in Registrary Heerbrand, 'is it not possible to fall into a certain dream-like state while one is awake? It once happened to me that while drinking coffee in the afternoon, in the meditative state required for physical and mental digestion, I suddenly recalled, as though by inspiration, where to find a document that I had lost. And in the same way, only yesterday, I beheld a magnificent Latin text in black-letter type dancing before my open eyes.'

'With all due respect, Registrary,' rejoined Sub-Rector Paulmann, 'you have always had a taste for poetical matters, which makes it easy to fall prey to romantic fancies.'

Anselmus, however, was glad that someone had come to his defence when he was so unfortunate as to be considered mad or drunk, and although it was by now rather dark, he noticed for the first time what beautiful dark-blue eyes Veronica seemed to have, never giving a thought to those wondrous eyes that he had seen in the elder-tree. In fact, the incident under the elder-tree had suddenly vanished from Anselmus's mind; he felt cheerful and at ease, and when they were getting out of the boat his high spirits even induced him to offer a helping hand to his defender Veronica; she put her arm in his, and without further ado, he conducted her homewards so adroitly and with such good fortune that he only tripped up once, and as this was on the only muddy patch on the entire way, Veronica's white dress was hardly splashed at all.

Sub-Rector Paulmann did not fail to notice how Anselmus had changed for the better; the student was again in his good books, and he apologized for the harsh words he had uttered a little earlier. 'Indeed,' added the Sub-Rector, 'there are cases of people being downright terrified and tormented by certain species of apparition; but this is a physical illness which can be alleviated by applying leeches*—saving your presence—to the backside, as was demonstrated by a famous scholar now deceased.'

Anselmus no longer had any idea whether he had been drunk, mad, or ill, but at all events he was sure there was no need for leeches, since all apparitions, of whatever species, had entirely vanished, and he was feeling more and more cheerful the more he managed to lavish his attentions on the fair Veronica. After the frugal meal, as usual, they played music. Anselmus seated himself at the piano, and Veronica let the company listen to her clear voice.

'My dear young lady,' said Registrary Heerbrand, 'you have a voice like a crystal bell!'

'Nothing of the sort!' burst out Anselmus, quite involuntarily.

Everyone stared at him in embarrassed amazement.

'Crystal bells sound wonderful in elder-trees! Wonderful!' continued Anselmus in an undertone.

Then Veronica put her hand on his shoulder and said: 'What are you talking about, Mr Anselmus?'

The student promptly regained his spirits and began to play. Sub-Rector Paulmann gave him a black look, but Registrary Heerbrand placed some sheet music on the stand and delighted the company by singing a bravura aria by Graun.* After that

Anselmus played the accompaniment to some more songs, and a fugue for two voices, performed by himself and Veronica, and composed by the Sub-Rector himself, put everyone in a thoroughly cheerful mood.

It was late in the evening, and Registrary Heerbrand was picking up his hat and stick, when Sub-Rector Paulmann went over to him with an air of mystery and said: 'My dear Registrary, I believe you meant to tell our good friend Anselmus— you know!—the matter we discussed previously . . .'

'With the greatest of pleasure', rejoined the Registrary, and after they had sat down in a circle, he began, without further ado, as follows.

'There is in this town a strange, eccentric old man, who is said to study all kinds of occult science; but as there are no such things in reality, I am inclined to believe that he is a scholarly antiquary and also something of an experimental chemist. I refer, of course, to our Privy Archivist Lindhorst. As you know, he lives all alone in his old house in a remote part of town, and when he is not occupied with his duties, he may be found in his library or in his chemical laboratory, to which, however, no one else is admitted. Besides many rare books, he owns a number of manuscripts, some written in Arabic and Coptic, and even in strange characters which belong to no known language. He wants these to be expertly copied, and for this purpose he requires someone skilled in line-drawing, who can copy all these characters on parchment, in Indian ink, with the utmost exactitude and accuracy. The person he employs will work in a special room in his house under his supervision, and receive not only free board but also a thaler for each day's work; and the Archivist also promises a substantial gratuity when the copies have been successfully completed. The working hours are from twelve to six daily, with a break for eating between three and four. Having employed two or three other young men to copy the manuscripts, but found that they were not up to the task, he finally asked me to recommend an expert calligrapher. I at once thought of you, my dear Anselmus, for I know that you not only write a good clear hand but can also make exact and elegant line-drawings. If, in these hard times, while waiting for a salaried post, you are willing to earn a thaler daily, not to mention the gratuity, then you must call upon the Archivist tomorrow at twelve o'clock precisely; doubtless you know where he lives. But take care not to make a single blot! If a blot falls on the copy, then there is nothing for it but to start all over again; if it falls on the original, then the Archivist is quite capable of throwing you out of the window, for he is a hot-tempered man.'

Anselmus was overjoyed by the Registrary's proposal, for not only did he write a clear hand and make line-drawings, but he was passionately fond of copying letters with the most laborious calligraphic skill. He therefore thanked his patrons very courteously and promised not to miss the appointment at twelve o'clock the next day. That night Anselmus could see and hear nothing but gleaming thalers and their pleasant jingling. And who can blame the poor fellow, since the whims of fortune had dashed so many of his hopes, and he was obliged to look on both sides of every penny and deny himself many of the enjoyments that appeal to the vigour of youth. Early in the morning he gathered together his pencils, his raven's quills, and his Indian ink; 'for', thought he, 'these materials are better than anything the Archivist could invent'. Above all, he inspected and arranged his masterpieces of calligraphy and his drawings, in order to show them to the Archivist as proof of his ability to perform what was required of him. All went well; a lucky star seemed to have taken charge; he tied his cravat neatly at the first attempt, he did not burst a seam or tear a stitch in his black silk stockings, and his hat did not fall into the dust again after being brushed clean.

To cut a long story short: at precisely half-past eleven the student Anselmus was standing in Conradi's shop in Castle Lane, in his bluish-grey tail-coat and black satin knee-breeches, a rolled-up bundle of line-drawings and calligraphic exercises under his arm, and drinking not just one but two glasses of the best liqueur; 'for this', thought he, tapping his empty pocket, 'will soon have thalers jingling in it'. Although it was a long walk to the lonely street in which Archivist Lindhorst's old house was situated, Anselmus was outside the front door by twelve o'clock. Standing there, he looked at the fine big bronze door-knocker; but as the last stroke of the bell of the Cross

Church smote the air, and he was about to seize hold of the knocker, its metal features were hideously obscured by fiery blue rays and contorted into a grin. Alas! it was the apple-woman from the Black Gate! Her pointed teeth were rattling in her loose mouth, and their rattling said: 'You gr-r-reat gorm-less fool! Just you wait! Why did you run through the gate? You fool!' Anselmus reeled back in horror; he tried to hold on to the doorpost, but his hand grasped the bell-pull and tugged it; the bell rang more and more loudly in jarring discords, and its mocking echo could be heard throughout the deserted house: 'Into glass you must pass!'

Such terror gripped Anselmus that a convulsive shudder ran through his every limb. The bell-pull sank to the ground and turned into a transparent white boa constrictor which coiled itself round him and squeezed him ever more tightly in its folds, until his limbs were crushed to pulp and the blood spouted from his veins, seeping into the serpent's transparent body and dyeing it red. In his frightful terror he tried to shriek: 'Kill me, kill me!' but his cries were no more than hollow gurglings. The serpent raised its head and placed its long, pointed, red-hot metal tongue upon Anselmus's chest; a stab-bing pain suddenly severed his vital artery, and he lost con-sciousness.

When Anselmus regained his senses, he was lying on his wretched pallet; but Sub-Rector Paulmann was standing before him, and saying: 'In Heaven's name, my dear Anselmus, what on earth have you been up to!'

THIRD VIGIL

News of Archivist Lindhorst's family. Veronica's blue eyes.
Registrary Heerbrand.

'The spirit looked upon the waters, whereupon they stirred and surged up in foaming waves and plunged thundering into the abysses, which opened their black jaws greedily to swallow them. Like victors in triumph, the granite rocks raised their jagged heads, guarding the vale, until the sun took it into her maternal lap to nurse and warm it, enfolding it with her rays as though with blazing arms. A thousand seeds that had been slumbering under the sandy waste now woke from their deep sleep and stretched their green shoots and leaves towards the face of their mother; like smiling children in a green cradle, flowers nestled in the bud, until they too, roused by their mother, awoke and bedecked themselves with the lights which their mother, to give them pleasure, had tinged with a thousand hues. But in the midst of the vale there was a black hill, which rose and sank as does man's breast when it heaves with ardent yearning. Vapours mounted from the abysses, gathering in mighty clouds, and strove fiercely to obscure their mother's face; but she called upon the gale, which descended upon them and scattered them, and when the pure ray again touched the black hill, excess of delight gave birth to a splendid fiery lily, opening its petals like lovely lips to receive sweet kisses from its mother.

'Now a brilliant light entered the vale. It was the youth Phosphorus, and when the fiery lily beheld him, she was overcome by passionate yearning love, and besought him: "Be mine eternally, fair youth! for I love you, and I must perish if you should leave me."

'Then said the youth Phosphorus: "I would gladly be yours, fair flower, but, like a thankless child, you will leave your father · and mother, you will forget your playfellows, you will desire to be greater and mightier than any of the flowers that now share your happiness as equals. The yearning that now suffuses you will be split into countless rays and will torture you, for the mind will give birth to the senses, and the supreme joy kindled by the spark that I now cast into you is the agonizing despair in which you will perish, to grow anew in an alien guise. This spark is *thought!*"

'"Alas!" lamented the lily, "cannot I be yours in the ardour that now burns within me? Can I love you more than I do now, and can I behold you as I do now, if you destroy me?"

'Then the youth Phosphorus kissed her, and she burst into flame as though filled with radiant light. From the flames sprang forth an alien being which swiftly escaped from the vale and roamed through infinite space, caring not a whit for its childhood playfellows nor for the youth it had loved. He for his part mourned his lost beloved, for it was only his infinite love for the beautiful lily that had induced him to enter the lonely vale, and the granite rocks bowed their heads in sympathy with the youth's lamentations. But one of the rocks opened its lap and brought forth a black dragon, its wings fluttering and whirring. The dragon said: "My brothers, the metals, are asleep within, but I am always wide awake, and am willing to help you." Rising and falling on his pinions, the dragon at last succeeded in catching the being that had sprung from the lily, bore it to the hill, and enfolded it in his wings. It became the lily once more, but thought remained to lacerate her, and her love for the youth Phosphorus was an agony which breathed poisonous vapours upon the flowers that had once rejoiced in her gaze, and made them wither and die. The youth Phosphorus put on gleaming armour that shed innumerable dazzling rays, and fought with the dragon, who struck the armour with his wing and made it ring loudly. Restored to life by its mighty clang, the flowers fluttered around the dragon like brightly coloured birds; the dragon's strength vanished, and he hid himself, defeated, in the depths of the earth. The lily was freed, the youth Phosphorus embraced her in the ardent passion of heavenly love, and in an exultant chorus the flowers, the birds, and even the lofty granite rocks paid homage to her as the queen of the vale.'

'Forgive me, my dear Archivist, but that's a lot of Oriental bombast!' said Registry Heerbrand, 'and we asked you, you know, to do as you usually do and recount some incident from your remarkable life, such as an adventure you had on your travels, provided it was true.'

'Let me assure you,' replied Archivist Lindhorst, 'what I have just told you is the truest story I can regale you with, my friends, and in a sort of a way it does form part of my life. For I come from that very vale, and the fiery lily who ended up reigning as a queen is my great-great-great-great-grandmother, so that I am really a prince.'

The entire company burst out laughing.

'Laugh as heartily as you please,' continued the Archivist; 'what I have given you is of course a very inadequate account, and you may well think it mere crazy nonsense; nevertheless, it is very far from absurd or even allegorical, but literally true. If I had known, though, that the splendid love-story to which I owe my existence would give you so little pleasure, I would instead have told you some of the news that I heard from my brother when he visited me yesterday.'

'Why, how is that? Have you really got a brother, Archivist? Where is he? Where does he live? Is he too employed by the King, or is he a private scholar?' asked a chorus of voices.

'No!' replied the Archivist, coolly and calmly taking a pinch of snuff, 'he went to the bad and joined the dragons.'

'Did I understand you correctly, my worthy Archivist?' asked Registrary Heerbrand. 'Joined the dragons?'

'Joined the dragons?' echoed the chorus.

'Yes, he joined the dragons,' continued the Archivist; 'it was a desperate move. You know, gentlemen, that my father died only very recently, a mere three hundred and eighty-five years ago, which is why I still wear mourning. As I was his favourite, he left me a magnificent onyx, which my brother very much wanted. We quarrelled about it beside my father's body in a most unbecoming fashion, until the late lamented lost his patience, leapt to his feet and threw my wicked brother downstairs. This irritated my brother so much that he joined the dragons on the spot. He now lives in a grove of cypresses near Tunis, where he has the task of guarding a famous mystical carbuncle. A necromancer, a devil of a fellow, who has just moved into a summer residence in Lapland, has his eye on this carbuncle, so that my brother can only leave his post for the odd quarter of an hour, while the necromancer is tending his salamander-beds in the garden, to bring me the latest news from the source of the Nile.'

For the second time the assembled company burst into a roar of laughter, but the student Anselmus was overcome by an uncanny feeling, and he could scarcely meet the Archivist's grave and intent gaze without trembling inwardly in a way that he himself found inexplicable. In particular, the Archivist's harsh but strangely metallic-sounding voice had a mysterious penetrating quality that shook Anselmus to the core.

There seemed no chance today of attaining the real purpose for which Registrary Heerbrand had taken him to the coffee-house. After the incident outside the Archivist's house, nothing could persuade Anselmus to attempt a second visit; for he was firmly convinced that a mere accident had saved him, if not from death, then from the danger of madness. Sub-Rector Paulmann had been walking along the street and found Anselmus lying insensible outside the front door, being tended by an old woman who had put down her basket of cakes and apples. The Sub-Rector had promptly summoned a sedan-chair and had Anselmus carried home in it. 'Think of me as you please,' said Anselmus, 'call me a fool, or not, as you wish; but I tell you, the accursed face of the old witch from the Black Gate was grinning at me from that door-knocker; as for what happened next, I'd rather not talk about it, but if I had recovered from my swoon and seen that accursed apple-woman in front of me (for that's who the old woman was who was tending me), I should have had heart failure there and then, or else gone mad.' No amount of persuasion and rational argument on the part of the Sub-Rector and the Registrary had the slightest effect, and even Veronica, with her blue eyes, could not divert him from his pensive and preoccupied mood. They concluded that his mind must be disordered, and sought ways of distracting him. The Registrary opined that the best means would be the employment offered by Archivist Lindhorst, namely the copying of manuscripts. All that was necessary was to introduce Anselmus to the Archivist in some suitable fashion, and since the Registrary knew that the latter spent almost every evening in a certain well-known coffee-house, he invited Anselmus to drink a glass of beer and smoke a pipe there every evening at his, the Registrary's, expense, until he should somehow be introduced to the Archivist and agree to undertake the copying of the manuscripts. Anselmus accepted this offer with the utmost gratitude.

'God will reward you, my dear Registrary,' said Sub-Rector Paulmann, 'if you can restore the young man to his senses.'

'God will reward you!' repeated Veronica, piously raising her eyes heavenwards and thinking what a charming young man Anselmus was, with or without his senses.

Just as Archivist Lindhorst, having picked up his hat and stick, was about to leave, Registrary Heerbrand hastily seized Anselmus by the hand, stepped in front of the Archivist with him, and said: 'My most esteemed Privy Archivist, this is the student Anselmus, who is exceptionally skilled in calligraphy and draughtsmanship, and would like to copy your rare manuscripts.'

'I'm exceedingly obliged to you,' replied the Archivist quickly, putting on his three-cornered military hat, elbowing the Registrary and the student aside, and hurrying noisily downstairs. They both stood there in astonishment, gaping at the door which he had just slammed in their faces so hard that the hinges were rattling.

'What a very peculiar old man!' said the Registrary.

'Peculiar old man', stammered Anselmus, feeling as though a stream of ice-cold water were flowing through his veins and turning him as rigid as a statue. But all the other customers laughed and said: 'The Archivist was in one of his moods today, but tomorrow he's sure to be as meek as a lamb and won't say a word; he'll just watch the smoke coiling from his pipe or read the newspapers; you mustn't mind him.'

'True enough,' thought Anselmus, 'why should anyone mind such behaviour! Didn't the Archivist say he was exceedingly obliged to me for offering to copy his manuscripts? And why did Registrary Heerbrand have to step in front of him just as he was setting off home? No, Privy Archivist Lindhorst is a decent chap at heart, and astonishingly liberal—though he does say some very odd things. But what's that to me? I'll go to his house tomorrow at twelve o'clock sharp, even if a hundred bronze apple-women try to stop me.'

FOURTH VIGIL

*The melancholy mood of the student Anselmus. The emerald mirror.
How Archivist Lindhorst flew away in the shape of a kite and
Anselmus met nobody at all.*

Let me ask you outright, gentle reader, if there have not been
hours, indeed whole days and weeks of your life, during which
all your usual activities were painfully repugnant, and everything you believed in and valued seemed foolish and worthless?
At such times you did not know what to do or where to turn;
your breast was stirred by an obscure feeling that a noble desire
for an object surpassing all earthly pleasures must somewhere,
sometime be fulfilled, a desire which your mind, like a timid
child brought up by severe parents, dared not put into words;
this yearning for something unknown obsessed you wherever
you went, like a translucent dream whose airy shapes dissolve
when looked at too closely, and you lost all interest in your
surroundings. You crept to and fro with downcast gaze like a
rejected lover, and none of humanity's many and varied activities gave you either joy or pain, as though you had ceased to
belong to this world. If you have ever felt such a mood, gentle
reader, then you know from your own experience the state in
which Anselmus found himself.

  And indeed, kind reader, I should like to think that I have
managed by now to bring the student Anselmus vividly before
your eyes. For in the night watches in which I am recording his
extraordinary story, I have still to recount many peculiar events,
which, like a ghostly apparition, turned the everyday lives of
ordinary people topsy-turvy, and I fear that you may end up
believing neither in Anselmus nor in Archivist Lindhorst; you
may even have some unjustified doubts about Sub-Rector Paulmann and Registrary Heerbrand, although the latter two
worthy gentlemen, at least, are still walking the streets of
Dresden. You are now, kind reader, in the fairy realm of glorious
wonders, whose mighty strokes summon up both supreme bliss
and extreme horror, and where the grave goddess raises her veil

so that we may fancy we see her face—but her grave expression often breaks into a smile, and that is the impish humour that teases us with the bewilderments of magic, as a mother often teases her dearest children. In this realm, which our spirit so often reveals to us, at least in our dreams, try, kind reader, to recognize the well-known shapes that, as the saying goes, cross your path every day. You will then believe that this magnificent realm is much nearer at hand than you had previously thought; and that is what I heartily wish you to believe, and what the strange story of Anselmus is supposed to convey.

As I told you, then, after his meeting with Archivist Lindhorst, the student Anselmus sank into a dreamy, brooding state which made him insensible to all contact with ordinary life. He felt some unknown force stirring within him and causing that blissful pain, that yearning, which assures humanity of another and higher existence. What pleased him most was to wander by himself through fields and forests, as though no longer tied to his impoverished life, and to behold the diverse images arising from the depths of his being, in which he seemed to recognize himself. So it chanced that one day, returning from a long walk, he passed that remarkable elder-bush under which, as though enchanted, he had seen so many strange sights. He felt curiously drawn to the welcoming green patch of grass, but no sooner had he sat down there than all the visions that he had seen in what seemed like heavenly ecstasy, and that a kind of alien force had since banished from his mind, reappeared as vividly as though he were seeing them for the second time. Indeed he discerned even more plainly than before that the lovely blue eyes were those of the green and gold snake which was twining itself round the trunk of the elder-tree, and that the wonderful sound of crystal bells that had so delighted and enraptured him must be radiating from the coils of its slender body. Again, just as he had done on Ascension Day, he embraced the elder-tree and called up into its branches and foliage: 'Oh, let me see you twining and twisting and coiling in the branches just once more, you lovely green snake! Give me just one more glance from your lovely eyes! I love you, I love you, and if you do not return I must perish of sorrow and pain!'

All was silent, however, and the elder-tree only rustled its boughs and leaves unintelligibly, just as it had done before. But Anselmus thought he now knew what was stirring within his breast and lacerating his heart in the agony of infinite yearning. 'Isn't it simply that I love you with all my heart, you wonderful gold snake', he said, 'and that I shall love you till I die? I can't live without you, and I must perish in hopeless misery unless I see you again, unless you become the beloved of my heart—but I know you will be mine, and then all the wonderful dreams that have reached me from another, higher world will come true.'

Every evening, when the sun strewed its sparkling gold only in the tops of the trees, Anselmus went to the elder-tree, and called in heartfelt and pitiable tones into the foliage and boughs, addressing his fair beloved, the little green and gold snake. One day, as he was doing this in his usual fashion, a tall gaunt man, wrapped in a capacious pale-grey frock-coat, suddenly appeared in front of him, darted a fiery glance at him, and exclaimed: 'Hey, hey! Who's doing all this weeping and wailing? Well now, it's Mr Anselmus, who has offered to copy my manuscripts.'

Anselmus was not a little frightened by this powerful voice, for it was the very same voice that had called out on Ascension Day: 'Hey, hey, who's whispering and muttering . . .' and so forth. His astonishment and alarm made him unable to utter a word.

'What's the matter with you, Mr Anselmus?' continued Archivist Lindhorst (for the man in the light-grey frock-coat was none other than he); 'what do you want from the elder-tree, and why have you not come to my house to start work?'

In fact, Anselmus had not yet managed to bring himself to call on the Archivist, although he resolved to do so every evening. At this moment, however, seeing his beautiful dreams destroyed by the wrathful voice that had robbed him of his beloved on the previous occasion, he was seized by a kind of desperation and burst out impetuously: 'You may think me crazy or not, Archivist, I don't care two pins, but it was in this very tree, on Ascension Day, that I saw the green and gold snake, the eternal beloved of my soul, and she spoke to me in wonderful crystal notes, but you—yes, you, Archivist!—you uttered such frightful cries and yells from across the river.'

'How can that be, my good sir?' interrupted the Archivist, smiling strangely as he took a pinch of snuff.

Anselmus felt a weight being lifted from his heart now that he had managed to start talking about his wondrous adventure, and he felt quite justified in virtually accusing the Archivist of producing the distant thunderous cry. He pulled himself together and said: 'Very well, I'll tell the whole story of the fateful events that befell me on Ascension Day, and then you can do and say what you like and think whatever you please about me.' And he did indeed relate the whole curious sequence of events, from his unfortunate collision with the apple-basket right down to the departure of the three green and gold snakes across the water, and how people had thought him drunk or mad. 'I saw all this,' concluded Anselmus, 'with my own eyes, and deep in my heart I can still hear the echo of the delightful voices that spoke to me; it was certainly not a dream, and if I am not to die of love and yearning, I have no choice but to believe in the green and gold snakes, though from your smile, Archivist, I can see that you consider the snakes no more than the product of my overheated imagination.'

'Not in the slightest,' rejoined the Archivist with perfect calm and composure; 'the green and gold snakes that you, Mr Anselmus, saw in the elder-tree, were my three daughters, and you have obviously fallen head-over-heels in love with the blue eyes of my youngest, whose name is Serpentina. What is more, I knew all this on Ascension Day, and since I got tired of hearing the muttering and tinkling as I was sitting at my desk, I called to the young hussies and told them it was time to hurry home, for the sun was already setting and they had amused themselves quite enough by singing and sunbathing.'

Anselmus felt as though he were now being told in so many words something he had long suspected. Although he felt as if the elder-tree, the wall, and the grassy patch, and all the other things around him, were beginning gently to spin, he got a grip on himself and was about to say something. Instead of letting Anselmus get a word out, however, the Archivist swiftly removed the glove from his left hand, held up a ring with a wondrous sparkling, flaming stone before Anselmus's eyes, and said: 'Look at this, my good Mr Anselmus, you will enjoy what you see.'

Anselmus looked, and, wonderful to relate! beams of light were radiating from the stone, as though from a fiery focus, and joining together to form a shining crystal mirror. In the mirror the three green and gold snakes were dancing and coiling, now dodging one another, now twined together. And every time their slender, sparkling bodies touched, glorious chords rang out like crystal bells, and the snake in the middle stretched her head right out of the mirror, as though full of yearning desire, and her dark-blue eyes said: 'Do you know me—do you believe in me, Anselmus? Only in faith is there love—can you really love?'

'Oh, Serpentina, Serpentina!' shrieked Anselmus, beside himself with rapture; but Archivist Lindhorst quickly breathed upon the mirror, the rays returned to the focus with a crackling of electricity, and once again there was only a small emerald flashing on the hand of the Archivist, who drew his glove over it.

'Did you see the gold snakes, Mr Anselmus?' asked the Archivist.

'Oh heavens, I did indeed!' replied the student, 'and the fair and lovely Serpentina.'

'Hush!' continued the Archivist, 'that's enough for today, and, what is more, if you decide to work for me, you can see my daughters often enough, or rather, I will give you this treat if you do a good job of work, and copy every character with the utmost accuracy and neatness. But you have never once called on me, although Registrary Heerbrand assured me that you would come forthwith, so that I have been vainly expecting you for several days.'

As soon as the Archivist had uttered the name Heerbrand, Anselmus once more felt that his feet were firmly planted on solid ground and that he really was the student Anselmus and the man before him Archivist Lindhorst. The latter's matter-of-fact tone, sharply contrasting with the wondrous apparitions which he had summoned up like a veritable necromancer, had something horrible about it, and this effect was heightened by the piercing gaze of his blazing eyes, which shone from their bony sockets in his craggy, wrinkled face as though from some kind of casing. The student was gripped by the uncanny feeling that had taken possession of him in the coffee-house when the Archivist had related so many wondrous incidents. With an effort he controlled his emotions, and when the Archivist repeated the question: 'Why have you not called on me?', he brought himself to recount all that had befallen him at the front door.

'My dear Mr Anselmus,' said the Archivist, when the student had finished his story, 'I know the apple-woman whom you deigned to mention; she is an abominable creature who has played all sorts of tricks on me, but to have herself made into a bronze door-knocker in order to frighten away welcome visitors is really too bad—quite insufferable. If you call on me at twelve tomorrow, my good Mr Anselmus, and notice her grinning and growling at you, please be kind enough to dab a little of this liquid on her nose, and then everything will be all right. Now goodbye, my dear Mr Anselmus; I walk rather fast, so I can hardly expect you to accompany me back to town. Goodbye! We'll see each other tomorrow at twelve.'

The Archivist had given Anselmus a small bottle of golden yellow liquid, and now he strode rapidly away. Twilight had fallen, and the Archivist seemed to be floating rather than walking into the valley. As he approached Kosel's Garden, the wind seized his capacious coat and blew its tails apart, so that they fluttered in the air like a huge pair of wings. To Anselmus, as he looked after the Archivist in astonishment, it seemed as though a great bird were spreading its pinions in order to fly swiftly away. As the student gazed into the twilight, a whitish-grey kite rose into the air with a harsh scream, and he perceived that the fluttering white object, which he had supposed was the Archivist striding away, must all along have been the kite, even though he could not work out how the Archivist had vanished so suddenly.

'But he may have flown away in his own person, Archivist Lindhorst,' said Anselmus to himself, 'for I can see and feel that all the strange figures from a distant world of wonders, which before I saw only in rare and remarkable dreams, have now entered my waking life and are making me their plaything. But never mind! You are alive and glowing in my heart, sweet and lovely Serpentina, you alone can appease the infinite longing that lacerates my innermost being. Oh, when shall I gaze into your lovely eyes—my dear, dear Serpentina!' cried the student Anselmus loudly.

'That's a vile unchristian name', muttered the bass voice of somebody near him who was returning home from a walk. On receiving this timely reminder of where he was, Anselmus hastened away, thinking to himself: 'Wouldn't it be unfortunate if I were now to meet Sub-Rector Paulmann or Registrary Heerbrand?' But he met neither.

FIFTH VIGIL

Counsellor Anselmus's lady. Cicero's De Officiis. Monkeys and other such rapscallions. Old Lizzie. The equinox.

'That Anselmus is simply good for nothing,' said Sub-Rector Paulmann; 'all my good advice, all my exhortations are wasted, he won't apply himself to anything, even though he has excellent school-leaving certificates, which are the foundation of all future achievement.'

Registrary Heerbrand, however, replied with a sly and mysterious smile: 'Let Anselmus go his own way, dear Sub-Rector! He's an odd fish, but with plenty of ability, and when I say "ability", I mean that he might end up a Privy Secretary, or even a Counsellor.'

'Couns—' began the Sub-Rector in the utmost amazement, but the word stuck in his throat.

'Hush!' continued the Registrary, 'I know what I know! He has been sitting in Archivist Lindhorst's house, copying manuscripts, for the past two days, and last night in the coffee-house the Archivist said to me: "The man you recommended is a sterling fellow, my worthy friend!—he'll go far," and now just think of the Archivist's contacts—not another word—we'll talk about this in a year's time!' With these words, still smiling slyly, the Registrary went out of the door, leaving the Sub-Rector motionless in his chair and speechless with amazement and curiosity.

Veronica, however, had drawn her own conclusions from this conversation. 'Didn't I know all along', thought she, 'that Mr Anselmus was a very clever and amiable young man, who will do great things? If only I knew whether he really is fond of me! But didn't he squeeze my hand twice that evening when we crossed the Elbe? Didn't he look at me during the duet in a strange way that quite pierced my heart? Yes, he must really be fond of me—and I . . .'

Veronica abandoned herself, as young girls will, to delicious dreams of a happy future. She was a Counsellor's lady, living in a handsome residence in Castle Lane, or on the New Market, or in Moritz Street; her fashionable hat, her new Turkish shawl, suited her perfectly; she took her breakfast in the window alcove, wearing an elegant morning gown and giving the cook instructions for the day. 'But don't spoil the meat course, for it's the Counsellor's favourite dish!' Passing dandies cast upward glances at her, and she overhears them saying: 'What a charming woman the Counsellor's lady is, and how beautiful she looks in that lace cap!' The lady of Privy Counsellor Y. sends a domestic to ask whether the Counsellor's lady would care to visit Linke's Restaurant today. 'Give your mistress my very best compliments and say that I am very sorry, but I have promised to have tea with the lady of President Z.' Then Counsellor Anselmus returns, having gone out early to attend to his duties. He is dressed in the latest fashion. 'It's ten o'clock already, I declare', he cries, making his gold watch strike the hour, and giving his young wife a kiss. 'How are you, my pet, can you guess what I've brought you?' he goes on teasingly, and from his waistcoat pocket he produces a pair of magnificent ear-rings in the latest style, which he puts in her ears to replace those she was wearing before. 'Oh, what lovely dainty ear-rings', cries Veronica out loud, throwing away her work and jumping up out of her chair to look at the ear-rings in the mirror.

'What on earth is the matter?' said Sub-Rector Paulmann, who had been so engrossed in Cicero's *De Officiis* that he now nearly dropped the book; 'you're getting as bad as Anselmus with your crazy fits.'

At that moment, however, the student Anselmus entered the room. Contrary to his normal habits, he had not paid a visit for several days. To Veronica's alarm and amazement, his whole manner had changed. In a confident tone which was quite uncharacteristic of him, he spoke of a new direction his life was taking and of wonderful prospects which had disclosed themselves to him but which many people were quite unable to see. Sub-Rector Paulmann, recalling the Registrary's mysterious remarks, was still more taken aback, and could scarcely utter a syllable. After mentioning something about work that urgently needed doing for Archivist Lindhorst, and kissing Veronica's hand with elegant ease, Anselmus hastened downstairs and was gone.

'That was the Counsellor already', murmured Veronica to herself, 'and he kissed my hand without slipping or treading on my toes as usual! He gave me such a tender look—he must really be fond of me.' She abandoned herself once more to her day-dreams, but now it seemed as though a hostile figure kept appearing among the lovely sights that filled her future domestic life as a Counsellor's lady, and the figure laughed scornfully and said: 'All this is stupid, commonplace stuff, and none of it is true anyway, for Anselmus will never marry you and become a Counsellor; he doesn't love you one bit, even though you have blue eyes and a slender build and a well-shaped hand.' A stream of icy water flowed through Veronica's heart, and a deep horror destroyed the contentment with which she had seen herself a moment earlier wearing the lace cap and the elegant ear-rings. She very nearly burst into tears as she said aloud: 'Oh dear, it's quite true, he doesn't love me, and I'll never be a Counsellor's lady!'

'Romantic capers, romantic capers!' shouted Sub-Rector Paulmann, seizing his hat and stick and hurrying off in a rage!

'That was all I needed', sighed Veronica, feeling very cross with her twelve-year-old sister, who had been quietly sitting and sewing the entire time. By now it was almost three o'clock, time to tidy the room and lay the table for coffee; for the Misses Oster had promised to call on their friend Veronica. But from behind every cabinet that Veronica moved, from behind the music-books that she removed from the piano, from behind every cup, from behind the coffee-pot that she took from the cupboard, that figure sprang forth like a mandrake, laughing scornfully, snapping its spidery little fingers, and crying: 'He'll never be your husband, he'll never be your husband!' And when she dropped everything and fled to the centre of the room, the creature grew to a huge size and stuck its long nose from behind the stove, groaning and growling: 'He'll never be your husband!'

'Don't you hear anything? Don't you see anything, Frances?' called Veronica, whose fear and trembling made her unable to touch another thing. Her younger sister rose from her sewing-frame, calm and unmoved, and said: 'What's the matter with you today, Veronica? You're making a mess of everything, and shaking all the furniture; I'd better give you a hand.'

But just then the merry girls entered, laughing heartily, and Veronica promptly realized that what she had taken for a living being was really the stove-lid and that the mocking words were really the creaking of the stove door, which would not shut properly. Yet such inner terror had gripped her that she could not recover her good spirits immediately, and her friends could not but notice the unusual nervousness revealed even by her pallor and her alarmed expression. They stopped short on the point of recounting a jolly story and besought their friend for heaven's sake to tell them what had befallen her. Veronica was obliged to confess that she had fallen prey to most peculiar ideas and suddenly been overcome in broad daylight by a strange fear of ghosts, which was not like her at all. She recounted so vividly how a little grey manikin had been peeping from every corner of the room to tease and mock her, that the Misses Oster cast timid glances all round them and soon had quite an uncanny and ghastly sensation. Then Frances entered with the steaming coffee, and all three quickly recollected themselves and laughed at their own folly.

Angelica (such was the name of the elder Miss Oster) was betrothed to an officer who was serving with the army, and he had not been heard of for so long that he must surely be dead, or at least badly wounded. This had plunged Angelica into the deepest grief, but today she was cheerful and almost boisterous, which Veronica, as she frankly declared, found most surprising.

'My dear girl,' said Angelica, 'do you think that my Victor is not constantly in my heart and my mind?—but that's why I'm so cheerful!—good heavens—so happy, so blissful in my very soul—for Victor is well, and I shall soon see him again as a captain of horse, decorated with medals that his boundless courage has earned him. A serious but not dangerous wound in his right arm, caused by a stroke from the sword of an enemy hussar, prevents him from writing, and since he refuses to leave his regiment he is continually moving from place to place and therefore cannot send me news, but this evening he will receive firm instructions to take leave in order to convalesce. He will set off tomorrow for our town, and as he is about to enter the carriage, he will be informed of his promotion to captain.'

'But, dear Angelica,' interrupted Veronica, 'how do you know all this?'

'Don't make fun of me, my dear friend', continued Angelica, 'but I know you won't, for might not the little grey manikin peep out from behind the mirror to punish you? At any rate, I cannot rid myself of the belief in certain mysterious things, because they have often entered my life in visible and even, I might say, tangible form. In particular, I don't find it nearly as strange and incredible as many others might to think that some people can possess a kind of second sight, and have infallible means of setting it in motion. There is in this town an old woman who possesses this gift to an exceptional degree. She is not like other people of her breed who tell fortunes from cards, molten lead, or coffee-grounds. After certain preparations, in which her client must take part, a wondrous medley of shapes and figures appears in a polished metal mirror; these the old woman interprets, and extracts from them the answer to the question. I went to see her last night and obtained the news about my Victor, and I don't doubt its truth for a single moment.'

Angelica's story cast a spark into Veronica's mind and soon ignited the idea of questioning the old woman about Anselmus and her hopes. She learnt that the old woman was called Mrs Rauer, lived in a distant street near the Lake Gate, was to be found exclusively on Tuesdays, Wednesdays, and Fridays from seven o'clock throughout the night until sunrise, and preferred one to come alone. That day was a Wednesday, and Veronica resolved to seek out the old woman under the pretext of accompanying the Osters home; and that is what she did.

Her friends lived in the New Town, and no sooner had she taken leave of them at the Elbe Bridge than she flew to the Lake Gate and soon found herself in the secluded alley which had been described to her and saw at its far end the little red house in which Mrs Rauer was said to live. As she stood outside the front door, she could not withstand a certain uncanny feeling, indeed an inner shudder. Finally, despite her inner repugnance, she pulled herself together and tugged the bell, whereupon the door opened and she groped her way through the dark corridor towards the stairs leading to the first floor, as described by

Angelica. On seeing nobody, she called into the dismal hallway: 'Does Mrs Rauer live here?' Instead of an answer, there rang out a long clear 'Miaow', and a large black tom-cat, arching its back and curling its tail, walked solemnly in front of her to the parlour door, which was opened in response to a second 'Miaow'.

'Well now, my daughter, here already? Come in—come in!' called the figure that stepped out of the room. The sight made Veronica stop as though transfixed. A tall, lean woman wrapped in black rags! As she spoke, her long pointed chin shook, her toothless mouth, overshadowed by her bony aquiline nose, was contorted into a grin, and her gleaming cat-like eyes threw off sparks as they flickered through her huge spectacles. Black bristly hairs stuck out of the many-coloured cloth wound round her head, and her loathsome countenance was rendered hideous by two large patches of scorched skin running from her left cheek across her nose.

Veronica could hardly breathe, and the scream that was about to break from her choking breast turned into a deep sigh as the witch's bony hand seized her and drew her into the room. Inside, all was life and motion; a bewildering mixture of squeaking and mewing and croaking and cheeping assailed her ears. The old woman struck the table with her fist and shrieked: 'Quiet, you rapscallions!' And the monkeys climbed, whining, on top of the high four-poster bed, and the guinea-pigs scurried beneath the stove, and the raven fluttered on to the circular mirror; only the black cat, apparently untroubled by the old woman's scolding, remained sitting calmly on the big padded chair on to which he had leapt after entering the room.

As soon as the noise had ceased, Veronica's spirits rose; she felt less uneasy than she had done out in the hallway, and even the woman no longer seemed so abhorrent. She now looked round the room for the first time. All manner of ugly stuffed animals hung from the ceiling, strange unknown instruments lay in a heap on the floor, and in the fireplace there burned a scanty blue fire which only sent up yellow crackling sparks now and again; but then a rustling noise came from the chimney, and loathsome bats with what seemed like contorted laughing human faces flitted to and fro, and sometimes the flame rose and licked the sooty wall, and such piercing howls and wails were heard that Veronica was gripped by fear and horror.

'Begging your pardon, missie', said the old woman with a chuckle. She took a large feather duster, dipped it in a copper cauldron, and sprinkled the fireplace with it. At once the fire went out and the room became pitch dark, as though filled with thick smoke; but the old woman, who had gone into a small chamber, returned with a light, and Veronica could no longer see the animals or the instruments; it was an ordinary, poorly furnished room.

The old woman came closer to her and said in a grating voice: 'I know what you want from me, my daughter; you'd like to know whether you will marry Anselmus once he is a Counsellor.' Veronica froze with amazement and terror, but the old woman continued: 'You told me everything at home with your Papa, when the coffee-pot was in front of you. *I* was the coffee-pot, didn't you recognize me? Listen, daughter! Give up Anselmus, give him up, he's a horrid creature; he kicked my sons in the face, my dear sons, the rosy-cheeked apples that wait to be bought and then roll out of people's pockets back into my basket. He is on the old fellow's side; the day before yesterday he poured the damned orpiment on my face and nearly blinded me; you can still see the marks where I was scorched, my daughter! Give him up, give him up! He doesn't love you, for he loves the green and gold snake; he will never be a Counsellor, for he has taken a job with the salamanders, and he wants to marry the green snake; give him up, give him up!'

Veronica, who in reality had a firm and steadfast character and was quick to overcome girlish terror, took a step backward and spoke in a serious and composed tone: 'Old woman! I have heard about your gift of seeing the future, and therefore, perhaps too rashly and inquisitively, I wanted you to tell me whether Anselmus, whom I love and esteem, will ever be mine. If you are not going to fulfil my wish, but only to tease me with your silly, mad chatter, then you are wrong, for I only wanted what I know you grant to others. Since it appears that you know my inmost thoughts, it might have been an easy matter for you to reveal many things that now worry and torment me, but after your foolish slanders of the good Anselmus I want nothing more to do with you. Good night!'

As Veronica was about to hurry away, the old woman fell on her knees, weeping and moaning, gripped the girl's dress, and cried: 'Little Veronica, don't you recognize old Lizzie, who has so often held you in her arms and nursed you and petted you?' Veronica could hardly believe her eyes; for though the old woman's appearance was distorted by her great age and, above all, by the scorched patches, she was recognizably the old nurse who had vanished from Sub-Rector Paulmann's house several years before. The old woman also looked quite different now: as she had formerly done, she was wearing a decent cap instead of the ugly coloured cloth, and a flowered jacket instead of the black rags. She got up from the floor, took Veronica in her arms, and went on:

'Everything I have told you may seem crazy, but I'm afraid it is true. Anselmus has done much to injure me, but not deliberately; he has fallen into the hands of Archivist Lindhorst, who wants to marry him off to his daughter. The Archivist is my greatest enemy, and I could tell you all manner of things about him, but you would not understand or else you would be too terrified. He is the wise man, but I am the wise woman—so let it be! I can see that you have set your heart on Anselmus, and I'll help you with all my powers to end up happily married to him, as you wish.'

'But for heaven's sake, tell me, Lizzie!' began Veronica—

'Hush, child—hush!' interrupted the old woman, 'I know what you are going to say, I have become as I am because I had to, there was no choice. Now then! I know the remedy that will cure Anselmus of his foolish love for the green snake and bring him to your arms as the most lovable of Counsellors; but you must help.'

'Tell me plainly, Lizzie! I'll do anything, for I love Anselmus dearly!' lisped Veronica in barely audible tones.

'I know', continued the old woman, 'that you were a brave child; it was in vain for me to tell you about the bogy man to make you go to sleep, for you promptly opened your eyes in order to see him; you would go into the most distant room without a light, and you often gave the neighbour's children a fright by putting on your father's powdered coat. Now then! If you are serious about wanting to defeat Archivist Lindhorst and the green snake through my art, if you are serious about wanting Anselmus to be a Counsellor and your husband, then slip out of your father's house at eleven o'clock on the night of the next equinox and come to me; I'll go with you to the crossroads in the open country not far from here, we'll prepare what is needed, and none of the peculiar things you may see will do you any harm. And now good night, daughter, your Papa is waiting with your soup.'

Veronica hurried away, firmly resolved not to miss the night of the equinox; 'for', thought she, 'Lizzie is right, Anselmus is entangled in strange toils, but I shall free him from them and call him mine for ever and ever; he is mine and always will be, Counsellor Anselmus.'

SIXTH VIGIL

Archivist Lindhorst's garden, with some mocking birds.
The golden pot. English cursive script. Horrid pot-hooks.
The prince of the spirits.

'After all,' said the student Anselmus to himself, 'it may have
been the extra-special strong liqueur, of which I partook somewhat too freely in Mr Conradi's shop, that created all the wild
phantoms that frightened me outside the Archivist's front door.
Today, therefore, I shall remain completely sober, and bid defiance to whatever adverse forces I may meet.'

Just as he had done before, when equipping himself for
his first visit to Archivist Lindhorst, he packed up his pen-
drawings and calligraphic masterpieces, his ink-horns, and his
well-sharpened raven's-quill pens. As he was about to walk out
of the door, his eye fell on the vial of yellow liquid that the
Archivist had given him. All his strange adventures returned
to his memory in vivid colours, and his heart was pierced by a
nameless feeling of bliss and pain. Unable to prevent himself,
he cried in a lamentable tone: 'Lovely and gracious Serpentina,
isn't it just to see you that I am going to the Archivist?' At that
moment he felt as though Serpentina's love might be the reward
for undertaking a dangerous and arduous task, and that this task
was none other than copying the Lindhorst manuscripts. He was
firmly convinced that he might encounter all manner of wondrous things as soon as he entered the house, or even outside it,
as had happened before. Instead of giving another thought to
Conradi's liqueur, he quickly put the vial into his waistcoat
pocket, so that he might faithfully follow the Archivist's instructions if the bronze apple-woman should venture to grin at
him. And did she not poke out her pointed nose, and flash her
narrow green eyes at him from the door-knocker, as he was
about to lift it at twelve o'clock precisely?

Without a second thought, Anselmus squirted the liquid into
the hideous face, which instantly smoothed itself into a gleaming round door-knocker. The door opened, the bells rang de-

lightfully throughout the house: 'ting-a-ling—young man—quick—quick—skip along—ting-a-ling'. He cheerfully climbed the fine wide staircase, enjoying the scent of the rare perfumes that were wafting through the house. In the hallway he paused uncertainly, not knowing at which of the many handsome doors he should knock; but at that moment Archivist Lindhorst appeared, wearing a voluminous damask dressing-gown, and called out: 'I'm glad you've kept your word at last, Mr Anselmus; I had better take you to the laboratory right away, so just follow me.'

With these words he strode across the long hallway and opened a small side-door leading into a corridor. Anselmus cheerfully followed the Archivist. From the corridor they entered a large hall, or rather a magnificent conservatory, for on both sides there stood all manner of rare and wondrous flowers, reaching to the ceiling. A dazzling magical light was everywhere, though one could not tell where it came from, since not a single window was to be seen. As Anselmus looked into the bushes and trees, long avenues seemed to stretch into the far distance. In the shadows of thick cypress bushes he saw the gleam of marble basins, from which wondrous figures rose and scattered crystal jets that fell splashing into the cups of luminous lilies; strange voices murmured and whistled amid the forest of wondrous plants, and glorious perfumes rose and descended. The Archivist had vanished, and Anselmus could see before him only a gigantic bush of glowing orange lilies. Intoxicated by the sight and by the sweet perfumes of the fairy garden, Anselmus stood as though rooted to the spot by enchantment. Then a giggling and tittering was heard from all sides, and small, clear voices began teasing and mocking him.

'Where have you come from, my scholarly friend? Why are you dolled up so nicely, Anselmus? Will you come and chat with us about how Grandmother squashed the egg under her bottom, and the young gentleman got a stain on his best waistcoat? Have you learnt the new aria by heart that Papa Starling has just sung to you, Anselmus? You're a sight for sore eyes in your glass wig and your brown paper top-boots!'

From every corner, and from right beside Anselmus, this teasing and tittering could be heard. Only now did the student realize that all manner of many-coloured birds were fluttering round him and making fun of him with continual laughter. At that moment the orange lily walked towards him, and he saw that it was Archivist Lindhorst, and that the brilliant red and yellow flowers on the Archivist's dressing-gown had deceived his sight.

'Forgive me for leaving you, my honoured friend,' said the Archivist, 'but I wanted to take a quick look at my fine cactus, which will flower tonight—but how do you like my little garden?'

'Good heavens!' replied the student, 'it is beautiful beyond description, my esteemed Archivist; but the birds are having no end of fun at the expense of my poor self!'

'What's all this nonsense?' called the Archivist angrily, turning to the bushes.

Out fluttered a great grey parrot, which perched on a myrtle bough beside the Archivist, looked at him with the utmost gravity through the spectacles on its curved beak, and croaked: 'Please don't take it amiss, Archivist; my naughty boys are in high spirits, but your scholarly friend is himself to blame, because . . .'

'Not another word!' interrupted the Archivist, 'I know these rascals, but you ought to keep them in better order , my friend! Let's go on, Mr Anselmus!'

The Archivist strode through many more rooms with exotic decorations, so fast that the student, following him, had scarcely time even to glance at the gleaming, strangely shaped furniture and other unfamiliar objects with which they were all filled. Finally they entered a large room in which the Archivist paused with upturned gaze, giving Anselmus time to feast his eyes on the magnificent sight afforded by the simple ornaments in this chamber. From the azure walls there emerged the bronze-coloured trunks of lofty palm-trees, whose colossal leaves, gleaming like sparkling emeralds, formed an arch just below the ceiling. In the middle of the room three Egyptian lions made of dark bronze supported a porphyry slab on which stood a simple golden pot. As soon as he saw it, Anselmus could not take his eyes away from the pot. All manner of shapes seemed to be playing on the polished gold in a thousand shimmering reflections: at times he glimpsed himself with arms outstretched in longing, alas! beside the elder-bush, and Serpentina slithered up and down, gazing at him with her lovely eyes. Anselmus was beside himself with wild delight. 'Serpentina, Serpentina!' he shrieked, but Archivist Lindhorst turned round quickly and said:

'What do you mean, my good Mr Anselmus? I believe you have just done my daughter the honour of calling to her; but she is in her room on the far side of the house, having her piano lesson. Let's go on.'

As the Archivist strode away, Anselmus followed, barely conscious of his surroundings. He neither saw nor heard anything more until the Archivist seized him by the hand and said: 'Here we are!'

Awaking as though from a dream, Anselmus perceived that he was in a lofty room with bookcases all round the walls and in no way different from an ordinary library and study. In the middle stood a large desk and an upholstered armchair.

'This', said the Archivist, 'is your place of work for the present. Whether you will also work in future in the blue library, where you suddenly called out my daughter's name, I don't yet know. But now I should like some evidence of your ability to perform your work according to my wishes and requirements.'

Anselmus now took courage and produced his drawings and calligraphic exercises from his pocket, feeling rather pleased with himself and certain of delighting the Archivist by his remarkable talent. The Archivist had scarcely set eyes on the first sheet, a piece of handwriting in the most elegant English style, when he gave a strange smile and shook his head. He did the same with every other sheet, so that the blood rushed to Anselmus's face; and finally, as the Archivist's smile became altogether mocking and contemptuous, Anselmus burst out angrily: 'Archivist, you seem less than satisfied with my modest talents?'

'My dear Mr Anselmus,' said the Archivist, 'you have an excellent natural gift for the art of calligraphy; but for the present, I see, I must rely more on your hard work and good will than on your skill. Part of the trouble may be the bad materials that you have been using.' The student spoke at some length about how everyone else had acknowledged his skill, and

about his Indian ink and his specially chosen raven's-quill pens.
But the Archivist handed him the sheet in English style and
said: 'Judge for yourself!'

Anselmus was thunderstruck to see how wretched his handwriting looked. The strokes were not rounded, the pressure had
not been properly applied, the capitals and small letters were
out of proportion; here and there a line was written with moderate success, but spoiled by horrid pot-hooks such as schoolboys
might scrawl.

'Besides', went on the Archivist, 'your ink is not durable.' He
dipped his finger in a glass of water, and dabbed it gently on
the letters, whereupon all the writing vanished without a trace.

Anselmus felt as though some monster were clutching his
throat. Unable to utter a single word, he stood there with the
unlucky sheet of paper in his hand. The Archivist, however,
laughed loudly and said: 'Don't be downcast, my esteemed Mr
Anselmus; the feats that you have not yet accomplished may
prove easier here. In any case, you will probably find better
materials here than you had before. Pluck up your spirits and
set to work!'

The Archivist now unlocked a cupboard and fetched a black
semi-liquid substance which emitted a very peculiar smell,
sharp-pointed pens in strange colours, a sheet of paper of exceptional whiteness and smoothness, and finally an Arabic manuscript. As soon as Anselmus had sat down to work, he left the
room.

Anselmus had often copied Arabic script before, and so the
first task did not seem too difficult. 'How the pot-hooks got
into my beautiful English cursive script, only God and the
Archivist can tell,' said he, 'but I'll take my oath that they are
not of *my* making.' Every word that he managed to inscribe on
the parchment increased his spirits and likewise his skill. The
pens were indeed splendid to write with, and the mysterious
pitch-black ink flowed obediently on to the dazzling white
parchment. As he worked away diligently, with intense concentration, he felt more and more at home in the lonely room,
perfectly contented with the task before him, and hopeful of
accomplishing it and earning his reward. On the stroke of three
the Archivist called him into the next room, where an excellent

lunch was ready. At table the Archivist was in an exceptionally cheerful mood; he inquired about Anselmus's friends, Sub-Rector Paulmann and Registrary Heerbrand, and had many good stories to tell about the latter in particular. Anselmus greatly enjoyed the old Rhine wine, which made him more talkative than he generally was. On the stroke of four he got up to go to his work, and the Archivist seemed well pleased by his punctuality. The copying of Arabic characters had gone well even before the meal, but now the work went better still: Anselmus was himself astonished at the rapidity and ease with which he managed to copy the curlicues of the foreign script. But there seemed to be a voice coming from his innermost heart and whispering audibly: 'Ah! could you accomplish this if *she* were not in your heart and mind, if you did not believe in *her* and her love?' Then a faint, faint lisping, a crystal tinkling, could be heard floating through the room: 'I am near, near, near you! I will help you. Be brave, be steadfast, dear Anselmus! I am working with you, so that you shall be mine!' And as soon as he heard these sounds with inward delight, he began to understand the unknown characters. He scarcely needed to look at the original any more—it was as though the characters were already traced on the parchment, and needed only to be filled in with black ink by his practised hand.

Anselmus went on working, with lovely sounds floating around him like sweet delicate breathings, until the clock struck six and Archivist Lindhorst entered the room. He went over to the table with a strange smile; Anselmus stood up in silence, while the Archivist continued to smile at him as though in scornful mockery. Hardly had he looked into Anselmus's copy, however, than his smile vanished and all his facial muscles moved to express a profound and solemn gravity. He no longer seemed the same man. His eyes, instead of their usual fiery sparkle, now turned upon Anselmus a look of indescribable gentleness; a mild blush mantled his pallid cheeks, and his soft and well-shaped lips, no longer pursed in irony, seemed about to open and deliver words of penetrating wisdom. His entire figure was taller and more dignified; the ample folds of his dressing-gown covered his shoulders and chest like a royal robe, and the white curls on his broad and lofty forehead were enclosed by a narrow circlet of gold.

'Young man,' began the Archivist in a solemn tone, 'young man, long before you suspected them, I already perceived all the hidden links binding you to my dearest and most sacred possession! Serpentina loves you, and a strange destiny whose fateful threads were spun by malign powers will be fulfilled when she is yours and you receive the golden pot, which belongs to her, as an indispensable dowry. But your happiness in a higher life can only be born from struggle. You are beset by malign forces, and only the inner strength with which you resist their attacks can save you from disgrace and perdition. By working here you will pass your apprenticeship; and provided you persevere in the task you were obliged to begin, faith and insight will lead you to your goal, which is close at hand. Carry *her* always in your heart—Serpentina, who loves you—and you will behold the magnificent wonders of the golden pot, and be happy for evermore. Farewell! Archivist Lindhorst will expect you tomorrow at twelve in your study! Farewell!'

The Archivist gently thrust Anselmus out of the door and locked it. Anselmus found himself in the room where he had eaten; its only door opened on to the hallway. As he paused outside the front door, astounded by all the wonders he had seen, a window was opened above his head. He looked up, and there was Archivist Lindhorst, restored to his usual guise as an old man in a whitish-grey coat. The Archivist called to him:

'Why, Mr Anselmus, what are you ruminating about? I suppose you can't get all that Arabic out of your head? Give my regards to Sub-Rector Paulmann, if you should happen to call on him, and come back tomorrow at twelve o'clock on the dot. The honorarium for today's work is already in the right-hand pocket of your waistcoat.'

And indeed Anselmus found the gleaming silver thaler in the pocket referred to, but it gave him no pleasure. 'What will come of all this, I can't tell,' said he to himself, 'but even if I am caught up in nothing more than some mad mystification, still the charming Serpentina dwells in my heart, and I would sooner perish than leave her, for I know that the thought within me is eternal, and no malign force can destroy it; but is the thought anything other than Serpentina's love?'

SEVENTH VIGIL

How Sub-Rector Paulmann knocked out his pipe and went to bed.
Rembrandt and Hell Brueghel. The magic mirror and
Dr Eckstein's prescription for an unknown ailment.

At last Sub-Rector Paulmann knocked out his pipe and said: 'It is high time to retire to bed.'

'It is indeed,' replied Veronica, who was alarmed by her father's staying up so long; for ten o'clock had long since struck. No sooner had the Sub-Rector entered his study and bedroom, no sooner had Frances's heavier breathing announced that she was fast asleep, than Veronica, who had got into bed in order to ward off suspicion, got up again, very, very quietly, dressed, put on her cloak, and slipped out of the house.

Ever since she had left old Lizzie, the image of Anselmus had been constantly before Veronica's eyes. A mysterious alien voice inside her had been continually repeating that his resistance was due to somebody hostile to her, and that this person held Anselmus in bonds which Veronica could break by the mysterious methods of magical art. Her trust in old Lizzie grew daily, and even the uncanny and horrifying impression made by the old woman faded from her mind, so that everything strange and weird in their relationship came to seem merely unusual and romantic, and thus was the kind of thing that attracted her. Hence she was firmly resolved to go through with the adventure of the equinox, even though she risked getting into endless trouble if her family noticed her absence. Now the fateful night of the equinox, on which old Lizzie had promised to aid and abet her, had at last arrived, and Veronica, having had ample time to get used to the idea of a nocturnal expedition, felt full of courage. She flew as swiftly as an arrow through the deserted streets, paying no heed to the gale that was whistling through the air and dashing big drops of rain in her face.

The clock of the Cross Church was just striking eleven, with a dull resounding clang, as Veronica, soaked to the skin, stood in front of the old woman's house.

'Why, my pet, here already! here already! Wait, just wait!'
came a cry from the upper storey; and a moment later the old
woman, laden with a basket and accompanied by her cat, was
also standing outside the door. 'Let us go and do deeds befitting
the night that favours our deeds', said she, seizing the trembling Veronica with a chilly hand. Veronica was given the heavy
basket to carry, while the old woman unpacked a cauldron, a
tripod, and a spade. By the time they emerged into the open
country, the rain had ceased, but the gale had grown stronger,
and howled in the air with a thousand voices. Frightful sounds
of heart-rending lamentation descended from the black clouds,
which swiftly gathered together and enveloped everything in
thick darkness. But the old woman strode rapidly onwards,
crying in piercing tones: 'Light the way, my boy, light the way!'
Thereupon flashes of blue lightning curled and crossed on their
path, and Veronica realized that the cat, as it sprang to and fro
in front of them, was scattering sparks which glimmered and
crackled, and that its fearful, hideous caterwauling could be
heard whenever the gale dropped for a moment. She could
hardly breathe, she felt as though ice-cold claws were clutching
at her heart, but she pulled herself together with a violent
effort, clung more closely to the old woman, and said: 'We must
go through with this business, no matter what comes of it!'

'That's right, daughter!' replied the old woman, 'remain
steadfast, and I'll give you something nice, and Anselmus into
the bargain!'

Finally the old woman stopped and said: 'Here we are!' She
dug a hole in the earth, filled it with coal and placed the tripod
over it, with the cauldron on top. All this was accompanied by
strange gestures, while the cat walked round and round her.
Sparks shot from his tail and formed a fiery ring. Soon the coal
began to glow, and blue flames finally leapt up under the
tripod. Veronica was made to remove her cloak and veil and to
crouch down beside the old woman, who seized her hands and
clasped them tight, staring at the girl with sparkling eyes. The
strange substances which the old woman had taken out of the
basket, and which might have been flowers, lumps of metal,
herbs, or animals (one could not tell which) now began to boil
and bubble. The old woman let go of Veronica and seized an

iron spoon, which she dipped in the glowing mass in order to stir it, while Veronica, on her instructions, had to gaze steadily into the cauldron and bend all her thoughts upon Anselmus. Now the old woman threw some gleaming pieces of metal into the cauldron, along with a lock of hair which she had cut from the crown of Veronica's head, and a ring Veronica had worn for a long time. While doing so she uttered unintelligible, hideous sounds that pierced the darkness, and the cat whined and whimpered as it ran round the cauldron.

I wish, kind reader, that you had been travelling to Dresden on the night of 23 September! As darkness fell, people tried in vain to detain you at the last stage of your journey; the kindly landlord pointed out that the wind and rain were too bad for travel, and that the night of the equinox was in any case an uncanny time to be journeying into the murk; but you disregarded him, reasoning justly: 'If I tip the postilion a whole thaler, I can be in Dresden by one o'clock at the latest, where a well-prepared supper and a soft bed will be awaiting me at the Golden Angel, or the Helmet, or the City of Naumburg Hotel.' Travelling through the darkness, you suddenly perceive a strange flickering little light in the distance. Approaching closer, you see a fiery ring, within which two figures are seated beside a cauldron that emits thick smoke and red flashes and sparks. Your way leads straight through the fire, but the horses snort and stamp and rear; the postilion curses and prays, and lashes the horses mercilessly, but they will not budge from the spot. Without thinking, you jump out of the carriage and run forward a few steps. Now you can distinctly make out the slim, beautiful girl who is kneeling beside the cauldron, dressed in her thin white night-dress. Her plaits have come undone in the gale, and her long chestnut hair is fluttering in the wind. Her angelic face is illuminated by the dazzling light of the flames flickering from under the cauldron, but an icy stream of terror has frozen it in deathly pallor, and in her vacant gaze, her raised eyebrows, her mouth vainly opened to utter a cry of mortal fear, which is strangled by the nameless agony clutching her bosom, you behold her horror, her terror. Her delicate hands are raised and clasped together, as though she were invoking her guardian angel to preserve her from the infernal monsters which are about to appear in obedience to the mighty spell! Thus she kneels as motionless as a marble statue. Opposite her, crouching on the ground, sits a tall, skinny woman with a coppery complexion, a hooked and pointed nose, and the sparkling eyes of a cat; her bare, bony arms protrude from her black cloak, and, as she stirs the hellish brew, she laughs and shouts in her croaking voice through the raging and roaring of the gale.

Even if you are not normally a shy or timid character, kind reader, I think that this scene, a picture by Rembrandt or Hell Brueghel come to life, would make the hair on your scalp rise in terror. But you cannot take your eyes off the girl caught up in such devilry, and an electric shock trembling through every nerve and fibre of your body instantly awakens in you the courageous idea of defying the mysterious powers of the fiery circle; this idea banishes your terror, indeed the idea itself germinated amid the terror and fright that produced it. You feel yourself to be one of the guardian angels to whom the girl is appealing in her mortal fear; you feel that you need only draw your pocket-pistol and shoot the old woman dead on the spot! But as this thought passes vividly through your mind, you cry: 'Hallo there!' or 'What's going on?' or 'What on earth are you up to?' The postilion blows a deafening blast on his horn, the old woman spins round and topples into her own brew, and everything vanishes instantly in a cloud of smoke. You then search for the girl in the darkness with intense longing. Whether you would have found her, I should not like to say; but you would have destroyed the old woman's charms, and broken the spell cast by the magic circle which Veronica had so thoughtlessly entered.

But neither you, kind reader, nor anyone else was travelling that way on 23 September in the stormy night that was so suitable for witchcraft, and Veronica had to remain by the cauldron in mortal terror until the work was close to completion. She heard the howling and roaring all around her, she heard all manner of horrible voices bleating and gibbering in a wild medley, but she did not raise her eyes, for she felt that the sight of the ghastly and terrifying beings by which she was surrounded might destroy her by plunging her into incurable madness. The old woman had stopped stirring the cauldron, the smoke grew weaker and weaker, till at last only a small flame, like that produced by strong spirit, was burning at the bottom of the cauldron.

'Veronica, my child!' cried the old woman, 'my pet! look down into the depths! What can you see? What can you see?'

Veronica, however, was unable to answer, although all manner of confused figures seemed to be coiling in the cauldron; the shapes became more and more distinct, until suddenly the student Anselmus stepped forth from the depths of the cauldron, smiling at her and holding out his hand.

'Oh, it's Anselmus! It's Anselmus!' cried Veronica.

The old woman quickly opened the cauldron's vent, and red-hot metal, hissing and crackling, flowed into a small mould which she had placed beside it. Up she sprang, whirling around with wild and hideous gestures, and screamed: 'The work is done. Thanks, my boy! You kept good watch. Hey, here he comes! Bite him to death, bite him to death!'

But suddenly a mighty beating of wings was heard in the air, as though a huge eagle were descending on them, and a terrible voice cried: 'Hey, hey, you rapscallions! That's enough, that's enough, be off with you!' The old woman collapsed howling in a heap, but Veronica lost consciousness.

When she came to, it was broad daylight; she was lying in her bed, and Frances was standing in front of her with a cup of steaming tea, and saying:

'Do tell me what the matter is, Veronica; I've been standing here for an hour or more, and you've been lying insensible as though you were in a fever, moaning and groaning, and frightening us out of our wits. Father hasn't gone to teach his class today, because of you, and he'll be here with the doctor any minute.'

Veronica took her tea in silence. As she gulped it down, the hideous images of the past night appeared vividly before her mind's eye. 'Have I just been tormented by a nightmare?' she wondered. 'But I really did go to the old woman's house last night, surely, and after all, wasn't it the twenty-third of September? No, I must already have been ill yesterday and have imagined the whole thing; and the only reason for my illness was that I never stopped thinking about Anselmus and the strange old woman who claimed to be old Lizzie, though I expect she was just teasing me.'

At this point Frances, who had gone out, returned carrying Veronica's dripping cloak in her hand. 'Just look, Veronica,' said she, 'what has happened to your cloak; the gale blew open a window during the night and knocked over the chair on which your cloak was lying; the rain must have come in through the window, for the cloak is wet through.'

Veronica's heart sank, for now she realized that, far from being tormented by a mere dream, she really had visited the old woman. Gripped by fear and horror, she shuddered in every limb. Trembling convulsively, she pulled the blanket over herself; but then she felt something hard pressing against her breast, and when she reached for it, it seemed to be a medallion. She drew it out as soon as Frances had taken away her cloak. It was a little round mirror of brightly polished metal. 'It's a present from the old woman', she exclaimed, feeling as though rays of fire were shooting out of the mirror, penetrating her innermost heart, and spreading a pleasant warmth. Her shivering fit was over, and she was filled with an indescribable sense of comfort and well-being. She could not help thinking of Anselmus, and as she bent her thoughts on him more and more intently, he smiled at her out of the mirror, like a miniature portrait come to life. Soon, however, she seemed to be seeing, not the picture—no!—but Anselmus himself in flesh and blood. He was sitting in a lofty, strangely decorated room and writing busily. Veronica wanted to walk over to him, tap him on the shoulder, and say: 'Mr Anselmus, look round, it's me!' But this was impossible, for he seemed to be surrounded by a shining stream of fire, though when Veronica looked more closely, it turned out only to be big books with their pages edged in gold leaf. At last, however, she managed to catch Anselmus's eye; it seemed to require some thought before he remembered who she was, but finally he smiled and said: 'Oh, it's you, my dear Miss Paulmann? But why do you see fit now and again to pretend to be a snake?'

Veronica could not help laughing loudly at these strange words; this woke her, as though she had been fast asleep and dreaming, and she quickly concealed the little mirror as the door opened and Sub-Rector Paulmann entered the room with Dr Eckstein. Dr Eckstein went straight to her bed, took her pulse, remained immersed in thought for a long time, and finally said: 'Well, well!' Thereupon he wrote a prescription, took her pulse once more, repeated: 'Well, well!' and left the patient. From Dr Eckstein's utterances, however, Sub-Rector Paulmann was unable to derive any clear conception of what might be wrong with Veronica.

EIGHTH VIGIL

*The library of palm-trees. The fortunes of an unhappy salamander.
How the black feather caressed a mangel-wurzel and Registrary
Heerbrand got very drunk.*

The student Anselmus had now been working in Archivist
Lindhorst's house for several days. The time he spent there was
the happiest of his life, for, constantly hearing lovely sounds
and Serpentina's comforting words, indeed occasionally feeling
the gentle touch of her breath, he was filled by a sense of
well-being that he had never known before, and that sometimes
rose to the highest pitch of bliss. All the hardships and petty
worries of his wretched existence had vanished from his mind,
and in the new life which had opened up before him like bright
sunlight, he was able to understand all the wonders of a higher
world which would otherwise have filled him with amazement,
indeed with horror. His copying went on very fast, for it seemed
more and more that he was only inscribing the parchment with
long-familiar characters, and scarcely needed to glance at the
original in order to reproduce everything with the utmost precision. The Archivist was rarely to be seen, except at mealtimes,
but he always appeared at the precise moment when Anselmus
had finished the last character of a manuscript, and gave him
another; he then departed in silence, after stirring the ink with
a small black rod and replacing the used pens with new and
sharper ones.

One day, when Anselmus had climbed the stairs on the stroke
of twelve, the door by which he normally entered proved to be
locked, and the Archivist, in his wondrous dressing-gown
strewn with images of brilliant flowers, appeared from the other
side.

'Come in by this door today, my dear Anselmus,' he called,
'for we must go into the room where the Masters of Bhagavadgita* are awaiting us.'

The Archivist strode along the corridor and led Anselmus
through the same large and small rooms as on his first visit.

Once more Anselmus was astonished by the magnificence of the conservatory, but he could now perceive that many of the strange flowers hanging on the dark bushes were in fact insects resplendent in gleaming colours, flapping their little wings and dancing and flitting in a swarm as though caressing one another with their probosces. As for the rose-pink and sky-blue birds, they had turned into fragrant flowers, and the scent they emitted rose from their cupped petals in soft, lovely tones, which mingled with the whisper of distant fountains and the murmuring of the lofty trees and shrubs to form mysterious chords that uttered a deep, sorrowful yearning. The mocking birds which had teased and tormented him before now fluttered round his head once more, incessantly crying in their small clear voices: 'Not so fast, my scholarly friend—don't keep staring into the clouds, you might fall flat on your face! Hee, hee! Put on your powdered coat, my scholarly friend—Neighbour Screech-owl will dress your wig.' And so they went on, uttering all manner of foolish chatter, until Anselmus had left the conservatory.

Finally the Archivist entered the azure room; the porphyry stand with the golden pot had vanished, and in their place in the middle of the room was a table draped in purple velvet. On it lay the writing materials with which Anselmus was familiar, and before it stood an armchair with similar drapery.

'My dear Anselmus,' said the Archivist, 'you have now, to my great satisfaction, copied many manuscripts quickly and accurately; you have gained my confidence; but the most important task remains to be done, and that is to copy, or rather paint, certain works written in special characters, which I keep in this room, and which can only be copied on the spot. You will therefore work here in future, but I must urge you to exercise the utmost care and concentration; one wrong stroke, or— Heaven forfend!—a blot on the original, would plunge you into misfortune.'

Anselmus noticed small emerald-green leaves protruding from the golden trunks of the palm-trees; the Archivist grasped one of these leaves, and Anselmus realized that the leaf actually consisted of a roll of parchment, which the Archivist spread out on the table before him. Anselmus was astonished by the strangely intertwined characters, and at the sight of the many dots, strokes, dashes, and curlicues, which seemed by turns to represent plants, or mosses, or animal shapes, his courage almost failed him. Wondering if he would be able to copy all these signs exactly, he fell into deep meditation.

'Take heart, young man!' exclaimed the Archivist, 'if you have proven faith and true love, Serpentina will help you!'

His voice rang like sonorous metal, and as Anselmus looked up in sudden alarm, the Archivist stood before him in the kingly form which Anselmus had beheld on his first visit to the library. The awestruck Anselmus was about to fall on his knees when the Archivist suddenly climbed up the trunk of a palm-tree and vanished among the emerald foliage. Anselmus understood that the prince of the spirits had spoken to him and had ascended to his study, where perhaps he would confer with the rays, sent to him as emissaries from some of the planets, about what should happen to Anselmus and the lovely Serpentina. 'Or else', thought Anselmus, 'he may be about to receive news from the source of the Nile, or a visit from a Magus of Lapland. But I had better set diligently to work.' And he began to examine the strange characters on the roll of parchment. The wondrous music from the conservatory reached his ears and surrounded him with sweet and delightful scents, and he could also hear the giggling of the mocking birds, but he could not make out the words, much to his relief. Sometimes, too, the emerald leaves of the palm-trees seemed to rustle, and the room was filled by the lovely crystalline notes which Anselmus had heard under the elder-tree on that fateful Ascension Day. Wondrously invigorated by these sounds and gleams, Anselmus concentrated ever more firmly on the inscriptions on the parchment, and soon an inner intuition told him that the characters could have no other meaning than 'Of the Marriage of the Salamander and the Green Snake'. At that moment a trio of clear crystal bells rang out. The words 'Anselmus, dear Anselmus', wafted from the leaves and, wonderful to relate, the green snake came twining its way down the trunk of the palm-tree.

'Serpentina! Lovely Serpentina!' cried Anselmus, in the rapture of supreme delight, for, as he looked more closely, it was a beautiful girl who was floating towards him, gazing at him with unspeakable yearning in her dark-blue eyes, just as he had pictured them in his mind. The leaves seemed to descend and stretch out; thorns sprouted from the trunks; but Serpentina wound and twined her way skilfully through them, and her fluttering, gleaming, iridescent dress clung so close to her slender body that it did not catch on the projecting thorns of the palm-trees. She sat down beside Anselmus on the same chair, put her arm round him, and held him so close that he could feel the breath from her lips and the electric warmth of her body.

'Dear Anselmus,' began Serpentina, 'you will soon be mine entirely; you will win me through your faith and your love, and I will bring you the golden pot, which will make us both happy for evermore.'

'Oh, fair and lovely Serpentina,' said Anselmus, 'if only I had you, what would I care about all the world besides? If only you were mine, I would gladly perish amid the strange and wondrous things in which I have been entangled since first I saw you.'

'I know,' continued Serpentina, 'that you have been alarmed and horrified by the unfamiliar and wondrous atmosphere which my father, often merely following his whims, has created around you, but now I hope it will never happen again, for I am here at this moment, my dear Anselmus, only to tell you, from the bottom of my heart, from the depths of my soul, everything you need to know, down to the smallest detail, in order to realize who my father is, and to understand quite distinctly how matters stand with him and me.'

To Anselmus it seemed as though her sweet and lovely form were embracing and enfolding him so completely that he could only live, move, and have his being in her, and as though it were only the beat of her pulse that sent tremors through all his fibres and nerves. He listened to every word she uttered, and each one resounded through the depths of his being and, like a ray of light, awoke in him a sensation of heavenly bliss. He had put his arm round her slender body, the slenderest there could be, but the glistening iridescent material of her dress was so smooth, so slippery, that he felt she might slide from his embrace and slip away, without letting him detain her; and he trembled at the thought.

'Oh, don't leave me, lovely Serpentina!' he cried involuntarily, 'you alone are my life!'

'I shall not leave you today', said Serpentina, 'until I have told you everything that your love for me enables you to understand. Know then, beloved! that my father is descended from the wondrous race of the salamanders, and that I owe my existence to his love for the green snake. In ancient times the wondrous land of Atlantis was ruled by Phosphorus, the mighty prince of spirits, and the elemental spirits were his servants. One day the salamander whom he loved most dearly (it was my father) was walking in the splendid garden which Phosphorus's mother had magnificently adorned with her fairest gifts, and heard a tall lily singing in soft tones: "Close your eyes tightly, till my beloved, the morning wind, awakens you." He stepped closer; touched by his glowing breath, the lily opened her petals, and he beheld the lily's daughter, the green snake, asleep within the cup. Thereupon the salamander was seized by passionate love for the green snake, and he stole her from the lily, whose perfumes, in a nameless lament, called for their beloved daughter everywhere in the garden. For the salamander had brought her to Phosphorus's castle, and implored him: "Marry me to my beloved, for she shall be mine for evermore."

'"Foolish being, what are you asking!" said the prince of the spirits; "know that the lily was once my beloved and shared in my rule, but the spark I cast in her threatened to destroy her, and only my victory over the black dragon, whom the earth-spirits now keep bound in chains, kept the lily's petals strong enough to enclose and preserve the spark within them. But if you embrace the green snake, your heat will burn up her body, and a new being will swiftly grow up and escape from you."

'The salamander did not heed the prince's warning. Filled with burning desire, he enfolded the green snake in his arms; she crumbled to ashes, and a winged being, born from the ashes, shot away through the air. Then the salamander was seized by the madness of despair; emitting fire and flames, he ran through the garden and laid it waste in his wild fury, so that the fairest flowers and blossoms sank down, burnt to ashes, and the air was filled with their lamentations.

'The wrathful prince of the spirits laid hold of the salamander in his anger, saying: "Your fire has spent its fury, your flames are extinguished, your beams have lost their light; sink down to the earth-spirits, and let them tease you and mock you and keep you captive, till your fiery substance catches light again and rises radiantly from the earth with you as a new being."

'The poor salamander sank down, his light extinguished, but the gruff old earth-spirit who was Phosphorus's gardener came to him and said: "Master! Who has more reason to complain of the salamander than I? Did I not use my finest metals to polish all the fair flowers that he has burnt? Did I not tend their seeds honestly, and waste many fine colours on them? And yet I shall plead the cause of the poor salamander, for it was only love—in which you, Master, have often been entangled!—that drove him to the despair in which he laid waste the garden. Spare him such harsh punishment!"

'"His fire is extinguished for the present," said the prince of the spirits. "In the unhappy time when the degenerate race of men will no longer understand the language of nature, when the elemental spirits, each confined in his own region, will speak to men only in faint and distant sounds, when man will be estranged from the harmonious circle and only an infinite yearning will bring him obscure tidings of the wondrous realm that he once inhabited, while faith and love dwelt in his heart—in that unhappy time the salamander's fiery substance will catch light anew, but he will rise only to the level of mankind and must accommodate himself to their wretched life and endure its privations. But not only will he retain the memory of his primal state; he will again live in holy harmony with all of nature, he will understand its marvels, and the power of his brothers among the spirits will once more be at his command. In a lily bush he will again find the green snake, and his marriage to her will bring forth three daughters, who will appear to men in the same guise as their mother. In springtime they will hang in the dark elder-bush and let their lovely crystal voices ring out. If, in that wretched time of inner obduracy, a youth shall be found to hear their song, and if one of the little snakes gazes at him with her lovely eyes, and if her gaze arouses in him an awareness of the distant land of wonders to which he

can courageously ascend by shaking off the burden of common
cares, and if there grows in him, along with his love for the
snake, a living and ardent faith in the wonders of nature, and
in his own existence amid these wonders, then the snake will
be his. But not until three such youths have been found and
married to his three daughters may the salamander cast off his
weary burden and join his brothers."

'"Permit me, Master," said the earth-spirit, "to give these
three daughters a present which will add splendour to their
lives once they have found their husbands. Each will receive
from me a pot made of the fairest metal I possess, and I shall
polish it with rays taken from the diamond; its lustre will reveal
a splendid and dazzling reflection of our wondrous realm, as it
now exists in harmony with all of nature, but from inside it
there shall rise a fiery lily, whose everlasting bloom will enfold
the tested and true youth in sweet perfumes. Soon he will learn
its language and understand the wonders of our realm, and
himself dwell with his beloved in Atlantis."

'You must have realized by now, dear Anselmus, that the
salamander I have been telling you about is none other than my
father. Despite his superior nature, he was obliged to submit to
the pettiest privations of common life, and that explains the
malicious whims with which he teases many people. He has
often told me that the spiritual character that Prince Phosphorus stipulated as the condition for marriage to me and my sisters
now has a name, though one that is only too often improperly
abused. It is called a child-like poetic spirit. Such a spirit is
often found in youths who are mocked by the rabble because of
the lofty simplicity of their behaviour and because they lack
what people call worldly manners. Oh, dear Anselmus! Now
you understand my song under the elder-bush, my gaze, you
love the green snake, you believe in me, and want to be mine
for evermore! The beautiful lily will bloom from the golden
pot, and we shall live together, blissfully happy, in Atlantis!

'But I cannot conceal from you that after a hideous battle with
the salamanders and earth-spirits the black dragon broke free
and rushed away through the air. Although Phosphorus keeps
him in chains once more, the black feathers that fell to the earth
during the struggle gave birth to malign spirits who every-

where oppose the salamanders and earth-spirits. That woman who is so hostile to you, dear Anselmus, and who, as my father well knows, is striving for possession of the golden pot, owes her existence to the love between one such feather, fallen from the dragon's wing, and a mangel-wurzel. She is aware of her origin and of her power, for the groans and heavings of the captive dragon reveal to her the secrets of many wondrous planetary conjunctions, and she tries by all possible means to work on people's innermost thoughts, while my father fights her with the lightning-flashes that shoot forth from within the salamander. She collects all the malign principles that dwell in harmful herbs and poisonous animals, mixes them under a favourable conjunction, and calls up many an evil sprite that bemuses man's mind with horror and terror and subjects him to the power of the demons created by the defeated dragon. Beware of the old woman, Anselmus; she is your foe, because your innocent child-like spirit has already foiled many of her evil spells. Be true, true, true to me, and soon you will reach your aim!'

'Oh, my—my own Serpentina!' cried Anselmus, 'How could I ever leave you, how could I do other than love you eternally!'

With a kiss burning on his lips, he awoke as though from a deep dream. Serpentina had disappeared. The clock struck six, and he realized with a shock of remorse that he had not copied a single stroke; full of concern at what the Archivist might say, he looked at the sheet, and, wondrous to relate, the copy of the mysterious manuscript was complete and flawless, and as he looked more closely at the characters, he was sure that he had copied out Serpentina's story about her father, the favourite of Prince Phosphorus in the wondrous land of Atlantis.

At this point Archivist Lindhorst entered, wearing his whitish-grey topcoat, with his hat on his head and his stick in his hand; he examined the parchment on which Anselmus had been writing, took a large pinch of snuff, and said with a smile: 'I thought as much! Well, here's your silver thaler, Mr Anselmus, and now let's be off to Linke's Restaurant! Follow me!'

The Archivist strode rapidly through the conservatory, in which there was such a confused jumble of singing, cheeping, and talking that Anselmus was quite deafened and thanked his

NINTH VIGIL

How the student Anselmus acquired some common sense. The punch-drinkers. How the student Anselmus took Sub-Rector Paulmann for a screech-owl, and the latter was greatly incensed. The ink-blot and its consequences.

The wonders and marvels which Anselmus met with every day had altogether estranged him from ordinary life. He no longer saw any of his friends, and each morning he waited impatiently for twelve o'clock, which admitted him to his paradise. And yet, although his whole heart was committed to the lovely Serpentina and the wonders of the fairy realm in Archivist Lindhorst's house, there were times when he could not help thinking of Veronica; sometimes, indeed, she seemed to come to him and confess amid blushes how dearly she loved him and how she was striving to tear him away from the phantoms which were merely teasing and mocking him. Now and again an alien power seemed to intrude and draw him irresistibly to Veronica, whom he had otherwise forgotten, compelling him to follow her wherever she might wish, as though he were firmly chained to the girl.

It was the night after Serpentina had first appeared to him in the form of a wondrous, lovely maiden, and revealed to him the wondrous secret of the marriage of the salamander with the green snake, that Veronica came more vividly to his mind than ever before. Yes, only on waking did he clearly realize that he had merely been dreaming, for he had been convinced that Veronica really was with him, complaining with every sign of deep, heart-rending sorrow that he was sacrificing her intense love to the fantastic apparitions which, though merely products of his deranged mind, would yet lead him into misfortune and ruin. Veronica was more lovable than he had ever seen her before; he could hardly stop thinking about her, and this state of mind caused him such torment that he went for a morning stroll in the hope of ridding himself of it. A secret magical force drew him to the Pirna Gate, and he was just about to turn into a side-street, when Sub-Rector Paulmann called from behind him: 'Why! Anselmus, my dear fellow! *Amice! Amice!* Where on earth have you been? You haven't been seen for ages. Did you know that Veronica is longing for you to accompany her singing again? Do come along; after all, you were going to call on me!'

Anselmus had no choice but to go with the Sub-Rector. On entering the house they were met by Veronica, very neatly and smartly dressed, so that the Sub-Rector asked in astonishment: 'Why are you dolled up like that, were you expecting a visitor? Look, I've brought Mr Anselmus!'

As Anselmus kissed Veronica's hand with all propriety and politeness, he felt a gentle pressure, which ran through all his fibres and nerves like a warm stream. Veronica was cheerfulness and charm personified, and when Paulmann had gone to his study, she managed, through roguish teasing, to work Anselmus up to such a pitch of excitement that he ended up forgetting his shyness and chasing the high-spirited girl round the room. Then, however, the imp of clumsiness took hold of him: he knocked against the table, and Veronica's dainty sewing-box fell down. Anselmus picked it up; the lid had opened, disclosing a little round metal mirror, into which he gazed with inexplicable pleasure. Veronica crept softly up behind him, put her hand on his arm, nestled close to him, and gazed likewise into the mirror. Thereupon Anselmus felt a struggle beginning within him: thoughts, images, flashed out and disappeared again—Archivist Lindhorst, Serpentina, the green snake—at last he calmed down, and his confused thoughts combined to form lucid consciousness. It was now clear that he had been thinking all the time only of Veronica, and that the form which had appeared to him in the blue room the previous day had likewise been Veronica, and that the fantastic legend of the marriage of the salamander with the green snake had only been written by him, but certainly not told to him. He wondered at his own dreamy fancies, and attributed them solely to the exalted state of mind produced by his love for Veronica, as well as to his work in the Archivist's rooms, where there were such strangely intoxicating perfumes. He could not help laughing heartily at the ridiculous notion of being in love with a little

snake and mistaking a respectable Privy Archivist for a salamander.

'Yes, it's Veronica!' he cried, but as he turned his head, he
looked straight into Veronica's blue eyes, which radiated love
and yearning. A soft moan escaped her lips, and instantly they
were pressed, burning, upon his.

'Happy man that I am,' sighed the enraptured student, 'my
dreams of yesterday are now coming true.'

'And will you really marry me once you have become a Counsellor?' asked Veronica.

'Of course!' answered Anselmus. At that moment the door
creaked, and Sub-Rector Paulmann entered, saying: 'Now, my
dear Anselmus, I won't let you go today; you must make do
with a plate of soup, and afterwards Veronica will make us some
delicious coffee, which we shall enjoy together with Registrary
Heerbrand, who has promised to visit us.'

'But, Sub-Rector,' replied Anselmus, 'don't you know that I
must go to Archivist Lindhorst's house, to do my copying?'

'Look here, *amice*!' said Sub-Rector Paulmann, holding out his
pocket-watch, which showed half-past twelve.

Anselmus now realized that it was much too late to walk to
the Archivist's house, and fell in with the Sub-Rector's wishes
all the more readily, since he would now be able to gaze at
Veronica all day long and hoped to receive many surreptitious
glances, squeeze her hand tenderly, and perhaps even extort a
kiss. Such were now the soaring ambitions of the student Anselmus, and the more he persuaded himself that he would soon
be freed from the fantastic notions that could have driven him
out of his senses altogether, the more comfortable he felt. After
dinner the Registrary did indeed turn up, and when the coffee
had been consumed and twilight had fallen, he gave the company to understand, chuckling and cheerfully rubbing his
hands, that he had something with him, which, if mixed by
Veronica's fair hands and given the appropriate form—foliated
and classified, so to speak—would be pleasing to all of them on
such a chilly October evening.

'Do tell us without more ado, my good Registrary,' exclaimed
the Sub-Rector, 'what this mysterious substance is that you
have with you.'

The Registry reached into the deep pocket of his coat and produced first, a bottle of arrack; second, some lemons; and third, some sugar. Before half an hour had passed, a bowl of delicious punch was steaming on Paulmann's table. Veronica offered the drink to the company, and all manner of cheerful and pleasant conversation ensued. But as soon as the alcohol mounted to Anselmus's head, all the images of his recent strange and wondrous experiences returned. He saw Archivist Lindhorst in his damask dressing-gown that shone like phosphorus—he saw the azure room, the golden palm-trees, indeed he felt as though he should believe in Serpentina after all—he was shaken by a seething inner tumult. Veronica gave him a glass of punch, and as he took it he gently touched her hand. 'Serpentina! Veronica!' he sighed inwardly, sinking into a profound reverie.

Registrary Heerbrand, however, exclaimed loudly: 'He's a strange old man, is Archivist Lindhorst, and nobody knows what to make of him. Good health to him! Clink glasses, Anselmus!'

Anselmus, suddenly emerging from his reverie, clinked glasses with the Registrary, and said: 'The reason, my honoured Registrary, is that Archivist Lindhorst is really a salamander, who laid waste the garden of Prince Phosphorus in a fury, because the green snake had flown away.'

'Eh? What?' asked Sub-Rector Paulmann.

'Yes,' continued Anselmus, 'that is why he must now be a Royal Archivist and keep house here in Dresden with his three daughters; they, however, are none other than little green and gold snakes, who sunbathe in elder-bushes, sing enchantingly, and allure young men, like the Sirens.'

'Anselmus, Mr Anselmus,' cried the Sub-Rector, 'have you gone out of your wits? For heaven's sake, what is this absurd drivel you're spouting?'

'He's quite right,' interrupted the Registrary, 'that fellow, the Archivist, is an accursed salamander, who lights a fire by snapping his fingers, and burns holes in your top-coat like red-hot tinder. Yes, you're absolutely right, Anselmus, old chap, and anyone who doubts it is no friend of mine!' And as he said this, the Registrary pounded the table with his fist so hard that the glasses tinkled.

'Registrary! Are you crazy?' shouted the infuriated Sub-Rector. 'My scholarly friend, what mischief are you up to this time?'

'Oh!' said the student, 'you're nothing but a bird yourself—a screech-owl who dresses wigs, Sub-Rector!'

'What? Me, a bird? A screech-owl? A hairdresser?' shouted the Sub-Rector wrathfully. 'You're mad, sir, mad!'

'But the old woman is a match for him', cried the Registrary.

'Yes, the old woman is powerful', interrupted Anselmus, 'though she's of very humble origins, for her papa is only a dirty old feather duster and her mother a horrid mangel-wurzel, but she owes most of her strength to all sorts of malign creatures and poisonous vermin that surround her.'

'That's an abominable slander,' cried Veronica, her eyes gleaming with anger, 'old Lizzie is a wise woman, and the black cat is not a malign creature; he's a handsome young man with refined manners, and her first cousin.'

'Can he eat salamanders without singeing his beard and perishing miserably?' said the Registrary.

'No, no!' shouted Anselmus. 'He'll never manage that in all his days; and the green snake loves me, for I have a child-like spirit and have gazed into Serpentina's eyes.'

'The cat will scratch them out', cried Veronica.

'Salamander, Salamander will defeat them all', roared Sub-Rector Paulmann in a towering rage; 'but am I in a mad-house? Am I mad myself? What's this crazy nonsense I'm talking? Yes, I'm mad—I'm mad too!' With these words the Sub-Rector sprang to his feet, tore off his wig, and hurled it at the ceiling, so that the locks were squashed and fell apart with a creaking noise, scattering powder all over the room. Thereupon Anselmus and the Registrary seized the punch-bowl and the glasses and threw them with jubilant yells at the ceiling, so that the pieces fell all over the room, clinking and tinkling.

'Long live the Salamander, down with the old woman, smash the metal mirror, hack out the cat's eyes! Little birds—birds of the air—eheu—eheu—evoe Salamander!' Thus all three shouted and bellowed at once. Frances rushed out, weeping loudly, but Veronica lay on the sofa, whimpering in sorrow and anguish.

Then the door opened, everyone suddenly fell silent, and in

came a little man in a short grey coat. His face had an oddly grave expression, and his hooked nose, with a large pair of spectacles perched on it, surpassed anything of the kind that had ever been seen. In addition, he wore such a peculiar wig that it rather resembled a feathered bonnet.

'A good evening to you all,' croaked the funny little man, 'I believe my scholarly friend Mr Anselmus is among the company? Archivist Lindhorst sends his humble compliments, and he waited in vain today for Mr Anselmus, but he respectfully requests him to appear at the usual time tomorrow.'

That said, he again left the room, and it was clear to everyone that the grave little man was really a grey parrot. Sub-Rector Paulmann and Registrary Heerbrand uttered a roar of laughter that resounded through the room, while Veronica whimpered and moaned as though lacerated by unutterable sorrow. The student Anselmus, however, was pierced by the madness of inner terror, and without knowing what he was doing he ran out of the house and through the streets. He found his way mechanically to his lodgings and his room. Soon afterwards Veronica came to him, in a calm and friendly spirit. She asked why he had given her such a fright when he was tipsy, and warned him to beware of new fancies when he was working in the Archivist's house. 'Good night, good night, my dear friend', lisped Veronica, breathing a kiss on his lips. Anselmus wanted to clasp her in his arms, but the dream-vision had disappeared. He awoke cheerful and refreshed, and could not help laughing heartily at the effects of the punch. When he thought of Veronica, however, he was filled by a feeling of comfort.

'I have her alone to thank', said he to himself, 'for my recovery from these foolish fancies. Truly, I was in as bad a state as the man who thought he was made of glass, or the one who wouldn't leave his room for fear of being eaten by chickens, because he imagined he was a grain of barley.* But as soon as I'm a Counsellor, I'll marry Miss Paulmann straight away, and be happy.'

At noon, walking through the Archivist's conservatory, he was astonished that the objects there should ever have seemed to him so strange and wondrous. He could see nothing but ordinary potted plants, various kinds of geraniums, myrtle-bushes, and so forth. Instead of the brilliantly coloured birds that had teased him in the past, there were only a few sparrows fluttering to and fro, which made an unintelligible and unpleasant noise on catching sight of Anselmus. The blue room also looked quite different, and he could not understand how the garish blue colour and the unnatural golden trunks of the palm-trees with their shapeless gleaming leaves could have appealed to him for one minute.

The Archivist looked at him with a curious ironic smile, and asked: 'Well, how did you enjoy the punch yesterday, my good Anselmus?'

'Oh, I suppose the parrot must have . . .', replied Anselmus shamefacedly, but he paused, recalling that the parrot's appearance must likewise have been a delusion of his fuddled senses.

'Why, I was myself among the company,' interrupted the Archivist, 'didn't you see me? But your mad antics came close to doing me a serious injury; for I was sitting in the punch-bowl just as Registrary Heerbrand laid hold of it in order to dash it against the ceiling, and I had to beat a hasty retreat into the Sub-Rector's pipe. Now adieu, Mr Anselmus! Work hard! I'll pay you a thaler for the day you missed, since you did such good work until then.'

'What silly rubbish the Archivist talks', said the student Anselmus to himself, sitting down at the table to begin copying the manuscript which the Archivist, as usual, had spread out before him. But on the roll of parchment he saw such a jumble of crooked lines and curlicues, which bewildered the eye without giving it a moment's respite, that it seemed wellnigh impossible to copy. Indeed, as he surveyed it all, the parchment seemed to be only a lump of marble with coloured veins, or a stone with patches of moss. Nevertheless, he was resolved to do all he could, and cheerfully dipped his pen in the ink-well, but the ink would not flow; he impatiently pressed the pen, and—oh heavens!—a big blot fell on the original.

From the blot, with a hiss and a roar, came blue lightning, which coiled its way through the room, crackling as it went, until it reached the ceiling. A thick cloud of steam gushed from the walls, the leaves began to rustle as though shaken by a storm, and gleaming basilisks, surrounded by flickering fire, shot forth from them, setting fire to the steam, so that a crackling mass of flame surged around Anselmus. The golden stems of the palm-trees turned into giant snakes which struck their hideous heads together with a piercing metallic clang, and enfolded Anselmus in their scaly bodies.

'Fool! endure the punishment for your impudent crime!' cried the frightful voice of the crowned salamander, appearing above the snakes like a dazzling ray of light amid the flames.

The snakes' gaping jaws scattered torrents of fire upon Anselmus. The fiery streams seemed to thicken around his body into a solid ice-cold mass. Anselmus's limbs were squeezed more and more tightly until they were rigid, and he lost consciousness. When he came to himself, he could not stir; he seemed to be surrounded by a brilliant light, and to knock against it every time he tried to raise his hand or make any other movement. Alas! he was sitting in a tightly stopped crystal bottle on a shelf in Archivist Lindhorst's library.

TENTH VIGIL

The sufferings of the student Anselmus in the glass bottle. Happy
life of the sixth-formers and solicitors' clerks. The battle in
Archivist Lindhorst's library. The salamander's victory and the
liberation of the student Anselmus.

I may be permitted, kind reader, to doubt whether you have
ever been enclosed in a glass bottle, unless some vivid dream
has teased you with such magical mishaps. If that has been the
case, then you will sympathize warmly with poor Anselmus's
misery; but if you have never had such dreams, then you will
do me and Anselmus a favour by letting your active imagination
enclose you in the crystal for a few minutes. You are enfolded
by a dazzling glitter, all the objects on every side appear illuminated and surrounded by rays of light in all the colours of the
rainbow—this shimmering light makes everything quiver,
shake, and rumble—you are floating, unable to move a muscle,
in what seems like frozen ether, squeezing you so tightly that
it is in vain for your spirit to issue commands to your lifeless
body. The huge burden presses more and more heavily upon
your chest; each breath you take consumes more of the scanty
supply of air circulating in the confined space; your veins swell,
hideous terror afflicts you, and your every nerve twitches as it
bleeds in mortal agony.

Have pity, kind reader, on the student Anselmus, who suffered these unutterable tortures in his glass prison. He was well
aware, however, that death could not release him; for, having
fainted through excessive suffering, did he not awaken as the
morning sun was shining brightly and cheerfully into the room,
and did his tortures not begin afresh? He could not lift a finger,
but his thoughts knocked against the glass with a discordant
sound that dulled his senses, and instead of the clear voice of
his inner spirit, he could apprehend only the muffled roaring
of madness. In despair he shrieked: 'Oh Serpentina, Serpentina,
rescue me from this infernal torment!'

And he seemed to feel the wafting of gentle sighs, which

settled on the bottle like the translucent green leaves of the elder-tree. The ringing ceased, the bewildering, dazzling glitter disappeared, and he could breathe more freely.

'Am I not solely to blame for my misery? Alas! have I not offended against you, gracious and beloved Serpentina? Was I not base enough to doubt you? Did I not lose my faith, and with it everything that was to have made me supremely happy? Alas, you will never be mine, I have lost the golden pot, I shall never be permitted to behold its wonders. Oh, if only I could see you just once, and hear your sweet, melodious voice, lovely Serpentina!'

Cut to the quick by his bitter sorrow, Anselmus was lamenting in this manner, when someone said right beside him: 'I don't know what's the matter with you, my scholarly friend; why are you kicking up such an unholy row?'

Anselmus realized that there were five more bottles standing next to him on the same shelf, and in them he perceived three sixth-formers from the Cross School* and two solicitors' clerks.

'Gentlemen,' he exclaimed, 'companions in misfortune, how can you possibly be so calm, indeed so merry, as your cheerful faces show? You are confined in glass bottles, just as I am, and can't move a muscle, nor even have a sensible thought, without a dreadful ringing and clanging, and without feeling as if your heads were spinning. But I don't suppose you believe in the salamander and the green snake.'

'You must be raving, my scholarly friend,' replied one of the sixth-formers; 'we have never been so well off as we are now, thanks to the silver thalers which the mad Archivist paid us for copying out his strange squiggles. We don't have to learn any more Italian choruses; now we can go every day to Joseph's Bar, or to other inns, enjoy the strong beer, stare the occasional pretty girl in the face, and sing "Gaudeamus igitur", just like real students. We're having the time of our lives.'

'The gentlemen are quite right,' put in a solicitor's clerk; 'I am likewise well supplied with silver thalers, as is my cherished colleague here beside me, and I spend all my time strolling in the Vineyard Gardens, instead of sitting indoors copying out dusty documents.'

'But, my good sirs!' said Anselmus, 'can't you feel that every one of you is sitting in a glass bottle, unable to move a muscle, let alone go strolling about?'

Thereupon all the sixth-formers and solicitors' clerks let out a peal of laughter and shouted: 'Our scholarly friend is mad; he thinks he's in a glass bottle, when he's standing on the Elbe Bridge and looking down into the water. Let's go on!'

'Alas,' sighed the student, 'they have never beheld the lovely Serpentina, they have no inkling of freedom and life in faith and love; that is why they do not feel the pressure of the prison to which the salamander confined them because of their folly and mean-spiritedness; but I, wretch that I am, will perish in misery and disgrace, unless I am rescued by *her* whom I love so inexpressibly.'

At that moment Serpentina's voice wafted and murmured through the room: 'Anselmus! Have faith, love, and hope!'

And every sound she uttered radiated into Anselmus's prison, and the glass was compelled to yield to her power and extend itself, letting the captive's chest move and expand! His situation became steadily less agonizing, and he realized that Serpentina still loved him and that it was she who was making his confinement in the glass bearable. He no longer troubled himself about his empty-headed companions in misfortune, but bent all his thoughts upon the lovely Serpentina.

Suddenly, however, a dull, unpleasant muttering arose from his other side. Soon he perceived that this muttering came from an old coffee-pot with a broken lid, standing on a small cupboard opposite him. As he looked more closely, the odious features of an old woman's shrivelled face became more and more distinct, and a moment later the apple-woman from the Black Gate was standing in front of the shelf. Grinning and laughing in his face, she cried in her harsh voice: 'Well, well, my lad! You must be patient! Into glass you shall pass—didn't I foretell this long ago?'

'Jeer and fleer as much as you like, you damned old witch,' said Anselmus, 'you are to blame for everything, but the salamander will catch you, you nasty mangel-wurzel!'

'Ho, ho!' replied the old woman, 'don't put on such airs! You kicked my little sons in the face, you scorched my nose, but I still like you, you rascal, because you used to be a decent person, and my little daughter likes you too. But you'll never get out of the glass unless I help you; I can't reach up to you, but my neighbour the rat, who lives in the attic just above you, will gnaw the shelf you're standing on till it breaks; then you'll tumble down and I'll catch you in my apron, so that you'll keep your nice smooth face instead of breaking your nose, and I'll carry you straight to Miss Veronica; she's the one you must marry, once you have become a Counsellor.'

'Leave me alone, you limb of Satan,' shouted Anselmus in a rage, 'it is only your hellish arts that provoked me into the crime for which I must now do penance. But I'll endure it all patiently, for I can be nowhere else but here, where the lovely Serpentina comforts me and enfolds me with her love! Listen, old woman, and despair! I defy your power, I love only Serpentina in all eternity. I'll never be a Counsellor, never look at Veronica, who has lured me into evil through you! If the green snake cannot be mine, I'll perish in yearning and sorrow! Be off with you—be off with you—you horrible changeling!'

At this the old woman gave a harsh laugh that rang through the room, and cried: 'Stay there and perish, then! But now it's time to set to work, for I have business here of another kind.'

Casting off her black cloak, she stood there in loathsome nakedness, then spun round in a circle; great folios fell to the floor, and from them she tore out leaves of parchment; sticking the pages skilfully together and drawing them over her body, she was soon clad in what resembled a strange armour of coloured scales. The black cat, spitting fire, sprang out of the ink-well that stood on the desk and greeted the old woman by caterwauling; she uttered a cry of delight and disappeared with the cat through the door. Anselmus noticed that she had gone to the blue room, and soon he heard a distant hissing and roaring; the birds in the garden were screaming, and the parrot was croaking: 'Hurry! Hurry! Robbers! Robbers!'

At that moment the old woman rushed back into the room, carrying the golden pot under her arm, gesturing hideously, and shrieking: 'Good luck! Good luck! My son, kill the green snake! Up, my son, and at her!'

Anselmus thought he heard a deep moan—it was Serpentina's voice. Horror and despair seized hold of him. Gathering all his strength, he pushed against the glass with such force that his nerves and veins almost burst. A sharp clang resounded through the room, and there in the doorway stood the Archivist, wearing his gleaming damask dressing-gown.

'Hey, hey! You rapscallions, you mad sprites—witches' work—come here—huzza!' he shouted.

The old woman's black hair rose like bristles, her red burning eyes gleamed with hell-fire, and, clenching the pointed teeth in her wide jaws, she hissed: 'We'll show you! We'll seize our prey!', with a jeering, mocking laugh like the bleat of a goat. Clutching the golden pot tightly, she took from it fistfuls of shining earth and threw them at the Archivist, but as soon as the earth touched his dressing-gown it turned into flowers which fell to the ground. Then the lilies on the dressing-gown flickered up in flames, and the Archivist hurled the crackling, burning lilies at the witch, who howled with pain; but when she sprang into the air and shook her parchment armour, the lilies were extinguished and crumbled into ash. 'To your prey, my boy!' screeched the old woman. The cat rose into the air and flew over the Archivist's head towards the door, but the grey parrot fluttered over and grasped the cat's neck in his crooked beak. Fiery red blood gushed from the cat's throat, and Serpentina's voice cried: 'Saved! Saved!'

Filled with rage and despair, the old woman threw herself upon the Archivist, dropping the pot behind her and spreading out her long, dried-up fingers in order to seize him in her claws; but the Archivist pulled off his dressing-gown and hurled it at the old woman. Blue crackling flames came hissing and spitting and roaring from the leaves of parchment, and the old woman rolled to and fro, howling and lamenting. She kept trying to take more earth from the pot and pull more leaves from the books to douse the blaze, and every time she managed to throw earth or parchment upon herself, the fire went out. But then she was assailed by flickering, hissing bolts of fire that seemed to come from inside the Archivist. 'Hey, hey! In for the kill! Victory to the Salamander!' rumbled the voice of the Archivist, and a hundred flashes of lightning coiled themselves in fiery rings round the screeching old woman. Locked in a furious struggle, the cat and the parrot flew whizzing round the room, but finally the parrot struck the cat to the floor with his power-ful wings, and piercing him and holding him with his claws, so that he howled and moaned hideously in his death-agony, the parrot's sharp beak hacked out the cat's glowing eyes, so that burning foam spouted from the sockets.

Thick smoke was rising from the spot where the old woman had been lying on the floor under the dressing-gown. Her howling, her terrible piercing yells of lamentation, were dying away in the distance. The clouds of smoke evaporated, along with their penetrating stench. The Archivist raised the dressing-gown, and beneath it lay a nasty mangel-wurzel.

'Honoured Archivist, I bring you the defeated enemy', said the parrot, presenting the Archivist with a black hair held in his beak.

'Very good, my friend', answered the Archivist; 'here lies *my* defeated enemy; be so kind as to do what is needful. This very day, as a small honorarium, you shall receive six coconuts and a new pair of spectacles, since I see the cat has broken your old glasses to smithereens.'

'Yours to command, as long as I live, my esteemed friend and benefactor!' rejoined the parrot in high good humour. Taking the mangel-wurzel in his beak, he fluttered with it through the window which the Archivist had opened for him. The latter seized the golden pot and called in a loud voice: 'Serpentina, Serpentina!'

However, when Anselmus, delighted by the downfall of the vile old woman who had done him such injury, looked at the Archivist, he again beheld the lofty majestic figure of the prince of spirits, gazing up at him with indescribable grace and dig-nity.

'Anselmus', said the prince, 'your loss of faith was not your fault, but that of a malign and destructive principle which strove to penetrate your heart and estrange you from yourself. You have proved your loyalty. Be free and happy!'

A flash of lightning pierced Anselmus's heart, the splendid trio of crystal bells rang out louder and clearer than he had ever heard it—all his fibres and nerves trembled—but the chord swelled and resounded more and more loudly through the room, the glass enclosing Anselmus was shattered, and he plunged into the arms of the fair and lovely Serpentina.

ELEVENTH VIGIL

Sub-Rector Paulmann's annoyance at the outbreak of madness in his family. How Registrary Heerbrand became a Counsellor, and went out in shoes and silk stockings during a sharp frost. Veronica's confessions. An engagement beside a steaming dish of soup.

'But do tell me, my dear Registrary, however was it possible for the confounded punch yesterday to addle our wits and lead us into all kinds of tomfoolery?'

These words were uttered by Sub-Rector Paulmann the next morning, as he entered the room where fragments of crockery were still lying all over the floor, with the unfortunate wig, reduced to its original components, floating in their midst. After the student Anselmus had rushed out of the door, the Sub-Rector and the Registrary had staggered and reeled about the room, shouting like men possessed and butting each other with their heads. Finally Frances had managed, with much effort, to put her fuddled papa to bed, while the Registrary, in the last stages of exhaustion, sank on to the sofa which Veronica had left in order to flee to her room.

The Registrary's head was wrapped in his blue handkerchief, and he looked very pale and melancholy. 'Oh, my dear Sub-Rector,' he groaned, 'don't blame the punch, which Miss Veronica prepared so deliciously! No, the whole thing is entirely the fault of that damned student. Haven't you noticed that for a long time now he has been *non compos mentis*? And don't you know that insanity is infectious? One fool, many fools; I beg your pardon, but that's an old proverb; particularly when one has taken a drop too much, it's easy to fall into a fury, and then you find yourself joining in the manœuvres and imitating all the exercises demonstrated by the mad drill-sergeant. Believe it or not, Sub-Rector, I still feel giddy whenever I think of the grey parrot.'

'Stuff and nonsense!' interrupted the Sub-Rector, 'it was the little old amanuensis to the Archivist, who had put on a grey cloak and come in search of Anselmus.'

'Perhaps,' rejoined the Registrary, 'but I must confess that I feel quite wretched; there was such a strange noise of whistling and organ-music all last night.'

'That was me,' returned the Sub-Rector, 'for I snore very loudly.'

'Well, maybe,' continued the Registrary, 'but Sub-Rector, Sub-Rector! I had sound reasons for trying to provide some good cheer last night, but Anselmus spoiled all my efforts. You don't know—oh, Sub-Rector, Sub-Rector!'

The Registrary leapt to his feet, tore the handkerchief from his head, embraced the Sub-Rector, squeezed his hand ardently, cried again in heart-rending tones: 'Oh, Sub-Rector, Sub-Rector!', seized his hat and stick, and rushed off at full tilt.

'Anselmus will never again cross my threshold', said Sub-Rector Paulmann to himself, 'for I see clearly that with his obdurate madness he robs the best people of such reason as they possess. The Registrary is another such case; *I* have kept my wits about me so far, but the devil who rapped so hard at the door yesterday may eventually break in and do his worst. So get thee behind me, Satan! away with you, Anselmus!'

Veronica had become very pensive. She never uttered a word, but occasionally gave a strange smile, and preferred being on her own.

'Anselmus has her on his conscience too,' said the enraged Sub-Rector, 'but it is as well that he does not show his face; I know he is afraid of me, that Anselmus, and that is why he never comes here.'

As the Sub-Rector uttered these last words out loud, Veronica, who happened to be present, burst into tears, and sighed: 'How could Anselmus come here? He's been imprisoned in a glass jar for ages.'

'What?' cried the Sub-Rector. 'Heavens above, she's beginning to talk nonsense like the Registrary; it won't be long before she has a fit. That damned, abominable Anselmus!'

He promptly ran to Dr Eckstein, who smiled and once more said: 'Well, well!' Instead of prescribing anything, however, the Doctor, as he left, added to the few words he had spoken: 'Attack of nerves! It will pass off by itself—fresh air—go for a drive—amuse herself—theatre—*Sunday's Child—Sisters of Prague**—it will pass!'

'I've seldom known the Doctor so eloquent,' thought the Sub-Rector; 'he was positively loquacious.'

Several days, weeks, and months went by; Anselmus had disappeared, but Registrary Heerbrand did not show his face either, until 4 February. On the stroke of noon that day he entered the Sub-Rector's study, wearing a new suit of the best material and in the latest fashion, with shoes and silk stockings, despite the sharp frost, and with a large bouquet of fresh flowers in his hand. The Sub-Rector was not a little surprised to see his friend so smartly turned out. The Registrary walked solemnly up to the Sub-Rector, embraced him with the best of good breeding, and said: 'Today, on the name-day of your charming and esteemed daughter Miss Veronica, I will state frankly what has been on my mind for so long! On that unfortunate evening, when I brought the ingredients of that ill-fated punch in my coat pocket, I intended to acquaint you with some pleasing news and celebrate the happy day with all good cheer. I had just learnt that I was to become a Counsellor, and I have now had this elevation confirmed by the patent *cum nomine et sigillo principis* which I have in my pocket.'

'Good heavens, Reg— Counsellor Heerbrand, I mean', stammered the Sub-Rector.

'But it is you, esteemed Sub-Rector,' pursued Counsellor Heerbrand, as we must henceforth call him, 'it is you who can add the crowning glory to my happiness. I have long cherished a secret affection for Miss Veronica, and can justly claim that she has given me many friendly glances which convince me that she would not be averse to my proposal. In a word, esteemed Sub-Rector, I, Counsellor Heerbrand, request the hand of your charming daughter Miss Veronica, and if you are agreeable, I mean to lead her to the altar forthwith.'

Sub-Rector Paulmann clapped his hands in amazement and exclaimed: 'Why! Why! Reg— Counsellor, I mean, who ever would have thought it! Well, if Veronica really loves you, I for my part have no objection; and perhaps her present low spirits come from being secretly in love with you, my dear Counsellor! We know what tricks young girls are capable of.'

At that moment Veronica entered the room, with the pale and haggard look that she now habitually wore. Counsellor

Heerbrand walked over to her, mentioned her name-day in a few well-chosen words, and presented her with the fragrant bouquet and a small package, from which, when she opened it, a pair of gleaning ear-rings shone forth. The colour mounted to her cheeks, her eyes glistened more brightly, and she exclaimed: 'Good heavens! These are the very ear-rings that I took such pleasure in wearing a few weeks ago!'

'How can that be?' interrupted Counsellor Heerbrand, somewhat dismayed and offended, 'I bought these jewels with base coin in Castle Lane, an hour ago.'

But instead of listening, Veronica was standing in front of the mirror, examining the effect of the ear-rings, which she had already hung in her ears. The Sub-Rector informed her, with a grave countenance and in a serious tone, of their friend Heerbrand's elevation and of his proposal of matrimony. Veronica gave the Counsellor a penetrating look, and said:

'I've known for a long time that you wanted to marry me. All right! I promise you my heart and my hand, but I must tell you—both of you, my father and my future husband—a number of things which have been weighing very heavily on my mind; and I must tell you this at once, even if it means letting the soup get cold that Frances, I see, is just putting on the table.'

Without waiting for answers from the Sub-Rector and the Counsellor, though words were plainly hovering on their lips, Veronica went on: 'You must believe me, my dear father, when I say that I loved Anselmus with all my heart, and when Registrary Heerbrand, who is now a Counsellor, declared that Anselmus might rise to such a rank, I resolved that he and none other should be my husband. But then it seemed as though hostile alien forces were trying to wrest him from me, and I resorted to old Lizzie, who used to be my nurse, and is now a wise woman and a great sorceress. She promised to help me and to deliver Anselmus to me. At midnight on the equinox we went to the crossroads, where she summoned up infernal spirits, and with the help of the black cat we created a little metal mirror. When I bent my thoughts upon Anselmus, I needed only to look into the mirror to control his mind entirely. But I now heartily repent of all this, and I vow that I will never again

have anything to do with Satanic arts. The salamander defeated
the old woman, I heard her lamenting, but there was no way I
could help; as soon as the parrot had devoured her in the form
of a mangel-wurzel, my metal mirror broke in two with a
piercing clang.'

Veronica fetched the pieces of the broken mirror and a lock
of hair from her sewing-box. Handing both to Counsellor Heerbrand, she continued: 'Beloved Counsellor, take the fragments
of the mirror, and at midnight tonight throw them off the Elbe
Bridge, from the place where the cross stands, into the river,
which is not frozen at that point. As for the lock of hair, keep
that next to your faithful heart. I vow once more to have nothing more to do with Satanic arts and I hope Anselmus is happy,
now that he is attached to the green snake, who is much wealth-
ier and more beautiful than I am. Beloved Counsellor, I will
love and honour you as your true and faithful wife!'

'Oh heavens,' cried the Sub-Rector in deep distress, 'she's
mad, she's mad—she can never be a Counsellor's lady—she's
mad!'

'Nothing of the sort', interrupted Counsellor Heerbrand; 'I
am well aware that Miss Veronica had a soft spot for that
tiresome fellow Anselmus, and it may well be that in her over-
wrought state she turned for help to the wise woman. This
woman, I perceive, can be none other than old Mrs Rauer, who
lives outside the Lake Gate and tells fortunes from cards and
coffee-grounds. Nor can it be denied that there are indeed
arcane arts which exercise a malign influence upon mankind;
one reads of such things in classical authors. But what Miss
Veronica says about the salamander's victory and Anselmus's
attachment to the green snake can be no more than a poetic
allegory—a metrical work, so to speak, telling of her final and
entire parting from the student.'

'Regard it as whatever you please, my dear Counsellor!' interrupted Veronica; 'as a silly dream, if you like.'

'I shall certainly not do that', rejoined Counsellor Heerbrand,
'for I am well aware that Anselmus is also in the grip of hidden
forces, which mislead him into all manner of crazy pranks.'

Sub-Rector Paulmann could contain himself no longer. He
burst out: 'Stop, for heaven's sake, stop! Have we overindulged

in the damned punch again, or has Anselmus's madness affected us? What sort of nonsense are you talking, Counsellor? I'll assume that your wits have been addled by love; but marriage will soon set that right. Otherwise I should be afraid, esteemed Counsellor, that you too had been touched by madness, and I should be worried about your progeny, which might inherit its parents' mania. Now, I give my fatherly blessing to your happy engagement, and you have my permission to exchange kisses as a betrothed couple.'

This was done on the spot, and the engagement was formally agreed before the soup had time to get cold. A few weeks later, Counsellor Heerbrand's lady was indeed sitting, as she had earlier imagined, in the window alcove of a fine house on the New Market, smiling down upon the passing dandies, who gazed up at her through their monocles and said: 'What a charming woman Counsellor Heerbrand's lady is!'

TWELFTH VIGIL

News from the estate where Anselmus took up residence on becoming Archivist Lindhorst's son-in-law. His life there with Serpentina. Conclusion.

Very deeply did I feel the sublime happiness of the student Anselmus, once he was wedded to the lovely Serpentina and had departed for the wondrous and mysterious realm which he acknowledged as his home and for which his heart, filled with strange premonitions, had so long been yearning. But it was in vain for me, kind reader, to try to convey in words any notion of the splendours by which Anselmus was surrounded. I perceived with disgust the inadequacy of every possible expression. I felt entangled in the petty tedium of daily life; my tormenting dissatisfaction made me ill; I crept around as though lost in dreams; in a word, I fell into the state of mind endured by Anselmus, as I described, gentle reader, in the Fourth Vigil. When I glanced through the eleven Vigils that I had successfully completed, I became quite fretful, thinking that I might never be permitted to add the twelfth as the keystone; for every time I sat down at night to round off the work, it seemed as though malicious spirits (doubtless relatives of the dead witch, if not her first cousins) were holding up a brilliantly polished mirror in which I beheld my own self, pale and melancholy from lack of sleep, like Registrary Heerbrand after getting drunk on punch. Then I flung my pen away and went straight to bed, so that I might at least dream about the happy Anselmus and the lovely Serpentina. After this had gone on for several days and nights, I at last received a quite unexpected note from Archivist Lindhorst, in which he wrote as follows:

Sir: It has come to my attention that you have recounted the strange fortunes of my worthy son-in-law, the sometime student, who is now the poet Anselmus, in eleven Vigils, and that you are now labouring to say something in the twelfth and final Vigil about his happy life in Atlantis, where he has taken up residence with my daughter on the fine estate I possess there. I cannot say that I am overjoyed at having my true character disclosed to the reading public, since it may expose me to innumerable difficulties in my employment as Privy Archivist, and may indeed inspire His Majesty's advisers to raise the question to what extent a salamander may take a legally binding oath as a public servant, and to what extent he may be entrusted with weighty responsibilities, since it is averred by Gabalis* and Swedenborg* that elemental spirits are by no means to be trusted. Moreover, my best friends will now shun my embrace, fearing that sudden exuberance might induce me to emit a flash of lightning and singe their wigs and their Sunday suits. None the less, despite all these considerations, I am willing to assist you, Sir, in the completion of your work, since it contains many complimentary references to myself and my dear married daughter (I wish I were well rid of the other two). If, therefore, you wish to write the Twelfth Vigil, then leave your garret, come down your damned five flights of stairs, and pay me a visit. In the blue room with the palm-trees, with which you are already familiar, you will find suitable writing materials, and you may then acquaint your readers in a few words with what you have beheld. That will please them better than a lengthy account of a way of life which you yourself know only from hearsay.

> I remain Sir, your devoted
> Salamander Lindhorst
> (*pro tem*. Privy Archivist to His Majesty)

This friendly, though rather crusty note from Archivist Lindhorst was extremely welcome. There seemed little doubt that the eccentric old man was well aware of the strange way in which I had learnt of his son-in-law's fortunes, something which the promise of secrecy obliged me to conceal even from you, kind reader, but he had not taken it so much amiss as I had feared. Indeed, he himself was offering me a helping hand to complete my work, which allowed me to conclude that he was at bottom content to have his strange spiritual existence revealed in print. 'Perhaps', thought I, 'the Archivist hopes that this will make it easier for him to dispose of his two remaining daughters, for a spark may enter the heart of some youth and awaken in him the yearning for the green snake, whom he will then seek and find in the elder-tree on Ascension Day. Anselmus's misfortune in being confined in the glass bottle will warn such a youth to beware of doubt and incredulity.'

On the stroke of eleven I extinguished the lamp on my desk and went to the house of the Archivist, who was already waiting for me in the hallway.

'So you've come, my worthy friend! I'm glad to see that you have not mistaken my good intentions. Come along!' With these words he led me through the conservatory, bathed in dazzling light, to the azure room, where I saw the purple desk at which Anselmus had worked. The Archivist disappeared but returned immediately holding a fine gold goblet, from which a blue flame crackled aloft.

'Here,' said he, 'I bring you the favourite drink of your friend Kapellmeister Johannes Kreisler. It is flaming arrack in which I have sprinkled some sugar. Take a sip of it while I remove my dressing-gown, so that as you sit and gaze and write, I may entertain myself, and enjoy your esteemed company, by swimming up and down in the goblet.'

'Just as you please, my worthy Archivist,' I rejoined, 'but if I partake of this drink, I hope you won't . . .'

'Don't worry, my friend', exclaimed the Archivist, quickly taking off his dressing-gown. To my considerable astonishment, he climbed into the goblet and vanished amid the flames. Undeterred, I blew the flames gently aside and took a sip of the drink. It was delicious!

Are not the emerald leaves of the palm-trees stirring with gentle sighs and murmurs, as though caressed by the breath of the morning wind? Aroused from sleep, they rise and move, whispering mysteriously of the wonders proclaimed by the sweet and distant notes of a harp. The azure, leaving the walls, floats to and fro like scented mist, but rays of dazzling light dart through the haze, and as though rejoicing in child-like pleasure it whirls and revolves and rises to the immeasurable heights of the vault above the palm-trees. The rays of light, each more dazzling than the last, gather in a body, until the bright sunlight discloses the vistas of the grove in which I see Anselmus.

Glowing hyacinths, tulips, and roses lift their beautiful heads, and their perfumes call in delightful tones to the happy man: 'Walk among us, beloved, who understands us—our fragrance is the yearning of love—we love you and are yours for evermore!'

The golden rays burn in glowing tones: 'We are fire which love has lit. Fragrance is yearning, but fire is passion, and do we not dwell within your breast? We are yours!'

The dark bushes, the lofty trees rustle and murmur: 'Come to us! Happy one! Beloved! Fire is passion, but our cool shade is hope! We will enfold your head with our loving sighs, for you understand us, because love dwells within your breast.'

The springs and streams gush and plash: 'Beloved, do not walk past so quickly, gaze into our crystal—your image dwells in us, and we preserve it with love, for you have understood us!'

Bright-hued birds twitter and sing in an exultant chorus: 'Listen to us, listen to us, we are the joy, the bliss, the rapture of love!'

But Anselmus casts a yearning look at the magnificent temple rising in the distance. The finely wrought columns seem to be trees, and the capitals and mouldings to be acanthus leaves, whose wondrous wreaths form a magnificent ornament. Anselmus walks towards the temple, gazing with deep bliss at the coloured marble, the wonderful moss-covered steps. 'No,' he cries, as though in supreme rapture, 'she is no longer distant!'

Thereupon Serpentina, in all her beauty and grace, emerges from the temple, carrying the golden pot, from which a magnificent lily has sprung. The unspeakable bliss of infinite yearning glows in her lovely eyes, and as she looks at Anselmus she says: 'My beloved, the lily has opened its petals; our utmost hopes are fulfilled. Can there be a happiness that resembles ours?'

Anselmus embraces her with the ardour of intense passion, the lily burns above his head in flaming rays of light. And the trees and bushes stir more audibly, and the springs and the birds exult in clearer and more joyful tones; all manner of colourful insects dance in the eddying breezes; in the air, in the water, on the earth, a glad, joyous, jubilant tumult celebrates the feast of love! Flashes of lightning dart through the bushes, diamonds peep from the earth like sparkling eyes, lofty fountains gush forth, strange perfumes waft by like whirring wings: these are the elemental spirits, paying homage to the lily and proclaiming Anselmus's happiness.

Anselmus raises his head, as though transfigured by radiant

light. Is it his gaze, his words, his song? It rings out clearly: 'Serpentina! Faith in you, love for you has disclosed to me the innermost being of nature! You brought me the lily which sprang from the gold, from the primal force of the earth, even before Phosphorus awakened thought. The lily is the knowledge of the holy harmony of all living things, and in this knowledge I shall live in the utmost happiness for evermore. Yes, I am a supremely happy man who has been granted supreme knowledge—I cannot do other than love you eternally, Serpentina! The golden rays of the lily will never fade, for as faith and love are eternal, so is knowledge.'

For the vision in which I had seen Anselmus in bodily form on his estate in Atlantis I was indebted to the arts of the salamander. It was splendid, too, that when the scene had dissolved into mist, I found it clearly and legibly described in my own handwriting on the paper that was lying on the purple table. Now, however, I felt pierced and lacerated by sudden anguish.

'Happy Anselmus, who has cast off the burden of daily life! Your love for Serpentina made you spread your wings and move them vigorously, and now you are living in joy and bliss on your estate in Atlantis! But as for poor me, in a few minutes I shall have left this fine room, which is far from being an estate in Atlantis, to return to my garret; the petty cares of my poverty-stricken life will absorb my thoughts, and my gaze is obscured by a thousand ills as though by thick mist, so that I doubt if I shall ever behold the lily.'

At that moment Archivist Lindhorst tapped me gently on the shoulder and said: 'Hush, my worthy friend! Don't complain like that! Weren't you in Atlantis yourself a moment ago, and haven't you at least got a pretty farm there, as the poetic property of your mind? Indeed, is Anselmus's happiness anything other than life in poetry, where the holy harmony of all things is revealed as the deepest secret of nature?'

THE SANDMAN

...•———◆———•...

Nathanael to Lothar

You must all be very worried by my not having written for so long. Mother is probably angry, and Clara, I dare say, thinks that I am living in the lap of luxury and have completely forgotten the lovely, angelic image which is so deeply imprinted on my heart and mind. That is not so, however; I think of you all, daily and hourly, and in my sweet dreams the amiable figure of my lovely Clara passes, smiling at me with her bright eyes as charmingly as she used to whenever I called on you. Oh, how could I possibly have written to you in the tormented state of mind which has distracted all my thoughts until now! Something appalling has entered my life! Dark forebodings of a hideous, menacing fate are looming over me like the shadows of black clouds, impervious to any kindly ray of sunlight. It is time for me to tell you what has befallen me. I realize that I must, but at the very thought mad laughter bursts from within me. Oh, my dear Lothar, how am I ever to convey to you that what happened to me a few days ago has indeed managed to devastate my life so cruelly! If only you were here, you could see for yourself; but now you must undoubtedly consider me a crack-brained, superstitious fool. To cut a long story short, the appalling event that befell me, the fatal memory of which I am vainly struggling to escape, was simply this: a few days ago, at twelve noon on 30 October to be precise, a barometer-seller entered my room and offered me his wares. Instead of buying anything, I threatened to throw him downstairs, whereupon he departed of his own accord.

You will apprehend that this incident must gain its significance from associations peculiar to myself, reaching far back into my own life, and that it must have been the personality of this unfortunate tradesman that had such a repulsive effect on me.

That is indeed the case. I am using all my strength to compose myself so that I may calmly and patiently tell you enough about my early youth for your lively imagination to visualize everything in distinct and luminous images. As I prepare to begin, I hear you laugh, while Clara says: 'What childish nonsense!' Laugh, I beg you, laugh and mock me as much as you please! But, God in heaven! the hair is rising on my scalp, and I feel as though I were begging you to mock me in mad despair, as Franz Moor begged Daniel.* Now, let me get on with the story!

During the day, except at lunch, my brothers and sisters and I saw little of our father. He was no doubt heavily occupied with his duties. After dinner, which was served at seven in accordance with the old custom, all of us, including our mother, would go into our father's study and sit at a round table. Our father would smoke tobacco and drink a big glass of beer with it. He would tell us many wondrous tales, and would become so excited over them that his pipe always went out; I would then have to light it again by holding out burning paper, which I greatly enjoyed. Often, however, he would give us picture-books and sit silent and motionless in his armchair, blowing such clouds of smoke that we all seemed to be swathed in mist. On such evenings our mother would be very melancholy, and hardly had the clock struck nine than she would say: 'Now, children, time for bed! The Sandman is coming, I can tell.'

Whenever she said this, I would indeed hear something coming noisily upstairs with rather heavy, slow steps; it must be the Sandman. On one occasion I found this hollow trampling particularly alarming, and asked my mother as she was shepherding us away: 'Mother! who is the wicked Sandman who always chases us away from Papa? What does he look like?'

'There is no such person as the Sandman, dear child,' replied my mother; 'when I say the Sandman is coming, that just means that you are sleepy, and can't keep your eyes open, as though someone had thrown sand in them.'

My mother's answer did not satisfy me; indeed my childish mind formed the conviction that our mother was only denying the Sandman's existence so that we should not be afraid of him; after all, I could always hear him coming upstairs. Filled with curiosity about this Sandman and his relation to us children, I finally asked my youngest sister's old nurse what kind of man the Sandman was.

'Why, Natty,' replied the old woman, 'don't you know that yet? He's a wicked man who comes to children when they don't want to go to bed and throws handfuls of sand into their eyes; that makes their eyes fill with blood and jump out of their heads, and he throws the eyes into his bag and takes them into the crescent moon to feed his own children, who are sitting in the nest there; the Sandman's children have crooked beaks, like owls, with which to peck the eyes of naughty human children.'

I now formed a hideous mental picture of the cruel Sandman, and as soon as the heavy steps came upstairs in the evening, I would tremble with fear and horror. My mother could extract nothing from me except the stammering, tearful cry: 'The Sandman! the Sandman!' I would then run to my bedroom and be tormented all night by the frightful apparition of the Sandman.

Soon I grew old enough to realize that the nurse's tale of the Sandman and his children's nest in the crescent moon could not be exactly true; yet the Sandman remained for me a fearsome spectre, and terror, indeed horror, would seize upon me when I heard him not only coming upstairs but also pulling open the door of my father's room and entering. Sometimes he would stay away for a long period; then he would come several times in quick succession. This went on for years, during which I never became accustomed to these sinister happenings, and my image of the hideous Sandman lost nothing of its vividness. His dealings with my father began increasingly to occupy my imagination; I was prevented from asking my father about them by an unconquerable timidity, but the desire to investigate the mystery myself grew stronger as the years went by. The Sandman had aroused my interest in the marvellous and extraordinary, an interest that readily takes root in a child's mind. I liked nothing better than hearing or reading horrific stories about goblins, witches, dwarfs, and so forth; but pride of place always belonged to the Sandman, and I kept drawing him, in the strangest and most loathsome forms, with chalk or charcoal on tables, cupboards, and walls.

When I was ten, my mother made me move from my nursery to a little bedroom just along the corridor from my father's

room. We were still obliged to go to bed whenever the clock
struck nine and we heard the unknown being in the house.
From my bedroom I could hear him entering my father's room,
and soon afterwards a fine, strange-smelling vapour seemed to
spread through the house. As my curiosity increased, so did my
resolve to make the Sandman's acquaintance by some means or
other. Often, when my mother had gone past, I would slip out
of my bedroom into the corridor, but I never managed to discover anything; for the Sandman had always entered the room
before I reached the spot at which he would have been visible.
Finally, impelled by an irresistible urge, I decided to hide in
my father's room and await the Sandman's arrival.

One evening I perceived from my father's silence and my
mother's low spirits that the Sandman was coming; accordingly
I pretended to be very tired, left the room before nine, and
concealed myself in a recess just beside the door. The front door
creaked and slow, heavy, rumbling steps approached the staircase. My mother hastened past me with my brothers and sisters.
Gently, gently, I opened the door of my father's study. He was
sitting, as usual, silent and motionless with his back to the
door, and did not notice me; I slipped inside and hid behind
the curtain which was drawn in front of an open wardrobe next
to the door. The rumbling steps came closer and closer; strange
sounds of coughing, scraping, and muttering could be heard.
My heart was quaking with fear and anticipation. Right outside
the door, a firm step, a violent tug at the latch, and the door
sprang open with a clatter. Bracing myself with an effort, I
peeped cautiously out. The Sandman was standing in the
middle of the room, facing my father, with the lights shining
brightly in his face. The Sandman, the frightful Sandman, was
the old advocate Coppelius,* who sometimes had lunch with
us!

But the most hideous of shapes could not have filled me with
deeper horror than this same Coppelius. Imagine a big, broad-
shouldered man with a massive, misshapen head, a pair of piercing, greenish, cat-like eyes sparkling from under bushy grey
eyebrows, and a large beaky nose hanging over his upper lip.
His crooked mouth was often distorted in a malicious smile,
and then a couple of dark red spots appeared on his cheeks, and

a strange hissing sound proceeded from between his clenched teeth. Coppelius was always seen wearing an ash-grey coat of old-fashioned cut, with waistcoat and breeches to match, but with black stockings and shoes with little jewelled buckles. His small wig scarcely covered more than the crown of his head, his greasy locks stood on end above his big red ears, and a large, tightly tied pigtail stuck out from the back of his neck, disclosing the silver buckle that fastened his crimped cravat. His entire appearance was repellent and disgusting; but we children had a particular aversion to his big, gnarled, hairy hands, and anything touched by them ceased at once to be appetizing. Once he noticed this, he took delight in finding some pretext for fingering a piece of cake or fruit that our kind mother had surreptitiously put on our plates, so that our loathing and disgust prevented us, with tears in our eyes, from enjoying the titbit that was supposed to give us pleasure. He behaved in just the same way on special days, when our father would pour out a small glass of sweet wine. Coppelius would then quickly pass his hand over it, or he would raise the glass to his blue lips and utter a fiendish laugh on seeing us unable to express our vexation other than by suppressed sobs. He used to refer to us only as 'the little beasts'; in his presence we were forbidden to utter a sound, and we cursed the ugly, unfriendly man, who was deliberately intent on spoiling our slightest pleasures. Our mother seemed to hate the odious Coppelius as much as we did; for as soon as he showed himself, her good spirits, her cheerful, relaxed manner, were transformed into sorrowful and gloomy gravity. Our father behaved towards him as though Coppelius were a higher being whose foibles must be endured and who had to be kept in a good mood at whatever cost. Coppelius had only to drop a hint, and his favourite dishes were cooked and rare wines opened.

On seeing Coppelius now, I realized with horror and alarm that he and none other must be the Sandman; but to me the Sandman was no longer the bogy man in the nursery story who brings children's eyes to feed his brood in their nest in the crescent moon. No! He was a hateful, spectral monster, bringing misery, hardship, and perdition, both temporal and eternal, wherever he went.

I was rooted to the spot. Despite the risk of being discovered and, as I was well aware, of being severely punished, I stayed there, listening, and poking my head between the curtains. My father welcomed Coppelius with much formality.

'Come on, let's get to work!' cried Coppelius in a hoarse, croaking voice, throwing off his coat.

My father, silent and frowning, took off his dressing-gown, and the two of them donned long black smocks. I did not notice where these came from. My father opened the folding doors of a cupboard; but I saw that what I had so long taken for a cupboard was instead a dark recess containing a small fireplace. Coppelius walked over to it, and a blue flame crackled up from the hearth. All manner of strange instruments were standing around. Merciful heavens! As my old father bent down to the fire, he looked quite different. A horrible, agonizing convulsion seemed to have contorted his gentle, honest face into the hideous, repulsive mask of a fiend. He looked like Coppelius. The latter, brandishing a pair of red-hot tongs, was lifting gleaming lumps from the thick smoke and then hammering at them industriously. It seemed to me that human faces were visible on all sides, but without eyes, and with ghastly, deep, black cavities instead.

'Bring the eyes! Bring the eyes!' cried Coppelius in a hollow rumbling voice.

Gripped by uncontrollable terror, I screamed out and dived from my hiding-place on to the floor. Coppelius seized me, gnashing his teeth and bleating, 'Little beast! Little beast!' He pulled me to my feet and hurled me on to the fireplace, where the flames began to singe my hair. 'Now we've got eyes—eyes— a fine pair of children's eyes', whispered Coppelius, thrusting his hands into the flames and pulling out fragments of red-hot coal which he was about to strew in my eyes.

My father raised his hands imploringly and cried: 'Master! Master! Let my Nathanael keep his eyes! Let him keep them!'

With a piercing laugh, Coppelius cried: 'All right, the boy may keep his eyes and snivel his way through his lessons; but let's examine the mechanism of his hands and feet.' And with these words he seized me so hard that my joints made a cracking noise, dislocated my hands and feet, and put them back in various sockets. 'They don't fit properly! It was all right as it was! The Old Man knew what he was doing!' hissed and muttered Coppelius; but everything went black and dim before my eyes, a sudden convulsion shot through my nerves and my frame, and I felt nothing more. A warm, gentle breath passed over my face, and I awoke from a death-like sleep; my mother was bending over me.

'Is the Sandman still there?' I stammered.

'No, my dear child, he's been gone for a long, long time, he'll do you no harm!' said my mother, kissing and cuddling her darling boy who was thus restored to life.

Why should I weary you, my dear Lothar? Why should I dwell on minute details, when so much remains to be told? Suffice it to say that I was caught eavesdropping and was roughly treated by Coppelius. Fear and terror brought on a violent fever, with which I was laid low for several weeks. 'Is the Sandman still there?' These were my first coherent words and the sign that I was cured, that my life had been saved. Now I need only tell you about the most terrifying moment of my early life; you will then be convinced that it is not the weakness of my eyesight that makes everything appear colourless, but that a sombre destiny has indeed veiled my life in a murky cloud, which perhaps I shall not penetrate until I die.

Coppelius did not show his face again, and was said to have left the town.

A year, perhaps, had gone by, and we were sitting one evening round the table, according to the old, unaltered custom. My father was in excellent spirits and told many delightful stories about the journeys he had made in his youth. Then, as it struck nine, we suddenly heard the front door creaking on its hinges, and slow, leaden steps came rumbling through the hall and up the stairs.

'That's Coppelius', said my mother, turning pale.

'Yes! It's Coppelius', repeated my father, in a dull, spiritless voice.

Tears burst from my mother's eyes. 'But, father, father!' she cried, 'does this have to happen?'

'This is the last time he will visit me, I promise you!' replied my father. 'Go, take the children away! Go to bed! Good night!'

I felt as though I were being crushed under a heavy, cold stone; I could hardly breathe! As I stood motionless, my mother seized me by the arm: 'Come along, Nathanael!' I allowed her to lead me away, and went into my bedroom. 'Keep quiet, and go to bed! Go to sleep!' my mother called after me; but I was so tormented by indescribable inner terror and turmoil that I could not sleep a wink. Before me stood the hateful, loathsome Coppelius, his eyes sparkling, laughing at me maliciously, and I strove in vain to rid myself of his image. It must already have been midnight when a frightful crash was heard, as though a cannon had been fired. The whole house trembled, a rattling, rustling noise passed my door, and the front door was slammed with a clatter.

'That's Coppelius!' I cried in terror, leaping out of bed. Suddenly a piercing scream of lament was heard; I raced to my father's room; the door was open, a cloud of suffocating smoke billowed towards me, and the maidservant shrieked: 'Oh, the master! the master!' On the floor in front of the smoking fireplace my father was lying dead, his face burnt black and hideously contorted, while my sisters wailed and whimpered all round him and my mother lay in a dead faint.

'Coppelius, you abominable fiend, you've murdered my father!' I shouted; then I lost consciousness.

Two days later, when my father was laid in his coffin, his features were once again as mild and gentle as they had been during his life. I was comforted by the realization that his alliance with the devilish Coppelius could not have plunged him into eternal perdition.

The explosion had roused the neighbours; the incident got out and came to the attention of the authorities, who wanted to call Coppelius to account. He, however, had vanished from the town without leaving a trace.

If I now tell you, my cherished friend, that the barometer-seller who called on me was none other than the abominable Coppelius, you will not blame me for interpreting his malevolent appearance as a portent of dire misfortune. He was differently dressed, but Coppelius's figure and features are too deeply engraved on my mind for any mistake to be possible. Besides,

Coppelius has not even changed his name. I am told that he claims to be a Piedmontese mechanic called Giuseppe Coppola.

I am determined to try conclusions with him and avenge my father's death, come what may.

Say nothing to my mother about the appearance of this hideous monster. Give my love to my dear Clara; I will write to her when my mind is calmer. Farewell!

Clara to Nathanael

It is true that you haven't written to me for a long time, but I am still convinced that I am in your thoughts. For you must have been preoccupied with me when, intending to send off your last letter to my brother Lothar, you addressed it to me instead of to him. I opened the letter joyfully and realized your mistake only on reading the words: 'Oh, my dear Lothar!' I should of course have read no further, but given the letter to my brother. You have sometimes teasingly accused me of such womanly calm and deliberation that if the house were about to collapse I would pause before taking flight, like the woman in the story, to smooth out a fold in the curtains; however, I need hardly tell you that I was deeply shaken by the first few sentences of your letter. I could scarcely breathe, and my head was spinning. Oh, my precious Nathanael, what terrible thing could have entered your life! The idea of parting from you, never seeing you again, pierced my heart like a red-hot dagger. I read and read! Your description of the odious Coppelius is horrible. I did not know that your good old father had met such a terrible, violent death. When I gave Lothar back his rightful property, he tried to soothe me, but without success. The frightful barometer-seller Giuseppe Coppola followed me about wherever I went, and I'm almost ashamed to confess that he disturbed even my usually sound and healthy sleep with all manner of strange dreams. But soon, on the very next day, I regained my normal state of mind. Don't be cross, dearly beloved, if Lothar happens to tell you that, despite your strange notion that Coppelius will do you an injury, I am as cheerful and relaxed as ever.

I will confess frankly that in my opinion all the terrors and horrors you describe took place only inside your head, and had very little to do with the real world outside you. Old Coppelius may have been odious enough, but it was his hatred of children that bred such a loathing of him in you children.

It was quite natural that your childish mind should connect the terrible Sandman in the nursery tale with old Coppelius, and that even when you no longer believed in the Sandman, Coppelius should seem a sinister monster, particularly hostile to children. As for his uncanny nocturnal goings-on with your father, I expect the two of them were simply conducting secret alchemical experiments, which could hardly please your mother, since a lot of money must have been squandered and moreover, as is said always to happen to such inquirers, your father became obsessed with the delusive longing for higher wisdom and was estranged from his family. Your father must have brought about his death by his own carelessness, and Coppelius cannot be to blame. Would you believe that yesterday I asked our neighbour, an experienced chemist, whether it was possible for such an explosion which killed people on the spot to occur in chemical experiments? He said, 'Why, of course', and gave me a characteristically long-winded account of how this could happen, mentioning so many strange-sounding names that I couldn't remember any of them. Now I expect you'll be angry with your Clara. You'll say: 'Her cold temperament cannot accept the mystery that often enfolds man in invisible arms; she perceives only the varied surface of the world and takes pleasure in it as a childish infant does in a glittering fruit which has deadly poison concealed within it.'

Oh, my precious Nathanael! don't you think that even a cheerful, relaxed, carefree temperament may have premonitions of a dark power that tries malevolently to attack our inmost selves? But please forgive a simple girl like me for venturing to suggest what I think about such inner conflicts. I probably shan't be able to put it into words properly, and you'll laugh at me, not because what I'm trying to say is stupid, but because I'm so clumsy at saying it.

If there is a dark power which malevolently and treacherously places a thread within us, with which to hold us and draw us down a perilous and pernicious path that we would never otherwise have set foot on—if there is such a power, then it must take the same form as we do, it must become our very self; for only in this way can we believe in it and give it the scope it requires to accomplish its secret task. If our minds, strengthened by a cheerful life, are resolute enough to recognize alien and malevolent influences for what they are and to proceed tranquilly along the path to which our inclinations and our vocation have directed us, the uncanny power must surely perish in a vain struggle to assume the form which is our own reflection. Lothar also says there is no doubt that once we have surrendered ourselves to the dark psychic power, it draws alien figures, encountered by chance in the outside world, into our inner selves, so that we ourselves give life to the spirit which our strange delusion persuades us is speaking from such figures. It is the phantom of our own self which, thanks to its intimate relationship with us and its deep influence on our minds, casts us down to hell or transports us to heaven. You see, my darling Nathanael, that Lothar and I have talked at length about dark powers and forces, and now that I have, with some labour, written down the main points, it seems to me quite profound. I don't quite understand Lothar's last words, I only have a dim idea of what he means, and yet it all sounds very true. I beg you to forget all about the hateful advocate Coppelius and the barometer-man Giuseppe Coppola. Be assured that these alien figures have no power over you; only your belief in their malevolent power can make them truly malevolent to you. If every line of your letter did not reveal the deep perturbation of your spirits, if your state of mind did not cause me pain in my very soul, then, indeed, I could make jokes about the advocate Sandman and the barometer-seller Coppelius. Keep your spirits up! If the hateful Coppola should presume to annoy you in your dreams, I am determined to appear in your presence like your guardian angel and to drive him away with loud laughter. I am not the slightest bit afraid of him or his horrid hands; I wouldn't let him spoil my appetite as an advocate, nor hurt my eyes as a Sandman.

Eternally yours, my most dearly beloved Nathanael, etc.

Nathanael to Lothar

I am very annoyed that Clara should have opened and read my recent letter to you, although admittedly the mistake was due to my own absent-mindedness. She has written me a most profound philosophical letter in which she demonstrates at great length that Coppelius and Coppola exist only in my mind and are phantoms emanating from myself which will crumble to dust the moment I acknowledge them as such. Really, who would have thought that the spirit which shines from such clear, gracious, smiling, child-like eyes, like a sweet and lovely dream, could draw such intellectual distinctions, worthy of a university graduate? She appeals to your opinion. You and she have talked about me. I suppose you have given her lectures on logic to teach her how to sift and search all problems with due subtlety. Well, stop it at once!

Anyway, it seems certain that the barometer-seller Giuseppe Coppola is not the same person as the old advocate Coppelius. I am attending the lectures given by the newly arrived professor of physics, who is called Spalanzani,* like the famous naturalist, and is likewise of Italian descent. He has known Coppola for many years, and besides, his accent makes it clear that he really is a Piedmontese. Coppelius was a German, though not an honest one, in my opinion. My mind is not completely at ease. You and Clara are welcome to think me a melancholy dreamer, but I cannot shake off the impression that Coppelius's accursed face made on me. I am glad he has left the town, as Spalanzani tells me.

This professor is an odd fish. A tubby little man with projecting cheek-bones, a delicate nose, thick lips, and small piercing eyes. But you will get a better idea of him than any description can convey if you take a look at Cagliostro* as he is depicted by Chodowiecki* in some Berlin magazine. That is what Spalanzani looks like.

Not long ago, as I was going up his stairs, I noticed that a narrow strip of the glass door was left unconcealed by the curtain which is normally drawn across it. I can't tell how it was that I peeped in inquisitively. Inside the room a tall, very slim woman, beautifully proportioned and magnificently dressed, was sitting in front of a small table on which she was leaning, with her hands folded. She was facing the door, so that I had a full view of her angelic face. She seemed not to notice me, and indeed there was something lifeless about her eyes, as though they lacked the power of sight; she seemed to be asleep with her eyes open. I had a rather uncanny feeling, and crept softly into the lecture-hall next door. Afterwards I learnt that the figure I had seen was Spalanzani's daughter Olimpia, whom, strangely and reprehensibly, he keeps locked up, so that nobody at all is allowed near her. There must be something peculiar about her; perhaps she is feeble-minded, for example. But why I am writing all this to you? I could have told you all this better and more fully by word of mouth. For let me tell you that in two weeks' time I shall be with you. I must see my dear sweet angel, my Clara, again. Her presence will blow away the mood of irritation which, I must confess, almost mastered me after that damnably sensible letter. That's why I won't write to her today.

Best wishes, etc.

No invention could be stranger or more extraordinary than the events which befell my poor friend, the young student Nathanael, and which I have undertaken to recount to you, dear reader. Have you, my kind patron, ever had an experience that entirely absorbed your heart, your mind, and your thoughts, banishing all other concerns? You were seething and boiling inwardly; your fiery blood raced through your veins and gave a richer colour to your cheeks. You had a strange, fixed stare as though you were trying to make out forms, invisible to any other eyes, in empty space, and your words faded into obscure sighs. 'What's wrong, my dear fellow? Whatever's the matter, old chap?' inquired your friends. And you, anxious to convey your inner vision with all its glowing colours, its lights and shadows, laboured in vain to find words with which to begin. But you felt as though you must compress the entire wonderful, splendid, terrible, hilarious, and hideous experience into your very first word, so that it should strike your hearers like an electric shock; yet every word, all the resources of language, seemed faded, frosty, and dead. You searched and searched, and stammered and stuttered, and your friends' matter-of-fact questions were like gusts of icy air blowing on your inner glow and wellnigh extinguishing it. But if, like a bold painter, you had first sketched the outlines of your inner vision with a few careless strokes, you had little trouble in adding ever brighter colours until the swirling throng of multifarious figures seized hold of your friends' imagination, and they saw themselves, like you, in the midst of the picture that arose from your mind!

I must confess, kind reader, that nobody has actually asked me to tell the story of young Nathanael; you are aware, however, that I belong to the curious race of authors, who, if they are filled with such a vision as I have just described, feel as though everyone who approaches them, and all the world besides, were asking: 'Whatever's the matter? Tell me everything, my dear fellow!' Thus I felt powerfully impelled to tell you about Nathanael's calamitous life. Its strange and wondrous character absorbed my entire soul; but for that very reason, and because, dear reader, I have to put you in the right mood to endure an odd tale, which is no easy matter, I racked my brains to find a portentous, original, and arresting way of beginning Nathanael's story. 'Once upon a time . . .'—the best way to begin any story, but too down-to-earth! 'In the small provincial town of S. there lived . . .'—somewhat better: at least it provides some build-up to the climax. Or why not plunge *medias in res*: '"Go to the Devil!"' cried the student Nathanael, wild-eyed with fury and terror, as the barometer-seller Giuseppe Coppola . . .'. I had in fact written this down, when I fancied there was something comical in the student Nathanael looking wild-eyed; this story, however, is no laughing matter. Unable to find words that seemed to reflect anything of the prismatic radiance of my inner vision, I decided not to begin at all. Be so good, dear reader, as to accept the three letters, kindly communicated to me by my friend Lothar, as the sketch for my portrayal; as I tell the story, I shall endeavour to add more and more colour to it. I may, like a good portraitist, succeed in depicting some figures so well that you find them good likenesses even without knowing the originals; indeed, you may feel as though you had often seen these persons with your very own eyes. Then, O my reader, you may come to believe that nothing can be stranger or weirder than real life, and that the poet can do no more than capture the strangeness of reality, like the dim reflection in a dull mirror.

In order to put you more fully in the picture, I must add that soon after the death of Nathanael's father, his mother had taken Clara and Lothar, the children of a distant relative who had likewise died and left them orphans, into the household. Clara and Nathanael became warmly attached to each other, and nobody could possibly have any objection to this; hence they were engaged by the time Nathanael left the town in order to continue his studies in G***. His last letter was written from G***, where he was attending lectures by the famous professor of physical sciences, Spalanzani.

I might now go on cheerfully with my story; but at this instant the image of Clara is so vividly present to me that I cannot look away, as always happened when she used to look at me with her lovely smile. Clara could by no means be called beautiful; that was the judgement of all professional authorities on beauty. Yet the architects praised her perfectly proportioned figure, while the painters raved about the chaste lines of her neck, her shoulders, and her breasts, fell in love with her wonderful hair, which reminded them of Battoni's Mary Magdalen,* and talked a lot of nonsense about Battoni's colouring techniques. One of them, however, a true fantasist, drew a very odd comparison between Clara's eyes and a lake by Ruysdael* which reflected the pure azure of the cloudless sky, the forests and flowery meadows, and the varied, happy life of the fertile landscape. Poets and musicians went further and said: 'Lake? Reflection? How can we look at the girl without perceiving wondrous, heavenly sounds and songs radiating from her gaze and penetrating and vivifying our very hearts? If we ourselves can't produce a decent song after that, we must be good for very little, and that indeed is the message of the sly smile that hovers around Clara's lips whenever we venture on some jingle that claims to be a song, though it consists only of a few incoherent notes.'

Such was the case. Clara had the vivid imagination of a cheerful, ingenuous, child-like child, a deep heart filled with womanly tenderness, and a very acute, discriminating mind. She was no friend to muddle-headed enthusiasts; for although she uttered few words, being taciturn by nature, her clear gaze and her sly, ironic smile said: 'Dear friends, how can you expect me to treat your shifting, shadowy images as real objects full of life and motion?' Many people accordingly criticized Clara for being cold, unresponsive, and prosaic; others, however, who saw life clearly and profoundly, were very fond of the warm-hearted, sensible, child-like girl, but none so much as Nathanael, who was energetic and cheerful in his approach to art and learning. Clara was intensely devoted to him, and their parting cast the first shadow on her life. With what rapture did she fly to his arms when he entered his mother's room, having returned home as he had promised in his last letter to Lothar. Nathanael's expectations were fulfilled; for on seeing Clara he thought neither about the advocate Coppelius nor about Clara's sensible letter, and all his irritation vanished.

Nathanael, however, was quite right when he told his friend Lothar that the figure of the repulsive barometer-seller Coppola had made a malevolent intrusion into his life. Even in the first few days of his visit, it was apparent to everyone that Nathanael's character had changed entirely. He fell into gloomy reveries and took to behaving in a strange and wholly unaccustomed way. To him, all life consisted of dreams and premonitions; he kept saying that each individual, fancying himself to be free, only served as a plaything for the cruelty of dark forces; that it was in vain to resist, and one must acquiesce humbly in the decrees of destiny. He went so far as to assert that artists and scholars were under a delusion when they believed that their creative endeavours were governed by the autonomy of their will: 'for', said he, 'the inspired state which is indispensable for creation does not arise from inside ourselves; it is due to the influence of a higher principle that lies outside us'.

The sensible Clara greatly disliked these mystical flights of fancy, but there seemed no point in trying to refute them. It was only when Nathanael maintained that Coppelius was the evil principle that had seized upon him when he was eavesdropping behind the curtain, and that this foul demon would wreak destruction upon their happy love, that Clara would become very serious and say: 'Yes, Nathanael, you're right! Coppelius is an evil, malevolent principle; he can do terrible harm, like the visible manifestation of a devilish power; but only if you fail to dismiss him from your mind. As long as you believe in him, he is real and active; his power consists only in your belief.'

Indignant that Clara conceded the existence of the demon only in his own mind, Nathanael would try to launch into the mystical doctrine of devils and evil forces, but Clara would irritably cut the conversation short by raising some trivial subject, to Nathanael's great annoyance. He concluded that such mysteries were inaccessible to cold and insensitive temperaments, without clearly realizing that he considered Clara's temperament to be such, and accordingly persevered in his attempts to initiate her into these mysteries. Early in the morning, when Clara was helping to make the breakfast, he would stand beside her, reading aloud from all manner of mystical books, until Clara asked: 'But, Nathanael dear, what if I were to scold *you* for being the evil principle exerting a malevolent influence on my coffee? For if I drop everything, as you demand, and gaze into your eyes while you read, the coffee will run over into the fire and none of you will get any breakfast!'

Nathanael would then clap the book shut and run angrily to his room.

In the past Nathanael had shown a special gift for composing charming and vivid stories which he would write down, and which Clara would listen to with heartfelt enjoyment. Now his compositions were gloomy, unintelligible, and formless, so that, even though Clara was too kind to say so, he was aware how little they appealed to her. Nothing had a more deadly effect on Clara than tedium; her unconquerable mental drowsiness would reveal itself in her expression and her speech. Nathanael's compositions were indeed very tedious. His annoyance with Clara's cold, prosaic temperament increased, while Clara could not overcome her irritation with Nathanael's dismal, obscure, tedious mysticism, and so, without noticing it, they became increasingly estranged from one another. Nathanael himself was obliged to confess that the figure of the hateful Coppelius had begun to fade from his imagination, and he often had difficulty in imparting lively colours to Coppelius in his compositions, where the latter appeared as a dreadful bogy man and emissary of fate. Finally he conceived the plan of writing a poem about his gloomy premonition that Coppelius would destroy his happy love. He portrayed himself and Clara as joined in true love, but every so often a black hand seemed to reach into their lives and tear out some newly discovered source of pleasure. Finally, when they are standing at the altar, the fearsome Coppelius appears and touches Clara's lovely eyes, which leap into Nathanael's breast, burning and singeing him; Coppelius seizes him and hurls him into a circle of flames which is rotating with the speed of a whirlwind, dragging him along in its fury. A tumult springs up, as when the savage hurricane lashes the ocean, whose foaming waves rear up like black giants with white heads, filled with the rage of combat. But through all the tumult he hears Clara's voice saying: 'Can't you see me? Coppelius deceived you; it wasn't my eyes that burned in your breast, but red-hot drops of your own heart's blood. I have my eyes, just look at me!' 'That is Clara', thinks Nathanael, 'and I am her own eternally.' At that moment his thought seems to reach down forcibly into the circle of flames, bringing it to a halt, and the tumult fades away in a black abyss. Nathanael gazes into Clara's eyes; but what looks at him from Clara's kindly eyes is death.

While composing this, Nathanael was calm and collected; he revised and polished every line, and, having submitted to the constraints of metre, he did not rest until the entire work was pure and melodious. Yet, when he had finished and read the poem aloud to himself, he was gripped by wild horror and terror, and shrieked: 'Whose hideous voice is this?' Before long, however, he again decided that it was a highly successful poem, which could not fail to animate Clara's cold temperament, though he had no clear idea what purpose this would serve or what might result from alarming her with hideous images prophesying the destruction of their love by a terrible fate.

They were sitting, Nathanael and Clara, in her mother's little garden. Clara was in good spirits, because during the past three days, while working on his poem, Nathanael had no longer tormented her with his dreams and premonitions. Besides, Nathanael talked in a lively, cheerful manner about pleasant matters, as in the past, so that Clara said: 'Now you're completely

, mine again. Do you see how we've driven that hateful Coppelius away?'

Only then did Nathanael remember that he had the poem in his pocket and had been meaning to read it aloud. He promptly drew it out and began reading, while Clara, resigned to the prospect of something tedious as usual, quietly began knitting. But as the cloud of gloom swelled up in ever-deepening blackness, she let her knitting fall from her hands and gazed fixedly at Nathanael. The latter was entirely carried away by his poem: his cheeks burned with the fire within him, tears gushed from his eyes. Finished at last, he gave a sigh of exhaustion. He seized Clara's hand and moaned miserably: 'Oh! Clara! Clara!'

Clara gave him a gentle hug and said in a low voice, but slowly and seriously: 'Nathanael, my darling Nathanael! Throw the crazy, senseless, insane story into the fire.'

Nathanael sprang up indignantly and exclaimed, thrusting Clara away: 'You accursed lifeless automaton!' He rushed away, while Clara, deeply hurt, shed bitter tears.

'Oh, he never loved me, because he doesn't understand me', she wailed.

Lothar entered the bower, and Clara could not help telling him what had occurred. Since he loved his sister with all his heart, every accusing word she uttered threw sparks into his mind, so that the irritation he had long felt with the dreamy Nathanael was inflamed into furious anger. He ran to Nathanael and rebuked him harshly for his senseless behaviour towards Lothar's dearly loved sister. Nathanael flew into a passion and replied in kind. They called each other a mad, fantastical coxcomb and a wretched, vulgar philistine. A duel was inevitable. They decided to meet next morning behind the garden and fight with sharpened rapiers, as was customary among the local students. In the mean time, they crept about, silent and scowling. Clara overheard their violent quarrel and saw the fencing-master bringing the rapiers at daybreak. She guessed what was afoot. Lothar and Nathanael arrived at the scene of their duel in gloomy silence; they removed their coats and were about to assail each other, their eyes burning with the blood-thirsty fury of combat, when Clara rushed through the garden gate.

'You dreadful savages!' she cried amid her sobs, 'strike me

down first before you attack each other; for how can I go on living if my lover has murdered my brother, or my brother has killed my lover!'

Lothar lowered his weapon and looked silently at the ground, but Nathanael, with a shock of heart-rending sorrow, recollected all the love he had felt for his adorable Clara in the most glorious days of his youth. The fatal implement fell from his hand and he threw himself at Clara's feet.

'Can you ever forgive me, my only, my beloved Clara! Can you forgive me, my beloved brother Lothar!'

Lothar was touched by his friend's agony; amid floods of tears, the three embraced in token of reconciliation and swore unfailing love and loyalty to one another.

Nathanael felt as though relieved of a heavy burden which had been crushing him, and as though, by resisting the dark forces which had ensnared him, he had saved his entire existence from the threat of annihilation. He spent three more blissful days among his dear ones, then returned to G***, where he intended to stay for another year before returning to his home town for good.

Everything relating to Coppelius was kept from his mother; for it was known that she could not think without horror of the man whom she, like Nathanael, held responsible for her husband's death.

On returning to his lodgings, Nathanael was astonished to discover that the whole house had been burnt to the ground. Nothing remained amid the ruins but the fire-walls separating it from the adjacent houses. Although the fire had broken out in the laboratory of the apothecary who lived on the ground floor, and the house had burnt from the bottom up, Nathanael's bold and energetic friends had managed to get into his upstairs room in time to save his books, manuscripts, and instruments. They had removed all these things, which were undamaged, to another house, and taken possession of a room there, which Nathanael immediately moved into. He paid no particular heed to the fact that he was now living opposite Professor Spalanzani; nor did he think it specially noteworthy that his window looked straight into the room where Olimpia often sat by herself, so that he could clearly make out her shape, although her features remained blurred and indistinct. He was eventually struck by the fact that Olimpia often spent hours sitting at a little table, just as he had previously glimpsed her through the glass door, without doing anything, but gazing rigidly across at him; he was also obliged to confess that he had never seen a more shapely woman, but, with Clara in his heart, he remained indifferent to the stiff and motionless Olimpia. Only occasionally did he glance up from his textbook at the beautiful statue: that was all.

Just as Nathanael was writing to Clara, there came a soft tap at the door. On his calling 'Come in!' it opened, and in peeped Coppola's repulsive face. Nathanael felt himself quaking inwardly; however, mindful of what Spalanzani had said about his fellow-countryman Coppola, and of his own sacred promise to Clara concerning the Sandman Coppelius, he felt ashamed of his childish superstition, pulled himself together with a great effort, and spoke as calmly and gently as he could: 'I don't wish to buy any barometers, my friend! Be off with you!'

Now, however, Coppola came right into the room; contorting his wide mouth into a hideous grin and giving a piercing look from under his long grey lashes, he said hoarsely: 'No barometer, no barometer! I 'ave beautiful eyes-a to sell you, beautiful eyes-a!'

'You madman,' cried Nathanael in horror, 'how can you have eyes to sell? Eyes?'

But Coppola had already put his barometers aside; he reached into the wide pockets of his coat and fetched out lorgnettes and pairs of spectacles, which he placed on the table.

'Now, now, glass-a, glass-a to wear on your nose-a, dese are my eyes-a, beautiful eyes-a!' And with these words he pulled out more and more spectacles, so that the whole table began strangely gleaming and shining. Innumerable eyes flickered and winked and goggled at Nathanael; but he could not look away from the table, and Coppola put more and more spectacles on it, and their flaming eyes sprang to and fro ever more wildly, darting their blood-red rays into Nathanael's breast. Overcome by mad terror, he shrieked: 'Stop! stop, you frightful man!'— and seized Coppola by the arm as the latter was reaching into his pocket for yet more spectacles, even though the entire table was now covered with them. Coppola freed himself gently, uttering a horrible hoarse laugh, and with the words: 'No good for you—but here, beautiful glass-a!' he swept up all the spectacles, packed them away, and produced from the side-pocket of his coat a number of large and small spyglasses. As soon as the spectacles had been removed, Nathanael became perfectly calm; thinking of Clara, he realized that the hideous apparition could only have proceeded from within himself, and that Coppola must be a thoroughly honest mechanic and optician, who could not possibly be the accursed double or ghost of Coppelius. Besides, the spyglasses that Coppola had now placed on the table had nothing remarkable about them, let alone the sinister qualities of the spectacles, and, in order to make amends for his behaviour, Nathanael decided to buy something from Coppola after all. He picked up a small, beautifully made pocket spyglass and tested it by looking out of the window. Never before in his life had he come across a spyglass that brought objects before one's eyes with such clarity, sharpness, and distinctness. He involuntarily looked into Spalanzani's room; Olimpia was sitting as usual at the little table, with her arms on it and her hands folded.

Only now did Nathanael behold Olimpia's wondrously beautiful face. It was only her eyes that seemed to him strangely fixed and dead. As he peered ever more intently through the glass, however, he thought he saw moist moonbeams shining from Olimpia's eyes. It was as though her power of vision were only now being awakened; her eyes seemed to sparkle more and more vividly. Nathanael remained at the window, as though rooted to the spot by a spell, gazing uninterruptedly at Olimpia's heavenly beauty. He was aroused, like somebody lost in a dream, by the sound of foot-scraping and throat-clearing. Coppola was standing behind him.

'Tre zecchini—three ducat!'

Nathanael, who had completely forgotten the optician, hastily paid the sum demanded.

'Beautiful glass-a, no? Beautiful glass-a?' asked Coppola in his repulsive hoarse voice, smiling maliciously.

'Yes, yes, yes!' replied Nathanael crossly. 'Good-bye, my friend!'

Coppola left the room, not without casting many strange side-glances at Nathanael, who heard him laughing loudly as he went downstairs.

'All right,' said Nathanael, 'he's laughing at me because I no doubt paid too high a price for the little spy-glass—too high a price!'

As he uttered these words in a low voice, a deep, deathly sigh seemed to send a grisly echo through the room. Nathanael caught his breath with fear. But no, it was he who had uttered the sigh, that was quite obvious.

'Clara', he said to himself, 'is probably right to think me tiresome and superstitious; but it's still a funny thing—oh, more than that, I suspect—that the silly idea that I paid too high a price for Coppola's spyglass makes me feel so oddly apprehensive; I can't think why this is.'

He then sat down in order to finish his letter to Clara, but one glance through the window convinced him that Olimpia was still sitting there, and at that instant, as though impelled by an irresistible force, he jumped up, seized Coppola's spyglass, and could not tear himself away from the alluring sight of Olimpia, until his friend and fellow-student Siegmund summoned him to Professor Spalanzani's lecture.

The curtain in front of the fateful room was drawn tight; Nathanael could neither glimpse Olimpia there nor, during the next two days, in her room, although he scarcely left his window and peered continually through Coppola's spyglass. On the third day the window was covered by drapery. In extreme despair, impelled by yearning and ardent desire, he ran out through the town gate. Olimpia's shape hovered in the air in front of him, stepped forth from the bushes, and looked at him with great radiant eyes from the clear water of the brook. The image of Clara had entirely departed from his mind; he thought only of Olimpia, and lamented out loud in a tearful voice: 'Oh, light of my life, you glorious, lofty star, did you rise upon me only to vanish again, leaving me in dark and hopeless night?'

Returning to his lodgings, he noticed a noisy upheaval going on in Spalanzani's house. The doors were open, all manner of utensils were being carried in, the first-floor windows had been taken off their hinges, busy maids were sweeping and dusting everywhere with large brooms, and inside joiners and decorators were tapping and hammering. Nathanael stood there in the street, beside himself with astonishment; Siegmund came up to him and said: 'Well, what do you think of our old Spalanzani?' Nathanael declared that he did not know what to think, since he knew nothing whatever about the Professor, but was extremely surprised to see such frantic activity going on in the quiet, gloomy house. Siegmund then informed him that Spalanzani was holding a ball and a concert the next day, and that half the university had been invited. It was rumoured abroad that Spalanzani would allow his daughter Olimpia, whom he had fearfully concealed from every human eye for so long, to make her first public appearance.

Nathanael obtained an invitation and went to the Professor's house at the appointed hour, his heart beating violently, as the carriages were rolling up and the lights were gleaming in the splendidly decorated rooms. A large and brilliant company was present. Olimpia made her appearance, sumptuously and tastefully dressed. Her beautifully moulded features and her shapely figure compelled general admiration. The slightly strange curve of her back and the wasp-like slenderness of her waist seemed to be the result of excessive tightlacing. There was something stiff and measured about her gait and posture, which many people found displeasing; it was ascribed to the constraint imposed by such a large company.

The concert began. Olimpia played the piano with great skill and likewise performed a bravura aria in a clear, almost shrill voice, like a glass bell. Nathanael was enraptured; standing in the back row, he was unable to make out Olimpia's features clearly in the dazzling light of the candles. Without anybody noticing, he therefore took out Coppola's spyglass and looked through it at the fair Olimpia. Ah! then he perceived that she was gazing at him yearningly, and that every note she uttered found its full expression in the amorous look that pierced his heart and set it afire. The artificial roulades seemed to Nathanael to be the heavenly jubilation of a heart transfigured by love, and when the cadenza was at last followed by a long trill which rang and resounded through the room, he felt as though red-hot arms had suddenly seized him; unable to restrain himself, he shrieked out in agony and rapture: 'Olimpia!'

Everyone looked round at him, and many people laughed. The cathedral organist, however, scowled yet more darkly than before and said only: 'Now, now!'

The concert was over; the ball began. 'To dance with her, with *her*!'—that was now the goal of all Nathanael's wishes and desires; but how was he to find the courage to ask her, the queen of the ball, for a dance? And yet, he himself could not tell how it came about that when the dance had already begun he found himself standing close to Olimpia, who had not yet been asked for a dance, and, scarcely able to stammer out a few words, he seized her hand. Olimpia's hand was ice-cold: a shudder went through him like a hideous, deadly frost. He stared into Olimpia's eyes, which beamed at him full of love and yearning, and at that moment a pulse seemed to begin beating in her cold hand and her life's blood to flow in a glowing stream. Love and desire flared up in Nathanael's heart; he embraced the fair Olimpia and flew with her through the ranks of the dancers.

Nathanael considered himself a good dancer, but the peculiar rhythmic regularity with which Olimpia danced often disconcerted him and made him realize how badly he kept time. However, he was reluctant to dance with any other woman, and would gladly have murdered everyone who approached Olimpia to ask her to dance. Yet this only happened on two occasions; to his astonishment, Olimpia then remained without a partner, and he did not fail to draw her on to the dance-floor again and again. If Nathanael had been capable of seeing anything other than the fair Olimpia, all manner of quarrels and disputes would have been inevitable; for the young people in various corners of the room were having difficulty in suppressing their laughter, and their tittering was evidently directed at the fair Olimpia, whom they were looking at strangely for some unaccountable reason. Excited by the dance and by generous quantities of wine, Nathanael entirely cast off his usual bashfulness. He sat beside Olimpia, clasping her hand, and spoke of his love in fiery, enthusiastic words which neither he nor Olimpia understood. But perhaps *she* did; for she gazed fixedly into his eyes and sighed repeatedly: 'Oh! oh! oh!' whereupon Nathanael said: 'O you splendid, divine woman! You ray shining from the promised afterlife of love! You profound spirit, reflecting my whole existence!' and much more along the same lines; but Olimpia only sighed repeatedly: 'Oh! oh!'

Professor Spalanzani passed the happy couple once or twice and smiled upon them with an air of strange satisfaction. Although Nathanael was in the seventh heaven, he suddenly felt as though down on earth, in Professor Spalanzani's house, darkness were falling; he looked round and noticed, to his consternation, that the last two lights in the empty ballroom had burnt down to their sockets and were about to go out. The music and dancing had long since ceased. 'Parting! Parting!' he cried in frantic despair; he kissed Olimpia's hand, he bent down to her mouth, his burning lips met ice-cold ones! Just as he had done on touching Olimpia's cold hand, he felt himself gripped by inward horror, and the legend of the dead bride* suddenly flashed through his mind; but Olimpia was clasping him tightly, and his kiss seemed to bring warmth and life to her lips.

Professor Spalanzani walked slowly through the empty ballroom; his steps sounded hollow, and his figure, surrounded by flickering shadows, had an uncanny, ghostly appearance.

'Do you love me—do you love me, Olimpia? Just this word! Do you love me?' whispered Nathanael, but Olimpia, rising to her feet, only sighed: 'Oh! oh!'

'Yes, you lovely, magnificent light of my life,' said Nathanael, 'you will shine on me, transfiguring my heart for evermore!'

'Oh, oh!' responded Olimpia, moving away. Nathanael followed her. They stood before the Professor.

'You have had a remarkably animated conversation with my daughter', said he with a smile. 'Well, my dear Nathanael, if you find pleasure in talking to the silly girl, I shall always welcome your visits.'

Nathanael was walking on air as he took his leave.

Spalanzani's ball was the main topic of conversation in the next few days. Although the Professor had endeavoured to display the utmost magnificence, the wags recounted all manner of oddities and improprieties, and criticism was levelled particularly at the rigid and silent Olimpia. Despite the beauty of her appearance, it was alleged that she was a complete imbecile, and that this was the reason why Spalanzani had kept her concealed for so long. Nathanael heard this with suppressed anger, but he held his peace; 'for', thought he, 'what would be the point of proving to these fellows that it is their own imbecility which prevents them from appreciating the wonderful depths of Olimpia's heart?'

'Do me a favour, old chap,' said Siegmund one day, 'and tell me how a sensible fellow like you could be besotted with that dummy, that wax doll?'

Nathanael was about to fly into a fury, but he controlled himself and replied: 'You tell me, Siegmund, how, with your sharp perceptions and your appreciation of beauty, you could fail to notice Olimpia's heavenly charms? But I thank the fates that, for that reason, I don't have you as a rival; otherwise one of us would have to perish.'

Observing his friend's state of mind, Siegmund backed down and remarked that in love there was no disputing about tastes. 'It's odd, though', he added, 'that many of us share the same opinion of Olimpia. We thought her—don't take this amiss, old chap!—strangely stiff and lacking in animation. Her figure is regular, certainly, and so is her face. She would be beautiful, but that her eyes seem to have no ray of life; they almost seem to lack the power of sight. Her gait is curiously measured, as though her every movement were produced by some mechanism like clockwork. She plays and sings with the disagreeably perfect, soulless timing of a machine, and she dances similarly. Olimpia gave us a very weird feeling; we wanted nothing to do with her; we felt that she was only pretending to be a living being, and that there was something very strange about her.'

Nathanael refrained from giving way to the bitterness that Siegmund's words aroused in him. He mastered his annoyance and only said, in grave tones: 'Olimpia may well inspire a weird feeling in cold, prosaic people like you. It is only to the poetic soul that a similarly organized soul reveals itself! I was the only one to arouse her loving gaze, which radiated through my heart and mind; only in Olimpia's love do I recognize myself. People like you may complain because she doesn't engage in trivial chit-chat, like other banal minds. She utters few words, certainly; but these few words are true hieroglyphs, disclosing an inner world filled with love and lofty awareness of the spiritual life led in contemplation of the everlasting Beyond. But you can't appreciate any of this, and I'm wasting my words.'

'God preserve you, my friend,' said Siegmund in very gentle, almost melancholy tones, 'but I feel you're in a bad way. Count on me if anything—no, I'd rather not say any more!' Nathanael suddenly felt that the cold, prosaic Siegmund was truly devoted to him, and when the latter extended his hand, Nathanael shook it very heartily.

Nathanael had entirely forgotten Clara's existence and his former love for her; his mother, Lothar, and everyone else had vanished from his memory; he lived only for Olimpia and spent several hours with her every day, holding forth about his love, the heartfelt rapport between them, and the elective affinities linking their souls, to all of which Olimpia listened with devout attention. From the darkest recesses of his desk Nathanael fetched everything he had ever written. Poems, fantasies, visions, novels, stories, were supplemented daily by all manner of incoherent sonnets, *ballades*, and *canzoni*, which he read to Olimpia for hours on end without ever wearying. But then, he had never had such a perfect listener. She did not sew or knit, she never looked out of the window, she did not feed a cage-bird, she did not play with a lap-dog or a favourite cat, she did not fiddle with scraps of paper or anything else, she never needed to conceal her yawns by a slight artificial cough: in a word, she stared fixedly at her lover for hours on end, without moving a muscle, and her gaze grew ever more ardent and more animated. Only when Nathanael finally rose and kissed her hand, and also her lips, did she say: 'Oh! Oh!' and then: 'Good night, my dear friend!'

'Oh, you wonderful, profound soul,' cried Nathanael, back in his room, 'no one but you, you alone, understands me perfectly.'

He trembled with heartfelt rapture when he considered how the marvellous harmony between his soul and Olimpia's was becoming more manifest by the day; for he felt as though Olimpia had voiced his own thoughts about his works and about his poetic gift in general; indeed, her voice seemed to come from within himself. This must indeed have been the case, for the only words Olimpia ever spoke were those that have just been mentioned. Although Nathanael did have moments of lucidity and common sense, for example just after waking up in the morning, when he recalled how entirely passive and taciturn Olimpia was, he nevertheless said: 'Words? What are words! The look in her heavenly eyes says more than any terrestrial language. Can a child of heaven ever adjust itself to the narrow confines drawn by miserable earthly needs?'

Professor Spalanzani seemed highly delighted at his daughter's relationship with Nathanael; he gave the latter many unmistakable signs of his goodwill, and when Nathanael finally ventured to hint that he might ask for Olimpia's hand in marriage, the Professor smiled broadly and declared that his daughter should have a free choice. Encouraged by these words, his heart burning with desire, Nathanael resolved that on the very next day he would implore Olimpia to tell him in so many words what her lovely eyes had told him long since: that she was willing to be his for evermore. He looked for the ring which his mother had given him on his departure, so that he might present it to Olimpia as a symbol of his devotion and of the newly budding and blossoming life that he owed to her. As he searched, Clara's and Lothar's letters fell into his hands; he tossed them indifferently aside, found the ring, put it in his pocket, and dashed off to find Olimpia.

As soon as he climbed the stairs and approached the landing, he heard an extraordinary hubbub which seemed to be coming from Spalanzani's study. There were sounds of feet stamping, glass tinkling, and blows falling on the door, mingled with curses and imprecations.

'Let go! Let go! Scoundrel! Villain! You staked your whole life? Ha, ha, ha!—that wasn't part of our wager—I made the eyes, I did—I made the clockwork—stupid wretch, you and your clockwork—you confounded brute of a half-witted clock-maker—get out—Satan—stop—you tinker—you devilish creature—stop—get out—let go!'

The voices howling and raving in such confusion were those of Spalanzani and the horrible Coppelius. In rushed Nathanael, gripped by nameless fear. The Professor had seized a female figure by the shoulders, while the Italian Coppola was holding it by the feet, and both were tugging at it for dear life, while quarrelling violently over it. Nathanael started back, filled with deep horror, on recognizing the figure as Olimpia; wild fury flared up in him, and he tried to tear his beloved from the hands of the enraged combatants, but at that moment Coppola turned round with gigantic strength, wrested the figure from the Professor's hands, and struck him such a terrible blow with it that he staggered and fell backwards over the table covered with phials, retorts, bottles, and glass cylinders, all of which were broken to smithereens. Coppola then threw the figure over his shoulder and rushed downstairs with a frightful yell of laughter, so that the figure's feet, which were hanging down in an unsightly way, gave a wooden rattling and rumbling as they knocked against the steps.

Nathanael stood stock still. He had perceived only too clearly that Olimpia's deathly pale wax face had no eyes, just black caverns where eyes should be; she was a lifeless doll. Spalanzani was writhing on the floor; his head, chest, and arms had been cut by broken glass, and blood was gushing out as though from a fountain. But he summoned all his strength and cried:

'After him, after him! Why are you standing there? Coppelius—he's stolen my best automaton—twenty years' work—I staked my life on it—the clockwork—language—walk—all mine—the eyes—he stole your eyes. The cursed scoundrel, the damned villain—after him—fetch Olimpia—here are her eyes!'

Thereupon Nathanael noticed a pair of bloody eyes lying on the floor and staring at him. Spalanzani picked them up with his unscathed hand and threw them at Nathanael, so that they struck him on the chest. Madness seized him with its red-hot claws and entered his heart, tearing his mind to pieces. 'Hey, hey, hey! Fiery circle, fiery circle! Spin, spin, fiery circle! Come on! Spin, wooden dolly, hey, spin, pretty wooden dolly . . .' and with these words he flung himself on the Professor and clutched him by the throat. He would have throttled him, but the hubbub had attracted a large number of people who forced their way into the room and pulled the frenzied Nathanael to his feet, thus rescuing the Professor, whose wounds were promptly bandaged. Siegmund, despite his strength, was unable to restrain the lunatic, who kept bellowing in a frightful voice: 'Spin, wooden dolly', and brandishing his fists. At last the united efforts of several people managed to overcome Nathanael by throwing him to the ground and tying him up. His words were swallowed up in a horrible animal-like bellowing. Raving in a hideous frenzy, he was taken to the madhouse.

Before continuing, kind reader, with the story of the unfortunate Nathanael, let me assure you, just in case you should feel any sympathy for the skilful mechanic and automaton-maker Spalanzani, that he made a complete recovery from his wounds. He was, however, obliged to leave the University, since Nathanael's story had created a stir, and public opinion considered it monstrously deceitful to foist a wooden doll instead of a living person upon respectable tea-parties (Olimpia had attended some and made quite a hit). Legal scholars described it as a subtle fraud which deserved a condign punishment inasmuch as it had been practised upon the public, and so adroitly conducted that nobody (except for the sharpest students) had observed it, although everyone was now trying to display sagacity by referring to all kinds of suspicious-looking details. These details, however, threw virtually no light on the matter. For could anyone's suspicions have been aroused by the fact that, according to one elegant *habitué* of tea-parties, Olimpia had defied convention by sneezing more than she yawned? Her sneezing, explained this exquisite gentleman, was the sound of the concealed mechanism winding itself up, for there had been an audible creaking. The professor of poetry and eloquence took a pitch of snuff, snapped his box shut, cleared his throat, and said in solemn tones: 'My most esteemed ladies and gentlemen! Don't you see what lies behind all this? The entire matter is an allegory—an extended metaphor! You take my meaning! *Sapienti sat!*'* But many esteemed gentlemen were not so easily reassured: the story of the automaton had made a deep impression on their minds, and a detestable distrust of human figures became prevalent. In order to make quite sure that they were not in love with wooden dolls, several lovers demanded that their beloved should fail to keep time in singing and dancing, and that, when being read aloud to, she should sew, knit, or play with her pug-dog; above all, the beloved was required not merely to listen, but also, from time to time, to speak in a manner that revealed genuine thought and feeling. The bonds between some lovers thus became firmer and pleasanter; others quietly dissolved. 'One really can't take the risk', said some. At tea-parties there was an incredible amount of yawning, but no sneezing, in order to avert any suspicion.

As mentioned earlier, Spalanzani was obliged to disappear in order to evade a criminal prosecution for fraudulently introducing an automaton into human society. Coppola had likewise vanished.

Nathanael awoke, as though from a terrible nightmare; he opened his eyes and felt an indescribable sense of bliss permeating his being with mild, heavenly warmth. He was lying in bed in his room in his father's house. Clara was bending over him, and his mother and Lothar were standing nearby.

'At last, at last, oh my darling Nathanael, you've recovered from your dangerous illness, now you're mine again!' said Clara, from the depths of her heart, folding Nathanael in her arms. The latter was so overcome by rapture and sorrow that bright, hot tears gushed from his eyes, and he uttered a deep sigh: 'My own, my own Clara!'

Siegmund, who had faithfully stood by his friend in time of trouble, entered the room. Nathanael held out his hand to him: 'My loyal friend, you did not abandon me.'

All traces of madness had vanished. Nathanael soon regained his health and strength, tended as he was by his mother, his sweetheart, his friends. Good fortune, meanwhile, had entered their house; for a miserly old uncle, from whom nobody had expected anything, had died and left Nathanael's mother not only a substantial fortune but also a small estate in a pleasant spot not far from the town. They all planned to remove thither: Nathanael's mother, Nathanael himself, with his bride-to-be Clara, and Lothar. Nathanael was now more gentle and childlike than ever before, and appreciated the heavenly purity of Clara's glorious soul for the first time. Nobody reminded him of the past, even by the slightest allusion. Only when Siegmund was leaving him did Nathanael say: 'By God, my friend, I was in a bad way, but at the right moment an angel guided me on to the path of light! Ah, it was Clara!' Siegmund prevented him from saying any more, fearing that painful memories might return with excessive clarity.

The four happy people were about to move to the estate. It was midday, and they were walking through the streets of the town. They had done plenty of shopping, and the lofty tower of the town hall was casting its gigantic shadow over the market-place.

'Why!' said Clara, 'let's climb up there one last time, and gaze at the distant mountains!'

No sooner said than done! Nathanael and Clara began the ascent, their mother went home with the maidservant, and Lothar, reluctant to climb the many steps, decided to remain below. Soon afterwards the two lovers were standing arm in arm on the highest gallery of the tower, gazing into the dim forests beyond which the blue mountains rose like a giant city.

'Look at that funny little grey bush, which really seems to be walking towards us,' said Clara.

Nathanael reached mechanically into his side-pocket; he found Coppola's spyglass, he looked sideways—Clara was standing before the glass! A convulsion ran through his every vein, he stared at Clara in deathly pallor, but an instant later rivers of fire were glowing and sparkling in his rolling eyes, and he uttered a horrible bellow, like a tormented animal; then he sprang aloft and cried in a piercing voice, interspersed with hideous laughter: 'Spin, wooden dolly! Spin, wooden dolly'— and with superhuman strength he seized Clara and was about to dash her to the ground below, but Clara clung firmly to the parapet in the desperation born of terror. Lothar heard the madman raving, he heard Clara's shriek of fright, a horrible suspicion shot through his mind, he rushed up the stairs, the door leading to the second flight of stairs was locked. Clara's shrieks grew louder. Beside himself with fury and fear, he hurled himself against the door, which flew open. Clara's cries were growing fainter and fainter: 'Help! Save me! save me!' she moaned, her voice dying away. 'She's dead—the madman has murdered her,' shrieked Lothar. The door leading to the gallery was locked as well. Desperation endowed him with prodigious strength; he pushed the door off its hinges. God in heaven! Clara, in the grip of the frenzied Nathanael, was suspended in the air, over the edge of the gallery—only one hand still clung to its iron railings. With lightning speed Lothar seized his sister, pulled her to safety, and dashed his fist in the madman's face, forcing the latter to reel back and relinquish his intended victim.

Lothar rushed downstairs, his sister unconscious in his arms. She was saved.

Meanwhile Nathanael was raving in the gallery, leaping into the air and shrieking 'Fiery circle, spin! Fiery circle, spin!'

People gathered below, attracted by his wild yells; in their midst loomed the gigantic figure of the advocate Coppelius, who had just arrived in the town and made directly for the market-place. As people began to climb the stairs in order to seize the lunatic, Coppelius laughed and said: 'Ha, ha—just wait, he'll soon come down by himself', and looked up, like the others. Suddenly Nathanael paused and stood stock still; he bent down, perceived Coppelius, and, with a piercing shriek of 'Beautiful eyes-a! Beautiful eyes-a!' he jumped over the parapet.

By the time Nathanael was lying on the pavement, his head shattered, Coppelius had vanished into the throng.

It is reported that several years later, in a distant part of the country, Clara was seen sitting hand in hand with an affectionate husband outside the door of a handsome country dwelling, with two merry boys playing in front of her. This would seem to suggest that Clara succeeded in finding the quiet domestic happiness which suited her cheerful, sunny disposition, and which she could never have enjoyed with the tormented, self-divided Nathanael.

PRINCESS BRAMBILLA

A Capriccio after Jacques Callot

•••••━━━◆━━━•••••

Preface

The fairy-tale *Little Zaches, otherwise Cinnabar** (Berlin: F. Dümmler, 1819) contains nothing more than a humorous idea, worked out in a loose and careless fashion. The author, therefore, was not a little surprised to come upon a review in which this jest, casually dashed off for a moment's amusement, was analysed with a solemn and serious air, and every source cited on which the author had supposedly drawn. This last did indeed give him pleasure, inasmuch as it made him seek out those sources for himself and extend his knowledge. In order to forestall any misunderstanding, the editor of these pages now declares in advance that *Princess Brambilla* is not, any more than *Little Zaches*, a book for people who like to take everything very seriously. The kind reader, however, who may be ready and willing to put gravity aside for a few hours and abandon himself to the whimsical and audacious play of a hobgoblin, even though it may occasionally be downright impertinent, is humbly requested by the editor not to forget the basis on which the whole affair rests, Callot's* fantastic caricatures, and also to consider what a musician may demand of a capriccio.

The author may venture to recall the saying of Carlo Gozzi (in the preface to the *Ré de' geni*),* that a whole arsenal of absurdities and apparitions cannot provide a fairy-tale with a soul, and that the soul comes only from its depths, from a governing idea drawn from some philosophical view of life. This indicates only what the author intended, not what he has achieved.

Berlin
September 1820

CHAPTER 1

The magical effect of a costly dress upon a young milliner.
Definition of the actor who plays lovers. On the smorfia *of Italian*
girls. How a venerable little man studies the sciences while sitting
in a tulip, and how respectable ladies make lace between the ears of
a mule. The mountebank Celionati and the tooth of the Assyrian
Prince. Sky-blue and pink. Pantaloon and the winebottle with its
wondrous contents.

Twilight was falling, the monastery bells were ringing the Ave; the sweet and lovely girl named Giacinta Soardi put aside the sumptuous dress of heavy red satin which she had been busily trimming, and looked with vexation out of the high window down into the narrow, drab, deserted alley.

Old Beatrice meanwhile was carefully gathering up the various colourful fancy-dress costumes which were lying on tables and chairs in the little room, and hanging them up one by one. She then stood in front of the open wardrobe, arms akimbo, and said with a chuckle: 'Well, Giacinta, we've really been working hard this time; I seem to have half the merry world of the Corso before my eyes. But then, Master Bescapi has never before ordered such sumptuous costumes from us. Well, he knows that our beautiful Rome will be truly glittering this year, in all its pleasure, splendour, and magnificence. Mark my words, Giacinta, what jubilation there will be tomorrow, on the first day of our Carnival! And tomorrow, tomorrow Master Bescapi will empty a whole handful of ducats into our laps—mark my words, Giacinta! But what's the matter, child? You're hanging your head, you're in a bad mood. Sulking? And tomorrow is Carnival?'

Giacinta was sitting in the chair where she worked and was staring at the floor with her chin on her hand, paying no heed to the old woman's words. Since, however, the latter would not stop chattering about the pleasures in store at the Carnival, Giacinta began: 'Do be quiet, old woman; do stop talking about a time which may be enjoyable enough for other people, but brings me nothing but vexation and boredom. What good does it do me to work day and night? What good are Master Bescapi's ducats to us? Aren't we as poor as church mice? Don't we have to make sure that what we earn in these few days is enough for us to live on meagrely the whole year round? What is left for us to enjoy ourselves with?'

'What has our poverty to do with the Carnival?' replied the old woman. 'Didn't we run about last year from early morning until late at night, and didn't I look fine and dignified as a Doctor? And you were arm-in-arm with me, looking charming as a gardener's girl (hee, hee!) and the handsomest masks ran after you and spoke to you in words as sweet as sugar. Well, wasn't that enjoyable? And what is to prevent us from doing the same this year? I need only brush my Doctor's outfit properly to get rid of all traces of the nasty confetti that was thrown at it, and your garden-girl costume is still hanging there. A couple of new ribbons and fresh flowers—what more do you need to be pretty and smart?'

'What are you saying, old woman?' exclaimed Giacinta. 'Am I to venture out in those wretched rags? No! A beautiful Spanish dress that clings to my body and then flows down in rich, thick folds, with wide slashed sleeves from which magnificent lace billows forth, a little hat with boldly waving plumes, a belt, a necklace of radiant diamonds: that's how Giacinta would wish to enter the Corso and take her place outside the Ruspoli Palace.* How the cavaliers would throng round her—"Who's the lady? She must be a Countess, a Princess"—and even Pulcinella would be struck with awe and forget his wildest pranks!'

'I am most astonished to hear you', rejoined the old woman. 'Tell me, since when have you been possessed by such an accursed spirit of pride? Well, if you are so ambitious that you want to imitate Countesses and Princesses, be good enough to get hold of a lover who can boldly reach into Fortunatus's purse* for the sake of your beautiful eyes, and send Signor Giglio packing. If that penniless rogue ever finds a couple of ducats in his pocket, he squanders it on fragrant pomades and titbits, and he still owes me two *paoli** for washing his lace collar.'

While uttering these words Beatrice had cleaned and lit the

lamp. Now that its bright light was shining in Giacinta's face, the old woman noticed that bitter tears were falling like pearls from her eyes. 'Giacinta,' she cried, 'by all the saints, Giacinta, what's wrong, what's the matter? Why, child, I didn't mean to be so unkind. Calm down, don't work so hard; after all, the dress will surely be ready at the time it's due.'

'Alas,' said Giacinta, resuming her work and keeping her eyes fixed on it, 'I think it is this dress, this horrid dress, that has filled me with all manner of foolish thoughts. Tell me, old woman, have you ever in your life seen a dress that could be compared with this one for beauty and splendour? Master Bescapi has indeed surpassed himself; a special spirit was guiding him when he cut out this magnificent satin. And then the splendid lace, the brilliant braid, the precious stones, which he has entrusted to us for the trimmings! I should dearly love to know the name of the happy woman who will adorn herself in this heavenly dress.'

'What concern is that of ours?' interrupted the old woman. 'We do the work and take our money. But it's true, Master Bescapi behaved so mysteriously, so strangely. Well, it must at least be a princess who will wear this dress, and though I'm not usually inquisitive, I'd be glad if Master Bescapi would tell me the name, and I'll pester him tomorrow until he does.'

'Oh, no, no,' exclaimed Giacinta, 'I don't want to know it, I'd sooner imagine that no mortal will ever put on this dress and that I'm working on a mysterious adornment for a fairy. I really feel as though all manner of tiny spirits were peeping at me from the glittering jewels, smiling and whispering: "Sew, sew your hardest for our beautiful queen; we'll help you, we'll help you!" And when I interweave the lace and the braid, it's as though charming little elves and gnomes in golden armour were skipping about and—oh no!' Giacinta gave a scream; just as she was sewing the bow on the bosom of the dress, she had pricked her finger so hard that the blood gushed forth like a fountain.

'Heaven help us!' cried the old woman, 'the beautiful dress!' She took the lamp, held it close to the scene of the accident, and plentiful drops of oil overflowed.

'Heaven help us, the beautiful dress!' cried Giacinta, almost fainting with fright. But although there was no doubt that both blood and oil had fallen on the dress, neither the old woman nor Giacinta could discover even the slightest trace of a stain. Giacinta now went on sewing briskly until she sprang up with a joyful cry of 'Finished!' and held the dress aloft.

'Oh, how beautiful,' cried the old woman, 'oh, how splendid, how magnificent! No, Giacinta, your dear little hands have never before made anything like that. And do you know, Giacinta, it seems to me that the dress would fit you perfectly, as though Master Bescapi had taken its measure from none other than yourself?'

'Fiddlesticks,' replied Giacinta, blushing scarlet, 'you're dreaming, old woman; am I as tall and slender as the lady for whom the dress must be intended? Take it, just take it, keep it carefully until tomorrow! Heaven grant that there's no nasty stain to be seen by daylight! Whatever would we do, poor wretches that we are? Just take it!'

The old woman hesitated.

'I must admit,' went on Giacinta, looking at the dress, 'while I was working I did sometimes have the feeling that the dress would fit me. I'm probably slender enough in the waist, and as for the length . . .'

'Giacinina,' exclaimed the old woman, with shining eyes, 'you've guessed my thoughts, and I've guessed yours. Never mind who wears the dress, princess, queen, or fairy; it's all one, my Giacinina must be the first to adorn herself with it . . .'

'Never', said Giacinta; but the old woman took the dress from her hands, hung it carefully over the back of the chair, and began to unbraid the girl's hair, which she then did up very neatly; next she fetched from the wardrobe the little hat decked with flowers and plumes, which she had trimmed on Bescapi's instructions, and fastened it on Giacinta's chestnut curls. 'Child, how charmingly the hat suits you! But now, off with your jacket!' cried the old woman, beginning to undress Giacinta, whose sweet modesty forbade her to resist.

'Hm,' murmured the old woman, 'the gentle curve of her neck, her lily-white breasts, her alabaster arms: the Medici Venus is not more shapely, Giulio Romano* painted nothing finer—I'd like to know what princess wouldn't envy my dear child for them!' As she dressed the girl in the magnificent gown, however, it seemed as though invisible spirits were helping her. Everything fitted neatly into place, each pin at once sat properly, each fold seemed to smooth itself: it was impossible to suppose that the dress could have been made for anyone but Giacinta.

'O all you saints!' cried the old woman, when Giacinta stood before her in such magnificent finery, 'you can't be my Giacinta! Oh, oh, how beautiful you are, Your Royal Highness! But wait, wait! We must have light, bright light in our little room!' And with these words the old woman fetched all the consecrated candles that she had saved from various Feasts of the Virgin Mary, and lit them, so that Giacinta was surrounded by rays of brilliant light.

Astonished by Giacinta's lofty beauty, and still more by the charming and yet dignified manner in which she walked to and fro in the room, the old woman clapped her hands and exclaimed: 'Oh, if only someone could see you, if only the entire Corso could behold you!'

At that moment the door sprang open; Giacinta shrieked and fled to the window; a young man took two steps into the room and remained rooted to the spot, as though petrified.

While the young man remains speechless and motionless, beloved reader, you may examine him at your leisure. You will find that he can scarcely be twenty-four or twenty-five, and that his appearance is most handsome and pleasing. His clothes must be called peculiar, because the colour and cut of each separate item is beyond reproach, yet the whole ensemble, instead of matching, presents a garish and repellent medley of colours. In addition, though his clothes are clean, they reveal his poverty: you can tell from his lace ruff that he has only one other to change it for; and his hat, worn at a rakish angle, is fantastically adorned with plumes which, as you can see, are laboriously held together with needle and thread. As you perceive, kind reader, the young man dressed in this fashion can be none other than a somewhat vain actor, whose earnings do not amount to much; and so he is. In a word, he is the self-same Giglio Fava who still owes old Beatrice two *paoli* for washing a lace collar.

'Ha! what do I see?' began Giglio Fava at last, as emphatically

as though he were in the Argentina Theatre;* 'Ha! what do I
see? Is it a dream that deceives me anew? No! it is she herself,
that divine being—may I venture to address her with audacious
words of love? Princess, oh Princess!'

'Don't be an ass,' cried Giacinta, turning round abruptly, 'and
save your antics for the next few days!'

'I know very well', replied Giglio, after drawing breath with
a forced smile, 'that it's you, my lovely Giacinta, but tell me,
what does this magnificent dress mean? Never before have you
looked so attractive; I wish I could always see you like this.'

'Really?' said Giacinta angrily; 'so it's my satin dress and my
plumed hat that you love?' And with these words she quickly
slipped into the adjoining room. Soon she reappeared in her
ordinary clothes, divested of all her adornments. In the mean
time the old woman had extinguished the candles and given the
impudent Giglio a good scolding for spoiling Giacinta's enjoyment of the dress intended for some aristocratic lady, and being
ungallant enough to indicate that such gorgeous attire could
heighten Giacinta's charms and make her appear more lovable
than before. Giacinta helped vigorously to administer this lesson, until at last poor Giglio, all humility and penitence, managed to calm them down enough for them to hear his assurance
that his astonishment had resulted from a strange coincidence
of unique circumstances.

'Let me tell you,' he began, 'my lovely child, my sweet life,
what a fantastic dream I had last night, when I had flung myself
on my couch, weary and worn out by the part of Prince Taer,*
which, as you know, and the world knows likewise, I play with
outstanding excellence. I fancied that I was still on the stage,
quarrelling bitterly with that dirty miser, the impresario, who
obstinately refused to advance me a miserable couple of ducats.
He loaded me with all manner of stupid reproaches; I tried to
defend myself better by making a fine gesture, but my hand
unexpectedly struck the impresario's right cheek, producing the
melodious sound of a good slap. The impresario promptly as-
saulted me with a large knife; as I retreated, my beautiful
Prince's cap fell on the ground, the cap that you, my sweet hope,
adorned so nicely with the fairest feathers ever plucked from an
ostrich. The monster, the barbarian, seized upon it in his rage,

and stabbed the poor thing with his knife, so that it writhed and whimpered at my feet in the agony of death. I wanted—I was compelled—to avenge the unfortunate cap. Throwing my cloak over my left arm, and drawing my princely sword, I assailed the infamous murderer. He, however, fled swiftly into a house, and from its balcony he fired at me with Truffaldino's rifle. Strangely enough, the flash of the fire-arm stopped in mid-air and shone upon me like sparkling diamonds. And as the smoke gradually dispersed, I realized that what I had taken for the flash of Truffaldino's rifle was nothing but the precious adornments on a lady's hat. O all ye gods! All ye seven blessed heavens! A sweet voice said—no, sang!—no, breathed out the fragrance of love in musical sounds: "Oh Giglio, my Giglio!" And I beheld a being of such heavenly grace, such lofty charm, that the scorching sirocco of ardent love shot through all my veins and nerves, and the fiery stream turned into lava surging forth from the volcano of my flaming heart. "I am," said the goddess, drawing closer, "I am the Princess . . ."'

'What?' said Giacinta angrily, interrupting Giglio's transports; 'you dare to dream about somebody other than me? You dare to fall in love looking at a stupid mindless dream-vision that was shot from Truffaldino's rifle?'

And now there came a storm of reproaches and complaints and insults and curses, and it was altogether in vain for poor Giglio to declare that the princess of his dream had had on the same dress that he had found his Giacinta wearing. Even old Beatrice, who was not usually inclined to side with Signor Penniless, as she called Giglio, was moved by compassion, and would not leave the stubborn Giacinta alone until she forgave her lover's dream, on condition that he should never again breathe a word about it. The old woman prepared a good dish of macaroni, and as the impresario, contrary to the dream, had in fact advanced Giglio a couple of ducats, he produced from his coat pocket a bag of sweets and a bottle of tolerably drinkable wine.

'I see you do think about me after all, Giglio dear', said Giacinta, popping a sugared fruit into her little mouth.

Giglio was even permitted to kiss her finger which had been injured by the nasty pin, and joy and bliss were restored. But if the Devil is among the dancers, the most graceful leaps are in vain. For it must have been the old enemy himself who, after Giglio had drunk a couple of glasses of wine, inspired him to speak as follows.

'I'd never have believed, my sweet life, that you could be so jealous of me. But you're right. I'm very handsome to look at, and endowed by nature with all manner of agreeable talents; but, more than that, I'm an actor. The young actor who, like me, plays lovelorn princes with divine grace, with suitable "Ohs" and "Ahs", is a walking romance, an intrigue on two legs, a love-song with lips to kiss, with arms to embrace, an adventure-story that has left its binding and jumped into real life and stands before the beautiful girl's eyes when she has closed the book. That is why we exercise an irresistible charm on the hapless females, who are madly in love with everything about us, our hearts, our eyes, our paste jewels, our plumes, and our ribbons. Rank and station count for nothing; a laundress or a princess, it matters not! Now I tell you, my lovely child, that unless I am deceived by certain mysterious presentiments, unless I am being teased by an evil goblin, the heart of the most beautiful of princesses is afire with love for me. If that has happened, or if it is about to happen, you won't blame me, my fairest hope, if I don't leave unused the gold-mine that has opened up before me, and if I neglect you a bit, since after all a poor little milliner . . .'

Giacinta had been listening with increasing attention, and moving closer and closer to Giglio, whose shining eyes reflected the dream-image of the previous night; now she leapt to her feet, gave the beautiful princess's fortunate lover such a box on the ear that all the fiery sparks from Truffaldino's fateful rifle skipped in front of his eyes, and rushed into her bedroom. It was in vain to beg and beseech her. 'Just go home quietly, she's got her *smorfia*, and that's that', said the old woman, lighting the sorrowful Giglio down the stairs.

There must be something peculiar about the *smorfia*, the strangely moody and headstrong character of young Italian girls; for the experts unanimously assert that, by wondrous magic, their character makes them so irresistibly lovable that their victim, instead of trying in vexation to break his bonds, becomes more and more firmly entangled; that the *amante* who has been disdainfully sent packing, far from offering an eternal 'Addio', sighs and pleads all the more fervently, as the folk-song says: 'Vien quà, Dorina bella, non far la smorfiosella!'* He who tells you this, dear reader, suspects that pleasure derived from displeasure can only flourish in the cheerful South, and that such a fair bloom of peace could not arise in our North. In the town where he lives, at any rate, the state of mind which he has often noticed in young girls who have just emerged from childhood is not at all comparable with that delightful smorfiosity. If these girls have been endowed by heaven with pleasant features, they contort them in a deplorable fashion; everything in the world is too small or too big for them, no suitable place for their little figures is to be found here on earth; they would rather endure the torture of a tight-fitting shoe than a friendly remark, let alone a witty one, and are fearfully cross with all the youths and men of the whole town for being mortally in love with them, though they can also entertain this idea without the slightest annoyance. There is no term to express this psychological state on the part of the fair sex. The substratum of ill manners contained in it is reflected, as in a concave mirror, among boys during the period when vulgar schoolmasters refer to them as hobbledehoys. And yet, considering his strangely excited state, poor Giglio was not in the least to be blamed for dreaming of princesses and wonderful adventures even while awake. On that very day, as he was walking along the Corso, looking somewhat like Prince Taer and feeling exactly like him, many extraordinary things had indeed occurred.

It so happened that, outside the church of San Carlo,* just where the Via Condotti crosses the Corso, amidst the booths of the sausage-sellers and macaroni-makers, the Ciarlatano* famed throughout Rome under the name of Signor Celionati had set up his platform, and was telling the assembled people fantastic tales about winged cats, leaping gnomes, mandrake roots, and so forth, and at the same time selling sovereign remedies for unrequited love and for toothache, for blanks in the lottery and for gout. Just then, far in the distance, a strange music composed of cymbals, pipes, and drums could be heard. The crowd broke up and streamed and rushed along the Corso to the Porta del Popolo, with loud cries of: 'Look, look! What, is the Carnival starting already? Look, look!'

They were right; for the procession moving slowly through the Porta del Popolo and along the Corso could only be deemed the strangest masquerade that had ever been seen. Beings swathed in red satin robes, seated on twelve little snow-white unicorns with golden hooves, were blowing very pleasingly on silver pipes and beating cymbals and little drums. Their robes had holes cut out for the eyes, in the manner of the Penitent Friars, and were embroidered all round with gold braid, which looked very curious. When the wind raised the robe of one of the little horsemen, a bird's foot could be seen, its claws adorned with diamond rings. After these twelve charming musicians came two mighty ostriches, drawing a cart to which was fixed a large gleaming golden tulip; in the tulip sat a little old man with a long white beard, wearing a robe of silvery material, and with a silver funnel stuck on his venerable head in place of a cap. The old man had a monstrous pair of spectacles on his nose and was very attentively reading a large book which was open in front of him. He was followed by twelve richly clad Moors, armed with long pikes and short sabres. Each time the old man turned over a page in his book he uttered a shrill and penetrating 'Kurre-pire-ksi-li-iii!', whereupon the Moors sang in loud booming voices: 'Bram-bure-bil-bal- Ala monsa Kikiburra-son-ton!' After the Moors, on twelve palfreys whose colour seemed to be pure silver, there came riding twelve figures wrapped up almost as thickly as the musicians, except that their robes were richly embroidered with pearls and diamonds on a silver ground and their arms were bare to the shoulders. The wondrous fullness and beauty of these arms, which were decorated with the most splendid bangles, was enough to reveal that the most beautiful of ladies must be concealed under the robes; and besides, each of them, as she rode, was industriously making lace, for which purpose large velvet cushions were fastened between the palfreys' ears. There followed a large coach which seemed made entirely of gold and was drawn by eight beautiful mules, each caparisoned in gold and led by tiny pages, prettily dressed in many-coloured feathered jerkins, on reins studded with diamonds. The animals shook their magnificent ears with indescribable dignity, whereupon sounds could be heard resembling those of musical glasses; the animals and the pages leading them accompanied these sounds with an outcry, which harmonized in the most delightful way. The people crowded around and tried to look into the coach, but could see nothing save the Corso and themselves; for the windows were clear mirrors. Many a one who thus beheld himself fancied for a moment that he himself was sitting in the splendid coach, and was beside himself with joy, just as the whole assembly was on being greeted in uncommonly pleasant and obliging terms by a delightful little Pulcinella standing on the roof of the coach. Amid this general jubilation, scarcely any further attention was paid to the brilliant procession, which now consisted of more musicians, Moors, and pages, dressed like the former, and including also some monkeys tastefully dressed in delicate colours, who danced on their hind legs with eloquent gestures and displayed unparalleled dexterity in turning somersaults. Thus the extraordinary procession moved down the Corso and through the streets until it reached the Piazza Navona, where it halted outside the palace of Prince Bastianello di Pistoia.

The gates of the palace sprang open. Suddenly the jubilation of the populace died down, and the miracle that followed was beheld amid a deathly hush of profound astonishment. Up the marble steps and through the narrow gateway went all the unicorns, the horses, the mules, the coach, the ostriches, the ladies, the Moors, the pages, without the slightest difficulty. When the last twenty-four Moors had entered in a gleaming file, the gate closed with a thunderous crash and an 'Ah!' from a thousand throats filled the air.

After the populace had gaped for a while in vain, and all remained quiet within the palace, they showed a strong inclination to mount an attack on the abode of the fairy-tale beings, and the *shirri** had some difficulty in dispersing them.

Thereupon the crowd again streamed up the Corso. Outside the church of San Carlo, Signor Celionati, abandoned by his audience, was still standing on his platform, shrieking and raging frightfully: 'Stupid people! Simpletons! Why are you running about bereft of your senses and abandoning your honest Celionati? You ought to have stayed here and heard from the lips of the sage, the experienced philosopher and adept, the true meaning of all the things you have been beholding with wide-open eyes and mouths, like foolish boys! Yet I shall make everything known to you! Listen, and I shall tell you who has entered the Pistoia Palace! Listen, listen! I shall tell you who is having the dust brushed from her sleeves in the Pistoia Palace!' These words suddenly brought the swirling crowd to a standstill; the people thronged round Celionati's platform and looked up inquisitively.

'Citizens of Rome!' began Celionati with great emphasis, 'citizens of Rome! Rejoice, exult, and throw your caps, your hats, or whatever else you happen to have on your heads, high in the air! Great good fortune has come to you; for the world-renowned Princess Brambilla from distant Ethiopia has come within your walls, a miracle of beauty and so rich in inestimable treasures that she could easily have the entire Corso paved with the most splendid diamonds and gems—and who knows what she may do to give you pleasure! I know that many of you are far from being asses, but are well versed in history. They will know that the most august Princess Brambilla is a great-granddaughter of wise King Cophetua,* who built Troy, and that her great-uncle, the great King of Serendippo,* a good-natured gentleman, has often eaten more macaroni than was good for him right here outside San Carlo, in your midst, dear children! If I add that the godmother to the noble lady Brambilla was none other than the Queen of Tarot,* Tartagliona by name, and that Pulcinella taught her to play the lute, then you know enough to go out of your wits! Do so, good people! Thanks to my occult learning, my white, black, blue, and yellow magic, I know that she has come because she thinks that among the masks on the Corso she will find her bosom friend and fiancé, the Assyrian Prince Cornelio Chiapperi, who left Ethiopia in order to have a tooth extracted here in Rome, which operation I have successfully performed! Behold it here in front of your eyes!'

Celionati opened a little gold box, produced a long, pointed, very white tooth, and held it aloft. The crowd shouted with joy and delight, and greedily bought the models of the princely tooth which the Ciarlatano now offered for sale.

'You see, good people,' continued Celionati, 'after the Assyrian Prince had endured the operation steadfastly and patiently, he somehow or other mislaid himself. Look for him, good people, seek the Assyrian Prince Cornelio Chiapperi, seek him in your parlours, bedrooms, kitchens, cellars, cupboards, and drawers! Whoever finds him and returns him intact to Princess Brambilla will receive a reward of 500,000 ducats. That is the sum that Princess Brambilla has placed on his head, not counting the pleasant and far from negligible amount of intelligence and wit that it contains. Seek him, good people, seek him! But are you capable of discovering the Assyrian Prince Cornelio Chiapperi, even if he is standing in front of your noses? Indeed, are you capable of perceiving the august Princess, even if she is walking close beside you? No, you cannot do either, unless you use the spectacles polished by the wise Indian Magus Ruffiamonte himself; and I shall provide you with some, out of pure goodness of heart and love for my fellow-man, provided you don't mind paying the *paoli* . . .' And with these words the Ciarlatano opened a chest and produced a number of exceedingly large spectacles.

Though the populace had already quarrelled bitterly over the princely teeth, the spectacles gave rise to much worse strife. Quarrelling was succeeded by jostling and punching, till at last, as is usual in Italy, the knives flashed, so that the *sbirri* had to intervene once more and disperse the crowd as they had done outside the Pistoia Palace.

While all this was happening, Giglio Fava, absorbed in a profound reverie, was still standing outside the Pistoia Palace and staring at the walls which had swallowed up the strangest of all masquerades in a quite inexplicable manner. To his wonderment, he could not withstand a certain uncanny yet sweet emotion which had taken entire possession of his mind; more wondrous still, he quite arbitrarily connected the extraordinary procession with his dream about the Princess who had sprung from the flash of the rifle and thrown herself into his arms. Indeed a presentiment told him that the person sitting in the coach with mirrors for windows was none other than the image of his dream. A tap on his shoulder roused him from his reverie: the Ciarlatano was standing in front of him.

'Why,' began Celionati, 'my good Giglio, you did wrong to abandon me and not to buy a single princely tooth or a magical pair of spectacles from me . . .'

'Don't be silly,' replied Giglio, 'and don't bother me with your childish antics, with the crazy nonsense that you tell the mob in order to dispose of your worthless trash!'

'Ho, ho!' went on Celionati, 'don't be so high and mighty, young sir! What you are kind enough to call my worthless trash contains many sovereign remedies that would benefit you, especially the talisman that could make you into an excellent, a good, or at least a tolerable actor—since you're now disposed to rant in a most lamentable fashion!'

'What?' cried Giglio angrily. 'Signor Celionati, you dare to call me a lamentable actor? Me, the idol of Rome?'

'You puppet!' replied Celionati, very calmly. 'That's just your fancy; there isn't a word of truth in it. You may at times have been inspired by a special spirit which enabled you to perform many parts successfully, but what little applause or fame it brought you will today be lost irrecoverably. For look, you have forgotten all about your Prince, and even if his image remains in your mind, it has become colourless, lifeless and mute, and you are unable to recall it to life. Your mind is entirely filled by a strange dream-image which you think has driven into the Pistoia Palace over there in a glass coach. Do you see how I read your mind?'

Giglio blushed and lowered his eyes. 'Signor Celionati,' he murmured, 'you are indeed a very strange man. You must have miraculous powers which enable you to guess my most secret thoughts—but then, your foolish performances in front of the crowd—I can't see how these things fit together, but—give me one of your big pairs of spectacles!'

Celionati gave a roar of laughter. 'You people are all like that!' he exclaimed. 'When you're running about with clear heads and healthy bellies, you believe in nothing except what you can touch with your hands; but if you're afflicted by mental or physical indigestion, you seize greedily on whatever you're offered. Ho, ho! The professor who hurled his anathemas at all the sympathetic remedies in the world, including mine, sneaked over to the Tiber the following day in surly solemnity and threw his left slipper into the water, as an old beggar-woman had advised him, thinking he would thus drown the malign fever which had so tormented him; and the wisest signor of all wise signori carried gentian root in the hem of his coat, to make him better at playing ball. I know, Signor Fava, you want to behold Princess Brambilla, the image of your dream, through my spectacles; but at present you won't succeed! Take a pair, though, and try!'

Giglio eagerly seized the beautiful gleaming pair of outsize spectacles which Celionati offered him, and looked at the palace. Wondrous to relate, the walls of the palace seemed to turn into transparent crystal; but nothing was visible save an indistinct and many-coloured throng of strange shapes, and only now and then did a ray of electricity flash through his heart, announcing the presence of the lovely imàge, which seemed to be struggling in vain to break free of the chaotic turmoil.

'May all the devils in hell fly down your throat!' cried a frightful voice all of a sudden, just beside Giglio, who, absorbed in gazing at the palace, felt himself being seized by the shoulder; 'you'll ruin me. The curtain must go up in ten minutes; you have the first scene, and you're standing here gaping at the old walls of that deserted palace, as though you were out of your wits!'

It was the impresario of the theatre where Giglio acted. He had run the length and breadth of Rome, sweating in terror, to find the vanished *primo amoroso*, and at last he had found him in the most unexpected place.

'Stop a moment!' cried Celionati, in turn seizing poor Giglio firmly by the shoulder, so that Giglio could no more move than could a pole rammed into the ground; 'stop a moment!' Then he added in a low voice: 'Signor Giglio, it is possible that you may see your dream-image on the Corso tomorrow. But you would be a great fool if you dolled yourself up in a beautiful mask; that would prevent you from getting a glimpse of the fair one. The more extraordinary and repulsive, the better! Put on a big nose that can wear my spectacles with dignity and calm! For you mustn't forget the spectacles!'

Celionati let go of Giglio, and the impresario promptly rushed off with his *amoroso*, like a tornado.

The very next day Giglio did not fail to procure a mask which seemed thoroughly extraordinary and repulsive, as Celionati had advised. A curious cap adorned with two lofty cock's feathers, a mask with a red nose whose hooked shape, immoderate length, and sharp point outdid all the excesses of the most profligate noses, a jerkin with thick buttons, somewhat resembling Brighella's, and a broad wooden sword. Giglio's self-denial in donning all these came to an end when he was invited to wear wide trousers that reached down to his slippers and concealed the most elegant pedestal upon which any *primo amoroso* ever stood and strutted.

'No,' exclaimed Giglio, 'it's impossible that the august Princess should set no store by a well-proportioned frame, and that she would not start back in horror on seeing me so vilely disfigured. I shall imitate the actor who had to assume a hideous disguise in Gozzi's play *The Blue Monster* but managed to stretch out from under the tiger's paw the well-shaped hand with which nature had endowed him and thus won the ladies' hearts even before his transformation! If his hand was elegant, so is my foot!' With these words, Giglio donned a pretty pair of sky-blue silk breeches with dark-red bows, along with pink stockings and white shoes with flimsy dark-red ribbons, all of which certainly looked very fetching, but formed rather a strange contrast with the rest of his outfit.

Giglio was convinced that Princess Brambilla would come to meet him in all her splendour and magnificence, followed by a brilliant retinue; seeing nothing of the sort, however, he recalled Celionati's saying that it was only by means of the magic spectacles that he would be able to behold the Princess, which implied that the fair one had concealed herself in some strange disguise.

And so Giglio ran up and down the Corso, inspecting every female mask, ignoring people's teasing remarks, until he found himself in a less frequented area. 'My dear Signor! My dear, good Signor!' croaked a voice in his ear. Before him stood a fellow whose droll and eccentric appearance surpassed anything Giglio had ever seen. The mask with the pointed beard, the spectacles, the goat-like hair, seemed to indicate a Pantaloon, as did the bodily posture of stooping with his right foot thrust forward; but the hat, pointed at the front and adorned with two cock's feathers, did not match the mask. The jerkin, the breeches, and the little wooden sword by his side obviously belonged to the worthy Pulcinella.

'My dear Signor,' said Pantaloon (let us call the mask thus, despite the change in his costume), 'it's a happy day that gives me the pleasure, the honour, of seeing you! Are you not a member of my family?'

'Much as that would delight me,' returned Giglio, bowing civilly, 'since it gives me, good sir, extreme pleasure to meet you, I do not know how any relationship . . .'

'O God!' interrupted Pantaloon, 'my good sir, have you ever been to Assyria?'

'I have a dim recollection,' answered Giglio, 'of setting out once on a journey there, but only getting as far as Frascati,* where the rogue of a *vetturino** overturned me outside the gate, so that my nose . . .'

'O God!' shrieked Pantaloon, 'so it's true! This nose, these cock's feathers—my dearest Prince! O my Cornelio! But I see you turning pale with joy at meeting me again! O my Prince! just a drop, a single drop!'

With these words Pantaloon lifted the great wicker bottle in front of him and handed it to Giglio. And at that moment a subtle reddish vapour arose from the bottle and solidified to form the sweet face of Princess Brambilla, and the charming little image rose up, though only as far as her waist, and stretched out her little arms to Giglio. The latter, beside himself with rapture, cried: 'O rise up completely, that I may behold you in your beauty!'

A mighty voice boomed in his ears: 'You lily-livered fop, in sky-blue and pink, how can you pretend to be Prince Cornelio! Go home and have a good sleep, you booby!'

'Brute!' exclaimed Giglio; but a sea of other masks came thronging around him, and Pantaloon and the bottle had vanished without a trace.

Sig. Lauinia.   *Cap. Cerimonia.*

Trastullo.   *Sig.ᵃ Lucia.*

CHAPTER 2

Of the strange state in which one wounds one's feet against sharp
stones, refrains from greeting distinguished persons, and knocks one's
head against locked doors. The influence of a dish of macaroni upon
love and enthusiasm. Frightful torments of the actors' hell and
Arlecchino. How Giglio, instead of finding his sweetheart, was
overpowered by tailors and given a blood-letting. The prince in the
box of sweets and his lost love. How Giglio wanted to be Princess
Brambilla's knight because a flag had grown out of his back.

Do not be angry, dear reader, if he who has undertaken to tell
you the extraordinary tale of Princess Brambilla just as he found
it suggested by the bold strokes of Master Callot's pen, assumes
that, at least until the last words of this little book, you will
readily surrender to the wondrous, and indeed believe a bit of
it. But perhaps, at the very moment when the fairy-tale procession took up its lodgings in the Pistoia Palace, or when the
Princess arose from the bluish fragrance of the winebottle, you
cried: 'Stuff and nonsense!' and threw the book away in vexation, paying no heed to the charming copperplate engravings?
In that case, everything I am about to say on behalf of the
strange enchantments of Callot's capriccios would come too
late, and that would be most unfortunate for me and for Princess Brambilla! But perhaps you were hoping that the author,
alarmed by some weird shape that suddenly confronted him,
was only making a detour through pathless thickets, and that
on calming down he would return to the broad, smooth way,
thus enabling you to go on reading! Good luck!

Now I can tell you, kind reader, that I have occasionally
managed (and perhaps you have had similar experiences) to
catch fairy-tale figures just at the moment when these airy
phantasms of the excited spirit were about to dissolve into
nothingness, and to give them such clear outlines that every eye
with the power to see such things beheld them in real life, and
believed in them accordingly. This may have encouraged me to
continue openly my convivial intercourse with a variety of

extraordinary figures and a plethora of wild and weird images, and to invite even the gravest readers into this strange and colourful company. You will scarcely, my dearest reader, mistake my courage for mere love of mischief, but see in it rather my pardonable eagerness to lure you out of the narrow confines of everyday life and to let you enjoy yourself as you please in an unfamiliar region. Yet this region, after all, is enclosed within the realm which, in true life and being, the human spirit governs according to its own pleasure.

Yet if all these reasons should be unacceptable, my last, desperate resort is to appeal to very serious books in which similar things occur, and whose entire veracity cannot admit of the slightest doubt. As regards Princess Brambilla's procession, which with all its unicorns, its horses, and the rest of its train, easily passed through the narrow gates of the Pistoia Palace, the *Wondrous Tale of Peter Schlemihl*, which we owe to the stout-hearted navigator Adalbert von Chamisso,* mentions a certain good-humoured man in grey, who performed a feat that puts the above-mentioned magic to shame. For, as you know, in response to people's wishes he drew some sticking-plaster, a telescopic tube, a carpet, a tent, and finally a carriage and horses, out of his coat pocket, without the slightest difficulty. Now, as for the Princess—but that will do! I should indeed mention that in life we often find ourselves unexpectedly standing in front of the gate that opens into a wondrous realm of magic, and are granted glimpses of the inner workings of the mighty spirit whose breath mysteriously surrounds us in our strangest premonitions. You, however, dear reader, could rightly maintain that you had never seen such a wild capriccio emerging from that gate as I claim to have beheld. I should therefore prefer to ask you if you have never in your life had a strange dream whose birth you could attribute neither to indigestion, nor to the fumes of wine, nor to fever; instead, the lovely magical image, which had previously spoken to you only in remote premonitions, seemed to have entered upon a mystic marriage with your mind and taken possession of your inner world, and in your timid amorous delight you neither sought nor dared to embrace the sweet bride who in all her gleaming finery had entered the gloomy, dismal workshop of your thoughts. But the lustre of the magic image filled your mind with bright light, and the yearning, the hope, the ardent desire to lay hold of the ineffable stirred and woke with flashes of lightning, and you wished to perish in unutterable pain, and become *her*, the lovely image itself! What difference did it make that you awoke from the dream? Were you not left with the nameless delight that, when transformed by outward life into a piercing agony, harrows your soul—were you not left with that? And did not everything around you appear dreary, sorrowful, and grey? Did you not fancy that the dream alone was your true existence, and that what you had previously taken for life was only the delusion of your befuddled senses? Did not all your thoughts focus on the fiery chalice of fervent emotion, where your sweet secret was concealed from the blind, chaotic labours of the everyday world? Hm! In such a dreamy mood one may well wound one's feet against sharp stones, forget to doff one's hat to distinguished persons, bid one's friends good morning in the middle of the night, and dash one's head against the first front door one comes to, because one had forgotten to open it; in short, the spirit wears its body like an ill-fitting garment that is everywhere too wide, too long, too uncomfortable.

It was in this state that the young actor Giglio Fava found himself after he had spent several days seeking Princess Brambilla without finding the slightest trace of her. All the wonders he had encountered on the Corso seemed to him only the continuation of the dream which had presented him with the lovely being whose image now arose from the fathomless ocean of yearning in which he was drowning, indeed dissolving. His dream alone was his real life, everything else was empty, trivial, and null; and so you can imagine that he completely neglected his acting profession. As if that were not enough, instead of uttering the words of his part, he spoke of his dream-image, Princess Brambilla; swore, in his mental turmoil, that he would overpower the Assyrian Prince, so that he himself would become the Prince; and lost himself in a labyrinth of confused and extravagant talk. Nobody could avoid concluding that he was mad, especially the impresario, who ended by abruptly dismissing him. The few ducats given him by the impresario from pure generosity at their parting could last only a short

time, and bitter poverty was fast approaching. At other times
this would have caused poor Giglio great alarm and worry; now,
however, he did not give it a thought, for he was floating in a
heavenly realm where earthly ducats are not needed.

As for the ordinary necessities of life, Giglio, not being fussy,
used to satisfy his hunger in passing at one of the cook-shops
which the *fritteroli*,* as is well known, keep on the street. So it
happened that one day he intended to consume a good dish of
macaroni whose steam was wafting towards him from the shop.
He approached, but on pulling out his purse in order to pay for
his scanty lunch, he was greatly dismayed to discover that it
contained not a single *baiocco*.* At that moment the physical
principle which here on earth keeps the spiritual one in base
slavery, whatever airs the latter may assume, made itself unmis-
takably felt. Giglio felt pangs of hunger such as he had never
known in the past, when he had consumed a substantial dish of
macaroni while filled by the sublimest thoughts. He assured the
keeper of the cook-shop that although he happened to have no
money on him, he would most certainly pay on the following
day for the dish he intended to consume. The shopkeeper, however, laughed in his face and remarked that, even if he had no
money, he could still satisfy his appetite; he had only to leave
behind the fine pair of gloves he was wearing, or his hat, or his
jacket. Only now did poor Giglio become vividly aware of his
unfortunate situation. He imagined himself before long as a
ragged beggar swallowing spoonfuls of soup outside monas-
teries. But he was still more cut to the quick when, on awakening from his dream, he caught sight of Celionati, who was
entertaining the people with his antics in his usual place outside
the church of San Carlo and, on meeting Giglio's gaze, threw
him a glance which the latter interpreted as cruel mockery. The
lovely dream-image had dissolved into nothingness, all his
sweet premonitions had vanished; he was certain that the villainous Celionati had led him astray by all manner of fiendish
spells and exploited his foolish vanity in a spirit of mockery and
malice in order to play a contemptible trick on him involving
Princess Brambilla.

He rushed off in a frenzy; he no longer felt hungry, but was
thinking only of how to be revenged on the old wizard.

He himself could not tell what the strange feeling was that pierced through all the anger and rage within him and compelled him to stand still, as though an unknown spell had suddenly fixed him to the spot. 'Giacinta!' came a cry from within him. He was standing outside the house where the girl lived, the steep stairs of which he had so often climbed under cover of twilight. Then he recalled how the deceitful dream-image had first aroused the sweet girl's vexation, how he had thereupon left her and never seen her, never thought about her; how he had lost his sweetheart and plunged himself into poverty and misery on account of Celionati's mad, accursed trickery. Weltering in sorrow and pain, he could not regain his self-control until he decided to go upstairs at once and win back Giacinta's favour, cost what it might. No sooner thought than done! But when he knocked at Giacinta's door, all within remained silent as the grave. He put his ear to the keyhole, but could not hear even a breath. He then called out Giacinta's name several times in a pitiable tone; and when no answer came, he began to confess his folly in the most touching manner, declaring that the Devil himself, in the shape of the accursed mountebank Celionati, had led him astray, and then offering the most high-flown assurances of his profound penitence and ardent love.

Thereupon a voice rang out from below: 'I'd like to know what donkey is groaning and lamenting in my house so early, for it's still a long time until Ash Wednesday!' It was Signor Pasquale, the fat landlord, who was laboriously climbing the stairs. On catching sight of Giglio, he called out: 'Ah! Is it you, Signor Giglio? Tell me, what evil spirit is making you whimper the tear-jerking part from some silly tragedy into an empty room?'

'Empty room!' shrieked Giglio, 'empty room? By all the saints, Signor Pasquale, tell me, where is Giacinta? Where is she, my life, my all?'

Signor Pasquale stared fixedly at Giglio and then said calmly: 'Signor Giglio, I know how things are with you; the whole of Rome has heard how you have had to leave the stage because you aren't in your right mind. Go to the doctor, go to the doctor, ask him to draw off a few pints of blood, and stick your head in cold water!'

'If I'm not mad yet,' yelled Giglio, 'I'll go mad if you don't tell me instantly where Giacinta is.'

'Do you expect me to believe, Signor Giglio,' continued Signor Pasquale calmly, 'that you don't know perfectly well how Giacinta left my house a week ago, followed by old Beatrice?'

However, when Giglio shrieked in fury: 'Where is Giacinta?' and roughly seized hold of the fat landlord, the latter roared 'Help! Help! Murderers!' so loudly that the whole house came to life. A burly lout of an errand-boy came running up, took hold of poor Giglio, ran downstairs with him, and flung him out of the house as adroitly as though he had a rag doll between his fists.

Ignoring his hard landing, Giglio picked himself up and rushed through the streets of Rome, driven now by something that really was close to madness. Just as the hour struck at which he had previously had to hurry to the theatre, a certain instinct produced by habit brought him to that very spot and into the actors' green-room. Only then did he realize where he was, and was deeply astonished to see Pantaloon and Arlecchino, Truffaldino and Colombina, and all the masks of the Italian *commedia dell'arte* flocking around him, in the place where tragic heroes, tricked out in silver and gold, were wont to strut solemnly and practise the sonorous verses with which they intended to cause amazement and *furore* in the audience. He stood there rooted to the spot, gazing around with staring eyes, like somebody who has just awoken from sleep and finds himself surrounded by a strange, wild company that he has never seen before.

Giglio's bewildered and grief-stricken appearance must have stirred something like remorse in the impresario, suddenly transforming him into a kindly, soft-hearted man.

'You're probably surprised, Signor Fava,' said he to the youth, 'to find everything so different from what it was when you left me? I must confess that the bombastic dramas which my theatre formerly boasted were beginning to bore the public extremely, and this boredom took possession of me too, especially as it was causing my purse to waste away with inanition. I've now got rid of all the tragic stuff and surrendered my theatre to the free jesting and delightful teasing of our masks, and I'm doing very well out of it.'

'Ha!' cried Giglio with burning cheeks, 'ha, Signor Impresario, confess that it was losing me that put an end to your tragedies. With the fall of the hero, the material to which his breath gave life crumbled into dust—did it not?'

'We had better not enquire too closely,' replied the impresario with a smile; 'but you seem to be in bad spirits, so I urge you to go down and watch my pantomime. It may cheer you up, or you may change your mind and enter my service again, though in a very different way; for it could well be that—but off you go! Here's a ticket; come to my theatre as often as you like!' Giglio did as he was bidden, more from apathetic indifference to his surroundings than from the desire to watch the pantomime.

Not far from him two masks were standing in animated conversation. Giglio heard his name mentioned several times; this roused him from his stupor, and he crept closer, covering his face below his eyes with his cloak, so that he might overhear all they were saying without being recognized.

'You're right,' said one of the masks, 'it's Fava's fault that we no longer see any tragedies in this theatre. Unlike you, however, I don't blame him for leaving the stage, but for the way he performed when he was on it.'

'How do you mean?' asked the other.

'Well,' went on the first, 'although Fava only too often managed to arouse a *furore*, I for my part have always considered him the most wretched actor in existence. A pair of flashing eyes, shapely legs, an elegant outfit, coloured plumes on one's cap, and huge ribbons on one's shoes—is that enough to make the young tragic hero? Indeed, when Fava emerged from the wings with measured steps like a dancer, when, ignoring his fellow-actors, he squinted towards the boxes and remained in a strangely affected posture long enough to give the fair ones ample time to admire him, he really seemed to me like a young cock with gaudy plumage, proudly taking his ease in the sun. And when he declaimed his verses stumblingly and badly, rolling his eyes, sawing the air with his hands, now rising on his toes and now doubling himself up like a pocket-knife, tell me, what sensible person could have his heart truly stirred by such behaviour? But we Italians are like that; we want exaggerated performances which convulse us for a moment but arouse our contempt as soon as we realize that what we took for flesh and blood is merely a lifeless puppet, moved by artificial threads, which deceived us with its strange movements. That would have happened to Fava, too; he would have perished gradually, if he had not hastened his early death.'

'I think', rejoined the other, 'that you are much too hard on poor Fava. When you criticize him for being vain and affected, when you maintain that he never played his part but only himself, and that he was unscrupulous in playing to the gallery, you may well be right; but he had quite a pleasing talent, and his final descent into madness surely calls for compassion, especially as it was probably caused by the strain of acting.'

'Don't believe that for a minute!' replied the first, laughing. 'Can you imagine that Fava went mad from pure amorous conceit? He thinks that a Princess is in love with him, and pursues her up hill and down dale. And since he is nothing but a wastrel, he has been reduced to poverty. Today, for example, he was obliged to leave his hat and gloves with the *fritteroli* in return for a dish of tough macaroni.'

'What are you saying?' cried the other. 'Are such follies possible? But we ought to find some way of helping poor Giglio out, since he gave us pleasure on many evenings. That dog of an impresario, into whose pockets he brought many ducats, ought to take charge of him and at least not let him starve.'

'There's no need,' said the first, 'for Princess Brambilla is aware of his madness and his poverty, and, as women always find the follies of love not just pardonable but attractive and surrender only too readily to compassion, she has just had a little purse filled with ducats put in his pocket.'

As the stranger uttered these words, Giglio reached mechanically, automatically, for his pocket and did indeed feel the little purse, filled with chinking gold pieces, which he had apparently received from the dream-Princess. An electric shock seemed to shoot through all his limbs. He could not yield to joy at the welcome miracle that had suddenly rescued him from his dismal situation, for he felt the icy breath of horror. He saw himself the plaything of unknown powers, and wanted to rush up to the masked stranger, but noticed at that moment that both the masks who had been conducting the fateful conversation had vanished without a trace.

To pull the purse out of his pocket and persuade himself still more conclusively of its existence was more than Giglio dared, fearing that the enchantment would melt away in his hands. As he pondered, however, and grew gradually calmer, it occurred to him that all the events which he had taken for the wilful teasing of magical powers might be nothing more than a farcical comedy, perhaps directed from the deep darkness of the wings by the strange and whimsical Celionati, with the aid of threads that were invisible only to Giglio himself. It occurred to him that the stranger might very well have slipped the purse into his pocket amid the thronging crowd, and that all he had said about Princess Brambilla might be an extension of the teasing which Celionati had begun. While, however, his mind was quite naturally dissolving all the magic into mundane reality, he also recollected all the pain of the wounds inflicted so mercilessly by his harsh critic. There can be no more hideous torments in the actors' hell than attacks on their vanity that cut right to the heart. And the very feeling that they are vulnerable and exposed to attack increases the victims' vexation and intensifies the pain of the strokes, for even if they try to suppress or deaden the pain, it reminds them that they have suffered a palpable hit. Thus Giglio could not forget the dreadful image of the young cock with his gaudy plumage who struts about complacently in the sun, and brooded and fretted over it obsessively, just because he was reluctantly compelled to acknowledge to himself that the caricature matched the original.

It was only to be expected that in this mood of irritation Giglio scarcely looked at the theatre and ignored the pantomime, although the auditorium often resounded with the laughter, the applause, the joyous cries of the spectators.

The pantomime presented hundreds of variations on the amorous adventures of the excellent Arlecchino with the sweet, lovely, coquettish Colombina. The charming daughter of the wealthy old Pantaloon had already refused the hand of the Knight in shining armour and the wise Doctor and roundly declared that she would love and marry none other than the agile little man with a black face and a jerkin patched together from a thousand rags; Arlecchino had already taken flight with his faithful maiden and, protected by a powerful spell, had happily evaded the pursuit of Pantaloon, Truffaldino, the Doctor, and the Knight. The point had been reached where Arlecchino, billing and cooing with his sweetheart, had at last been caught by the *shirri* and was about to be dragged to prison along with her. This did indeed happen; but just as Pantaloon and his followers were about to mock the poor couple unsparingly, and Colombina, shedding floods of tears in her agony, was kneeling to plead for her Arlecchino, the latter waved his slapstick and from all sides, from the ground, from the air, there appeared smart, neat, fine-looking people who bowed deeply to Arlecchino and led him and Colombina away in triumph. Pantaloon, frozen to the spot in astonishment, then sinks down in exhaustion on a stone bench in the prison, and invites the Knight and the Doctor to sit down likewise; all three put their heads together and discuss what to do next. Truffaldino stands behind them and inquisitively sticks his head between theirs, refusing to move, although blows rain on him from all sides. They then try to stand up, but find themselves magically fixed to the bench, which instantly grows a pair of mighty wings. Crying loudly for help, the entire company fly away through the air on the back of a monstrous vulture. The prison is then transformed into an open pillared hall adorned with wreaths of flowers, in the midst of which a lofty and richly decorated throne has been erected. The delightful music of drums, pipes, and cymbals can be heard. A brilliant procession approaches; Arlecchino is carried on a palanquin by Moors, followed by Colombina in a magnificent triumphal chariot. The two are led to the throne by sumptuously dressed ministers; Arlecchino raises his slapstick as a sceptre, and everyone kneels in homage; even Pantaloon and his followers can be seen among the kneeling multitude. The mighty Emperor Arlecchino rules with his Colombina over a beautiful, splendid, brilliant realm!

As soon as the procession entered the theatre, Giglio glanced up and found himself too surprised and astonished to look away, for he could make out every member of Princess Brambilla's train: the unicorns, the Moors, the ladies netting on the backs of mules, and so on. Nor did he miss the venerable scholar and statesman in the glittering golden tulip, who, as he passed, looked up from his book and seemed to give Giglio a friendly nod. The only difference was that, instead of the Princess's closed coach with mirrors for windows, Colombina rode in the open triumphal chariot.

In Giglio's mind there began to form a dim presentiment that this pantomime too was mysteriously connected with all the wondrous events that had befallen him; but just as a dreamer tries vainly to retain the images that arise from his own mind, so Giglio could arrive at no clear idea of how such a connection was possible.

In the nearest café Giglio established that Princess Brambilla's ducats, far from being an illusion, rang true and were properly minted. 'Hm!' he thought, 'Celionati has slipped me this purse out of mercy and compassion, and I shall pay my debt to him when I become the star of the Argentina Theatre; and that is bound to happen, for only the bitterest envy, the most ruthless intrigues, could malign me as a bad actor!' There were good grounds for the conjecture that the money came from Celionati; for the old man had indeed often helped him in dire need. Yet he was taken aback to find, embroidered on the dainty purse, the words: 'Remember the image of your dream!'

As he was pensively contemplating these words, somebody shouted in his ear: 'I've found you at last, you traitor, you deceiver, you lying, ungrateful monster!' A hideous Doctor seized him, sat down unceremoniously beside him, and continued to heap objurgations upon him.

'What do you want with me? Are you mad? Are you crazy?' cried Giglio; but on the removal of the Doctor's ugly face-mask, Giglio recognized old Beatrice.

'By all the saints,' cried Giglio, quite beside himself, 'is that you, Beatrice? Where's Giacinta? Where is the sweet, lovely child? My heart is breaking with love and yearning! Where's Giacinta?'

'You may well ask, you cursed scoundrel!' replied the old woman. 'Poor Giacinta is in prison, her young life is wasting away, and it is all your fault. For if her head hadn't been full of you, and she'd been able to wait patiently for the evening, she wouldn't have pricked her finger as she was sewing the trimmings on Princess Brambilla's dress, and the dress wouldn't have had a horrid stain; and then the worthy Master Bescapi, may hell swallow him up, wouldn't have demanded that she make good the damage, and when we were unable to find the large sum that he demanded, he couldn't have had her clapped into prison. You could have helped us—but no, we weren't grand enough for a good-for-nothing actor . . .'

'Stop!' cried Giglio, interrupting the garrulous old woman, 'you're to blame for not coming running to me and telling me everything. I'd give my life for that sweet girl! If it weren't midnight, I'd run straight to the abominable Bescapi—these ducats—my sweetheart would be free within the hour; but never mind midnight! Away, away, to her rescue!' And with these words Giglio stormed off, followed by the old woman's mocking laughter.

However, as it often happens that in our excessive anxiety to do something we forget the crucial point, so Giglio had run through the streets of Rome until he was out of breath before it occurred to him that he should have asked the old woman for Bescapi's address, which was entirely unknown to him. As fate or chance would have it, however, he eventually reached the Piazza di Spagna and was standing just outside Bescapi's house when he shouted: 'Where the Devil does Bescapi live!' Immediately a stranger took him by the arm and led him into the house, telling him that Master Bescapi lived there and that he could certainly collect the mask which he had doubtless ordered. Once they were indoors, the man asked him, since Master Bescapi was not at home, to say which mask he had requested; perhaps it was a simple *tabarro*,* or—but Giglio turned on the man, who was a worthy journeyman tailor, and ranted so wildly about bloodstains and prison and payment and setting someone free on the spot that the journeyman stared at him in astonishment, unable to utter a syllable in reply. 'Damn you, will nothing make you understand me? Bring your master here at once, the devilish dog!' bellowed Giglio, seizing hold of the journeyman. However, the same thing happened as in Signor Pasquale's house. The journeyman roared so loudly that people came flocking from all sides.

Bescapi himself rushed in; but as soon as he spied Giglio, he exclaimed: 'By all the saints, it's the mad actor, poor Signor Fava. Seize him, all of you, seize him!' All the people fell upon Giglio, overpowered him with ease, bound him hand and foot, and laid him upon a bed. Bescapi went over to him, but was met with a thousand bitter reproaches for his avarice and cruelty, and a harangue about Princess Brambilla's dress, the bloodstain, payment, and so forth.

'Please calm down,' said Bescapi mildly, 'do please calm down, my dear Signor Giglio, and shake off those ghosts that are tormenting you! In a few moments you will see everything in a quite different light.'

What Bescapi meant by this soon became apparent; for a surgeon entered and opened one of poor Giglio's veins, despite his attempts at resistance. Exhausted by the day's events and by the loss of blood, poor Giglio sank into a deep slumber, as though he had fainted.

When he woke, he was in pitch darkness; it cost him an effort to recall what had recently happened to him; he felt that he had been untied, but he was too feeble to move much. Through a crack, probably in a door, a faint ray of light penetrated into the room, and he seemed to hear deep breathing and then a soft whispering which finally turned into intelligible words: 'Is it really you, my precious Prince? And in such a condition? So small, so small, that I think you could fit into my box of sweets! But don't think that I like and esteem you any the less; for don't I know that you are a fine, upstanding, amiable gentleman, and that all this is only one of my dreams? Do be kind enough to show yourself to me tomorrow, even if it's only your voice! When you cast a glance at a poor maid like me, it was bound to happen, for otherwise . . .'. Here the words tailed off into an indistinct whisper. There was something uncommonly sweet and charming about the voice; Giglio felt himself quaking with inner tremors; but as he tried to listen attentively, the whispering, which almost resembled the plashing of a nearby spring, lulled him once more into deep sleep.

Bright sunlight was shining into the room when a gentle shaking roused Giglio from his sleep. Master Bescapi, standing in front of him, took his hand and said with a good-humoured smile: 'You're feeling better, aren't you, my dear Signor? Yes, thanks be to the saints! You're looking a little pale, but your pulse is steady. When your paroxysm attacked you, heaven led you into my house and permitted me to do a small service to the man whom I consider the finest actor in Rome, and whose loss plunged us all into the depths of sorrow.'

Bescapi's last words were certainly a powerful balm for Giglio's wounds; the latter, however, began to speak in a serious and sombre manner: 'Signor Bescapi, I was neither ill nor mad when I entered your house. You were hard-hearted enough to have poor Giacinta Soardi, to whom I am engaged, thrown into prison, because she could not pay for a fine dress which she had spoiled, or rather sanctified, by splashing it with rosy ichor from a wound inflicted by a needle on the tenderest of fingers. Tell me instantly how much you want for the dress; I shall pay the sum, and we shall then set out on the spot to free the sweet, lovely child from the prison where she is languishing on account of your avarice.' With these words Giglio got out of bed as quickly as he could and drew from his pocket the purse full of ducats, which he was resolved to empty if need be.

But Bescapi said, staring at him, 'How can you take such wild fancies into your head, Signor Giglio? I know nothing about any dress that Giacinta spoiled, nor about bloodstains or people being thrown into prison!' On Giglio's repeating the whole story he had heard from Beatrice, and in particular giving a minute description of the dress which he himself had seen in Giacinta's room, Bescapi declared that the old woman had undoubtedly made a fool of him; 'for I can assure you', said he, 'that there is not one word of truth in the whole story, and I never gave Giacinta any such dress to embroider as you describe'.

Giglio could not distrust Bescapi's words, since it would have been impossible to explain his refusal to take the money offered him, and became convinced that here, too, there was some weird magic at work, in whose clutches he was caught. There was nothing for it but to leave Master Bescapi and wait in the hope that fortune would bring back the sweet Giacinta, for whom his love now flared up once more.

There was someone standing outside Bescapi's door whom Giglio would have wished a thousand leagues away: old

Celionati. 'Why!' he called out to Giglio, with a laugh, 'what a good soul you are! Fancy wanting to give up the ducats that you owe to fortune's favour on behalf of your sweetheart, who isn't your sweetheart any longer.'

'You are a frightful, uncanny person!' replied Giglio. 'Why have you invaded my life? Why do you want to take control of my existence? You boast of an omniscience which I dare say costs you little effort; you surround me with spies who watch my every move; you stir up everyone against me; it is you whom I have to thank for the loss of Giacinta and of my job—your innumerable arts . . .'.

'I've got better things to do', exclaimed Celionati, laughing loudly, 'than to put such a guard on the illustrious person of the ex-actor Giglio Fava! But, Giglio, my son, you really do need a guardian to put you on the right path leading to your goal . . .'

'I'm an adult,' said Giglio, 'and I beg you, Ciarlatano, to let me take care of myself.'

'Ho, ho!' replied Celionati, 'don't be so headstrong! What if I were acting for your good? What if I were planning to give you the supreme earthly happiness, and were the intermediary between you and Princess Brambilla?'

'Oh, Giacinta, Giacinta, what a miserable wretch I am! I've lost her! Was there ever a day that brought me more dire misfortune than yesterday?' cried Giglio, quite beside himself.

'Now, now,' said Celionati comfortingly, 'the day wasn't as unfortunate as all that. The lessons you received in the theatre were very salutary, once you had got over your annoyance at the charge of abandoning your gloves, hat, and cloak to pay for a dish of tough macaroni; then you saw a most magnificent performance, which may be called the foremost in the world, if only because it utters the profoundest truths without need for words; then you found the ducats you lacked in your pocket . . .'.

'They came from you, I know', interrupted Giglio.

'Even if that were so,' continued Celionati, 'it makes no difference; suffice it to say that you took the gold, got back on good terms with your stomach, arrived happily in Bescapi's house, received a much-needed blood-letting, and finally spent the night under the same roof as your beloved!'

'What are you saying?' cried Giglio. 'With my beloved? Under the same roof as my beloved?'

'It is even so,' rejoined Celionati. 'Look up!'

Giglio did so, and felt a hundred lightning-bolts shoot through his heart as he saw his lovely Giacinta on the balcony, elegantly dressed, and more charming than he had ever seen her, with old Beatrice behind her. 'Giacinta, my Giacinta, my sweet life!' he called up yearningly. But Giacinta cast him a contemptuous glance and left the balcony, closely followed by Beatrice.

'She's still persisting in her damned smorfiosity', said Giglio crossly; 'but she'll come round.'

'Hardly!' replied Celionati; 'for, my good Giglio, you probably do not know that while you were boldly pursuing Princess Brambilla, a fine, upstanding, handsome prince wooed your *donna*, and, it seems . . .'

'All the devils in hell!' shrieked Giglio; 'that old fiend Beatrice has sold her to the fellow; but I'll poison the vile woman with ratsbane and plunge a dagger into the heart of the accursed Prince . . .'

'Do nothing of the sort, my good Giglio,' interrupted Celionati, 'go home quietly and have yourself bled again if any more wicked thoughts occur to you! May God guide you. No doubt we'll see each other again on the Corso.' With these words Celionati hastened away across the street.

Giglio remained rooted to the spot, casting furious glances towards the balcony, clenching his teeth, and murmuring the most dreadful curses. When Master Bescapi put his head out of the window and politely asked Giglio to enter and await the new crisis that seemed to be approaching, Giglio, assuming that Bescapi was leagued with the old woman in a plot against him, yelled out: 'Damned procurer!' and rushed madly away.

On the Corso he ran into a few former comrades with whom he entered a nearby wine-shop in order to drown all his vexation, his amorous chagrin, his despair in the heat of fiery Syracusan wine.

Such a decision is not usually very judicious, for the heat that consumes one's vexation tends to blaze up uncontrollably and set light to everything within one that should be protected from the flame; but in Giglio's case all went well. Revelling in a cheerful and convivial chat with the actors and in all manner of reminiscences and good stories about the theatre, he forgot all the misfortunes that had come his way. On leaving, he and his friends arranged to appear on the Corso that evening in the most fantastic masks that could be devised.

The outfit that he had worn once already struck Giglio as sufficiently grotesque, except that this time he did not despise the long, odd-looking pantaloons, and also wore his cloak hitched up on a stick, so that he almost looked as if a flag were growing out of his back. Dressed up in this fashion, he roamed through the streets and gave himself up to unrestrained enjoyment, thinking neither of his dream-image nor of his lost sweetheart.

He remained rooted to the spot, however, when, near the Pistoia Palace, a tall and noble figure suddenly approached him wearing the magnificent clothes in which he had once surprised Giacinta; or rather, as he beheld the image of his dreams in real, waking life. A flash of lightning seemed to penetrate his whole body; but he himself could not tell how it happened that all the unease and apprehension of yearning love, which normally paralyses one's mind when the gracious image of the beloved suddenly appears, was swallowed up in the cheerful courage given by a sensation of such pleasure as he had never before experienced. Putting his right foot forward, puffing out his chest and drawing in his shoulders, he promptly adopted the most elegant posture in which he had ever delivered his most extraordinary speeches, and lifted his beret with its long, pointed cock's feathers from his stiff wig. Staring at Princess Brambilla (for it was indubitably she) through his huge spectacles, he began, in the croaking voice that matched his disguise:

'The loveliest of fairies, the most gracious of goddesses now walks upon the earth; envious wax conceals the triumphant beauty of her countenance, but the radiance that enfolds her lets fly a thousand shafts of lightning which enter the hearts of old and young, and all alike, ablaze with love and rapture, pay homage to the heavenly being.'

'From what high-flown tragedy', replied the Princess, 'did

you borrow these fine phrases, Captain Pantaloon, or whoever you are? Tell me, what are the victories signified by the trophies which you are carrying so proudly on your back?'

'No trophy,' cried Giglio, 'for I am still fighting to gain the victory! It is the flag of hope, of the most ardent yearning, to which I am sworn; it is my signal of distress, announcing my unconditional surrender, my "Have pity on me", which the breezes waft towards you from the folds of my cloak. Accept me as your knight, Princess, and then I will do valiant combat, gain the victory and wear the trophies in homage to your grace and beauty.'

'If you want to be my knight,' said the Princess, 'then put on proper armour! Cover your head with the menacing helmet, and seize the good broadsword! Then I shall believe in you.'*

'If you will be my lady,' replied Giglio, 'Rinaldo's Armida,* then be wholly so! Discard the lavish finery, which bewilders my senses like perilous enchantment. This gleaming blood-stain . . .'

'You're not in your right mind!' exclaimed the Princess, walking rapidly away and leaving Giglio where he was.

Giglio felt as though it had not been he who spoke to the Princess, and as though he had automatically recited something he did not even understand; he was close to believing that Signor Pasquale and Master Bescapi were right in thinking him touched with madness. Just then a troop of masks approached, their hideous visages embodying the most grotesque products of a wild imagination. On recognizing his comrades, Giglio promptly regained his exuberant merriment. He mingled with the leaping, dancing group, calling loudly: 'Bestir yourselves, wild revellers! Move yourselves, mighty and mischievous spirits of impudent mockery! I'm entirely yours, and you may regard me as one of yourselves!'

Giglio thought that among his comrades he noticed the old man from whose bottle Brambilla's shape had arisen. Before he knew what was happening, the old man seized him, spun him round in a circle, and screeched in his ears: 'Little brother, I've got you! Little brother, I've got you!'

CHAPTER 3

Of fair-haired people who presume to find Pulcinella tedious and un-
funny. German and Italian humour. How Celionati, sitting in the
Caffè Greco, maintained that instead of sitting in the Caffè Greco
he was manufacturing Paris rappee on the bank of the Ganges. The
wondrous tale of King Ophioch, who ruled in the land of Urdar,
and Queen Liris. How King Cophetua married a beggar maid, a
noble Princess ran after a bad comedian, and Giglio girded on a
wooden sword and then knocked over a hundred masks on the Corso,
until he finally stopped because his own self had begun to dance.

'You young, proud people, with fair hair and blue eyes, whose
"Good evening, my pretty child!", uttered in a booming bass,
alarms even the cheekiest young wench! Is it possible for your
blood, frozen by a perpetual winter, to thaw in the wild gusts
of the Tramontana, or in the ardour of a love-song? Why do you
boast of your mighty zest for life, your unspoiled vital energy,
when you cannot appreciate the maddest, most comical comedy
of all comedy, which our blessed Carnival offers in rich abundance? And you even dare to find our worthy Pulcinella sometimes tedious and unfunny, and call the most exquisite creations
of humorous derision the productions of a disordered mind!'
These words were spoken by Celionati in the Caffè Greco,*
where, as usual, he had gone in the evening and joined the
German artists,* who were in the habit of visiting this house
in the Strada Condotti at that time, and who had just subjected
the grotesque antics of the Carnival to severe criticism.

'However can you say such things, Master Celionati!' replied
the German painter Franz Reinhold. 'They do not match the
favourable remarks you usually make about the German character. It is true that you have always reproached us Germans for
demanding that a joke should mean something more than simply the joke itself, and I admit that you are right, though in a
quite different way from what you probably suppose. May God
comfort you if you think us so stupid as to accept irony only in
an allegorical sense! You would be gravely mistaken. We un-

derstand very well that you Italians seem much more at home
with the pure joke, as such, than we are; but if only I could
make clear what a difference I find between your jokes and ours,
or rather, between your irony and ours! Well, we have just been
talking about the wild, grotesque figures roaming along the
Corso; and I can add a kind of simile. When I see such a weird
fellow rousing the people to laughter by his hideous grimaces,
I feel as though a primordial image had become visible to him
and were speaking to him; but he does not understand its
words, and just as one does in life when trying to grasp the
meaning of an unintelligible speech in a strange language, he
automatically imitates the gestures of that primordial image,
though in an exaggerated manner, because of the effort required. Our jokes are the very language of that primordial
image, which speaks from deep within us and necessarily produces the appropriate gestures by virtue of the inner principle
of irony, just as a hidden rock produces ripples on the surface
of the stream that flows over it. Don't imagine, Master Celionati, that I do not appreciate the burlesque humour which lies
in outward appearances and takes its material only from thence,
or that I deny your nation's outstanding ability to create such
burlesque humour. But forgive me, Celionati, if I say that for
burlesque to be tolerable, it must contain a dose of good humour, and that is what I miss in your comic characters. The
good humour that keeps our jokes pure is swallowed up in the
principle of obscenity that animates your Pulcinella and a hundred other such masks, and then behind all their grotesque
antics one glimpses that frightful, horrible fury of rage, hatred,
and despair that drives you to madness and murder. On that
day of the Carnival on which everyone carries a candle and tries
to blow out somebody else's candle, when amid the wildest
jubilation and roars of laughter the whole Corso trembles with
the furious yells of "Ammazzato sia, chi non porta moccolo",*
I am carried away by the insane delight of the crowd and am
second to none in blowing out candles and yelling "Ammazzato
sia!". But believe me, Celionati, at that very moment I am
seized by an uncanny trembling that entirely suppresses the
good humour which belongs to our German character.'

'Good humour?' said Celionati with a smile. 'Tell me, my

good-humoured German friend, what do you think of our the-atrical masks? Our Pantaloon, Brighella, Tartaglia?'

'Why,' replied Reinhold, 'I think these masks disclose a treas-ure trove of the most delicious mockery, the sharpest irony, the freest, not to say the most scurrilous fancy, although I should say that they concern the various outward guises of human nature rather than human nature itself, or, to put it better and more briefly, they concern *men* rather than *man*. Besides, Celion-ati, please don't think me mad enough to doubt that your nation contains men gifted with the profoundest humour. The invisible church knows no distinction of nations; it has its members everywhere. And let me just tell you, Master Celion-ati, your goings-on have long seemed to us most peculiar. You display yourself to the people as an eccentric Ciarlatano, but then you take pleasure in our company, forgetting your Italian character and delighting us with wonderful stories which make a profound impression on our hearts; but even when you tell us childish tales, you cast a strange spell which fascinates and enraptures us. Indeed, the crowd is right to denounce you as a wizard; I for my part think only that you belong to the invisible church, which has some extraordinary members, even though they all grow out of one body.'

'What on earth do you think of me?' cried Celionati vehe-mently, 'what fancies or suspicions do you have about me? Are all of you so certain that I am sitting here among you, point-lessly talking pointless stuff about things that you cannot begin to understand unless you have gazed into the clear watery mir-ror of the Fountain of Urdar,* unless Liris has smiled upon you?'

'Ho, ho!' cried everyone at once, 'he's back at his old tricks! On you go, wizard, on you go!'

'Has none of you any brains?' exclaimed Celionati, interrupt-ing the chorus by striking the table with his fist so violently that everyone suddenly fell silent.

'Has none of you any brains?' he continued more calmly. 'Tricks? Dances? I am only asking how you all come to be so sure that I really am sitting among you, holding a conversation which you all think you hear with your bodily ears, although it may be only a mischievous airy spirit who is teasing you? Who can guarantee that the Celionati whom you are trying to persuade that Italians don't understand irony is not even now strolling along the Ganges and picking fragrant flowers to make Paris rappee* for the nostrils of some mystic idol? Or perhaps he is walking among the dark and dreadful tombs at Memphis,* to request the most ancient of the kings for the little toe of his left foot to be used for medical purposes by the proudest princess in the Argentina Theatre. Or he may be sitting by the Fountain of Urdar, deep in conversation with his most intimate friend, the magician Ruffiamonte. But stop! I shall act as though Celionati really were sitting here in the Caffè Greco, and tell you about King Ophioch,* Queen Liris, and the watery mirror of the Fountain of Urdar, if you want to hear such things.'

'Do tell us, Celionati,' said one of the young artists; 'I can see this is going to be one of your stories that are wild and extra-ordinary enough for anyone, but very agreeable to listen to.'

'Let none of you suppose', began Celionati, 'that I am going to serve up senseless fairy-tales, and let none of you doubt that everything happened just as I am going to tell! All your doubts will be removed when I assure you that I learnt the whole story from the lips of my friend Ruffiamonte, who himself is in a way the central character in the story. It was scarcely more than two hundred years ago, as we were roaming through the fires of Iceland in search of a talisman born of fiery floods, and talked a good deal about the Fountain of Urdar. So prick up your ears, open your minds!'

At this point, my kind reader, you must be prepared to hear a story which seems quite unconnected with the events that I have undertaken to recount and is thus open to criticism as a mere episode. Sometimes, however, it happens that if you resol-utely follow the path that seemed to be leading you astray, you suddenly find yourself at your journey's end. And thus it may also be that this episode only appears to be a false trail but in fact leads straight to the heart of my main story. Hear therefore, O my reader, the wondrous

STORY OF KING OPHIOCH AND QUEEN LIRIS

A very, very long time ago, at a time, one might say, that

followed the dawn of time as closely as Ash Wednesday follows Shrove Tuesday, young King Ophioch ruled over the Land of Urdar. I do not know whether the German Büsching* has described the Land of Urdar with any geographical accuracy; but this much is certain, that, as the magician Ruffiamonte has assured me a thousand times, it was among the most favoured lands that there ever have been or will be. Its meadows produced such luxuriant grass and clover that no cow, however dainty her palate, ever wanted to leave her dear native country. Its extensive forests had not only trees, plants, first-rate game, but also such sweet fragrances that the morning and evening breezes never tired of rampaging among them. There were vines, and olives, and every kind of fruit in abundance. Clear silvery streams traversed the entire country, while gold and silver were the gift of mountains which, like truly wealthy men, were simply clad in a faded dark grey, and anyone who took the slightest trouble could scrape the finest jewels out of the sand and use them, if he so wished, as elegant buttons on his shirt or his waistcoat. If there were no cities built of brick, apart from the royal palace made of marble and alabaster, this was owing to the people's lack of civilization, which prevented them from realizing that it was better, after all, to sit in one's armchair, sheltered by stout walls, than to dwell by the murmuring stream in a humble cottage, surrounded by rustling bushes, exposed to the danger that some impertinent tree might hang its foliage in the windows and keep putting in a word, like an uninvited guest, or that vines and ivy might do the work of the paper-hanger. When you consider, furthermore, that the inhabitants of the land of Urdar were enthusiastic patriots, dearly loved the King even when he was not before their eyes, and even shouted 'Long live His Majesty!' on other days besides his birthday, then you see that King Ophioch should have been the happiest monarch under the sun. And so he would have been, were it not that he, and many of those considered the wisest people in the land, were assailed by a strange sorrow that prevented them from taking pleasure in the splendours around them. King Ophioch was an intelligent youth, bright and quick-witted, and even had some poetic sensibility. This would seem quite incredible and improper, were it not made conceivable and excusable by the age in which he lived.

In King Ophioch's soul there must still have lingered echoes of that wondrous dawn of time, with its supreme happiness, when nature nursed her favourite child, man, with loving care, and allowed him directly to contemplate the whole of being and therewith to comprehend the highest ideal and the purest harmony. For Ophioch often felt as though sweet voices were speaking to him in the mysterious rustling of the forest, in the whispering of the bushes and springs, as though shining arms were stretching down from the golden clouds to take hold of him, and his breast swelled with ardent yearning. But then all these thoughts were swallowed up in a wild, desolate chaos; he felt a blast of cold air from the icy pinions of the terrible, sombre demon which had estranged him from his mother, and saw himself helplessly abandoned by her wrath. The voice of the forest and the distant mountains, which had previously aroused his yearning and a sweet intuition of vanished happiness, died away amid the mockery of the sombre demon. But in King Ophioch's mind the burning breath of this mockery gave rise to the illusion that the demon's voice was the voice of his enraged mother, who was now striving to compass the destruction of her degenerate child.

As was stated earlier, many people in his land understood King Ophioch's melancholy and, understanding it, were seized by it themselves. The majority, however, failed to understand such melancholy, least of all the Council of State, which, fortunately for the kingdom, retained its health.

Thanks to its health the Council was persuaded that nothing could rescue King Ophioch from his melancholy musings except the acquisition of a pretty, cheerful, happy wife. They cast their eyes on Princess Liris, the daughter of a neighbouring king. Princess Liris was indeed as beautiful as any king's daughter you care to imagine. Although nothing in her surroundings, nothing that she saw or heard, left the slightest imprint on her mind, she was continually laughing, and since people in the land of Hirdar (this was the name of her father's country) were as much at a loss to account for her merriment as people in Urdar were to account for King Ophioch's sorrow, the two royal souls seemed made for each other. Moreover, the

Princess's sole pleasure that assumed any tangible form was netting, surrounded by her ladies-in-waiting, who were obliged likewise to net, just as King Ophioch seemed to take pleasure only in pursuing the beasts of the forest in utter solitude. King Ophioch had no objections to the spouse proposed for him; he considered the marriage a mere matter of state, and left the arrangements to his ministers who were so anxious for it to take place.

The marriage was soon consummated amid all possible splendour. Everything went off happily and magnificently, except for one small mishap: the court poet composed an epithalamium which King Ophioch flung at his head; thereupon the poet promptly went mad and fancied that he had poetic sensibility, which prevented him from composing any more poetry and rendered him incapable of serving any longer as court poet.

Weeks and months went by, but no trace of a change could be seen in King Ophioch's mood. His ministers, who liked the laughing Queen very much, reassured themselves and the people, saying: 'He'll soon come round!'

King Ophioch, however, did not come round: each day he became sadder and more serious than before, and, worst of all, a deep dislike of his laughing Queen germinated in his mind. The Queen seemed not to notice, and indeed it could never be established whether she noticed anything in the world, except the stitches in her netting.

One day, when King Ophioch was out hunting, it so happened that he found himself in the wild, desolate part of the forest, where a tower of black stone, as old as creation, jutted into the air as though it had grown out of the rock. The wind rustled in the tree-tops, and howls of heart-rending woe replied from the deep gorge. In this sinister place King Ophioch's breast was strangely moved. Yet he felt as though these terrible sounds of deep sorrow revealed a glimmer of hope that his estrangement might be overcome. It seemed no longer to be his mother's scornful wrath, but rather her piteous lament that he was hearing, and the lament comforted him by telling him that his mother's wrath would not last for ever.

As King Ophioch paused, lost in his own thoughts, an eagle swept through the air and hovered over the battlements of the tower. King Ophioch involuntarily seized his bow and fired an arrow at the eagle; instead of hitting it, however, the arrow lodged in the chest of a venerable old man standing on the battlements, whom King Ophioch had not seen until now. Terror gripped King Ophioch as he recollected that the tower was the observatory which, as legend had it, the ancient kings of the country had formerly ascended on mysterious nights, and where, as consecrated intermediaries between the people and the ruler of all being, they had proclaimed the will and the utterances of the mighty mother. He realized that he was in the place that everyone carefully avoided because it was said that the old Magus Hermod* was standing on the battlements of the tower, sunk in slumbers that had lasted for a thousand years, and that if he were roused from his sleep, the elements would rise in fury, and assail one another in a furious combat in which everyone and everything would inevitably perish.

The grief-stricken Ophioch was about to fall on his knees when he felt a gentle touch: the Magus Hermod was standing in front of him, holding in one hand the arrow that had struck his chest. A gentle smile softened the grave and venerable features of the Magus as he spoke: 'You have roused me from a long prophetic sleep, King Ophioch! I thank you, for it happened at the right moment. It is now time for me to betake myself to Atlantis and receive from the hands of the lofty and mighty Queen the gift which she promised me as a token of reconciliation, and which, O King Ophioch, will take the fatal sting from the pain which lacerates your breast. Thought destroyed intuition, but from the prism of the crystal, formed by the fiery flood in its nuptial conflict with the malevolent poison, intuition will radiate forth new-born, itself the foetus of thought! Farewell, King Ophioch! In thirteen times thirteen moons you will see me again, and I shall bring you your reconciled mother's fairest gift, which will dissolve your pain into supreme pleasure and melt the icy prison in which your spouse, Queen Liris, has so long been held captive by the most malevolent of all demons. Farewell, King Ophioch!'

With these mysterious words the old Magus left the young king, disappearing into the depths of the forest.

If King Ophioch had previously been sad and pensive, he now

became much more so. Old Hermod's words remained in his
soul, and he repeated them to the court astrologer, hoping that
the latter would interpret their unintelligible meaning. The
astrologer, however, declared that they had no meaning, for
there was no such thing as a prism or a crystal, or rather the
latter, as every apothecary knew, could not be produced from a
fiery flood and malevolent poison. As for Hermod's confused
remarks about thought and new-born intuition, he added, they
must remain unintelligible, if only because no astrologer, nor
any decently educated philosopher, could want anything to do
with the meaningless language of the unpolished age to which
the Magus Hermod belonged. Not only was King Ophioch
thoroughly dissatisfied with this excuse, but he also gave the
astrologer a furious tongue-lashing, and it was fortunate that
he happened to have nothing handy to throw at the head of the
unfortunate astrologer, as he had done with the court poet's
epithalamium. Ruffiamonte maintains that even if the
chronicles do not mention it, there is no doubt, according to
the popular legends of Urdar, that on this occasion King
Ophioch called the astrologer a—donkey.

Since the melancholy young king could not free his soul from
the Magus Hermod's mystical words, he finally resolved to
discover their meaning for himself, cost what it might. He
therefore caused the words 'Thought destroyed intuition', along
with the Magus's further utterances, to be inscribed in gold
letters on a black marble tablet, which he inserted in the wall
of a sombre room in a remote corner of his palace. He then
seated himself on a well-upholstered couch in front of this
tablet, rested his chin on his hand, and gave himself up to
profound meditation while contemplating the inscription.

Queen Liris, quite by chance, happened to enter the room
where King Ophioch was sitting before the inscription. Although, as usual, she was laughing so loudly that the walls
reverberated, the King seemed not to notice his dear and merry
spouse. His gaze remained rigidly fixed on the black marble
tablet. Scarcely had she read the mysterious words, however,
than her laughter died away and she sank down silently on the
cushions beside the King. After King Ophioch and Queen Liris
had stared at the inscription for a considerable time, they began

to yawn more and more loudly, then closed their eyes and sank into such a deep, death-like sleep that no human skill could arouse them. They would have been taken for dead and laid in the royal vault with the ceremonies usual in the land of Urdar, had not their soft breath, their beating pulses, and the colour of their faces been unmistakable signs of their continuing life. Since, moreover, the royal couple still had no children, the Council of State resolved to rule in place of the slumbering King Ophioch, and performed this task so skilfully that nobody had the slightest inkling of the monarch's torpor. Thirteen times thirteen moons went by from the day on which King Ophioch had had his momentous encounter with the Magus Hermod; then the inhabitants of Urdar were shown a more magnificent spectacle than any they had ever seen.

The great Magus Hermod arrived on a fiery cloud, surrounded by elemental spirits of every race, and while the breezes, in mysterious chords, proclaimed the harmony of all nature, he descended on to the colourful carpet of a beautiful fragrant meadow. A luminous star, whose fiery radiance was too much for the naked eye, seemed to be hovering above his head. This, however, was a prism of shining crystal, and as the Magus lifted it high in the air, it melted and ran into the earth in glittering drops, to gush forth a moment later, plashing cheerfully, as a magnificent silvery spring.

Around the Magus everything leapt into motion. While the earth-spirits descended into the depths and caused gleaming metal flowers to spring up, the spirits of fire and water surged to and fro in mighty jets of their respective elements, and a crowd of air-spirits whizzed and whistled, fighting and wrestling with one another as though in a merry tournament. The Magus ascended once more and spread out his broad cloak; everything was at once wrapped in a dense vapour that arose from the earth, and when it dissolved, the place where the spirits had been fighting was occupied by a magnificent pool like a watery mirror, as clear as the sky, surrounded by gleaming stone and wondrous herbs and flowers; in its midst the spring gushed up cheerfully, sending out ripples as though in mischievous play.

At the very moment when the Magus Hermod's mysterious

prism dissolved to become a spring, the royal couple awoke from their long enchanted sleep. King Ophioch and Queen Liris hastened to the spot, driven by irresistible desire. They were the first to gaze into the water. As they beheld the shining blue sky, the bushes, the trees, the whole of nature, and their own selves, mirrored upside-down in its infinite depths, they felt as though dark veils were being rolled back to disclose a magnificent new world full of life and joy, and as they perceived this world they felt a delight such as they had never known or suspected. After gazing into the pool for a long time, they rose, looked at each other—and laughed: for the physical expression not only of intense well-being but also of joy at the victory of inner spiritual forces must be called laughter. If the transfiguration of Queen Liris's countenance, which for the first time lent her beautiful features true life and heavenly charms, had not sufficiently testified to her entire change of heart, it would have been apparent to all from the way she laughed. For her laughter was now so completely different from the giggling with which she had formerly annoyed the King that many sound judges claimed that it was not she who was laughing, but a wondrous being concealed within her. The same applied to King Ophioch's laughter.

As both laughed in this remarkable manner, they cried almost simultaneously: 'Oh! We were lying and dreaming sad dreams in a dismal, inhospitable foreign region, and have woken to find ourselves at home. Now we recognize ourselves in ourselves, and are no longer orphan children!' And then they embraced each other with every sign of the most heartfelt love. While the two embraced, everyone who could press close enough looked into the water; those who had been infected by the King's sorrow and looked into the watery mirror felt the same effects as the royal couple; those, however, who had previously been merry remained in the same state. Many doctors considered that it was ordinary water, lacking mineral enrichment, and many philosophers urged people not to gaze into the watery mirror, on the grounds that seeing oneself and the world upside-down can easily make one dizzy. There were even some people among the most highly educated class in the kingdom who maintained that the Fountain of Urdar did not exist. (The Fountain of

Urdar was the name which the King and the people immediately bestowed on the magnificent water that had sprung from Hermod's mysterious prism.) King Ophioch and Queen Liris knelt down at the feet of the great Magus Hermod who had brought them happiness and healing, and thanked him in the most elegant words and phrases that they could muster. The Magus Hermod raised them to their feet with proper dignity, embraced first the Queen and then the King, and promised that, being deeply concerned for the welfare of the land of Urdar, he would sometimes show himself in the observatory in the event of critical situations arising. King Ophioch was anxious to kiss his worthy hand, but he would not suffer this, and instead promptly rose into the air. From his lofty position he called down, in a voice that rang like metal bells that have been vigorously struck:

'Thought destroys intuition, and man, once torn away from his mother's breast, reels around without a home, prey to mad illusions, blind and insensate, until the veritable mirror of thought supplies thought itself with the knowledge that he *is* and that in the deepest and richest mine which the maternal Queen has opened up to him he commands as a lord, even if he must obey as a vassal.'

HERE ENDS THE STORY OF
KING OPHIOCH AND QUEEN LIRIS.

Celionati fell silent, and the youths too remained absorbed in the silent contemplation induced by the old Ciarlatano's tale, which they had expected to be very different.

At last Franz Reinhold broke the silence. 'Master Celionati,' said he, 'your tale recalls the Edda,* the Voluspa, the Somskritt,* and I don't know what other old mythical books; but if I understand you correctly, the Fountain of Urdar which brought happiness to the inhabitants of Urdar is precisely what we Germans call humour, the wondrous power, born from deep intuitive understanding of nature, by which thought creates its own ironic double, whose strange antics give delight by revealing the antics—let me keep to this impertinent word—of thought itself and of all sublunary being. But indeed, Master

Celionati, you have shown by your myth that you understand other kinds of fun than that of your Carnival; I henceforth count you as a member of the invisible church, and bow the knee to you, as King Ophioch did to the great Magus Hermod; for you too are a mighty wizard.'

'What are you talking about?' exclaimed Celionati. 'A tale? A myth? Have I told you, or tried to tell you, anything more than a pleasant story from the life of my friend Ruffiamonte? You must know that this person, my intimate friend, is himself the great Magus Hermod, who cured King Ophioch of his sorrow. If you don't believe me, you can ask him yourselves, for he is here, living in the Pistoia Palace.'

No sooner had Celionati mentioned the Pistoia Palace than everyone remembered the extraordinary masquerade which had entered the palace a few days earlier, and rained questions about it on the strange Ciarlatano, assuming that such an extraordinary person must be better informed than anyone else about the extraordinary procession.

'I'm quite sure', exclaimed Reinhold, laughing, 'that the handsome old man who was sitting in the tulip deep in study was your friend, the great Magus Hermod, or the wizard Ruffiamonte.'

'That is so, my son!' replied Celionati calmly. 'However, the time is not yet ripe to say much about the dwellers in the Pistoia Palace. Still, if King Cophetua could marry a beggar-maid, the great and powerful Princess Brambilla can perfectly well run after a bad comedian . . .'

Saying this, Celionati left the café, and nobody had the least idea what he meant by his last words; but since this was often the case with Celionati's utterances, nobody troubled to think much more about it.

While all this was happening in the Caffè Greco, Giglio was roaming up and down the Corso in his weird mask. He had not failed to obey Princess Brambilla's instructions by putting on a hat whose upturned brim made it resemble a strange kind of helmet, and arming himself with a broad wooden sword. His mind was filled with the lady of his heart; but he himself could not understand how it was that to win the love of a Princess did not strike him as anything special, or as the happiness reserved for dreams; in his impertinent self-assurance he believed that she must inevitably be his, because she could do nothing else. And this idea gave rise to reckless merriment which vented itself in the most exaggerated grimaces and by which, in his heart of hearts, Giglio himself was frightened.

Princess Brambilla was nowhere to be seen; but Giglio, quite beside himself, shrieked: 'Princess! Darling! Precious pet! I'll find you, I'll find you!' and knocked a hundred masks out of his way, like a madman, until he caught sight of a couple of dancers who absorbed his whole attention.

A funny little fellow, dressed like Giglio down to the slightest detail, and in size, posture, and so forth, his perfect double, was playing the guitar and dancing with a very elegantly dressed female who was accompanying him with castanets. If Giglio was petrified by the sight of his dancing double, his breast glowed again when he looked at the girl. He thought he had never before seen so much beauty and grace; each of her movements revealed the excitement born of rare enjoyment, and it was this excitement that lent an unspeakable charm even to the wild abandon of the dance.

There was no denying that the weird contrast between the two dancers had something grotesquely comical about it which could not but provoke one to laughter, even while gazing adoringly at the lovely girl; but it was this very feeling, composed of the most contradictory elements, that inspired the excitement born of strange, unspeakable pleasure, which had seized hold of the dancing girl and the funny fellow. Just as Giglio was beginning to suspect who the girl might be, a mask beside him said: 'That is Princess Brambilla, dancing with her lover, the Assyrian Prince Cornelio Chiapperi!'

CHAPTER 4

*On those useful inventions, sleep and dreams, and what Sancho
Panza thinks of them. How a Württemberg official fell downstairs
and Giglio was baffled by his own self. Rhetorical fire-screens,
double gibberish, and the white Moor. How old Prince Bastianello
di Pistoia scattered orange-pips in the Corso and took the masks
under his protection. The* beau jour *of plain girls. News of the
famous sorceress Circe, who now ties-ribbon-bows, and of the
delightful snakeweed that grows in happy Arcadia. How Giglio
stabbed himself in pure desperation and thereupon sat down at table
and helped himself freely, but then bade the Princess good night.*

You must not be surprised, beloved reader, if something that
may call itself a capriccio, but in fact resembles a fairy-tale as
closely as though it were one, contains a great deal of weird
goings-on and dream-like delusions, such as the human spirit
nurtures; or rather, if the action of the story is at times transferred to the inner lives of its characters. May not that indeed
be the right place for it? Perhaps, O my reader, you agree with
me that the human spirit is itself the most wondrous fairy-tale
imaginable. What a magnificent world lies locked up in our
bosoms! No horizon sets bounds to it, and its treasures outweigh the incalculable riches of the entire visible creation! How
death-like would be our life, poorer than a beggar's and blinder
than a mole's, if the World Spirit had not supplied us, nature's
hirelings, with an inexhaustible diamond-mine within ourselves, from which, in glorious radiance, shines forth the wondrous realm that is our very own possession! How gifted are
those who are conscious of this possession! Still more gifted and
blessed are those who can not only behold the gems of their
inner Peru, but also bring them to the surface, polish them, and
coax a more splendid fire from them. Well! Sancho* was of the
opinion that God should honour the man who invented sleep,
for he must have been a smart fellow; still more honour, however, should be paid to the inventor of the dream. Not the
dream that arises from our minds only when we lie under the

soft blanket of sleep—no, the dream that we dream our whole lives long, the dream that often lifts the oppressive burden of earthly cares upon its wings and silences every bitter woe, every dismal lament of disappointed hope, being itself a heavenly ray kindled in our bosoms both to inspire our incessant yearning and to promise its fulfilment.

He who has undertaken to present you, O beloved reader, with the strange capriccio of Princess Brambilla, recalled these ideas just as he was about to describe the curious mood that overcame the disguised Giglio Fava on hearing the whisper: 'That is Princess Brambilla dancing with her lover, the Assyrian Prince Cornelio Chiapperi!' Authors can seldom bear to withhold from the reader their thoughts concerning this or that stage in their heroes' progress; they are only too fond of supplying the chorus for their own books, and they give the name 'reflection' to anything that, though not necessary to the story, may be added as an agreeable flourish. The thoughts with which this chapter began may therefore be considered an agreeable flourish; for indeed they contributed as little to the story as to the description of Giglio's mood, which was by no means so strange and unusual as one might think after reading the author's preamble. To cut a long story short: all that happened to Giglio Fava, on hearing those words, was that he instantly believed himself to be the Assyrian Cornelio Chiapperi who was dancing with Princess Brambilla. Any philosopher worth his salt, with some practical experience behind him, will be able to explain this so fully and so simply that the mental experiment can be understood by fourth-formers. Any such psychologist can do no better than consult Mauchardt's *Handbook of Empirical Psychology** and cite the case of the Württemberg official who fell downstairs while drunk and then told the clerk who was guiding him how sorry he was at the latter's accident. 'To judge from all that we have hitherto learnt about Giglio Fava,' the psychologist will continue, 'he is suffering from a condition fully comparable to intoxication, a kind of spiritual drunkenness, arising from the stimulating effect on his nerves of certain eccentric conceptions of the self, and since actors are particularly inclined to this form of intoxication, therefore . . .' and so on and so forth.

Accordingly Giglio believed himself to be the Assyrian Prince
Cornelio Chiapperi; and though this was nothing out of the
ordinary, it might be harder to explain the origins of the unknown happiness whose fiery glow pervaded his inner being.
He plucked the strings of the guitar with ever greater force, and
his grimaces grew wilder as he abandoned himself more and
more to the furious dance. But his self stood opposite him,
dancing and capering and pulling hideous faces just like him,
and aiming blows at him with the broad wooden sword. Brambilla had disappeared!

'Ho, ho,' thought Giglio, 'it's only because of my self that I
can't see my bride-to-be, the Princess; I can't understand my
self, and my accursed self is attacking me with a dangerous
weapon, but I'll play and dance it to death, and then I shall be
my self and the Princess will be mine!'

Amid these rather confused thoughts, Giglio cut wilder and
wilder capers, but at that moment the wooden sword wielded
by his self struck Giglio's guitar so hard that it was shattered
to smithereens and Giglio tumbled over, landing very ungently
on his back. The guffaws of the crowd which had gathered
around the dancers roused Giglio from his fantasies. His spectacles and mask having come off in his fall, he was recognized,
and a hundred voices cried: 'Bravo, bravissimo, Signor Giglio!'

Giglio picked himself up and hastened away, since it suddenly
occurred to him that it was highly improper for a tragic actor
to provide the crowd with a grotesque spectacle. On reaching
his room he flung off the eccentric mask, wrapped himself in a
tabarro, and returned to the Corso. His aimless wanderings
eventually brought him to the Pistoia Palace, where he felt
himself suddenly being clasped from behind in somebody's
arms, while a voice whispered to him: 'Am I deceived by your
gait and posture, or is it you, my worthy Signor Giglio Fava?'

Giglio recognized the Abbate Antonio Chiari.* The sight of
him suddenly recalled to Giglio's mind the happy past epoch
when he still played tragic heroes and then, having removed his
buskins, stole up the narrow stairs to the charming Giacinta.
Since early youth, the Abbate Chiari (perhaps an ancestor of the
famous Chiari who had a feud with Count Gozzi and had to
admit defeat) had spared no effort to train his mind and his

fingers in the production of tragedies, in which astounding stories were brought on stage in a most charming and pleasing fashion. Terrible events were not allowed to take place before the spectators' eyes except in a mild, watered-down form, and the horrors of some dreadful deed would be plastered in the glutinous gum of so many fine words and phrases that the hearers consumed the sweet pap without a shudder and did not taste its bitter core. He converted even the flames of hell into a source of friendly light by placing in front of them the oil-soaked fire-screen of his rhetoric, and sprinkled the smoky waves of Acheron with the rose-water of his Martellian verses,* so that the infernal flood should flow softly and gently and turn into a poetic flood. Many people like this sort of thing, and hence it is no wonder that the Abbate Antonio Chiari could be called a popular poet. And since he was also especially adept in composing what are known as 'meaty' parts, it was inevitable that the poetic Abbate should have become the idol of the actors. Some witty French poet* says there are two kinds of gibberish: one that is unintelligible to readers and hearers, and a second, higher variety, which is unintelligible even to its creator, be he poet or prose-writer. It is to the latter, more sublime kind that the dramatic gibberish belongs, which provides most of the 'meaty' parts in tragedies. Speeches full of sonorous words, which neither the audience nor the actor understands and which even the poet did not understand, receive the loudest applause. The Abbate was a past master in composing such gibberish, just as Giglio Fava excelled in speaking it, while pulling faces and striking mad and fearsome postures that were sufficient by themselves to make the spectators shriek in tragic ecstasy. Accordingly the two of them, Giglio and Chiari, reinforced each other's efforts, and, of course, held each other in the highest possible esteem.

'How fortunate,' said the Abbate, 'that I've found you at last, Signor Giglio! Now I can learn from your own lips about your goings-on; I've been hearing about them piecemeal, and they sound thoroughly crazy and foolish. You've been badly treated, haven't you? Didn't that ass of an impresario throw you out of the theatre because my tragedies produced in you an enthusiasm which he mistook for madness, and because you would speak nothing except my verses? A bad business! You know, of course, that the idiot has entirely abandoned tragedy, and puts nothing on in his theatre but silly masked pantomimes, which I hate like poison. And so that most imbecile of impresarios refuses to accept any more of my tragedies, although as an honest man I can assure you, Signor Giglio, that in my two works I have managed to show the Italians what a tragedy really is. As for the ancient tragedians—Aeschylus, Sophocles, and so on, whom I expect you've heard of—it goes without saying that their harsh, rugged character is entirely unaesthetic. They can be excused only by the fact that art was then in its infancy, but they must be entirely distasteful to us. Products of our early poetic period like Trissino's* *Sofonisba* and Speroni's* *Canace*, which, from sheer ignorance, are cried up as great masterpieces, will doubtless be forgotten once my plays have instructed the public about the strength, the overwhelming power, of the genuine tragic feeling that is created by suitable language. It's only unfortunate at present that not a single theatre will perform my plays, since your former impresario, that villain, has changed his tune. But just wait, "il trotto d'asino dura poco".* It won't be long before your impresario falls flat on his face, along with his Arlecchino and Pantaloon and Brighella and all the other vile products of a despicable insanity, and then . . . Indeed, Signor Giglio, your departure from the theatre was like a death-blow to me; for no actor on earth has succeeded as you have done in understanding my completely original, unprecedented ideas . . . But let's get out of this dreadful, deafening crowd! Come home with me, and I'll read you my latest tragedy, which will cause you more astonishment than you have ever felt before. I have entitled it *The White Moor*. Don't be put off by the strange name! It is perfectly appropriate to the extraordinary, unprecedented character of the play.'

Each word uttered by the garrulous Abbate helped to release Giglio from his previous state of tension. His heart swelled with joy when he imagined himself once more as a tragic hero, declaiming the incomparable verses of the Abbate Antonio Chiari. He asked the poet very insistently whether *The White Moor* contained a really 'meaty' part for him to play.

'Did I ever, in any tragedy, compose parts that were *not*

meaty?' replied the Abbate heatedly. 'It's a misfortune that my plays can't be performed entirely by first-rate actors, right down to the smallest part. *The White Moor* includes a slave, at the very beginning of the catastrophe, who speaks the lines:

> Ah, doleful day! most cruel of deceits!
> Ah, master most unfortunate! your death
> Makes me shed tears and instantly depart!

whereupon he does indeed instantly depart, never to appear again. The part is by no means extensive, I confess; but believe you me, Signor Giglio, it takes almost a generation for the best actor to deliver these lines in the spirit in which I received and composed them, and in such a way as to enchant the public and transport it into paroxysms of ecstasy.'

During this conversation the Abbate and Giglio reached the Via del Babuino, where the Abbate lived. They had to ascend such a rickety flight of stairs that Giglio, for the second time, had a vivid recollection of Giacinta and secretly wished he could meet that lovely creature rather than the Abbate's white Moor.

The Abbate lit two candles, moved an armchair in front of the table for Giglio's benefit, fetched out a fairly stout manuscript, sat down opposite Giglio and began very solemnly: 'The White Moor, a tragedy,' and so on.

The first scene began with a long monologue by some important character, who first talked about the weather, expressing the hope that the impending grape-harvest would be plenteous, and then reflected on the unlawfulness of fratricide.

Giglio himself could not tell how it was that the Abbate's verses, which he had previously thought supremely glorious, now seemed so silly, so puerile, so tedious. Yes, even though the Abbate made the walls shudder by delivering all the speeches in powerful, booming tones with the most exaggerated rhetorical effect, none the less Giglio sank into a reverie, recalling all the strange things that had befallen him since the day when the Pistoia Palace opened to receive the extraordinary masquerade. Wholly absorbed in these thoughts, he reclined in his armchair, folded his arms, and let his head sink lower and lower towards his chest.

A heavy blow on his shoulder shook him out of his reverie.

'What?' shouted the infuriated Abbate, who had sprung up and dealt him the blow, 'I really believe you're asleep! Don't you want to hear my *White Moor*? Ha! Now I understand everything. Your impresario was quite right to throw you out; you have turned into a wretched lad unable to comprehend or appreciate the highest flights of poetry. Do you realize that your fate is now sealed, that you can never again raise yourself from the slime into which you have sunk? You fell asleep listening to my *White Moor*; that is a crime which nothing can expiate, a sin against the Holy Ghost. Get out of my sight!'

Giglio was frightened out of his wits by the Abbate's outburst of rage. He pointed out, in melancholy and humble tones, that a strong and resolute spirit was needed to respond to his tragedies, whereas he (Giglio) felt crushed and overwhelmed by the events, some of them strange and ghostly, others unfortunate, in which he had been caught up during the last few days.

'Believe me, Signor Abbate,' said Giglio, 'I am in the clutches of a mysterious fate. I am like a broken zither that cannot receive or give out a single harmonious note. If you fancied that I fell asleep during your magnificent verses, then this much is certain, that I was so overpowered by an irresistible, morbid drowsiness that even the most powerful speeches in your incomparable *White Moor* seemed dull and tedious.'

'Are you off your head?' shouted the Abbate.

'Don't fly into such a rage!' went on Giglio. 'I revere you as the supreme master to whom I owe all my art, and I am seeking your advice and help. Permit me to recount everything that has befallen me, and stand by me in my hour of need! Help me to take my place in the brilliant sunshine of fame that will radiate from your *White Moor*, and recover from my desperate fever!'

Mollified by these words, the Abbate listened to the whole story of mad Celionati, Princess Brambilla, and so on. When Giglio had finished, the Abbate spent a few moments in deep thought and then began, in grave and solemn tones: 'From what you have told me, my son Giglio, I infer correctly that you are entirely blameless. I forgive you, and to show you that my magnanimity and my kindness are unlimited, I shall confer upon you the utmost happiness that you will ever encounter in your earthly career! Take the part of the White Moor, and let your most ardent yearning for the sublime be stilled when you play it! But, O my son Giglio, you are caught in the Devil's snares. An infernal cabal against sublime poetry, against my tragedies, against myself, is trying to employ you as a fatal tool. Have you never heard of old Prince Bastianello di Pistoia, who used to dwell in the old palace that the masked rabble entered, and who vanished from Rome without a trace, several years ago? Well, this old Prince Bastianello was an odd fish, silly and eccentric in all his words and actions. For example, he claimed to be descended from the royal line of a distant unknown country, and to be three or four hundred years old, although I myself knew the priest who baptized him here in Rome. He often spoke of mysterious visits from his family, and indeed the most extraordinary figures often appeared suddenly in his house, and then vanished as suddenly as they had come. Is anything easier than to dress servants and maids in strange costumes? For that's all that those figures were, although the stupid populace gaped at them in astonishment and took the Prince for something quite out of the ordinary, perhaps even for a magician. He was always up to some tomfoolery, and it's quite certain that once at Carnival he scattered orange-pips in the middle of the Corso, and the pips immediately burst and produced pretty little Pulcinellas, to the delight of the crowd; the Prince said these were the Romans' sweetest fruit.

'Anyway, why should I bore you by describing the Prince's crazy nonsense, instead of telling you straight away what makes the Prince such a dangerous person? Can you imagine that the old wretch was planning to undermine all good taste in literature and art? Can you imagine that, as regards the theatre, he defended the masks and would tolerate only ancient tragedy, but then spoke of a kind of tragedy that only an addled brain could devise? I never quite understood what he was getting at, but it sounded almost as though he were asserting that the highest tragedy must be produced by a special kind of humour. And—no, it's incredible, it's almost impossible to say—he claimed that my tragedies—do you understand?—*my* tragedies were uncommonly humorous, though in a different way, since in them the rhetoric of tragedy unwittingly parodied itself. Well, what harm can foolish ideas and opinions do? If only the

Prince had stopped there; but deeds, foul deeds, resulted from his enmity towards me and my tragedies! Even before you came to Rome, the terrible event had befallen me. My most magnificent tragedy (except for *The White Moor*), *The Brother's Ghost Revenged*, was being performed. The actors excelled themselves; never before had they grasped so well the inner meaning of my words, never before had their movements and postures been so truly tragic. Let me take this opportunity of telling you, Signor Giglio, that in your gestures, and especially in your postures, you still have a lot to learn. Signor Zechielli, my chief tragedian at that time, could stand with his legs wide apart, his feet planted firmly on the ground, his arms raised in the air, and gradually twist his body round until his face was looking over his back, so that his gestures and facial expressions made the audience think him a double-faced Janus. That kind of thing generally creates the most striking effect, but it has to be done every time I say "He begins to despair"! Bear that in mind, my son, and do your best to despair like Signor Zechielli! But to come back to my *Brother's Ghost*: the performance was the finest I had ever seen, yet at every speech my hero uttered the public burst into uncontrollable laughter. Since I could see the Prince di Pistoia in his box, intoning this laughter each time, there could be no doubt that he was responsible for this frightful misdeed, though God knows what devilish plots and ploys he used. How glad I was when the Prince disappeared from Rome! But his spirit lives on in the confounded old Ciarlatano, mad Celionati, who has already tried, albeit in vain, to ridicule my tragedies in puppet-theatres. And it is only too certain that Prince Bastianello is haunting Rome once more; that is shown by the grotesque masquerade that entered his palace. Celionati is pursuing you in order to do me harm. He has already managed to drive you off the boards and destroy your impresario's tragic theatre. Now you are to be tempted into complete apostasy from art, by having your head stuffed with all manner of crazy notions, phantasms of princesses, grotesque ghosts, and so forth. Take my advice, Signor Giglio, stay quietly at home, drink more water than wine, and apply your care and diligence to the study of my *White Moor*, which I'll give you to take with you! Only in *The White Moor* can you seek and find comfort and peace, followed by happiness, honour and fame. Farewell, Signor Giglio!'

The following morning Giglio tried to do as the Abbate had bidden him and study the fine tragedy of *The White Moor*. He was unsuccessful, however, because all the letters on every page melted before his eyes into the image of the sweet and lovely Giacinta Soardi. 'No,' cried Giglio impatiently at last, 'I can't stand it any longer, I must go to her, my fair one. I know she still loves me, she can't help it, and despite her *smorfia* she won't be able to conceal it when she sees me again. Then I'll surely be rid of the fever which that confounded fellow Celionati has cast on me, and from the mad confusion of dreams and fancies I shall rise again, new-born, as a White Moor, like the phoenix from the ashes! Blessed Abbate Chiari, you have guided me back to the right path.'

Giglio promptly put on his best clothes in order to betake himself to Bescapi's house where his sweetheart, as he thought, was to be found. He was just stepping out of the door when he suddenly felt the effects of *The White Moor* which he had been trying to read. Tragic rhetoric overcame him like a fit of strong fever! 'What?' he cried, thrusting out his right foot, leaning backwards, and extending both arms with his fingers spread out as though warding off a ghost; 'what if she no longer loves me? What if, seduced by the magical phantasms of the noble world of Orcus, drugged by a Lethean potion that brings oblivion and has blotted out the thought of me, she has forgotten me altogether? What if a rival . . . Horrible thought, born of black Tartarus and the fecund chasms of death! Ha, despair! Murder and death! Come hither, sweet friend, who expiates all dishonour in blood's roseate glow, who gives peace and comfort—and *revenge*.' Giglio roared out the last words so loudly that the whole house echoed. At the same time he reached for the naked dagger that was lying on the table, and put it in his belt. It was, however, only a stage dagger.

Master Bescapi seemed a good deal surprised when Giglio asked about Giacinta. He claimed that she had never stayed in his house, and Giglio's asseverations that he had seen her a few days before on the balcony, and spoken with her, were not of the slightest help; instead, Bescapi cut short the conversation and enquired with a smile how Giglio had enjoyed his recent blood-letting. The moment Giglio heard his blood-letting mentioned, he dashed headlong away. As he was crossing the Piazza di Spagna, he saw an old woman in front of him, laboriously carrying a covered basket, and recognized her as old Beatrice. 'Ha,' he murmured, 'you shall be my guiding star, I'll follow you!' He was a good deal surprised when the old woman crept, rather than walked, to the street where Giacinta had previously lived, and when she stopped outside Signor Pasquale's front door and put down her heavy basket. At that moment she caught sight of Giglio, who had been following close on her heels.

'Ha!' she cried, 'my sweet good-for-nothing, are you showing your face again at last? A fine faithful lover you are, gadding about wherever you have no business to be, and forgetting your sweetheart in the merry Carnival season! Now, just help me to carry this heavy basket upstairs, and then you can see whether little Giacinta is prepared to box your ears and set your shaky head to rights.'

Giglio heaped bitter reproaches on the old woman for mocking him with the foolish lie about Giacinta being in prison; the old woman, however, claimed to know nothing of this, but maintained that Giglio had imagined it all, and that Giacinta had never left the parlour in Signor Pasquale's house and had been more industrious during this Carnival than ever before. Giglio rubbed his brow, and tugged his nose, as though he were trying to rouse himself from sleep. 'It's only too certain,' said he, 'either I'm dreaming now, or else I've been having the most bewildering dream the whole time . . .'

'Take hold of the basket, if you don't mind', interrupted the old woman. 'The burden that weighs down your back will tell you better than anything else whether or not you're dreaming.'

Giglio promptly lifted the basket and ascended the narrow staircase, with the most wondrous sensations in his bosom. 'What on earth have you got in the basket?' he asked the old woman, who was walking in front of him.

'What a silly question!' she replied. 'I suppose you've never known me go to the market to shop for my little Giacinta?

Besides, we're expecting guests today . . .'

'Gue-e-ests?' repeated Giglio slowly. At that moment, however, they reached the top of the stairs. The old woman told Giglio to put the basket down and go into the parlour, where he would find Giacinta.

Giglio's heart was pounding with nervous anticipation and delicious fear. He knocked gently and opened the door. There was Giacinta, as usual, busily working at the table, which was laden with flowers, ribbons, all kinds of fabrics, and so forth.

'Why,' cried Giacinta, gazing at Giglio with shining eyes, 'Signor Giglio, where have you come from all of a sudden? I thought you had left Rome long ago?'

Giglio found his sweetheart so exceptionally pretty that he remained standing in the doorway, startled and speechless. And indeed everything about her seemed bathed in a rare and magical grace; a richer incarnadine was glowing on her cheeks, and her eyes were shining, as has been said, right into Giglio's heart. One need only say that Giacinta had her *beau jour*; but as this French word can no longer be tolerated, it may be remarked in passing that there is indeed such a thing as the *beau jour* and that it works in a particular way. A nice young lady who is lacking in beauty, or is even decidedly ugly, need only think (whether inspired by internal or external causes): 'I'm a very pretty girl, after all!' and she can be sure that this splendid idea and the sublime well-being within her will automatically produce the *beau jour*.

At last Giglio, quite beside himself, rushed over to his sweetheart, flung himself at her feet, and seized her hands with a tragic cry of 'My Giacinta, my sweet life!' Suddenly, however, he felt his finger being deeply pricked by a pin, so that he jumped up in pain and felt compelled to cut several capers amid cries of 'Damnation!'

Giacinta gave a peal of laughter, and then said, very quietly and calmly: 'You see, dear Signor Giglio, that served you right for your ill-mannered and impetuous behaviour. Apart from that, it is very good of you to call on me, for soon you may not be able to see me with so little ceremony. You have my permission to remain in my company. Sit down on this chair facing me and tell me how you have been all this while, what fine new parts you are playing, and so forth! You know I enjoy hearing about that, and so long as you avoid the confounded tearful rhetoric with which the Signor Abbate Chiari—may God not deny him everlasting bliss on this account!—has bewitched you, it is very pleasant to listen to you.'

'My Giacinta,' said Giglio, in agonies from love and the pinprick, 'let us forget the torture of parting! They have returned, the sweet and blissful hours of happiness, of love . . .'

'I don't know what nonsense you're talking,' interrupted Giacinta. 'You speak of the torture of parting, and I can assure you that for my part, if I really thought that you were leaving me, I wouldn't feel anything, and I certainly wouldn't feel tortured. If by blissful hours you mean those in which you did your best to bore me, then I don't think these will ever return. But between you and me, Signor Giglio, there's a lot about you that I like, you have sometimes been quite nice to me, and I will gladly permit you to see me in future as much as is proper, although circumstances that restrict any familiarity will oblige us to remain at a distance and place you under some restraint.'

'Giacinta!' cried Giglio, 'what a strange way to talk!'

'There's nothing strange about it', replied Giacinta. 'Just sit down quietly, my good Giglio! This may be the last time that we are together so familiarly. But you may always be sure of my favour; for, as I said, I shall never cease to feel goodwill towards you.'

Beatrice came in carrying a couple of plates with delicious fruit; she also had a decent-looking bottle under her arm. This was evidently what the basket had contained. Through the open door Giglio could see a merry fire crackling on the hearth, and the kitchen table was heavily laden with dainties of all kinds.

'Little Giacinta,' said Beatrice with a chuckle, 'if our modest meal is to honour our guest properly, I must have some more money.'

'Take as much as you need,' replied Giacinta, handing the old woman a little purse through which fine ducats could be seen gleaming. Giglio froze on recognizing it as the twin brother of the purse which, as he was compelled to assume, Celionati had slipped into his pocket, containing ducats which were now dwindling. 'Is this an infernal deceit?' he shrieked, tearing the purse from the old woman's hand and holding it in front of his eyes. He sank back into his chair in exhaustion, however, when he read on the purse the message: 'Remember the image of your dream!'

'Ho, ho, Signor Penniless!' growled the old woman, retrieving the purse from Giglio's outstretched hand. 'You're astonished to see such a fine sight, are you? Listen to this delightful music, and enjoy it!' With these words she shook the purse so that the gold in it chinked, and left the room.

'Giacinta,' said Giglio, beside himself with pain and misery, 'what hideous, frightful mystery . . . Speak! Pronounce my death!'

'You're just the same as ever', replied Giacinta, holding the slender needle towards the light between her tapering fingers and passing the silvery thread adroitly through the eye. 'You're so used to going into an ecstasy about everything that you walk about like a continual boring tragedy, uttering your still more boring "Oh, alas, woe is me!" There's no question here of anything hideous or frightful; but if you're capable of behaving properly, instead of cavorting around like a half-crazy person, I could tell you a thing or two.'

'Speak, and slay me!' murmured Giglio in a strangled voice.

'Do you remember, Signor Giglio,' began Giacinta, 'how you once told me, not so very long ago, what a wonderful being a young actor is? You described such an admirable hero as a walking love-intrigue, a living romance on two legs, and I don't know what else. Now I maintain that a young seamstress, endowed by heaven with a pretty figure, a nice face, and, above all, that inward magical power by virtue of which a girl is truly a girl, is a much more wonderful being. Such a favourite child of kindly nature really deserves to be called a delightful adventure floating in the air, and the narrow staircase that leads you to her is the heavenly ladder that admits you to the realm of youthfully audacious dreams of love. She is herself the delicate mystery of feminine adornment which, now in the luminous splendour of sumptuous colours, now in the gentle light of the moon's white rays, of roseate mists, or the blue haze of evening, casts a delightful spell over you men. Allured by yearning and desire, you approach the wondrous mystery, you behold the

mighty fairy amid her magical instruments; but then, touched
by her little white fingers, her lace becomes an amorous net,
and every ribbon she ties becomes a snare in which you are
caught. And her eyes reflect the delicious folly of love, which
is conscious of itself and takes heartfelt pleasure in itself. You
hear your sighs echoed from within the fair one's breast, but
with charming softness, as the yearning echo calls to the lover
from the distant magical mountains. Neither rank nor station
counts: for the wealthy prince and the poor actor, the little room
of his charming Circe* is the flowery, verdant Arcadia* offering
refuge in the barren desert of his life. And if some snakeweed
grows among the beautiful flowers of this Arcadia, what does
it matter? It is of the seductive kind, with magnificent blossoms
and a still more beautiful fragrance . . .'

'Oh, yes,' interrupted Giglio, 'and the flower itself conceals
the creature whose name is borne by that blossoming, fragrant
herb; it darts out and suddenly pierces you with its tongue, like
a sharp pin . . .'

'Whenever', resumed Giacinta, 'some strange man, who has
no business in Arcadia, sticks his stupid nose into it.'

'Nicely put, my sweet Giacinta!' replied Giglio wrathfully. 'I
must confess that since I last saw you you have become wondrously clever. You philosophize about yourself in a way that
astonishes me. I expect you fancy yourself as an enchanting
Circe in the charming Arcadia of your garret, which Master
Bescapi does not fail to provide with the instruments needful
for magic.'

'Perhaps it's the same for me as it is for you', went on Giacinta, very calmly. 'I too have had all sorts of pleasant dreams.
But, my good Giglio, as for all the things I said about the
character of a pretty seamstress, take them at least partly as a
joke, as mischievous teasing, and don't apply it to me, especially
as this may be the last piece of millinery I will ever do. Don't
be alarmed, my good Giglio! It's quite likely that on the last
day of Carnival I shall exchange this shabby dress for a purple
robe, and this little stool for a throne!'

'Heaven and hell!' shouted Giglio, springing up violently
with his clenched fist against his brow. 'Death and damnation!
So what that hypocritical villain whispered in my ear is true

after all? Ha! Open and spout thy flame, abyss of Orcus! Arise, ye sable sprites of Acheron! Enough!' Giglio launched into a hideous monologue expressing despair, taken from one of the Abbate Chiari's tragedies. Since he had declaimed this monologue to her a hundred times, Giacinta could remember every single line of it, and, without looking up from her work, prompted her despairing lover whenever his memory failed him. Finally he drew his dagger, plunged it into his breast, sank down so heavily that the room re-echoed, stood up again, dusted his clothes, wiped the perspiration from his brow, and asked with a smile: 'That's real professional stuff, isn't it, Giacinta?'

'Certainly,' replied Giacinta, without moving. 'You gave an excellent performance, Giglio dear. But now I think it's time for supper.'

Old Beatrice, meanwhile, had laid the table, served a couple of dishes from which a wonderful aroma issued, and placed beside them the mysterious bottle and gleaming crystal glasses. As soon as Giglio saw this, he seemed quite beside himself: 'Ha, the guest, the Prince . . . What is the matter with me? O God! I wasn't acting, I really am in despair. Yes, you have plunged me into the depths of mad despair, you faithless betrayer, serpent, basilisk—you crocodile! But revenge! Revenge!' As he uttered these words he brandished his stage dagger, which he had picked up from the floor, in the air. But Giacinta, having thrown her work on to her sewing-table and got to her feet, took him by the arm and said: 'Don't be a fool, Giglio dear! Give this dangerous instrument to old Beatrice, so that she can make it into tooth-picks, and sit down beside me at the table; for you really are the only guest I was expecting.' Mollified all of a sudden, Giglio was patience itself; he allowed her to lead him to the table, and helped himself to the dishes without the least constraint.

Giacinta continued to talk quietly and good-humouredly about her imminent happiness, and repeatedly assured Giglio that she would not become so puffed up with pride as to forget his face; on the contrary, if she saw him at a distance, she would undoubtedly recollect him and send him plenty of ducats, so that he should never be short of rosemary-coloured stockings and perfumed gloves. After Giglio had drunk a few glasses of wine, the whole wondrous fable of Princess Brambilla returned to his mind, and he replied in friendly tones that he was very glad that Giacinta was so kindly disposed towards him; but neither her pride nor her ducats would be of any use to him, as he was about to leap to the rank of a prince. He then recounted how the grandest and richest Princess in the world had chosen him to be her knight, and how at the end of the Carnival, as the husband of his noble lady, he hoped to bid farewell for ever to the impoverished life he had led hitherto. Giacinta seemed delighted by Giglio's good fortune, and the two of them had a pleasant chat about the pleasures and riches that were in store for them.

'It would be nice', said Giglio at last, 'if the kingdoms we are going to rule over were close together, so that we could keep up our acquaintance; but unless I'm mistaken, the domain of my adored Princess is beyond India, on your left after you pass Persia.'

'That's a pity', replied Giacinta; 'I expect I shall have to go a long way off, too, for the realm of my princely husband is supposed to be near Bergamo.* But I expect we can find a way of becoming and remaining neighbours.'

They both agreed that their future kingdoms must be transferred to the Frascati area.

'Good night, my dear Princess!' said Giglio.

'I wish you agreeable repose, my dear Prince!' replied Giacinta.

And so, as dusk fell, they parted peacefully and pleasantly.

CHAPTER 5

*How Giglio, during the period when the human spirit is perfectly
sober, arrived at a wise decision, put Fortunatus's purse in his
pocket, and cast a haughty glance at an exceedingly humble tailor.
The Pistoia Palace and its wonders. The wise man in the tulip
gives a reading. King Solomon the Prince of Spirits and Princess
Mystilis. How an old Magus put on a black dressing-gown, donned
a sable cap, and uttered prophecies in bad verses and with a tousled
beard. Unhappy fate of a feather-brain. The kind reader fails to
learn in this chapter what else happened when Giglio was dancing
with the fair unknown.*

It is written in some book stuffed with sage advice that anyone
endowed with a degree of imagination suffers from a kind of
insanity that ebbs and flows like the tide. Its time of high water,
when the billows rise and roar, is nightfall, just as the low water
comes in the early hours of the morning, when one has just
woken and is drinking one's cup of coffee. Hence the above-
mentioned book sagely advises us to use this period, when our
minds are so marvellously clear and lucid, for all the most
important matters in life. It is only in the morning that one
should marry, read unfavourable reviews, make one's will, beat
one's servant, and so forth.

It was in this pleasant low-water period, when the human
spirit rejoices in perfect sobriety, that Giglio Fava became
alarmed at his own folly and wondered why he had not long
since performed the action the necessity for which had been, so
to speak, staring him in the face. 'It's only too certain', he
thought, agreeably conscious of his perfectly sound intellect,
'that old Celionati is half mad, and that he not only enjoys his
madness but deliberately sets himself to draw other, perfectly
sane people into it. It's equally certain, however, that the richest
and most beautiful Princess in the world, the divine Brambilla,
has taken up residence in the Pistoia Palace, and—O heaven
and earth! can such a hope be deceitful, when it has been
confirmed by premonitions, by dreams, by the rosy lips of the

most charming mask of all—that the sweet ray of love, darted from her heavenly eyes, has fallen upon my fortunate self? Concealed by her veil, hidden behind the rails of a box, she saw me as I was acting some Prince or other, and her heart was mine! How could she approach me directly, after all? Doesn't the gracious being need intermediaries, confidantes, to spin the thread which will at last be entwined to form the sweetest of bonds? No matter how it happened, Celionati is beyond doubt the person who will lead me into the Princess's arms—but instead of straightforwardly taking a direct course, he plunges me head over heels in a sea of madness and mockery, persuades me that I must assume a ridiculous disguise in order to seek the fairest of princesses on the Corso, tells me of Assyrian princes, of magicians . . . Away with all this tomfoolery, away with mad Celionati! What prevents me from putting on smart clothes, walking straight into the Pistoia Palace and throwing myself at the feet of Her Serene Highness? O God, why didn't I do that yesterday, or the day before?'

To Giglio's displeasure, on conducting a hasty inspection of his wardrobe, he could not but confess that his plumed hat exactly resembled a plucked cockerel, that his jerkin, after being dyed three times, glistened with all the colours of the rainbow, that his cloak only too clearly disclosed the art of the tailor whose bold stitching bade defiance to devouring Time, and that his familiar blue silk breeches and pink stockings were autumnally faded. In a sorrowful mood, he reached for the purse which he assumed to be almost empty, and found it full to bursting 'Divine Brambilla!' he cried in rapture, 'yes, divine Brambilla, I remember you, I remember the lovely image of my dreams!'

You may imagine that Giglio, with what seemed to be Fortunatus's purse in his pocket, immediately scurried through all the tailors' shops and old-clothes shops in order to procure a suit as beautiful as any prince in the theatre ever wore. Nothing he was shown was rich or splendid enough for him. Finally he reflected that he would be satisfied only with a suit made by the skilled hand of Bescapi, and promptly betook himself to the master.

On hearing Giglio's request, Master Bescapi beamed radiantly, exclaimed: 'Oh, my dear Signor Giglio, I have just what you want', and led his eager customer into another room. Giglio, however, was not a little surprised to find no suits here except the complete outfits of the Italian comedy and, in addition, the wildest and most grotesque masks. Thinking that Master Bescapi had misunderstood him, he described in a rather irritated tone the grand and sumptuous costume in which he wanted to array himself.

'Oh, heavens!' cried Bescapi in a melancholy voice, 'what's this I hear? Surely, my dear Signor, your attacks have not . . .'

'If you are willing to sell me the suit I want, master tailor,' interrupted Giglio impatiently, rattling the ducats in his purse, 'well and good; if not, then forget about it . . .'

'Now, now,' said Master Bescapi apologetically, 'please don't be cross, Signor Giglio! Oh dear, you don't realize how much I want to help you. Oh, if only you had just a tiny bit of sense!'

'How dare you, master tailor?' cried Giglio angrily.

'Why,' went on Bescapi, 'if I'm a master tailor, I only wish that I could measure you for a suit with the measure that would serve you properly. You are heading for disaster, Signor Giglio, and I am sorry that I cannot repeat to you all the things that the wise Celionati has told me about you and your impending fate.'

'Oho?' said Giglio, 'the *wise* Signor Celionati? That fine fellow of a mountebank who is persecuting me in every possible way, who wants to trick me out of my greatest good fortune, because he hates my talents and myself, because he rebels against the gravity of superior natures, because he would like to turn everything into foolish mummery and witless jesting! Oh, my dear Master Bescapi, I know everything; the worthy Abbate Chiari has revealed all his schemes to me. The Abbate is the most splendid man and the most poetical character that you could hope to meet; for he created the white Moor for *me*, and nobody in the whole wide world, I tell you, could play the white Moor, except me.'

'What are you saying?' cried Master Bescapi with a roar of laughter. 'Has the worthy Abbate (whom I hope Heaven will soon summon to an assembly of superior natures), has he managed to wash a Moor white with the tears which he pours out so copiously?'

'Let me ask you once more, Master Bescapi,' said Giglio, suppressing his anger with difficulty, 'whether or not you are willing to sell me the suit I want in return for my good solid ducats?'

'With pleasure,' replied Bescapi cheerfully, 'with pleasure, my dear Signor Giglio!'

Thereupon the Master opened the room in which the most sumptuous and magnificent suits were hanging. Giglio's eye was immediately caught by a complete costume that was indeed very sumptuous, though its strange medley of colours made it look somewhat fantastic. Master Bescapi declared that this costume was very expensive and would probably be beyond Giglio's reach. However, when Giglio insisted on buying the costume, drew out his purse, and told the master to name whatever price he wanted, Bescapi explained that he could not dispose of the suit, as it was intended for a foreign prince, none other than Prince Cornelio Chiapperi.

'What?' cried Giglio, in a transport of ecstasy, 'what are you saying? In that case the costume was made for nobody but me. Happy Bescapi! It is none other than Prince Cornelio Chiapperi who stands before you, and who has found his innermost being, his true self, in your shop!'

The moment Giglio had spoken these words, Master Bescapi snatched the suit from the wall, and called one of his lads, whom he ordered to pack the suit in a basket and carry it after His Serene Highness.

'Keep your money, my honoured Prince!' cried the master, as Giglio was about to pay. 'You must be in a hurry. Your most humble servant will get his money in due course; perhaps the white Moor will settle this trifling account! God guard you, my excellent Prince!'

Casting a haughty glance at the master, who was almost touching the ground in his dainty and obsequious bows, Giglio slipped Fortunatus's purse in his pocket and departed thence with the beautiful Prince's costume.

The suit fitted so perfectly that Giglio's uncontrollable joy made him press a gleaming ducat into the hand of the tailor's lad who had helped him undress. The lad asked for a couple of good *paoli* instead, since he had heard that the gold of stage princes was worthless and that their ducats were only buttons or counters. Giglio, however, threw the boy out for being too clever by half.

After Giglio had sufficiently practised his beautiful and graceful gestures in front of the mirror, after he had memorized the fantastic language of lovesick heroes and convinced himself that he was totally irresistible, he made his way to the Pistoia Palace, just as dusk was beginning to fall.

The door, not being locked, yielded to the pressure of his hand, and he entered a spacious pillared hallway in which a funereal silence reigned. As he looked around in astonishment, dim pictures of the past arose from the deepest recesses of his mind. He felt as though he had been here at some earlier time, but as his soul could form no clear image, and all his efforts to visualize these pictures were in vain, he was overcome by a fear and apprehension that wholly destroyed his resolve to pursue his adventure.

Just as he was about to leave the palace, he almost collapsed with terror as his own self, seemingly veiled in mist, suddenly approached him. Soon, however, he realized that what he had taken for his double was his picture, reflected in a dark mirror on the wall. But at that moment he also felt as though a hundred sweet, tiny voices were whispering: 'Oh, Signor Giglio, how handsome you are, how wondrously good-looking!' Giglio struck a pose in front of the mirror, raised his head, put his left hand on his hip, raised his right hand, and exclaimed rhetorically: 'Courage, Giglio, courage! Your happiness is assured, make haste to seize it!' Thereupon he began to march up and down with ever firmer steps, clearing his throat and coughing, but all remained silent as the grave, and no living being was to be heard. He tried to open one or two doors that must lead into the rooms, but all were firmly locked.

What remained but to ascend the wide marble staircase that gracefully wound its way upwards on either side of the hallway?

Having reached the upper corridor, whose decoration was in keeping with the simple majesty of the whole building, Giglio thought he could hear, in the far distance, the sounds of a foreign and strange-sounding instrument. He crept cautiously onward and soon perceived a dazzling ray of light coming through the keyhole of the door opposite him in the corridor. He could now also make out that what he had mistaken for the sound of an unknown instrument was the voice of a man speaking, although the voice did indeed sound strange, since it resembled now the clashing of cymbals, now the blowing of a deep, hollow pipe. As soon as Giglio was beside the door, it opened very softly by itself. Giglio entered and remained rooted to the spot in profound astonishment.

Giglio found himself in an immense hall, the walls of which were covered with purple-streaked marble; from its lofty dome descended a lamp whose fiery radiance immersed the scene in burning gold. In the background, a rich drapery of gold brocade formed a canopy under which, on a dais with five steps leading up to it, stood a gilded armchair upon coloured rugs. Sitting in the chair, and wearing a silver brocade robe, was the little old man with the long white beard who had been pursuing his studies in the tulip when Princess Brambilla entered the palace. As before, he was wearing a silver funnel on his venerable head; as before, he had a monstrous pair of spectacles on his nose; as before, he was reading, though now out loud (Giglio had heard his voice in the distance), from a large book that lay open in front of him on the back of a kneeling Moor. On either side stood the ostriches, like mighty bodyguards; when the old man had finished a page, they alternately turned over the leaf with their beaks.

All round, in a closed semicircle, sat a good hundred ladies, as wondrously beautiful as fairies and clad in the sumptuous splendour for which fairies are renowned. All were industriously making lace. In the centre of the semicircle, in front of the old man, was a small porphyry altar, and on it were two odd little dolls, in the attitude of people plunged in slumber, with royal crowns on their heads.

When Giglio had in some measure recovered from his astonishment, he wanted to give notice of his presence. Scarcely, however, had he even thought of speaking, when he received a rough thump on his back. Only then, to his considerable alarm, did he notice a row of Moors armed with long pikes and short sabres, in whose midst he was standing; they were staring at him with flashing eyes and baring their ivory teeth at him.

Giglio realized that the best course was to be patient.

What the old man was reading to the lace-making ladies, however, ran more or less as follows.

'The fiery sign of Aquarius is over our heads; the dolphin is swimming eastward through surging waves and spurting pure crystal from its nostrils into the sombre floods! It is time for me to speak to you of the great mysteries that have been enacted, of the wondrous enigma whose solution will rescue you from perishing miserably.

'The Magus Hermod was standing on the battlements of the tower, observing the motion of the heavenly bodies. Just then four old men, swathed in robes whose colour resembled that of fallen leaves, strode through the forest towards the tower and, on reaching its base, raised a mighty lament. "Hear us! Hear us, great Hermod! Be not deaf to our appeal, awake from your deep sleep! If we only had the strength to bend King Ophioch's bow, we would shoot an arrow through your heart, as he did, and you would have to descend, instead of standing aloft in the gale, like an insensible block! But, worthy sage, if you will not awaken, we have some missiles in readiness, and we shall tap you on the chest with a few fair-sized stones, to arouse the human feelings locked therein! Awake, magnificent sage!"

'The Magus Hermod looked down, leant over the parapet, and spoke in a voice that resembled the roaring of the sea and the howling of the approaching tempest: "You people down below, don't be fools! I am not sleeping, and am not to be awakened by arrows and lumps of rock. I already have some idea what you are after, my dear people! Wait a little, I shall come down directly. In the meantime you can pick some strawberries, or play catch-as-catch-can on the grassy rocks. I'll be down directly."

'When Hermod had come down and seated himself upon a large rock covered by a soft and many-coloured carpet of the finest moss, one of the men, who appeared, from the white beard stretching to his belt, to be the oldest, began thus: "Great Hermod, doubtless you already know everything I am about to say, better than I do myself; but I must say it, just so that you may learn that I know it too."

'"Speak, young man!" replied Hermod. "I shall be glad to listen to you; for what you have just said shows that you possess a penetrating intellect, if not profound wisdom, although you are scarcely more than a child."

"'You know", continued the spokesman, "that one day King Ophioch's Council was discussing whether every vassal should be obliged to deliver a certain quantity of wit annually to the kingdom's central store of humour, with which the poor could be fed in the event of famine or drought, and that the King suddenly said: 'The moment in which man falls down is that in which his true self stands erect.' You know that as soon as he had spoken these words King Ophioch did indeed fall down, never to rise again, because he was dead. Since it happened that Queen Liris, in the same moment, had closed her eyes, never to open them again, the Council of State found itself in no small difficulties over the succession, since the royal pair had no progeny whatsoever. The court astronomer, an ingenious man, finally conceived a method of prolonging King Ophioch's wise reign for many long years. He proposed that the same procedure should be followed as in the case of a well-known prince of spirits, King Solomon, whom the spirits continued to obey long after his death. In accordance with this proposal, the Council was joined by the court carpenter, who made an elegant structure out of boxwood; after King Ophioch's body had been nourished by the most excellent spices, this structure was pushed under his rump, so that he sat upon it in great state. His arm, however, was controlled by means of a concealed pulley, one end of which hung down into the great council chamber like a bell-rope, so that he could wave his sceptre to and fro. Nobody doubted that King Ophioch was alive and in command. Wondrous things happened, however, to the spring of Urdar. The waters of the lake it had formed remained bright and clear; but while formerly all those who looked into it had felt an especial pleasure, there were now many who, on beholding all of nature and themselves in it, became vexed and angry at the sight, because they thought it contrary to propriety, to the human intellect, and to the wisdom that man had so laboriously accumulated, to see things, especially one's own self, upside-down. And more and more of them ended by maintaining that the vapours of the bright lake befuddled the senses and transformed proper gravity into folly. In their annoyance they threw all sorts of rubbish into the lake, so that it lost its glassy clarity and became darker and darker, until at last it resembled a horrid swamp. This, O wise Magus, has brought our country much misfortune; for the most refined people now strike one another in the face and claim that that is the true irony of the sages. The greatest misfortune, however, occurred yesterday, when good King Ophioch suffered the same fate as the prince of spirits. The evil woodworm had secretly been gnawing his seat, and suddenly, when in the middle of governing, His Majesty toppled over before the eyes of the populace who had crowded into the throne-room, so that his demise can no longer be concealed. I myself, great Magus, happened to be pulling the cord that worked the sceptre, and when His Majesty collapsed the cord broke and struck me in the face so hard that I have had my fill of string-pulling for the rest of my life. O wise Hermod, you have always been faithfully devoted to the good of the Land of Urdar; tell us, what are we to do to ensure that a worthy successor takes over the reins of government and the Lake of Urdar becomes bright and clear once more?"

'The Magus Hermod pondered deeply, and then replied: "Wait for nine times nine nights, then the Queen of this country will blossom from the Lake of Urdar! In the mean time, govern the country as best you can!"

'And it came to pass that fiery beams arose over the swamp which had formerly been the fountain of Urdar. These were the fire-spirits, gazing into the lake with burning eyes, while the earth-spirits scrabbled up from the depths. Once the ground had dried, a beautiful lily sprang up, and within its petals a lovely child lay sleeping. This was the Princess Mystilis. The four ministers who had consulted the Magus Hermod carefully removed her from her beautiful cradle and made her Regent of the country.

'These four ministers became the Princess's guardians, and tried to tend and cherish the dear child as much as was in their power. They were greatly distressed, however, when the Princess, on attaining the age when she should have been able to speak properly, began to talk in a language that nobody could understand. Linguists were summoned from far and wide to study the Princess's language, but as malign destiny would have it, the wiser and more learned the linguists were, the less they could understand of the child's utterances, which, moreover, sounded perfectly intelligent and articulate. Meanwhile the lotus had closed its petals again, but all round it pure crystal water was gushing up in tiny fountains. This gave the ministers great joy, for they could only suppose that in place of the swamp the beautiful watery mirror of the Fountain of Urdar would soon be gleaming again. As for the Princess's language, the wise ministers resolved to do what they should have done long before and consult the Magus Hermod.

'When they had entered the eerie shade of the mysterious forest, and could see the stonework of the tower through the dense vegetation, they came upon an old man who was sitting on a piece of rock and reading pensively in a large book, and whom they could not but identify as the Magus Hermod. As the evening was chilly, Hermod had put on a black dressing-gown and a cap of sable fur, which suited him quite well but gave him a strange and rather sinister appearance. The ministers also had the impression that Hermod's beard was somewhat untidy, for it resembled a tangled bush. When the ministers had humbly explained their business, Hermod rose, gave them such a terrible look from his fiery eyes that they almost fell on their knees there and then, and uttered a peal of laughter that resounded and echoed throughout the forest, so that the frightened animals fled through the bushes and the birds shot up from the thickets, screaming as though in deadly terror. Never having seen or spoken to the Magus Hermod in this contumacious mood, the ministers felt uneasy; but they waited in awestruck silence to see what the great Magus would do. The Magus, however, sat down once more on the large stone, opened the book, and read in solemn tones:

> "A black stone lies within the sombre hall
> In which the royal couple, laid in state,
> Pale, silent death upon their cheeks, await
> The magic word that breaks their slumber's thrall!

> "And deep below this stone there lies a treasure
> To light the life of Mystilis the fair,
> The princess born of flowers, sun, and air,
> A precious gift, compound of earthly pleasure.

"The gaudy bird will then in nets be caught
Which dainty fairies wove with magic art.
Blindness will cease, the mists will all depart,
Our foe will die of wounds his own hand wrought!

"Prick up your ears, and then perhaps you'll hear!
Take off your spectacles, perhaps you'll see,
If useful ministers you want to be!
But if you're donkeys still, you're lost, I fear!"

'With these words the Magus shut the book with such force that a veritable thunder-clap rang out and all the ministers tumbled over backwards. By the time they had recovered, the Magus had disappeared. They agreed that serving their father-land required them to undergo great suffering; for it would otherwise have been intolerable to let that rough bully of an astrologer and magician call them donkeys for the second time. For the rest, they themselves were astonished at the wisdom which enabled them to penetrate the Magus's riddle. On arriving in Urdar they promptly went to the hall where King Ophioch and Queen Liris had been asleep for thirteen times thirteen moons, lifted the black stone that was set in the middle of the floor, and found, deep in the earth, a little box, magnificently carved from the finest ivory. They gave it to Princess Mystilis, who immediately pressed a spring, so that the lid flew open, and took out the dainty lace that was in the box. No sooner had she the lace in her hands than she gave a peal of joyous laughter and said perfectly intelligibly: "Granny put it in my cradle; but you rascals stole my treasure and wouldn't have given it back to me, if you hadn't fallen down flat in the forest!"

'Thereupon the Princess at once began industriously making lace. The delighted ministers were about to execute a collective leap to signify their joy, when the Princess suddenly went rigid and shrank into a dainty little china doll. If the ministers' joy had been great, so now was their sorrow. They wept and blubbered so loudly that they could be heard throughout the palace, until one of them, in a pensive mood, suddenly paused, dried his eyes with the two ends of his robe, and spoke as follows: "Ministers, colleagues, comrades, I almost think that the great

Magus is right, and we are . . . Never mind what we are! Has the riddle been solved? Has the gaudy bird been caught? This lace is the net woven by tender fairies in which it must be caught."

'On the ministers' orders the most beautiful ladies in the kingdom, veritable fairies in their charm and grace, were assembled in the palace and obliged to keep making lace amid the most magnificent splendour. But what good did this do? The gaudy bird was nowhere to be seen; Princess Mystilis remained a china doll; the gushing springs of the Fountain of Urdar continued to dry up, and all the kingdom's vassals sank into the bitterest ill-humour. Then it came to pass that the four ministers, on the verge of despair, sat down beside the swamp that had once been the clear and beautiful Lake of Urdar, burst out in loud lamenting, and besought the Magus Hermod in the most affecting terms to take pity upon them and on the wretched Land of Urdar. A hollow groaning came from underground; the lotus opened its petals and from them arose the Magus Hermod, who spoke in wrathful tones.

'"Unhappy, blind creatures! It was not I with whom you spoke in the forest; it was the evil demon, Typhon* himself, who played a foul magical trick upon you and summoned up the fateful secret of the lace-box! To his own detriment, however, he has spoken more truth than he meant to. Let the tender hands of fairy-like ladies make lace, let the gaudy bird be caught; but listen to the true riddle, whose solution will also release the Princess from her enchantment."'

Having read as far as this, the old man paused, rose from his seat, and addressed the little dolls, which were standing on the porphyry altar in the centre of the circle, as follows: 'Most excellent royal couple, most dear Ophioch, most revered Liris, disdain no longer to follow us on our pilgrimage in the comfortable travelling-costumes I gave you! I, your friend Ruffiamonte, will deliver what I promised!'

Ruffiamonte then looked around the circle of ladies and said: 'It is now time to put aside your spinning and utter the mysterious saying of the great Magus Hermod, spoken from within the petals of the wondrous lotus-flower.'

While Ruffiamonte kept time with firm strokes of a silver rod, the ladies, having left their seats and formed a closer circle around the Magus, uttered the following verses in chorus:

'Where is the land whose sky's perpetual blue
Calls forth the richest bloom of all earth's joys?
Where is the city where a merry crew
Keeps jest and gravity in equipoise?
Where is the little world of gaudy hue,
Filled by the shapes of fantasy and mirth?
Where does the might of fair illusion reign?
Where is the self whose self can bring to birth
The not-self,* self-divided without pain,
And keep the utmost happiness on earth?

'The land, the world, the city, and the self,
Have all been found; the self perceives in clarity
The world from which it once disjoined itself,
And folly is transformed to wise hilarity
(Whatever dull sobriety may deem),
Through spirit fortified by life and verity;
The master's wondrous needle indicates
A kingdom lost, and those who merely seem
Humble and low, he slyly elevates,
To rouse the couple from their pleasant dream.

'All hail to Urdar's fair and distant land!
Its spring at last shines purified and bright,
Freed from the servitude a demon planned,
And boundless bliss arises to the light.
Now every bosom stirs with joy serene;
All pain has melted into high delight.
What radiance shines amid the forest green?
What jubilation greets our glad release?
Run, run to welcome our most gracious Queen
Who found her self! and Hermod is at peace!'

The ostriches and the Moors now made a confused outcry, and the strange voices of many other birds could be heard piping and chirruping. But the loudest cries came from Giglio, who had suddenly regained his composure, as though waking from a trance, and felt as though he were in some burlesque play.

'What's happening, in the name of heaven? Do put an end to these crazy antics! Be sensible and tell me where I can find Her

Serene Highness, the magnificent Princess Brambilla! I am
Giglio Fava, the most famous actor in the world, and Princess
Brambilla loves me and is going to confer high honours upon
me—listen to me, won't you? Ladies, Moors, ostriches, don't
pay any attention to that silly nonsense! I know what I'm
talking about, better than that old fellow; for I, and none other,
am the white Moor!'

As soon as the ladies noticed Fava, they uttered a long, resounding peal of laughter and rushed to seize him. Giglio
himself could not tell why he suddenly felt so horribly frightened and did his best to evade their clutches. This would have
been impossible, had he not spread out his cloak and managed
to flutter up into the lofty dome of the room. The ladies chased
him to and fro, throwing large pieces of cloth at him, until he
sank down in exhaustion. Then the ladies threw a net over his
head, and the ostriches fetched a splendid golden cage, in which
Giglio was unmercifully imprisoned. At that moment the lamp
went out and the entire scene vanished as if by magic.

Since the cage stood beside a large open window, Giglio could
look down into the street, but as the populace had just flocked
to the theatres and *osterie*, it was completely empty and deserted,
so that poor Giglio, squeezed into his prison, found himself in
dismal solitude.

'Is this the happiness I dreamt of?' he burst out lamenting.
'Is this the wondrous, delicate mystery concealed in the Pistoia
Palace? I saw them, the Moors, the ladies, the little old fellow
sitting in the tulip, the ostriches, just as they entered through
the narrow gateway; only the mules and the page-boys were
missing! But Brambilla wasn't among them. No, the lovely
image of my yearning desire, my ardent love, is not here! Oh
Brambilla, Brambilla! And I must languish miserably in this
vile captivity, and shall never play the white Moor! Oh! Oh!
Oh!'

'Who's making such a din up there?' came a cry from the
street. Giglio instantly recognized the voice of the old Ciarlatano, and a ray of hope entered his terrified bosom.

'Celionati,' said Giglio in heartfelt tones, 'dear Signor Celionati, is it you I see there in the moonlight? I'm sitting in this
cage, in a miserable state. They've locked me in here, like a

bird! Oh, heavens! Signor Celionati, you are a virtuous man who wouldn't abandon his neighbour; you have wondrous powers at your disposal, help me, oh, help me out of my confounded painful situation! Oh freedom, golden freedom, who treasures you more than he who is in a cage, even if the bars are made of gold?'

Celionati gave a loud laugh and said: 'You see, Giglio, this is what comes of your confounded folly and your wild fancies! Who told you to enter the Pistoia Palace in such a ridiculous get-up? How could you sneak into a gathering to which you weren't invited?'

'What?' cried Giglio, 'my beautiful costume, the only one in which I could present myself worthily to my adored Princess, you call it a ridiculous get-up?'

'Your beautiful costume', replied Celionati, 'is the reason why you have been treated like this.'

'But am I a bird?' cried Giglio in vexation and anger.

'The ladies', continued Celionati, 'certainly took you for a bird, of a kind they are always very anxious to get hold of—a feather-brain!'

'Oh heavens!' said Giglio, quite beside himself, 'me, Giglio Fava, the renowned tragic hero, the white Moor! Me, a feather-brain!'

'Now, Signor Giglio,' cried Celionati, 'just be patient, and sleep, if you can, quietly and softly! Who knows what good fortune the coming day has in store for you!'

'Have mercy, Signor Celionati,' shrieked Giglio; 'release me from this confounded prison! Never again will I enter the accursed Pistoia Palace.'

'Really,' replied the Ciarlatano, 'you don't deserve any help from me, for you disdain all my good advice and wish to throw yourself into the arms of my mortal enemy, the Abbate Chiari, who, let me tell you, has plunged you into your present misfortune by his vile deceitful doggerel. But . . . you are a good boy really, and I am an honest, soft-hearted fool, as I have often shown; and so I will rescue you. I hope that tomorrow, in return, you will buy a new pair of spectacles and an Assyrian tooth from me.'

'I'll buy whatever you want from you; just give me freedom,

freedom! I'm nearly suffocated already!' said Giglio. The Ciarlatano climbed up to him on an invisible ladder, and opened one side of the cage; the unhappy feather-brain squeezed through the opening with some difficulty.

But at that moment a confused uproar began in the palace, and a medley of horrible voices started squealing and howling.

'By all the powers!' cried Celionati; 'people have noticed your escape, Giglio, hurry up and get away!'

With strength born of desperation, Giglio squeezed his way out of the cage, and threw himself recklessly down into the street, where, not having suffered the slightest injury, he picked himself up and ran off at full tilt.

On arriving in his garret and perceiving the eccentric costume in which he had fought with his own self, he cried, quite beside himself: 'Yes, the spirit of madness lying there in bodily form is my self, and these princely garments were stolen by the dark demon from the feather-brain and forced upon me, so that the beautiful ladies should be deceived into mistaking me for the feather-brain! I know I'm talking nonsense; but that's all right, for I really have gone crazy, because the self has no body—ho, ho! Off we go, off we go, my dear sweet self!' With these words, he furiously tore off the beautiful garments, put on the wildest and weirdest of masquerade costumes, and ran to the Corso.

All the delight of heaven ran through his veins, however, when an angelically charming girl, with a tambourine in her hand, invited him to dance. The copperplate engraving attached to this chapter shows Giglio dancing with the fair unknown; what further happened, however, will be made known to the kind reader in the following chapter.

Gian Farina .   Fracischina .

Fracasso .   Taglia Cantoni

CHAPTER 6

How someone became a Prince while dancing, fainted in the arms of a charlatan, and then at supper doubted the talents of his cook.
Liquor anodynus *and much ado without cause. A knightly combat between two friends consumed by love and melancholy, and its tragic outcome. The disadvantages and impropriety of taking snuff.*
A girl's freemasonry and a newly invented flying-machine. How old Beatrice put a pair of spectacles on her nose and took them off again.

SHE. Spin, spin harder, whirl unceasingly, mad, merry dance! Ha, how quickly everything flies past! No rest, never a pause! All manner of colourful shapes blaze up like the sparks scattered by fireworks and vanish into the black night. Delight pursues delight and cannot catch it, and that is the very essence of delight. Nothing more tedious than to be rooted to the spot and have to answer every look, every word! So I wouldn't like to be a flower; rather, a gold beetle, humming and buzzing round your head until you can't hear yourself think for the noise! What happens to thinking, anyway, when reason is pulled along in the whirlpools of wild delight? Now it is too heavy, tears the threads and drops into the abyss; now it is too light, and flies up into the misty heavens. It's impossible to keep one's reason rational while dancing; so let's give it up entirely as long as our figures and *pas* go on. And so I shan't answer any of your questions, you smart, nimble fellow! See how I circle round you and slip away from you, just when you think you're about to catch me and hold me tight! And again! And again!

HE. Oh yes! No, missed you! But it all depends on knowing how to observe and maintain the correct equilibrium when dancing. Any dancer must therefore hold something in his hand as a balancing-rod; and therefore I shall draw my broad sword and brandish it in the air—like that! What do you think of this caper, of this attitude, in which I entrust my entire self to the centre of gravity formed by the tiptoes of my left foot? You call that careless folly; but that precisely is the reason

which you despise, although without it one cannot understand anything, even equilibrium, which has many uses! But
what's this? Your coloured ribbons are waving, and, like me,
you're floating on the tiptoes of your left foot, holding your
tambourine high above your head; and you ask me to dispense
entirely with reason and balance? I'll throw you the hem of
my cloak, so that you'll fall into my arms, blinded and
staggering! But no, no! The moment I seized you, you'd no
longer be there, you'd vanish into nothingness! Who are you,
you mysterious being, born of air and fire, yet an inhabitant
of the earth, who peeps alluringly from the water! You can't
escape me. Or can you? You're trying to descend, I fancy I
can hold you tight, and you float up into the air. Are you
truly the honest elemental spirit who set life alight and
brought it to life? Are you the melancholy, the ardent desire,
the delight, the heavenly rapture of true being? But always
the same *pas*, the same figures! And yet, fairest one, nothing
is eternal but your dance, and that is indeed the most wonderful thing about you . . .

THE TAMBOURINE. When you hear me rattling, rapping and
ringing, O dancer, you either think that I'm trying to pull
the wool over your eyes with all manner of silly nonsense, or
else you take me for a clumsy idiot who can't grasp the tone
and rhythm of your melodies; and yet it's me alone who
preserves your tone and your rhythm. So listen! Listen! Listen
to me!

THE SWORD. You think, O dancer, that because I'm made of
dull, deaf wood and have no tone or rhythm, I can be of no
use to you. But let me tell you that the tone and rhythm of
your dance proceed solely from my oscillations. I am both
sword and zither, and can wound the air with song and music,
cut and thrust. And I preserve your tone and rhythm; so
listen! Listen! Listen to me!

SHE. How the harmony of our dance keeps increasing! Why,
what steps, what capers! Bolder and bolder, and yet it still
works, because we understand our dance better and better!

HE. Ha! a thousand rings of fire are all around us! What
delight! Magnificent fireworks, you can never go out; for
your material is everlasting, like time itself—but stop, stop;

I'm burning, I'm falling into the fire.

TAMBOURINE and SWORD. Hold on tight! Hold on to us tightly, dancers!

SHE and HE. Alas! The whirling, twirling, swirling abyss— seizes us—down we go!'

So ran, word for word, the extraordinary dance that Giglio Fava danced in the most graceful fashion with the fair one, who could be none other than Princess Brambilla herself, until the delirium of riotous delight brought him close to fainting. Instead of doing so, however, Giglio heard the tambourine and sword again advising him to hold on tightly, and felt as though he were collapsing into the fair one's embrace. Yet he did not do this either: he found himself in the arms, not of the Princess at all, but of old Celionati.

'I don't know, my dear Prince', began Celionati, '(for I recognized you at a glance despite your peculiar get-up), how you can have been taken in by such crude deception, since you are usually a sensible gentleman. It's lucky that I happened to be standing here and caught you in my arms just as that wanton wench was about to take advantage of your fainting-fit by carrying you off.'

'Thank you very much indeed for your goodwill, dear Signor Celionati', replied Giglio; 'but I don't understand a word you say about crude deception, and I'm only sorry that my wretched fainting-fit prevented me from finishing my dance with the fairest and loveliest of Princesses, which would have made me perfectly happy.'

'What are you saying?' replied Celionati. 'Do you think that that really was Princess Brambilla who was dancing with you? No! The vile deceit lies in the fact that the Princess foisted on you a person of mean station so that she might pursue other love affairs without hindrance.'

'Could I possibly be deceived?' exclaimed Giglio.

'Consider', pursued Celionati, 'that if your dancing-partner had really been Princess Brambilla, and you had successfully finished your dance, the great Magus Hermod must instantly have appeared to lead you and your lovely bride into your kingdom.'

'That's true', replied Giglio; 'but tell me what did happen, and who I was really dancing with!'

'You shall and must learn everything', said Celionati. 'But, if you don't mind, I shall accompany you into your palace, where we can have a more relaxed conversation, O my princely master.'

'Be good enough', said Giglio, 'to guide me thither! For I must confess that my dance with the supposed Princess has had such an effect on me that I seem to be walking in a dream, and at this moment I really don't know where in Rome my palace is situated.'

'Just come with me, Your Highness!' exclaimed Celionati, taking Giglio's arm and marching off with him.

He went straight to the Pistoia Palace. Standing on the marble steps leading to the gateway, Giglio examined the palace from top to bottom, and then said to Celionati: 'If that really is my palace, which I don't doubt for a moment, then I've been attacked by some very strange inhabitants, who get up to high jinks in the finest rooms and carry on as though the house belonged to them and not me. Bold hussies, tricked out in borrowed finery, mistake decent, sensible people—and, may the saints preserve me, I think this has happened to me, the owner of the house—for a rare bird that they must catch in nets woven by fairies' tender hands, and this causes great upset and disturbance. I have a feeling that I was imprisoned here in a horrid bird-cage, and so I don't really want to go in again. If it were possible, my dear Celionati, for my palace to be situated somewhere else, just for today, I should be extremely pleased.'

'Your palace, Your Highness,' replied Celionati, 'can be situated nowhere but here, and it would be against all the rules of etiquette to turn round and enter someone else's house. You need only reflect, O my Prince, that everything done here, by ourselves or others, far from being real, is only a capriccio without a word of truth in it, and then you will not be in the least put out by the mad people and their antics up there. Pluck up your courage, and let's go in!'

'But tell me,' cried Giglio, restraining Celionati as the latter was about to open the door, 'didn't Princess Brambilla enter this palace with the magician Ruffiamonte and a numerous train of ladies, pages, ostriches, and mules?'

'Certainly', replied Celionati; 'but since you are at least as much the owner of this palace as the Princess is, that can't keep you from entering likewise, even if for the moment you do so inconspicuously. You'll soon find yourself quite at home here.'

With these words Celionati opened the door of the palace and pushed Giglio in ahead of him. The vestibule was dark and silent as the grave, but, when Celionati knocked gently on a door, there soon appeared a very pleasing little Pulcinella carrying lighted candles.

'If I am not mistaken,' said Giglio to the little fellow, 'I have already had the honour of seeing you, my dear Signor, on the roof of Princess Brambilla's coach.'

'That is so', replied Pulcinella; 'at that time I was in the Princess's service, and in a way I still am, but above all I am the loyal valet of Your Highness's self, my Prince!'

Pulcinella lighted the two new arrivals into a splendid room and then modestly withdrew, remarking that whenever and wherever the Prince should command his services, he would promptly appear on the touch of a spring; for, although he was the only joke in livery on the ground floor, his boldness and quickness enabled him to replace a whole staff of servants.

'Ha!' cried Giglio, looking round the magnificently decorated room, 'now at last I see that I really am in my palace, in my princely room. My impresario had it painted but did not pay for it, and when the painter presented his bill, the impresario boxed his ears, whereupon the machinist beat the impresario with a Fury's torch! Yes, I'm in my princely home! But you were going to free me from the terrible delusion I was under concerning the dance, my dear Signor Celionati. Speak, I beg you, speak! Let's sit down!'

When Giglio and Celionati had seated themselves in soft armchairs, the latter began: 'Know, my Prince, that the person who was foisted on you instead of the Princess is none other than a pretty little milliner by the name of Giacinta Soardi!'

'Can this be?' exclaimed Giglio. 'But didn't that girl take as her lover a wretched comedian without a penny to his name, called Giglio Fava?'

'Certainly,' replied Celionati; 'but can you imagine that this miserable penniless comedian, this stage prince, is being pursued up hill and down dale by Princess Brambilla, who for that reason brought you together with the milliner, hoping that by some crazy misunderstanding you would fall in love with the latter and seduce her away from the hero of the boards?'

'What an idea,' said Giglio, 'what a criminal idea! But believe me, Celionati, it's only an evil, demonic spell that is getting everything mixed up and confused, and I shall destroy the spell with this sword, wielding it with a courageous hand, and annihilate the wretch who dares to permit my Princess to love him.'

'Do that,' replied Celionati with a mischievous smile, 'do that, my dear Prince! It's very important to me that the silly fool should be got out of the way, and the sooner the better.'

Giglio now bethought himself of Pulcinella and the service the latter had offered. He pressed a concealed spring; Pulcinella promptly appeared, and being, as he had asserted, able to replace a whole staff of diverse servants, the cook, the cellarer, the table-layer, and the cupbearer were all present, and a tempting meal was ready in a few seconds.

After eating and drinking his fill, Giglio felt that the food and wine revealed rather too clearly that only one person had prepared, fetched, and served them; for they all tasted alike. Celionati remarked that that might be the reason why Princess Brambilla had dismissed Pulcinella from her employment, because his impetuous vanity made him want to do everything single-handed, and this had often brought him into conflict with Arlecchino, who presumed to do just the same.

At this point there is a gap in the remarkable original capriccio which the narrator is meticulously copying. To speak in musical terms, the transition from one key to the next is missing, so that the new chord begins with none of the requisite preparation. Indeed one might say that the capriccio breaks off with an unresolved dissonance. For we are told that the Prince (meaning presumably none other than Giglio Fava, who was threatening to kill Giglio Fava) was suddenly afflicted by a frightful stomach-ache which he attributed to Pulcinella's cooking; after Celionati had provided him with *liquor anodynus*,* however, he fell asleep, whereupon a loud noise began. We are told neither what this noise signified, nor how the Prince, or

Giglio Fava, along with Celionati, left the Pistoia Palace.

The next instalment runs more or less as follows.

As the day was drawing to its close, a mask appeared in the Corso which aroused everyone's attention by its strangeness and weirdness. On its head it wore a peculiar cap adorned with two lofty cock's feathers; its face was concealed by a huge nose like an elephant's trunk, on which was perched a large pair of spectacles; it also wore a jerkin with thick buttons and a pretty pair of sky-blue breeches with dark red bows, rose-coloured stockings, white shoes with dark-red ribbons, and a beautiful pointed sword by its side.

The kind reader will recognize this mask from Chapter 1 and therefore knows that it could conceal none other than Giglio Fava. This mask, however, had scarcely walked twice up and down the Corso, when a wild Captain Pantaloon Brighella, who has likewise made several appearances in this capriccio already, leapt forth and accosted the mask with eyes gleaming with rage, crying: 'Have I found you at last, you infamous stage hero, you vile white Moor! You shan't escape me this time! Draw your sword, poltroon, defend yourself, or I'll run my wooden sword through your body!'

While uttering these words, the eccentric Captain Pantaloon brandished his broad wooden sword in the air; Giglio, however, was not in the least put out by this unexpected assault, but said in calm and composed tones: 'Who is this vulgar ruffian who wishes to fight a duel with me and yet has not the least notion of chivalrous behaviour? Listen, my friend! If you really recognize me as the white Moor, then you must be aware that I am a hero and a knight without peer, and that it is only true courtesy that bids me appear in sky-blue breeches, pink stockings, and white shoes. This is a ballroom costume *à la* King Arthur. I still have my good sword shining at my side, however, and I shall face you like a true knight if you challenge me as a knight, and if you are the real thing and not a buffoon in Roman guise!'

'Forgive me, O white Moor,' replied the mask, 'for ignoring even for a moment my duty to the hero and the knight! But as sure as princely blood flows through my veins, I shall show you that I have read the best romances of chivalry with as much profit as you.'

Thereupon the princely Captain Pantaloon took a few steps backward, held out his sword to Giglio in a fencer's attitude, and said in a tone of hearty goodwill: 'Do you mind?' Elegantly acknowledging his adversary, Giglio drew his rapier from its sheath, and the combat commenced. It was soon apparent that both Captain Pantaloon and Giglio were highly adept in chivalrous behaviour. Their left feet were planted solidly on the ground, while their right feet alternately advanced resolutely to the attack, or withdrew to a defensive position. The blades glittered as they crossed, and blow followed blow with lightning speed. After a hot and perilous passage of arms the combatants were obliged to rest. They looked at each other, and along with the rage of battle they felt such mutual love that they fell into each other's arms and shed copious tears. The combat then began afresh with redoubled strength and skill. But, just as Giglio was about to parry a well-aimed thrust from his opponent, the latter's sword caught in the bow attached to the left leg of Giglio's breeches, tearing it off with a rending sound.

'Stop!' cried Captain Pantaloon.

The wound was examined and found to be insignificant. A couple of pins sufficed to fasten the bow again.

'I shall now,' said Captain Pantaloon, 'take my sword in my left hand, because the weight of the wood is tiring out my right arm. You, however, can keep your light rapier in your right hand.'

'Heaven preserve me,' replied Giglio, 'from doing you such a malfeasance! I too shall take my rapier in my left hand; for that is proper and practical, since I shall be better able to hit you.'

'Come to my bosom, dear and noble comrade', exclaimed Captain Pantaloon.

The combatants embraced once more, so moved by the magnificence of their actions that they howled and sobbed like anything, and then assailed each other ferociously.

'Stop!' cried Giglio, perceiving that his thrust had caught the brim of his opponent's hat. The latter at first stoutly denied having received any injury, but since the brim was hanging down over his nose, he was obliged to accept Giglio's noble-hearted ministrations. The wound was insignificant; the hat, once Giglio had put it straight, remained a fine piece of felt. The combatants gazed at each other with enhanced love, for each had proved the other's chivalry and valour. They embraced each other and wept, and the ardour of the fray again sprang into a blaze. Giglio dropped his guard, his adversary's sword struck his chest, and he fell over backwards, bereft of life.

Despite this tragic outcome, the crowd watching Giglio's corpse being carried away laughed so heartily that the whole Corso shook, while Captain Pantaloon coolly replaced his broad wooden sword in its sheath and strode off proudly down the Corso.

'Yes,' said old Beatrice, 'that's settled; if that ugly old mounte-bank, Signor Celionati, shows his face here again, and tries to turn the head of my sweet lovely girl, I'll send him about his business. And I think even Master Bescapi aids and abets his follies.'

Old Beatrice may have been right in a way; for ever since Celionati had taken to visiting the charming milliner Giacinta Soardi, the latter seemed inwardly transformed. She appeared to be lost in a perpetual dream, and sometimes talked such wild and whirling nonsense that the old woman was concerned for her sanity. Giacinta's principal obsession, as the kind reader may suspect from Chapter 4, was that the wealthy and magnificent Prince Cornelio Chiapperi loved her and was going to ask for her hand. Beatrice, however, was of the opinion that Celionati, Heaven alone knew why, was trying to hoodwink Giacinta; for if the Prince really loved her, there was no conceivable reason why he should not have visited his beloved's dwelling long before, since Princes are not usually bashful in such matters. Besides, Beatrice added, the few ducats they received from Ce-lionati were by no means worthy of a Prince's lavishness. Most likely, she concluded, there was no such person as Prince Cor-nelio Chiapperi; and even supposing there was, old Celionati himself, to her certain knowledge, had proclaimed to the pop-ulace from his platform outside San Carlo that the Assyrian

Prince Cornelio Chiapperi, after having a tooth extracted, had got lost, and was being sought by his betrothed, Princess Brambilla.

'Don't you see?' cried Giacinta with shining eyes, 'that's the key to the whole mystery, that's the reason why the good and noble Prince takes such care to remain hidden. Since he is wrapped up in his ardent love for me, he is afraid of Princess Brambilla and her claims, and yet cannot make up his mind to leave Rome. It is only in the strangest of disguises that he ventures to show himself on the Corso, and it is on the Corso that he gave me the clearest proof of his tender affection. Soon, however, the golden star of happiness will rise upon him, the dear Prince, and myself. Do you remember a foppish comedian who used to pay court to me, one Giglio Fava?'

The old woman remarked that that didn't require a particularly retentive memory, since poor Giglio, whom she still preferred to an unmannerly Prince, had called on her only two days before and had greatly enjoyed the delicious meal she had cooked for him.

'Can you believe it, old woman', went on Giacinta, 'Princess Brambilla is actually chasing this miserable wretch? That's what Celionati tells me. But just as the Prince is still reluctant to appear in public as my betrothed, so the Princess cannot yet decide to renounce her former love and elevate the comedian Giglio Fava to her throne. At that moment, however, when the Princess gives Giglio her hand, the enraptured Prince will receive mine.'

'Giacinta,' cried the old woman, 'what folly, what silly fancies!'

'And as for what you said', continued Giacinta, 'about the Prince having hitherto disdained to visit his beloved in her own home, there isn't a word of truth in it. You have no idea what charming devices the Prince employs in order to see me without anyone knowing. For let me tell you that besides the other admirable qualities and skills that he possesses, the Prince is also a great magician. Never mind that he once visited me at night, so small, so delightful, so adorable, that I'd have liked to eat him up. But often, even when you are present, he suddenly appears right here in our little room, and it is your fault alone that you see neither the Prince nor the glorious things that are then revealed. Our cramped room spreads out and becomes a vast, magnificent hall with marble walls, gold-brocaded tapestries, damask couches, and tables and chairs of ebony and ivory; but I like it even more when the walls disappear altogether and I walk hand in hand with my beloved in the most beautiful garden anyone could imagine. I'm not at all surprised, old woman, that you can't smell the heavenly fragrance that floats through this paradise, since you have the nasty habit of cramming your nose full of snuff, and even in the Prince's presence you can't restrain yourself from pulling out your snuff-box. But you should at least remove the scarf that covers your ears in order to hear the singing in the garden, for it entirely captivates the senses and banishes all earthly suffering, including toothache. You can't find it in the least improper that I permit the Prince to kiss me on both shoulders; for you can see how I instantly sprout the most beautiful, colourful, glistening butterfly wings and soar high up into the air. Ha! that alone is true delight, when the Prince and I sail together through the heavenly azure. All the splendours of earth and heaven, all the riches, all the treasures thought to lie concealed in the depths of creation, are revealed to my intoxicated gaze, and they are all, all mine! And you say, nurse, that the Prince is mean and leaves me in poverty, despite his love? Perhaps you think that I'm only rich when the Prince is present; but even that isn't true. See, nurse, how at this moment, when I'm doing no more than talking about the Prince and his magnificence, our room has been so beautifully adorned. Look at these silk curtains, these carpets, these mirrors, and, above all, this precious wardrobe, whose exterior is worthy of its sumptuous contents! For you need only open it and bars of gold tumble into your lap. And what do you think of these smart ladies-in-waiting, maids, and pages, whom the Prince has appointed to serve me in the mean time, before the whole glittering retinue of his court surrounds my throne?'

As she uttered these words, Giacinta stepped in front of the wardrobe which the gentle reader has already beheld in Chapter 1; it contained the sumptuous, but strange and eccentric costumes which Giacinta had trimmed on Bescapi's orders, and to which she now began speaking softly.

The old woman watched Giacinta's behaviour, shaking her head, and then began: 'God comfort you, Giacinta! you are under a terrible delusion, and I'm going to fetch our father confessor to drive away the devil who haunts you. But I tell you, it's all the fault of that crazy mountebank who put the Prince in your head, and of that silly tailor who gave you the absurd masque outfits to work on. Still, I'm not going to scold you! Come to your senses, my sweet child, my dear Giacinti-netta, be yourself, be a good child as you were before!'

Giacinta sat down silently in her armchair, propped her delic-ate head on her hand, and gazed meditatively at the floor in front of her.

'And', went on the old woman, 'if our good Giglio would give up his escapades—but stop—Giglio! Why! as I look at you like this, little Giacinta, I remember what he once read to us from that little book—wait, wait, wait—it fits you perfectly.' From a basket filled with ribbons, laces, scraps of silk, and other trimmings, the old woman fetched a small, neatly bound vol-ume; putting her spectacles on her nose, she crouched down in front of Giacinta and read:

'Was it on the lonely mossy bank of a purling brook, was it in a fragrant bower of jasmine? No, I now recall, it was in a cosy little room lit by the rays of the setting sun that I set eyes on her. She was sitting in a low armchair, her head propped on her right hand, so that her dark curls, wilfully ruffled, spilled out between her white fingers. Her left hand, lying in her lap, was playfully tugging at the silk ribbon which had come un-fastened from the slender body it girded. It was as though the movement of this hand was involuntarily imitated by the little foot whose toes, just peeping out from beneath the ample folds of her dress, were gently tapping on the floor. Her entire figure, I assure you, was bathed in such grace, such heavenly charm, that my heart trembled in nameless bliss. I wished for Gyges's ring,* so that she might not see me; for were she to feel my gaze, I feared that she might dissolve into air, like a dream-image! A sweet and gracious smile played round her mouth and cheeks, gentle sighs forced their way through her ruby lips and struck me like burning arrows of love. I started in terror, thinking that I had called her name aloud in the sudden agony of fervent bliss! She did not perceive me, however; she could not see me. Thereupon I ventured to look into the eyes which seemed fixed rigidly upon me, and reflected in this gracious mirror I beheld the wondrous magical garden to which the angelic being had taken flight. Castles of luminous air opened their gates, and there streamed forth a merry, colourful crowd who, with shouts of rejoicing, laid rich and splendid gifts before the fair one. But these gifts were all the hopes, all the yearning desires, that arose from the inmost depths of her heart to animate her bosom. The lace that covered her shining bosom swelled ever higher, like a flood of lilies, and a shimmering incarnadine gleamed upon her cheeks. For only now did the mystery of music awaken, uttering the supreme truth in heavenly tones. You may believe me when I say that I myself, reflected in this wondrous mirror, was now standing in the midst of the magic garden.'

'That', said the old woman, shutting the book and taking her spectacles from her nose, 'is very nicely and prettily said; but, heavens above, what extravagant language, just to say that there is nothing more charming, and for men of sense and feeling nothing more alluring, than a beautiful girl sitting lost in thought and building castles in the air. And as I say, that fits you perfectly, my Giacintina, and all the nonsense you have told me about the Prince and his tricks is nothing more than the words that match the dream in which you are absorbed.'

'And', replied Giacinta, rising from her chair and clapping her hands like a joyful child, 'if that were so, wouldn't I resemble the charming magical image that you have just been reading about? And you may as well know that these were the Prince's words which, when you tried to read from Giglio's book, flowed involuntarily from your lips.'

CHAPTER 7

How a neat young man in the Caffè Greco was accused of abomin-
able things; how an impresario repented, and the model of an actor
died of the Abbate Chiari's tragedies. Chronic dualism, and the
double prince whose thoughts ran sideways. How somebody saw
things upside-down because of an eye complaint, lost his land, and
did not go for a walk. Trouble, strife, and parting.

The kind reader cannot possibly complain that in this story the
author has wearied him by covering too much ground. All its
settings—the Corso, the Pistoia Palace, the Caffè Greco, and so
on—are conveniently close together within a small area which
can be traversed in a few hundred steps; and, leaving aside the
inconsiderable detour to the Land of Urdar, all the events are
confined to this small and manageable area. Hence only a few
steps are now required for the kind reader to return to the Caffè
Greco, where, only four chapters back, the mountebank Celionati told some German youths the wonderful and curious tale of
King Ophioch and Queen Liris.

Well then! A good-looking, neatly dressed young man was
sitting all by himself in the Caffè Greco, seemingly absorbed in
profound thought; so that when two men entered and approached him, they had to call two or three times, 'Signor!
Signor! My dear Signor!', before he awoke, as though from a
dream, and enquired with cultivated politeness: 'What can I do
for you, gentlemen?'

The Abbate Chiari—for it must be explained that the two
men were none other than the Abbate Chiari, the celebrated
author of the yet more celebrated *White Moor*, and the impresario who had replaced tragedy with farce—promptly began:
'My dear Signor Giglio, how is it that you don't appear in
public any longer, and one has to hunt through the whole of
Rome in order to find you? Behold here a repentant sinner,
converted by the power and force of my words, who wishes to
make amends for the wrong he has done you and recompense
you in full measure for your losses!'

'Yes, Signor Giglio,' put in the impresario, 'I freely confess my folly, my infatuation. How could I possibly mistake your genius? How could I doubt, even for a moment, that you alone were my sole support? Come back to me, and receive once more, in my theatre, the admiration and the deafening, tumultuous applause of the world!'

The neat young man gazed at the Abbate and the impresario in astonishment, and replied: 'Gentlemen, I don't know what you want from me. You address me by an unfamiliar name, you talk about things that mean nothing to me—you behave as though we were acquainted, although I can scarcely remember ever seeing you before in my life!'

'You are quite right, Giglio,' said the impresario, with tears in his eyes, 'to treat me so harshly and behave as if you didn't know me; for I was an ass to drive you away from the boards. But, Giglio, my boy, please don't be obstinate! Give me your hand!'

'Think of me, dear Signor Giglio,' interrupted the Abbate, 'think of the white Moor, and remember that you cannot gain more fame and honour anywhere than on the stage of this stout fellow, who has sent Arlecchino and his train of riff-raff packing, and has regained the happiness of receiving and performing my tragedies.'

'Signor Giglio,' continued the impresario, 'you shall decide your own salary; in fact, you shall have a completely free choice of the costume for the white Moor, and we shan't quarrel about a few yards of false braid or an extra packet of sequins.'

'And I tell you,' exclaimed the young man, 'that everything you say is and remains an insoluble puzzle to me.'

'Ha!' shrieked the enraged impresario, 'I understand you, Giglio Fava, I see what your game is; I see it all now. That cursed devil of a—well, I won't name him, so as not to poison my mouth—*he* has caught you in his toils, he has you firmly in his clutches. You are already engaged. But ha, ha, ha! you will repent too late when that villain, that miserable master tailor who has gone mad from ridiculous conceit, when he . . .'.

'I beg you, my dear Signor,' said the young man, interrupting the angry impresario, 'keep your cool and don't excite yourself! I see what the misunderstanding consists in. Aren't you mistaking me for an actor by the name of Giglio Fava, who, I have been told, used to be reputed an outstanding actor, although he was really never any good?'

The Abbate and the impresario stared at the young man as though they had seen a ghost.

'Probably', continued the young man, 'you have been away from Rome, gentlemen, and have only just returned; for otherwise I should be surprised that you had not heard the news that the whole of Rome is talking about. I should be sorry to be the first to tell you that Giglio Fava, the actor you are seeking and set such store by, was fatally injured in a duel yesterday on the Corso. I myself am only too convinced of his death.'

'Oh, wonderful!' cried the Abbate, 'how unspeakably fine and wonderful! So it was the celebrated actor Giglio Fava who was knocked to the ground yesterday by a ridiculous grotesque fellow, and kicked both legs in the air? Really, my dear Signor, you must be a stranger in Rome, with little knowledge of our Carnival pranks, or else you would know that when people were about to lift the supposed corpse and carry it away, they found only a handsome cardboard model, whereupon the crowd burst into gales of laughter.'

'I do not know', went on the young man, 'to what extent the tragic actor Giglio Fava was made of cardboard, instead of flesh and blood; but it is certain that on being dissected, his body was found to be crammed with sheets from the tragedies of a certain Abbate Chiari, and that the doctors ascribed the fatal blow that Giglio had received from his opponent to his having monstrously overstuffed himself and ruined his digestive system by excessive indulgence in watery and insubstantial fare.'

As the young man uttered these words, the entire circle burst into a roar of laughter. For, during this remarkable conversation, the Caffè Greco had gradually filled up with its usual customers, and the German artists, in particular, had formed a circle round the speakers.

If the impresario had previously been angry, the Abbate now unleashed his wrath with much greater fury. 'Ha!' he shrieked, 'you did it on purpose, Giglio Fava; you are to blame for the disgrace I suffered on the Corso! Just wait! My revenge shall find you—crush you . . .'

The offended poet delivered a torrent of scurrilous abuse and seemed about to seize the neat young man forcibly, together with the impresario. Accordingly the German artists laid hold of them both and flung them somewhat roughly out of the door, so that they shot past old Celionati as he was about to enter. 'Have a good trip!' he called after them.

On catching sight of Celionati, the neat young man hurried up to him, took him by the hand, led him into a remote corner of the room, and began: 'If only you had come earlier, dear Signor Celionati, to free me from those two tormentors! They mistook me for the actor Giglio Fava, whom—you know this, alas!—I fatally injured during my unfortunate paroxysm yesterday on the Corso, and they accused me of all manner of abominable things. Tell me, do I really resemble Fava enough to be mistaken for him?'

'You need have no doubt, sir,' replied the Ciarlatano politely, indeed almost deferentially, 'that your pleasing features do indeed resemble those of that actor, and you were therefore very wise to dispose of your double, which you accomplished with great dexterity. As for the foolish Abbate Chiari and his impresario, my Prince, count on me! I shall contrive to free you from any irritation that might delay your complete recovery. Nothing is easier than to sow discord between a director and a poet so that they fall on each other and devour each other, like the two lions of which nothing was left but their two tails, which were found on the scene of combat as a dreadful memorial that murder had been done. Don't be upset by your resemblance to the cardboard tragedian! For I have just learnt that the young men there who freed you from your persecutors are likewise under the impression that you are none other than Giglio Fava.'

'Oh, my dear Signor Celionati,' said the neat young man in a low voice, 'for heaven's sake, don't betray my identity! You know why I must remain concealed until I am fully recovered.'

'Have no fear, my Prince,' replied the mountebank, 'without giving you away, I shall say as much about you as is needful to gain these young men's esteem and friendship, while ensuring that it does not occur to them to enquire about your name and station. Behave for the moment as though you were paying us no attention! Look out of the window, or read the newspapers, and then you can join in our conversation later. To make sure that what I say does not embarrass you, however, I shall use the only language that is really appropriate for matters concerning you and your illness, although at present you do not understand it.'

Signor Celionati took his place, as usual, among the young Germans, who were still describing amid hearty laughter how, on seeing the Abbate and the impresario about to assault the neat young man, they had thrown the pair out with all possible dispatch. Several of them then asked the old man if it was not the well-known actor Giglio Fava who was leaning out of the window over there; and after Celionati had replied in the negative, explaining that it was in fact a young stranger of noble birth, the painter Franz Reinhold (whom the gentle reader has already seen and heard in Chapter 3) remarked: 'I can't see how anyone could find a resemblance between that stranger and the actor Giglio Fava. I grant that they may look superficially alike as far as their eyes, mouths, noses, foreheads, and build are concerned; but what creates a real resemblance is the spiritual expression, which most portrait-painters, or rather face-copiers, can't capture, so that they can never supply pictures that truly resemble their subjects; and there is such a world of difference between the spiritual expressions of these two that I, for my part, could never have mistaken the stranger for Giglio Fava. Fava had a vacuous face, whereas this stranger's face has something strange about it which I can't fathom.'

The young people urged the old mountebank to tell them another story like the wondrous tale of King Ophioch and Queen Liris, which they had enjoyed so greatly, or rather to tell them the sequel to that tale, which he must have heard from his friend the magician Ruffiamonte or Hermod in the Pistoia Palace.

'Sequel?' cried the mountebank. 'What sequel? Did I pause suddenly, clear my throat, and say with a bow: "To be continued at a later date"? And besides, my friend the magician Ruffiamonte has already read the subsequent course of the story aloud in the Pistoia Palace. It's your fault, not mine, that you missed his lecture, which was attended by ladies in search of instruction, as is now the fashion; and were I to repeat it all, that would arouse hideous boredom in one person who is always with us and who was also present at that lecture, and hence knows everything. I mean of course the reader of the capriccio entitled *Princess Brambilla*, a story in which we all appear and act. So no more about King Ophioch and Queen Liris and Princess Mystilis and the gaudy bird! But I'll talk about myself, if that is of any use to you, you frivolous people!'

'Why frivolous?' asked Reinhold.

'Because', continued Master Celionati in German, 'you look on me as someone whose only purpose is to tell you fairy-tales which sound droll merely because of their drollery and serve to pass your time. But I assure you that when the author invented me he intended me for a quite different purpose, and if he saw how you sometimes take me for granted, he might think I had gone to the bad. Anyway, none of you shows me the respect and deference that I deserve for my profound knowledge. Thus you cherish the contemptible opinion that I have never made any thorough study of the science of medicine, but simply pass ordinary nostrums off as occult remedies and try to cure all diseases by the same means. Now, however, the time has come to open your eyes. From far, far away, from a land so distant that Peter Schlemihl, despite his seven-league boots, would have to run for a whole year to get there, a very distinguished young man has travelled to enjoy the benefits of my art. He suffers from a disease which may well be called the strangest and at the same time the most dangerous disease in existence, and its cure really does depend on an occult remedy whose possessors must have been initiated by magical ceremonies. The young man suffers from chronic dualism.'

'What?' cried his hearers, all bursting into laughter. 'What are you talking about, Master Celionati? Chronic dualism? What on earth is that?'

'I can see', said Reinhold, 'that you are about to tell us another fantastic tale, and afterwards you'll deny it all.'

'Why, my son Reinhold,' replied the mountebank, 'you are the last person who should level that reproach at me; for with you I have always stood by my claims, and since I think you correctly understood the story of King Ophioch, and have yourself looked into the clear watery mirror of the Fountain of

Urdar, then . . . But before I say any more about this disease, let me tell you, gentlemen, that the patient whom I have undertaken to cure is none other than that young man who is looking out of the window, and whom you mistook for the actor Giglio Fava.'

Everyone looked inquisitively at the stranger and agreed that his features, though highly intelligent in all other respects, had something uncertain and confused about them which suggested a dangerous illness, possibly concealed insanity.

'I think, Signor Celionati,' said Reinhold, 'that by your chronic dualism you mean simply that strange form of insanity in which the self is estranged from itself, so that the personality can no longer remain intact.'

'Not bad, my son!' replied the mountebank, 'but you've missed the mark all the same. If, however, I am to give you an account of my patient's strange illness, I fear that I may be unable to tell you about it clearly and intelligibly, especially as you are not physicians and I must therefore avoid all terms of art. Well, let's see how we get on! First of all I must observe that the author who invented us, and whom we must obey if we want really to exist, has prescribed no particular time for us to live and have our being. Fortunately for me, therefore, I can assume, without committing an anachronism, that you have read the works of a certain extremely witty German writer, Georg Christoph Lichtenberg,* and therefore know about the double crown prince. A queen found herself (to borrow the expression of another witty German writer, Jean Paul)* in a more interesting condition than her country. Her people hoped for a prince; the queen, however, gave them twice as much as they had asked for by producing two charming little princes, who were twins of the Siamese variety, being joined together by the hindquarters. Although the court poet claimed that nature had not found enough room in a single human body for all the virtues which the heir to the throne would embody, although the ministers comforted the king, who was rather taken aback by this double blessing, by pointing out that four hands would wield sceptre and sword more firmly than two, just as the whole sonata of government would have a fuller, richer sound in a four-handed rendition—despite all this, there were plenty of circumstances that gave rise to justified concern. First of all, the extreme difficulty of inventing a practical and at the same time elegant model for a certain kind of seat gave grounds for worry about what shape would in future be appropriate for the throne. Likewise, a commission composed of philosophers and tailors took 365 meetings to decide what kind of four-legged trousers would be simultaneously the most comfortable and the most graceful. What seemed worst of all, however, was the complete mental disparity between the two that was gradually revealed. When one prince was sad, the other was merry; when one wanted to sit down, the other wanted to run; in short, their wishes never agreed. And yet it could not be claimed that either had a specific character; for the nature of each seemed to pass over into the other, in an endlessly changing cycle. The reason for this was doubtless that they had grown together not only physically but also spiritually, and that caused the dissension between them. You see, their thoughts always ran sideways, so that neither of them could ever be sure whether his thoughts had been thought by him or by his twin; and if that isn't a muddle, I don't know what is. Now if you imagine somebody having such a double prince, with thoughts running sideways, lodged in his body as *materia peccans*, then you have the illness I am talking about, whose principal symptom is the patient's inability to make sense of himself.'

During this speech the young man had approached the company without being noticed, and as they were all gazing silently at the mountebank as though expecting him to continue, the young man bowed politely and began: 'I do not know, gentlemen, if you have any objection to my joining you. When I have my health and spirits, I am generally popular everywhere; but Master Celionati has doubtless told you such extraordinary things about my illness that you will not want me to bother you.'

Reinhold assured the new guest, on behalf of the rest of the company, that he was welcome, and the young man took his seat in the circle. The mountebank took his leave, after reminding the young man once more to follow the diet prescribed for him.

As always happens, the person who had left the room immediately became the subject of discussion, and the young man was questioned about his extraordinary physician. He assured the company that Master Celionati had acquired a fine body of knowledge and had profitably attended lectures in Halle and Jena, so that one could have perfect confidence in him. In other respects, too, he considered Celionati to be an excellent and congenial man, whose only fault was the very great one of frequently lapsing into allegorical language, much to his own detriment. Master Celionati had indeed, added the young man, spoken in a very extraordinary fashion about the illness he had undertaken to cure. Reinhold explained how, according to the mountebank's assertion, the young man⁻ had a double crown prince lodged in his body.

'Don't you see, gentlemen,' said the young man with a pleasant smile, 'that again is a pure allegory, and yet Master Celionati is precisely acquainted with my illness and knows that I am suffering only from an eye complaint, incurred by wearing spectacles prematurely. There must be something wrong with my retina; for unfortunately I see most things upside-down, and so the most serious matters often strike me as exceedingly comical, and the most comical matters, conversely, as exceedingly serious. This often terrifies me and makes me so giddy that I can hardly stay on my feet. The main thing necessary for my cure, according to Master Celionati, is frequent and vigorous exercise; but, heavens above, how am I to start?'

'Well, my dear Signor,' exclaimed one of the company, 'since I see you're quite steady on your feet, I know . . .'

At that moment there entered a person well known to the kind reader, the celebrated master tailor Bescapi. He went up to the young man, bowed very low, and began: 'Your Royal Highness!'

'Royal Highness?' cried all the artists at once, looking at the young man in astonishment.

The latter, however, said calmly: 'My secret has been accidentally revealed, against my wishes. Yes, gentlemen, I am indeed a prince, and an unfortunate one moreover, since I am striving in vain for possession of the mighty and magnificent kingdom which is my inheritance. If I said a moment ago that I was unable to take the exercise I need, that is because I have no land,

and hence no space in which to move. It is precisely because I am enclosed in such a little box that all the figures I see are in such confusion, shooting across one another's paths like skittles, so that I cannot see them distinctly; which is extremely unpleasant, since my true and inmost nature is such that I can only live in clarity. Thanks, however, to the efforts of my physician and of this venerable minister, I think that a happy alliance with the fairest of princesses can restore me to the health, greatness and power which ought to be mine. I solemnly invite you, gentlemen, to visit me in my territories, in my capital city. You will find yourselves perfectly at home there and will never wish to leave me, because it is only in my domains that you can lead the true life of an artist. Do not fancy, good gentlemen, that I am exaggerating, or that I am given to vain boasting! Wait until I am again a healthy prince, who can recognize his subjects even if they are standing on their heads, and you will learn how anxious I am to do you good. I shall keep my word, as sure as I am the Assyrian Prince Cornelio Chiapperi! For the time being I shall keep my name and country concealed from you, but you shall learn both at the proper time. I must now consult with this excellent minister about certain important affairs of state, then pay a call on folly and walk through the court to see whether any good jokes have sprouted from my hotbeds.' With these words the young man gave the master tailor his arm, and the two of them departed.

'What do you say to all this, my friends?' said Reinhold. 'I feel as though all sorts of figures were running in circles with ever-increasing speed, driven on by the colourful masquerade of some wild, fanciful game, until the eye can no longer recognize them or tell them apart. Let's put on masks, however, and go to the Corso! I suspect that the wild Captain Pantaloon, the victor in yesterday's furious duel, will show himself again today, and do all manner of extraordinary things.'

Reinhold was right. Captain Pantaloon was walking up and down the Corso with measured steps, as though still bathed in the glorious light of his victory the previous day, but without doing anything eccentric as in the past, although his boundless gravity made him look even funnier than usual. The gentle reader has already guessed, and is now certain, who is concealed behind this mask: none other than Prince Cornelio Chiapperi, the fortunate bridegroom of Princess Brambilla. And Princess Brambilla herself could only be the beautiful lady, carrying a wax mask in front of her face and dressed in sumptuous and splendid clothes, who was walking majestically along the Corso. The lady seemed anxious to meet Captain Pantaloon; for she managed to corner him so adroitly that it seemed impossible for him to avoid her, and yet he slipped aside and continued his measured promenade. Finally, however, as he was about to advance with rapid steps, the lady took him by the arm and spoke in sweet and charming tones: 'Yes, it's you, my Prince! Your gait gives you away, and so does the attire worthy of your rank—you never wore anything finer! O speak, why do you flee from me? Do you not recognize your life and hope in me?'

'I really don't know who you are, fair lady!' said Captain Pantaloon. 'Or rather, I dare not guess, since I have so often been the victim of foul deceit. Princesses transform themselves into milliners before my very eyes, comedians turn into cardboard figures, and yet I have resolved not to tolerate illusions and phantasms any longer, but to destroy them wherever I encounter them.'

'Then', exclaimed the lady wrathfully, 'you should begin with yourself! For you yourself, worthy Signor, are nothing more than an illusion! But no,' continued the lady in gentle, tender tones, 'no, beloved Cornelio, you know what sort of Princess it is who loves you, and how she has travelled from distant lands to seek you and be yours! And did you not swear to remain my knight? Speak, beloved!'

The lady had once more taken hold of Pantaloon's arm; he, however, held out his pointed hat towards her, drew his broad sword, and said: 'Behold! I have removed the sign of my knighthood and taken the cock's feathers away from my unvisored helmet; I have quitted the ladies' service; for all of them reward me with ingratitude and faithlessness!'

'What are you saying?' exclaimed the lady angrily. 'Are you mad?'

'The sparkling diamond on your brow', continued Captain Pantaloon, 'may glitter as much as you please! The feather plucked from the gaudy bird may wave in my face! I shall resist

CHAPTER 8

*How Prince Cornelio Chiapperi, unable to console himself, kissed
Princess Brambilla's velvet slipper, and both were then caught in
netting. New marvels of the Pistoia Palace. How two magicians
rose through the Lake of Urdar on ostriches and took their seats in
the lotus-flower. Queen Mystilis. Old acquaintances reappear, and
the capriccio entitled* Princess Brambilla *comes to a joyful
conclusion.*

It did not look, however, as though our friend Captain Pantaloon, or rather the Assyrian Prince Cornelio Chiapperi (for the
gentle reader must now be aware that the wild, grotesque mask
concealed none other than this esteemed princely personage), it
did not look as though he had any idea how to console himself.
For the next day on the Corso he lamented loudly that he had
lost the fairest of all princesses, and that, unless he found her
again, he would run himself through the body with his wooden
sword in sheer desperation. Since, however, his cries of woe were
accompanied by the funniest gestures imaginable, he of course
soon found himself surrounded by all manner of masks who
were enjoying his antics.

'Where is she?' he cried in piteous tones, 'where has she gone,
my lovely bride, my sweet life? Was it for this that I let Master
Celionati extract my finest tooth? Is this why I pursued myself from one corner to another, in order to find myself? And
did I succeed in finding myself, only to languish wretchedly,
deprived of love, pleasure, and the territories which are mine
by right? Good people! If any of you knows where the Princess
is hidden, let him open his mouth and tell me, instead of
leaving me to lament uselessly here; or let him run to the fair
one and inform her that the truest of knights, the smartest of
bridegrooms, is ranting and raving with pure yearning, with
ardent desire, and that all of Rome, like a second Troy, may
perish in the flames of his amorous fury, unless she comes
instantly to cool my ardour with the moist moonbeams of her
gracious eyes!'

The crowd burst into hoots of laughter, but a piercing voice cried: 'Mad Prince, do you think that Princess Brambilla should make any concession to you? Have you forgotten the Pistoia Palace?'

'Ho, ho,' replied the Prince, 'be silent, impudent feather-brain! Be glad that you've escaped from the cage! Good people, look at me and say whether *I* am not the real gaudy bird that is to be caught in netting?'

The crowd uttered renewed hoots of laughter; but at that very moment Captain Pantaloon fell on his knees, as though bereft of his senses; for before him stood the fair one herself, in the full glory of her grace and charm, and in the same clothes as she had been wearing on her first appearance on the Corso, except that instead of her little hat she was wearing a magnificent sparkling diadem on her brow, from which rose brightly coloured plumes.

'I am yours', cried the Prince in the utmost rapture, 'I am entirely yours. Behold these plumes on my burgonet! They are my white flag, the sign of my complete and unconditional surrender!'

'That was inevitable', replied the Princess; 'you had no choice but to submit to such a wealthy potentate as myself, for otherwise you would have no home of your own, and would remain a wretched Prince. Now, however, swear eternal fealty to me, by this symbol of my absolute sovereignty!'

With these words the Princess drew forth a dainty little velvet slipper and handed it to the Prince, who first swore eternal and unshakeable fealty to the Princess as truly as he intended to exist, and then kissed the slipper three times. As soon as he had done so, there rang out a loud, piercing cry of 'Brambure bil bal! Alamonsa kikiburva son-ton!' The couple was surrounded by the ladies swathed in sumptuous robes who, as the gentle reader will remember, entered the Pistoia Palace in Chapter 1. Behind them stood the twelve richly dressed Moors, but instead of pikes the Moors were holding lofty peacocks' feathers, which gleamed wondrously as they waved them to and fro through the air. The ladies, however, threw veils of netting over the couple, swathing them in denser and denser folds and finally in complete darkness.

When the mists of the netting fell away, amid the loud music of horns, cymbals, and kettle-drums, the couple found themselves in the Pistoia Palace, in the very hall into which, a few days earlier, the impudent actor Giglio Fava had intruded.

But the hall now looked far more magnificent than it had done then. For instead of the single lamp illuminating the hall, there were now hundreds suspended all around, so that the hall seemed ablaze. The marble pillars supporting the lofty dome were wreathed in luxuriant garlands; the strange foliation on the ceiling, interwoven with forms that might have been birds with gaudy plumage, delightful children, or wondrous animal shapes, seemed to stir with life, and from the folds of the gilded drapery that canopied the throne the merry, laughing faces of lovely maidens could be seen glinting forth, now here, now there. The ladies were standing in a circle as before, but dressed with greater splendour; instead of netting, however, they were strewing the hall with magnificent flowers from golden vases, or swinging censers which emitted a delectable fragrance. On the throne stood the magician Ruffiamonte and Prince Bastianello di Pistoia, affectionately embracing. It need hardly be said that the latter was none other than the mountebank Celionati. Behind the princely couple—that is, behind Prince Cornelio Chiapperi and Princess Brambilla—stood a small man in a robe of many colours, holding a neat little ivory box; the lid was open, but the box contained nothing but a sparkling little needle, which the small man was gazing at with an extremely cheerful smile.

The magician Ruffiamonte and Prince Bastianello di Pistoia finally loosened their embrace and only squeezed each other's hands. Then the Prince called loudly to the ostriches: 'Hey, good people! Fetch the big book, so that my friend here, honest Ruffiamonte, may read aloud what still has to be read!' The ostriches hopped away, flapping their wings, and fetched the big book, which they placed on the back of a kneeling Moor and then opened.

The Magus, looking remarkably handsome and youthful in spite of his long white beard, stepped over to the book, cleared his throat, and read the following verses:

Italy! Land whose sky's perpetual blue
  Calls forth the richest bloom of all earth's joys!
  Rome, where at Carnival a merry crew

Keeps gravity and jest in equipoise!
  Upon an oval stage of gaudy hue
  Cavort the shapes of fantasy and mirth;

That is the world, ruled by a merry sprite.
  The guardian spirit here can bring to birth
  The not-self from the self in sheer delight,

Creating joy where once were pain and dearth.
  The land, the world, the city, and the self
  Have all been found. In pure celestial clarity

And truly matched, the couple knows itself,
  And apprehends life's last and deepest verity.
  Now dull sobriety must quit the field,

Since folly is transformed to wise hilarity;
  The master's wondrous needle has revealed
  The kingdom lost. Wild magic with its whims

Gives power to the spirit we all revere,
  Arousing him from his delusive dreams.
  Hark! what sweet sounds accost the listening ear?

The azure vault of heaven softly gleams;
  The multitude obeys the music's spell,
  By many a murmuring spring and rustling tree.

O magic land where endless pleasures dwell,
  Where yearning calls to yearning, fain to see
  Its likeness true displayed in love's clear well!

Now plunge yourselves into the surging foam
  That you may taste, beyond the mounting swell,
  The lofty rapture of your fiery home!

The Magus clapped the book shut; but at that moment a fiery vapour arose from the silver funnel on his head, and gradually filled the hall. And amid the harmonious sounds of bells, harps, and trumpets, everything began stirring and surging with life. The dome rose and turned into the cloudless vault of heaven, the pillars turned into lofty palm-trees, the gilding fell down to form the ground strewn with glistening many-coloured flowers, and the great crystal mirror melted and became a magnificent bright lake. The fiery vapour from the Magus's funnel had now dispersed, and cool, balmy breezes wafted through the immeasurable spaces of the magic garden filled with the most magnificent and delightful bushes and trees and flowers. The music grew louder, and amid general jubilation a thousand voices sang:

> All hail and happiness to Urdar's land!
>   Its spring at last shines purified and bright,
>   Freed from the servitude a demon planned!

Suddenly the music, the jubilation, and the singing all ceased; amid profound silence the Magus Ruffiamonte and Prince Bastianello di Pistoia mounted their ostriches and swam towards the lotus-flower which rose from the middle of the lake like a radiant island. They climbed into its calyx, and those with the sharpest eyes among the people assembled round the lake quite clearly perceived the magicians removing a very small, but very dainty china doll from a box and inserting it into the calyx of the flower.

It came to pass that the loving couple, Prince Cornelio Chiapperi and Princess Brambilla, woke from their stupor and involuntarily gazed into the bright, clear, mirror-like lake on whose shore they found themselves. But on seeing themselves in the lake, they *knew* themselves for the first time, gazed at each other, burst out into laughter of such a wondrous kind that it could be compared only to the laughter of King Ophioch and Queen Liris, and then fell into each other's arms in the utmost rapture.

And no sooner did the couple laugh than—O wondrous miracle!—there rose from the lotus-flower's calyx a divine female figure which grew taller and taller until her head towered into the blue of the sky, while her feet were seen taking root in the furthest depths of the lake. In the sparkling crown on her head sat the Magus and the Prince, gazing down upon the crowd of people who, transported and intoxicated with rapture, were rejoicing and shouting: 'Long live our lofty Queen Mystilis!' while the music of the magic garden rang out in full chords.

And again a thousand voices sang:

> Yea, boundless bliss arises from the deep
>   And flies aloft where sunlit heaven gleams.
>   Behold our Queen, restored from magic sleep!

Her god-like head is wreathed in lovely dreams,
    Her footsteps open many a jewelled shaft.
Life's fairest truth—what is, and not what seems—
    Is given to those who knew themselves—and laughed!

Midnight was past, and the crowds were streaming out of the theatres. Old Beatrice closed the window through which she had been peering, and said: 'It's time now for me to get everything ready; for my master and mistress will soon be here, and they'll probably bring good Signor Bescapi with them.' Just as before, when Giglio had to carry the basket filled with delicacies up the stairs, the old woman had bought everything requisite for a delicious meal. But no longer was she obliged to struggle in the narrow space that was supposed to represent a kitchen, and in the miserable cramped room let by Signor Pasquale. Instead, she had a spacious hearth and a brightly lit room at her command, and her master and mistress had three or four fair-sized rooms to move about in, furnished with handsome tables, chairs, and other quite decent domestic objects.

As the old woman spread a fine linen cloth over the table, which she had moved into the middle of the room, she said with a chuckle: 'Hm! It is nice of Signor Bescapi, not only to give us this pretty flat, but to supply us so amply with everything we need. Now, I hope, poverty has left us for ever!'

The door opened and in walked Giglio Fava and his Giacinta.

'Come to my arms, my sweet, lovely wife!' said Giglio. 'Let me tell you, from the bottom of my heart, that since the moment when we were first joined together, I have been filled by life's purest and most glorious delight. Whenever I see you playing Smeraldine, or other roles conceived by true humour, or stand by your side as Brighella, Truffaldino, or some other fantastic humorist, I perceive inwardly a whole world of the wittiest and most daring irony, which gives life to my acting. But tell me, my life, what rare spirit came over you today? Never before have you let loose such flashes of charming feminine humour; never have you been so unspeakably lovable in your pert, fantastic moods.'

'I might say the same about you, my beloved Giglio!' replied Giacinta, pressing a gentle kiss on Giglio's lips. 'You too were more magnificent than ever today, and you may not have noticed that we continued our big scene by improvising for over half an hour, amid prolonged and good-humoured laughter from the audience. But hasn't it occurred to you what a day this is? Don't you realize at what a fateful time this exceptional inspiration seized hold of us? Don't you remember that it is exactly a year since we gazed into the magnificent clear waters of the Lake of Urdar, and knew ourselves?'

'Giacinta,' cried Giglio, in joyful astonishment, 'what are you saying? It seems like a beautiful dream, the Land of Urdar—the Lake of Urdar! But no, it wasn't a dream, we knew ourselves! Oh, my dearest Princess!'

'Oh,' replied Giacinta, 'my dearest Prince!' And now they embraced afresh, with loud laughter and confused exclamations: 'There's Persia—there's India—but here's Bergamo, and here's Frascati—our kingdoms are side by side—no, no, it's one and the same kingdom which we rule over, a mighty and princely couple, it's the beautiful, magnificent Land of Urdar itself—ha, what fun!'

And now they danced round the room, rejoicing, falling into each other's arms, kissing, and laughing.

'Aren't they just like merry children!' muttered old Beatrice meanwhile. 'Married for a whole year, and yet they're still billing and cooing and jumping about and—O Saviour! almost knocking the glasses off the table! Ho, ho! Signor Giglio, keep the hem of your coat out of my ragout! Signora Giacinta, have mercy on the china and spare its life!'

But instead of paying any attention to the old woman, the two continued their antics. Finally Giacinta took hold of Giglio's arms, gazed into his eyes, and said: 'But tell me, dear Giglio, you must have recognized him, the little man standing behind us, wearing a robe of many colours and holding an ivory box?'

'Why not, my dear Giacinta?' replied Giglio. 'It was the good Signor Bescapi, with his creative needle, who is at present our faithful impresario, and who first put us on the stage in the guise that corresponds to our inmost natures. And who would have thought that that crazy old mountebank . . .'

'Yes,' interrupted Giacinta, 'that old Celionati in his ragged cloak and hat full of holes . . .'

'That he was really the fabulous old Prince Bastianello di Pistoia?' said the fine-looking, smartly dressed man who had just walked into the room.

'Oh, gracious sir,' cried Giacinta, her eyes shining with joy, 'is it really you? How happy we are, my Giglio and I, that you've called on us in our little flat! Don't refuse to take a modest meal with us, and then you can tell us the truth about Queen Mystilis, the Land of Urdar, and your friend the magician Hermod, or Ruffiamonte; I still can't make sense of it all.'

'There is no need, my sweet, lovely child,' said the Prince of Pistoia with a gentle smile, 'for any further explanation; it is sufficient that you can make sense of yourself, and have knocked some sense into that bold fellow who has fittingly become your husband. You see, bearing in mind that I am a mountebank, I could easily let loose a torrent of mysterious and boastful-sounding words; I could say that you are imagination, whose wings need humour if they are to soar aloft, but without the body of humour you would be nothing but a pair of wings and would drift away through the air, a plaything of the winds. But I won't do that, and one good reason is that I'd lapse into allegory, thus committing a fault for which Prince Cornelio Chiapperi rightly reproved old Celionati in the Caffè Greco. I'll simply say that there is indeed an evil demon who wears sable caps and black dressing-gowns, and, by passing himself off as the great Magus Hermod, is able to bewitch not only good people of ordinary stamp but even queens like Mystilis. It was extremely malicious of the demon to arrange that the Princess could only be freed from her spell by a miracle which he considered impossible. For it was necessary to find, in a little world known as the theatre, a couple of people who were not only animated by true imagination, true inward humour, but were also capable of recognizing this state of mind objectively, as though in a mirror, and of introducing it into external life in such a way that it should have the effect of a powerful spell upon the great world which surrounds the little world. Thus the theatre, if you like, could after a fashion represent the well of 'Urdar, in which people can look. I was convinced, dear children, that the spell could be broken through you, and I promptly wrote off to my friend the Magus Hermod. You know how he arrived forthwith, and put up in my palace, and you know how much trouble we took over you, and if Master Callot had not stepped in and teased you, Giglio, into taking off your heroic garb . . .'

'Yes, gracious sir,' interrupted Signor Bescapi, who had followed close on the Prince's heels, 'a hero's colourful garb—when you're talking to this charming couple, remember me, and the part I took in the great task!'

'Certainly,' replied the Prince, 'and because you were also a wonderful man in yourself, a tailor who found fantastic people to wear the fantastic garments you were skilled in making, I made use of your help and finally made you the impresario of the strange theatre where irony and true humour are what counts.'

'I have always thought of myself,' said Signor Bescapi, with an extremely cheerful smile, 'as someone who makes sure that things don't get spoiled when they are being cut out, like form and style, so to speak!'

'Well said, Master Bescapi!' cried the Prince of Pistoia.

While the Prince of Pistoia, Giglio, and Bescapi were talking of this and that, Giacinta busied herself charmingly by decorating the room and the table with flowers which old Beatrice had hastened to fetch, and by lighting many candles. When the room was brightly lit and looking festive, she insisted that the Prince should sit in the armchair, which she had adorned with so many cloths and rugs that it could almost be compared to a throne.

'Somebody', said the Prince before sitting down, 'of whom we should all be very much afraid, since he is sure to criticize us unmercifully and may dispute our very existence, might say that I have come here at night for no reason other than for his sake, and to tell him what you had to do with the freeing of Queen Mystilis, who is the true Princess Brambilla, from her spell. This Somebody is wrong; for I tell you that I came here, and will always come on the fateful anniversary of your self-knowledge, to share your pleasure in the idea that all people may be called rich and happy who, like us, have beheld and recognized their lives, themselves, and their entire existence in the wondrous sunlit mirror of the Lake of Urdar.'

At this point, O kind reader! the source on which the editor of these pages has drawn suddenly dries up. There is only an obscure legend to the effect that both the Prince of Pistoia and the impresario Bescapi greatly enjoyed the macaroni and the Syracusan wine in the company of the young couple. It may also be surmised that on that evening and also later, many wondrous things happened to the fortunate pair of actors who had come into such close contact with Queen Mystilis and the power of magic.

Master Callot is the only person who could provide further information.

MASTER FLEA

A fairy-tale in seven adventures of two friends

FIRST ADVENTURE

Introduction

In which the kind reader learns as much as he needs to know about the life of Mr Peregrinus Tyss. The distribution of Christmas presents in the house of the bookbinder Lämmerhirt in Kalbach Lane, and the beginning of the first adventure. The two Alines.

Once upon a time—what author nowadays dare begin his tale in such a way? 'Old-fashioned! Boring!' cries the kind or rather unkind reader, who, as the old Roman poet* sagely advises, wishes to be brought immediately *medias in res*. He feels as though some tedious, long-winded guest had just arrived and were taking a comfortable seat and clearing his throat in order to begin his endless sermon; and he impatiently shuts the book that he has scarcely opened. The present editor of the wondrous tale of Master Flea is indeed of the opinion that such a beginning is in fact a very good one, in fact the best that any story can have, which is why the best story-tellers, such as nurse-maids, old women, and so forth, have always made use of it. But since any author writes principally in order to be read, the aforementioned editor will by no means deprive the gentle reader of the desire to be *his* reader. He therefore informs the reader straight away and without more ado that Peregrinus Tyss, whose strange destinies this story will relate, had never on any previous Christmas Eve felt such tremulous excitement and joyous anticipation as on the evening when the narrative of his adventures begins.

Peregrinus was in a dark chamber next to the large room in which he was accustomed to receive his Christmas presents.

There he at times crept softly up and down, listening occasionally at the door; at times he seated himself quietly in the corner, closed his eyes, and inhaled the mystic scents of marzipan and gingerbread which were streaming out of the next room. He shivered deliciously in secret each time he opened his eyes suddenly and was dazzled by the bright rays of light that came through the cracks in the door and ran to and fro along the wall.

At last the silver bell tinkled, the door was opened, and Peregrinus rushed out to find a blazing ocean of flickering Christmas lights in many colours. He stopped stock still in front of the table on which the most beautiful gifts were neatly and delightfully arranged; only a loud 'Oh!' forced its way from his breast. Never before had the Christmas tree borne such rich fruit, for all the sweets you can possibly name, along with many golden nuts, many golden apples from the garden of the Hesperides, were hanging from the boughs, which bent under their sweet burden. And there is no describing the supply of the choicest toys, beautiful lead soldiers, huntsmen to match, opened picture-books, and so on. Peregrinus still did not venture to touch any of the wealth bestowed on him; it was all he could do to overcome his astonishment and to grasp the happy thought that all this really was now his.

'Oh, my dear parents! Oh, my good Aline!' cried Peregrinus in the utmost rapture.

'Now,' replied Aline, 'have I done it properly, Perry? Are you really pleased, my child? Don't you want to take a closer look at all these beautiful things? Wouldn't you like to try out your new horse, this handsome bay?'

'A magnificent horse,' said Peregrinus, looking at the harnessed and saddled rocking-horse with tears of joy in his eyes, 'a magnificent horse, of the true Arab breed.' He promptly mounted the noble steed; but though Peregrinus was normally an excellent horseman, he must have done something wrong on this occasion, for the untamed Pontifex (that was the horse's name) reared up, snorting, and threw him off, so that he landed with his legs in the air. However, before the terrified Aline could leap to his aid, Peregrinus picked himself up and seized the horse's bridle just as it was kicking its heels and making ready to bolt. Once more he swung himself into the saddle, and by fully exerting all his equestrian skill, managed to tame the wild stallion so that it trembled, panted, moaned, and acknowledged Peregrinus as its lord and master. Once Peregrinus had dismounted, Aline led the vanquished beast to its stable.

Now that the boisterous horsemanship, which had caused an excessive noise in the room and probably in the whole house, was over, Peregrinus sat down at the table in order to make a calm inspection of the other gleaming gifts. He contentedly ate some marzipan while putting various puppets through their paces, looking into some of the picture-books, and then reviewing his smartly uniformed army, which he deemed invincible for the good reason that none of the soldiers had a stomach. He then turned to hunting. To his annoyance he now noticed that there was only a rabbit-hunt and a fox-hunt; the stag-hunt and the wild-boar-hunt were completely missing. They should have been there, and nobody knew that better than Peregrinus, who had bought all the toys himself with indescribable trouble and care.

But wait! it seems essential to preserve the gentle reader from a serious misunderstanding into which he might fall if the author were to continue describing this feast without remembering that *he* knows the truth about the Christmas display of which he has spoken, but the kind reader does not; and the reader, of course, wants to learn something not known already.

It would be a great mistake to suppose that Peregrinus Tyss was a child receiving Christmas presents from his kindly mother or some other affectionate female with the romantic name of Aline. Not a bit of it!

Mr Peregrinus Tyss was thirty-six years old and hence almost in the prime of life. Six years before people had said that he was a handsome fellow; now they rightly called him a fine-looking man; but always, both then and now, everyone complained that Peregrinus was too much of a recluse, unacquainted with life, and obviously inclined towards morbid melancholy. Fathers with marriageable daughters opined that the best way for the good Tyss to cure himself of melancholy was to marry, for he had a free choice and need hardly fear a refusal. On this last point, at least, the fathers were correct, inasmuch as Mr Peregrinus was not only a fine-looking man, as has been stated, but also possessed a very substantial fortune left to him by his father, Mr Balthasar Tyss, a highly respected merchant. When such a gifted man asks a girl who has grown out of romantic infatuations, i.e. has reached at least the age of twenty-three or twenty-four, the innocent question: 'Will you make me happy by giving me your hand, my precious one?' she generally answers, with blushing cheeks and downcast eyes, 'Speak to my dear parents; I obey their command, I have no will of my own!' Her parents, however, fold their hands and say: 'If it is God's will, we can have no objection, dear son-in-law!'

Nothing seemed further from Mr Peregrinus Tyss's thoughts, however, than marriage. For besides being extremely timid in general, he displayed a strange idiosyncrasy with regard to the female sex in particular. A woman's presence brought out beads of perspiration on his forehead, and if a young and tolerably pretty girl spoke to him, he fell into a panic which made him completely tongue-tied and caused him to tremble convulsively in every limb. That may have been the reason why his old nurse was so singularly ugly that many people in the district where Mr Peregrinus Tyss lived considered her a curiosity of natural history. Her black, matted, greying hair matched her rheumy red eyes, her bulbous coppery nose matched her pallid lips, completing the image of a candidate for a witches' sabbath on the Blocksberg,* so that a couple of centuries earlier she could scarcely have avoided being burnt at the stake. Now, however, she was thought by Mr Peregrinus Tyss, and doubtless by many others, to be a very good-natured person. So indeed she was, and hence she might well be forgiven for catering to her bodily comfort by drinking many glasses of schnapps in the course of the day; she also, perhaps too frequently, drew a monstrous black lacquered snuff-box from her tucker and gave her protuberant nose an ample supply of genuine Offenbach snuff. The kind reader has by now perceived that this remarkable person is the very same Aline who arranged the Christmas presents. Heaven knows how she acquired the illustrious name of the Queen of Golconda.*

If fathers demanded that the rich and agreeable Mr Peregrinus Tyss should abandon his misogyny and enter into matrimony on the spot, old bachelors contradicted them by asserting that Mr Peregrinus was quite right not to marry, since his temperament was not suited for it.

The trouble was, however, that many of them, on uttering the word 'temperament', assumed an enigmatic expression and, in response to further enquiries, hinted rather distinctly that Mr Peregrinus Tyss was apt to go off his head from time to time, a failing which he had displayed from his earliest youth. The many people who thought that poor Peregrinus was off his head were chiefly of the sort who are firmly convinced that on life's great highway, which one must follow in accordance with sense and reason, the best guide and signpost is one's nose, and who would rather wear blinkers than be tempted by the fragrant shrubs and flowery meadows that lie alongside.

It is certainly true enough that Mr Peregrinus had many strange qualities which people found hard to accept.

We have already mentioned that the father of Mr Peregrinus Tyss was a very rich and respected merchant, and when we add that he also owned a splendid house on the pleasant Horsemarket, and that it was in this house, and in the very room where little Peregrinus had always received his Christmas presents, that the adult Peregrinus now received *his* presents, nobody can doubt that the scene of the wondrous adventures narrated in the story is none other than the famous and beautiful town of Frankfurt on the Main.

About Mr Peregrinus's parents there is nothing in particular to be said, save that they were decent quiet people of whom nobody could say anything but good. The boundless esteem which Mr Tyss enjoyed on the Stock Exchange was due to the fact that his speculations were always correct and secure, and that in gaining one large sum after another he never grew conceited, but remained as modest as before. Instead of showing off his wealth, he displayed it only by avoiding all niggardliness, whether with large amounts or small, and by his indulgence towards insolvent debtors who had fallen into misfortune, even if they were themselves to blame.

For a very long time Mr Tyss's marriage was childless, until after almost twenty years Mrs Tyss presented her husband with a fine healthy boy, who was of course our Mr Peregrinus Tyss.

You may imagine how boundless was the parents' joy, and even today everyone in Frankfurt still talks about the magnificent christening feast given by old Tyss, where the noblest and oldest Rhine wine was drunk, as though it were a coronation dinner. What is held even more to old Mr Tyss's credit, however, is that he invited to this christening feast a couple of people who had often injured him out of malice, as well as others whom he thought *he* had injured, so that the banquet turned into a true feast of peace and reconciliation.

Alas! little did good Mr Tyss know or suspect that that same boy whose birth so delighted him would soon cause him sorrow and grief.

Even in early childhood Peregrinus displayed a very peculiar temperament. For, after crying continuously, day and night, for several weeks, although no physical ailment could be found, he suddenly fell silent and became motionless, rigid, and unresponsive. He seemed incapable of the slightest reaction: his little face moved neither to laugh nor to cry, and seemed to be that of a lifeless doll. His mother maintained that while pregnant with him she had happened to look at the old bookkeeper, who had been sitting for the past twenty years silent and motionless, with the same lifeless face, in front of the ledger in the counting-house. She shed many tears over the little automaton.

At last Peregrinus's godmother had the happy thought of bringing him a garishly painted and, truth to tell, very ugly harlequin. The child's eyes came to life in a wondrous manner, his mouth formed a gentle smile, he stretched out his hand for the doll, and, on being given it, squeezed it tenderly. Then the child looked again at the coloured manikin with such an intelligent and eloquent expression as though his sensibility and understanding had suddenly been awakened into more activity than is usual in children of his age. 'He's too clever,' said his godmother, 'he won't live long! Just look at his eyes; he thinks much more than he ought to!'

This remark was a great comfort to old Mr Tyss, who had in some measure resigned himself to ending up with a simpleton after so many years of vain hopes. Soon, however, he acquired new worries.

The time when children usually begin to speak was long past, and yet Peregrinus had not uttered a sound. He would have been taken for a deaf mute if he did not sometimes look attentively at the person talking to him, and even indicate his response by a joyful or sorrowful expression, so that it was impossible to doubt that he not only heard but also understood everything that was said to him. His mother was greatly astonished when she found the godmother's remark confirmed. At night, when the child was in bed and thought nobody was listening, he uttered single words and even whole phrases, which were so far from being gibberish that they seemed the result of long practice. Heaven has endowed women with a singular and unfailing ability to respond tactfully to human nature as it follows diverse paths in its early development, and this is why they are generally much the best people to bring up children, at least in the earliest years of life. In keeping with such tactfulness, Mrs Tyss never thought of letting the child know what she had observed, or forcing him to speak; instead, she skilfully found other means of inducing him no longer to conceal his talent for speech, but to let it shine before all the world and to express himself, slowly but distinctly, to everyone's admiration. However, he always showed some reluctance to speak, and preferred being left to himself.

Mr Tyss was therefore relieved of his worry about Peregrinus's failure to speak, only to acquire much greater worries later on. When Peregrinus had grown into a boy of school age, it seemed impossible to teach him anything without extreme effort. Reading and writing followed the same wondrous course as speaking: at first all efforts seemed unavailing, and then all of a sudden he did it far better than anyone could have expected. Later, one tutor after another left the house, not because they disliked the boy, but because they could not come to terms with his character. Peregrinus was quiet, well-behaved, and industrious, and yet proper systematic learning, such as the tutors wanted, was out of the question, since he would not take an interest in or devote himself to anything that did not appeal to his deepest emotions, and everything else passed him by without leaving a trace. What appealed to his emotions was above all the wondrous. Whatever aroused his imagination became the element in which he lived and had his being. Thus he once received as a present an elevation of the city of Peking, with all its streets, houses, and so on, which took up a whole wall of his room. Looking at this fairy-tale city with the extraordinary people who seemed to be thronging its streets, Peregrinus felt as though the stroke of a magic wand had transported him to another world in which he wanted to make his home. He threw himself passionately upon anything he could find concerning China, the Chinese, or Peking; he found somewhere a list of the Chinese sounds, and laboured to pronounce them accurately in a shrill piping voice; he even tried, with the aid of the paper-scissors, to give his beautiful calamanco dressing-gown a Chinese cut, so that he might follow local customs and walk rapturously through the streets of Peking. Nothing else could attract his attention, much to the annoyance of his tutor, who was trying to teach him the history of the Hanseatic League at the express desire of old Mr Tyss. The latter was now obliged to learn, much to his sorrow, that Peregrinus could not be removed from Peking, whereupon he had Peking itself removed from the boy's room.

Old Mr Tyss had already considered it a bad omen when Peregrinus, as a small child, preferred counters to ducats, and later displayed a decided aversion to large money-bags, ledgers, and day-books. Strangest of all, he could not hear the phrase 'bill of exchange' being uttered without trembling convulsively and declaring that he felt as though somebody were scraping a pane of glass with the point of a knife. Mr Tyss was obliged to realize that there was no hope of making a merchant out of Peregrinus, and though he would have been glad to see his son following in his footsteps, he renounced this desire, on the assumption that Peregrinus would devote himself to a specific profession. It was a principle with Mr Tyss that even the wealthiest man must have an occupation and hence a definite standpoint in life. Dilettantes were an abomination to him, and yet Peregrinus showed every sign of becoming such a dilettante, having acquired in his own way a chaotic jumble of knowledge. This was old Tyss's greatest and most pressing worry. Peregrinus cared nothing about the real world, his father knew of no other; and so it was inevitable that, as Peregrinus grew older, this should give rise to an ever-increasing conflict between father and son. This caused great sorrow to Peregrinus's mother, for since he was generally good-natured, well-behaved, and an excellent son, she was perfectly happy to tolerate his activities, little as she understood his dreams and fancies, and she could not understand why his father was so anxious to impose a specific occupation on him.

On the advice of trusted friends old Tyss sent his son to the University of Jena. When Peregrinus returned after three years, however, the old gentleman exclaimed in vexation and anger: 'Just as I thought! John-a-Dreams went away, John-a-Dreams has come back!' Mr Tyss was quite right, inasmuch as Peregrinus's character had not changed a jot, but had remained just the same. However, Mr Tyss had not yet given up hope of persuading his wayward son to see sense, opining that if Peregrinus were forced into business, he might end up by liking it and changing his disposition. He sent him to Hamburg on some errands which required no special knowledge of commerce, and recommended him to a friend there, who was to assist him faithfully in all things.

Peregrinus arrived in Hamburg, presented his father's business acquaintance not only with the letter of recommendation but also with all the papers concerning his errands, and then vanished, nobody knew where.

Thereupon Mr Tyss's business acquaintance wrote to him:

Yours of the — to hand, delivered by your worthy son. The latter did not show his face again, but quickly departed from Hamburg without leaving a message.—Peppers are quiet here, cotton is bearish, only the middling brands of coffee are in demand; loaf sugar, however, is holding up well, and in indigo there continue to be sundry good opinions.—I have the honour to be, etc.

This letter would have caused Mr Tyss and his good lady no little dismay, had not the same post brought a letter from their prodigal son, apologizing in the most melancholy language for his entire inability to perform his errands according to his father's wishes, and explaining that he felt irresistibly drawn to remote regions, from which he hoped to return home, in better spirits, after a year.

'It's a good thing', said the old gentleman, 'for the lad to see

a bit of the world; they'll shake him out of his day-dreams.'
When Peregrinus's mother expressed concern that their son
might not have enough money for his long journey, so that he
was to be blamed for his carelessness in not telling them where
he was going, the old man replied with a laugh: 'If the lad is
short of money, he'll come to terms all the sooner with the real
world, and even if he hasn't told us where he's going, he knows
where to write to *us*.'

Nobody knows where Peregrinus actually journeyed; some
maintain that he went as far as India, others say that he only
imagined it; but it is certain that he must have been far away,
for it was not after a year, as he had promised his parents, but
only after three whole years had elapsed, that Peregrinus returned to Frankfurt. He arrived on foot and in considerable
poverty.

He found his parents' house bolted and barred. Nobody
stirred within, however hard he rang and knocked.

At last the next-door neighbour returned from the Stock
Exchange, and Peregrinus promptly asked him if Mr Tyss was
by any chance away on a journey.

His neighbour started back in astonishment and exclaimed:
'Mr Peregrinus Tyss! Is it you? Are you back at last? Don't you
know . . . ?'

Peregrinus stood speechless in front of his neighbour; for the
first time the sorrow of life pierced his heart, and he saw the
beautiful gleaming world, where he had once dwelt merrily,
shattered to pieces.

His neighbour saw clearly that Peregrinus was quite unable
to transact any necessary business, however small. He therefore
took him into his house and sorted everything out with the
utmost speed, so that Peregrinus found himself back in his
parents' house that same evening.

Exhausted and crushed by a feeling of desolation such as he
had never before known, he sank into his father's big armchair,
which was still standing in its former position. Then a voice
said: 'How good it is that you're back, dear Mr Peregrinus. Oh,
if only you had come sooner!'

Peregrinus looked up and saw, standing right in front of him,
the old woman whom his father had employed as a nurse in his

early childhood, mainly because her frightful ugliness made it difficult for her to find employment, and who had never left the house since.

After staring at her for a long time, Peregrinus at last began, with a strange smile: 'Is that you, Aline? My parents are still alive, aren't they?' With these words he rose and went through all the rooms, looking at each chair, each table, each picture, and so forth. Then he said calmly: 'Yes, everything is as I left it, and it shall remain so!'

From that moment on Peregrinus began the strange way of life referred to at the outset. Withdrawn from all society, he lived in the great spacious house with his old nurse in the deepest solitude. At first he was all alone, but later he rented a couple of rooms to an old man who had been a friend of his father's. This man seemed as much a hermit as Peregrinus. That was reason enough for Peregrinus and the old man to get on very well, since they never saw each other.

There were only four family anniversaries which Peregrinus celebrated with the utmost solemnity. These were his father's and mother's birthdays, the first day of Easter, and his own christening. On these days Aline had to lay a table for as many people as Peregrinus's father had generally invited, prepare the same dishes that had usually been served, and supply the same wine as in the past. It goes without saying that the same silver, the same plates, the same glasses, which had been bequeathed intact to Peregrinus, had to be used in the manner that had been customary for so many years. Peregrinus insisted strictly on this. Once the table was ready, Peregrinus sat down all alone at its head, ate and drank only a little, listened to the conversation of his parents and the imaginary guests, and gave modest replies to the occasional question put to him by one of the company. Once his mother had pushed back her chair, he rose with the others and took his leave of everyone with the greatest politeness. He then retired to a distant room and left his Aline to distribute the many untouched dishes and the wine to the poor. The faithful soul performed her master's command most conscientiously. On his parents' birthdays, Peregrinus began the celebration early in the morning, as he had done as a boy, by bringing a beautiful bouquet into the room where his parents were breakfasting and reciting some verses which he had learnt by heart. On his own christening feast he naturally could not sit at the table, as he had only just been born. Aline therefore had to take care of everything herself, such as urging the guests to drink and, as the phrase goes, doing the honours of the table; otherwise this was exactly like the other anniversaries. Apart from these, Peregrinus had one specially joyful day, or rather joyful evening, in the year, and that was the distribution of presents on Christmas Eve, which, more than any other enjoyment, had aroused sweet and pious rapture in his young heart.

Peregrinus himself purchased coloured Christmas lights, toys, and sweets, just as his parents had done for him in his boyhood, and then the presents were distributed as the kind reader has already been told.

'It's most annoying,' said Peregrinus, after playing a little longer, 'it's most annoying that the stag-hunt and the wild-boar-hunt have gone astray. Where on earth can they be? Oh, look!' At that moment he noticed a still unopened box, and hastily stretched out his hand towards it, supposing that it contained the missing hunt; on opening it, however, he found it empty, and started back as though shaken by sudden terror. 'Strange,' he murmured to himself, 'strange! What can be the matter with this box? I felt as though something dangerous, which my eyes were not sharp enough to perceive, had leapt out of it at me!'

On being questioned, Aline assured him that she had found the box among the toys, but had struggled in vain to open it; hence she had assumed that it contained something special, and that its lid would yield only to the expert hand of her master. 'Strange,' repeated Peregrinus, 'very strange! And I was particularly looking forward to that hunt; I hope this is not ominous! But who would dwell on such groundless fancies on Christmas Eve? Aline, bring the basket!' Aline promptly brought him a large white basket with a handle, into which Peregrinus carefully packed the toys, the sweets, and the lights; he then took the basket under his arm, and the big Christmas tree over his shoulder, and thus set out on his journey.

Mr Peregrinus Tyss had the kindly and laudable habit of

taking all the presents which he had laid out for himself and paying an unexpected visit to some needy family where he knew there were merry children, laden with colourful, shining presents like Father Christmas, so that he might relive his happy childhood for a couple of hours. When the children's joy was at its height, he would creep softly away and would often walk the streets for half the night, unable to control the deep emotion that weighed upon his heart, and feeling that his own house was a dismal tomb in which he and all his joys were buried. On this occasion the presents were destined for the children of a poor bookbinder named Lämmerhirt, a skilful and industrious man who had been working for Mr Peregrinus for some time, and whose three merry boys, aged from five to nine, were well known to him.

The bookbinder Lämmerhirt lived on the top floor of a narrow tenement in Kalbach Lane, and what with the whistling and raging of the winter gale, and the furious showers of sleet, you may imagine that Mr Peregrinus did not reach his destination without considerable effort. A couple of meagre lights were shining feebly from Lämmerhirt's windows as Peregrinus toiled up the steep stairs. 'Open up,' he cried, 'open up, open up! Father Christmas has brought presents for good children!'

The bookbinder opened the door in alarm, and gazed at the snow-covered Peregrinus for quite a while before recognizing him. 'Why, Mr Tyss, sir,' exclaimed Lämmerhirt in astonishment, 'for heaven's sake, Mr Tyss, sir, to what do I owe this honour, on Christmas Eve . . .'.

Instead of letting him finish, however, Mr Peregrinus shouted: 'Children, children! Look out, Father Christmas has brought you presents!', took command of the large gateleg table in the middle of the room, and began to fetch the Christmas presents from the basket where they had been safely protected from the weather. The dripping wet Christmas tree had of course been left outside the door. The bookbinder still could not understand what was happening; his wife was quicker to catch on, for she smiled at Peregrinus with tears in her eyes, but the children stood at some distance, silently devouring with their eyes each present that emerged from the wrappings, and could not refrain from uttering loud cries of joy and astonishment. Finally, when Peregrinus had cleverly divided up the presents and arranged them according to the age of each child, he turned on all the lights and cried: 'Come along, children, these are the presents that Father Christmas has brought you!' The children, who had scarcely grasped that all this was to be theirs, burst out in loud rejoicing and jumped up and down with cries of pleasure, while their parents prepared to thank their benefactor.

Being thanked by the parents and the children was just what Mr Peregrinus always tried to avoid, and so he was anxious to slip away quietly as usual. He had reached the door when it suddenly opened and before him, in the clear light of the Christmas candles, stood a young woman dressed in radiant garments.

It is seldom wise for an author to offer the kind reader a precise description of any very beautiful person who appears in his story, detailing that person's height, build, posture, colour of eyes and hair; instead, it seems preferable to give you this person wholesale instead of piecemeal. In any case, it would suffice to assure you that the woman approaching Peregrinus, to his mortal terror, was exceptionally pretty and charming, were it not important to mention certain special features that distinguished this little person.

The woman was indeed little, smaller, in fact, than anyone ought to be, but of very fine and delicate build. Although her face was shapely and expressive, it was given a somewhat strange and alien air by the fact that her pupils were larger and her finely drawn black eyebrows were higher than is normal. The little lady was dressed, not to say tricked out, as though she had just come from a ball. A magnificent diadem flashed amid her dark hair; the rich border of her dress only half concealed her full breasts; her lilac and yellow striped dress of heavy silk clung close to her slender body, its folds falling only far enough to reveal the daintiest little feet in white shoes; likewise, her lace sleeves and her white kid gloves were short enough to display the most beautiful part of her dazzlingly white arms. Her costume was completed by a rich collar and diamond ear-rings.

Of course the bookbinder was just as taken aback as Mr Peregrinus, and the children abandoned their toys to stare open-mouthed at the strange lady; but, since women are always the people least surprised by anything odd or unusual and are always the first to recover their composure, it was the book-binder's wife who spoke first, asking whether they could serve the beautiful stranger in any way.

As the lady now entered the room, the alarmed Peregrinus tried to seize this moment to make his escape. The lady, how-ever, took him by both hands and lisped in a sweet little voice: 'Fortune favours me, I have caught up with you! O Peregrinus, dear Peregrinus, what a happy and propitious reunion!'

With these words she raised her right hand so that it touched Peregrinus's lips and he was obliged to kiss it, despite the drops of cold perspiration that appeared on his brow. The lady then let go of his hands, and he could indeed have fled, but he felt himself under a spell, unable to move from the spot, like some wretched animal fascinated by the sight of the rattlesnake. 'Dearest Peregrinus,' said the lady, 'do let me take part in this beautiful festival, which you, with your noble character and your warm and tender heart, have arranged for these good children. And let me contribute something as well.'

Only now did they notice a dainty little basket hanging from her arm. From it she drew all manner of pretty toys which she busily arranged on the table. She led the boys to it, showed each one the presents intended for him, and behaved so nicely to the children that her charm was really indescribable. The book-binder thought he was dreaming, but his wife had a mischie-vous smile, for she was convinced that there was something special between Mr Peregrinus and the strange lady.

While the parents continued to wonder and the children to rejoice, the strange lady took her seat on a rickety old sofa and compelled Mr Peregrinus Tyss, who was beginning to doubt whether he was indeed that person, to sit beside her. 'My dear,' she began, lisping softly in his ear, 'my precious friend, how happy, how blissful I feel at your side.'

'But,' stuttered Peregrinus, 'but, my dear young lady . . .', then suddenly, heaven knows how, the strange lady's lips came so close to his that, before he had thought of kissing her, he had done so. You may imagine that this rendered him speechless once and for all.

'My sweet friend,' went on the strange lady, edging so close to Peregrinus that she was practically sitting on his lap, 'my sweet friend! I know what grieves you, I know what wounded your peaceful child-like heart this evening. But take comfort! I have brought you that which you lost and hardly dared hope ever to recover.'

With these words the strange lady took from her basket of toys a wooden box, and handed it to Peregrinus. It contained the stag-hunt and wild-boar-hunt that he had missed among his Christmas presents. It would be hard to describe the strange emotions that clashed in Peregrinus's mind.

If the strange lady's appearance, despite her delightful charm, had something ghostly about it that might have raised a shudder even in people less inclined than Peregrinus to shun female company, poor Peregrinus, who had already been sufficiently frightened, could not but be overcome by deep horror on realizing that everything he had done in utter solitude was known to the lady in minute detail. Yet amid his horror, when he looked up and saw her beautiful dark eyes shining triumphantly beneath her long silky lashes, when he felt the sweet breath of the gracious being, and the electric warmth of her body—then, with wondrous shivers, he began to sense the unspeakable pain of inexpressible desire, which he had never before known, stirring within him! For the first time, his whole way of life, especially the game with Christmas presents, seemed childish and silly, and he felt ashamed that the lady should know about it. It seemed as though her gift were the living proof that she understood him better than anyone else on earth, and that a deep, warm feeling of delicacy had led her to give him pleasure in this way. He resolved to keep the precious gift for ever and never let it out of his hands. Completely carried away by his feelings, he pressed the box containing the stag-hunt and wild-boar-hunt violently against his chest.

'Oh, what rapture!' lisped the lady. 'You are pleased with my gift! Oh, darling Peregrinus, my dreams, my premonitions did not deceive me!'

Mr Peregrinus Tyss regained his senses sufficiently to say, clearly and audibly: 'But my dear young lady, if only I had the least idea whom I have the honour . . .'.

'Naughty man,' interrupted the lady, tapping him gently on the cheek, 'pretending not to know your faithful Aline! But we mustn't take up these good people's room any longer. Accompany me, Mr Tyss!'

On hearing the name Aline, Peregrinus naturally thought of his old nurse, and he now felt just as though a windmill were spinning round inside his head.

The strange lady now took leave of the bookbinder, his wife, and his children in the most charming and cheerful way imaginable. Lämmerhirt's astonishment and awe allowed him only to stammer something unintelligible, while the children behaved as though the stranger were an old acquaintance. But Mrs Lämmerhirt said: 'Such a good-looking, generous gentleman as yourself, Mr Tyss, deserves to marry a beautiful, kind-hearted lady like this one, who helps you to do good works even at night. I congratulate you with all my heart!' The lady thanked her with visible emotion, declaring that their wedding-day should be a festival for the Lämmerhirts as well. She then forbade any of the family to accompany them, and took a small candle from the table to light them down the stairs.

You may imagine how Mr Tyss, now arm-in-arm with the strange lady, felt about all this! ' "Accompany me, Mr Tyss!" ' he thought, 'that must mean downstairs as far as the carriage which is standing outside the door and where the servant, or perhaps a whole staff of servants, is waiting; for this must be some mad princess, who . . . May heaven release me from this strange agony and leave me with such wits as I have!'

Mr Tyss had no idea that everything that had happened so far was only a prelude to the most extraordinary of adventures, and therefore, without realizing it, he did well in asking heaven in advance to preserve his wits.

When the couple had descended the stairs, the front door was opened by invisible hands and closed again in like manner once Peregrinus and the lady had gone out. Peregrinus paid no attention to this, for he was overcome by astonishment on finding not the slightest trace of a carriage or an attendant outside the building.

'For heaven's sake,' exclaimed Peregrinus, 'where is your carriage, my lady?'

'Carriage?' replied the lady, 'what carriage? Do you suppose, dear Peregrinus, that my impatience, my anxiety to find you, would have let me drive here slowly and calmly? I ran through rain and storm, urged on by hope and yearning, until I found you. Thanks be to heaven that I succeeded! Now, take me home, dear Peregrinus, I live not far from here.'

Mr Peregrinus forcibly dismissed the idea that it would have impossible for the lady, smartly dressed as she was in white silken shoes, to take even a few steps without spoiling her entire costume amid the sleet and snow, whereas her meticulous toilette revealed not the slightest discomposure. He resigned himself to accompanying her some distance further, and was glad that the weather had changed. The wild storm was over, there was not a cloud in the sky, the full moon shed its friendly beams, and only the bitingly cold air reminded them that it was a winter night.

Scarcely had Peregrinus taken more than a step, however, when the lady began first to whimper softly, then to lament loudly that she was freezing to death. Peregrinus's blood was coursing through his veins with such heat that he did not feel the cold and it had therefore not occurred to him that the lady was thinly clad, without even a shawl. Realizing his blunder, he tried to put his cloak round her. However, the lady fended off his efforts, moaning: 'No, my dear Peregrinus! That's no use! My feet! Oh, my feet! I shall die of this frightful pain!' Half-fainting, and about to collapse, she besought him in a weak voice: 'Carry me, carry me, my gracious friend!'

Peregrinus promptly took the little lady, who proved as light as a feather, in his arms like a child, and wrapped her carefully in the folds of his cloak. He had only gone a short distance with his lovely burden, however, when a frenzy of intense desire seized hold of him ever more strongly. As he rushed through the streets, almost beside himself, he rained ardent kisses upon the neck and bosom of the gracious being who was nestling close to his chest. Finally he seemed to wake abruptly from a dream: he was outside a door, and looking up he recognized his own house on the Horsemarket. Only now did it occur to him that he had not asked the lady where she lived. He pulled himself together with a violent effort and asked: 'Madame! you heavenly, divine being, where do you live?'

'Why, here, dear Peregrinus,' returned the lady, raising her dainty head, 'here in this house. I'm your Aline, I live with you! Open the door quickly.'

'No! Never!' shouted Peregrinus in terror, letting her sink to the ground.

'What!' cried the lady, 'you are about to drive me away, Peregrinus, and yet you know of my frightful fate, you know that as a child of misfortune I have no roof over my head, and that I must perish here miserably, unless you take me into your home as before! But perhaps you would rather I died—so be it! At least carry me to the fountain, so that people won't find my corpse in front of your house—ah—those stone dolphins may have more pity than you. Oh! oh! how cold it is.'

The lady collapsed in a faint, and panic and despair gripped Peregrinus's heart and squeezed it as though with ice-cold tongs. Shrieking wildly: 'Let things happen as they will, I cannot do otherwise!', he lifted the insensible lady, took her in his arms and tugged the bell-pull. When the footman opened the door, Peregrinus rushed past him; and instead of knocking gently at the top of the stairs, as was his wont, he shouted as he was half-way up, so loudly that the hallway re-echoed: 'Aline! Aline! Light! light!'

'Eh? What? What's this? What's all this in aid of?' said old Aline, staring, as Peregrinus removed his cloak from the still unconscious lady and placed her on the sofa with tender care.

'Quick,' cried Peregrinus, 'quick, Aline, light a fire! Bring smelling-salts, tea, punch, beds!'

Aline, however, did not stir from the spot, but continued to stare at the lady and repeat: 'Eh? What? What's this? What's all this in aid of?'

Peregrinus said something about a countess, perhaps even a princess, whom he had met in the house of the bookbinder Lämmerhirt and whom he had had to carry home after she had fainted in the street. As Aline remained motionless, he stamped his foot and shouted: 'In the Devil's name, I said light a fire! Tea! Smelling-salts!'

Thereupon a feline gleam appeared in the old woman's eyes, and her nose seemed to give off a phosphorescent light. She produced her large black snuff-box, opened the lid so violently that it clanged, and took a mighty pinch of snuff. Then, with arms akimbo, she said sarcastically: 'Why, just look! A countess, a princess! You find her in a poor bookbinder's house in Kalbach Lane, and she faints in the street! Ho, ho, I know where you find these painted ladies after dark! That's a good trick, that's a fine way to carry on! Bringing a loose woman into a respectable house, and adding to your sins by calling on the Devil on Christmas Eve. And I'm to lend a hand with this, am I, in my old age? No, Mr Tyss, you must look for another helper; it's no use asking me. I leave your service tomorrow.'

And with these words the old woman went out, slamming the door behind her so hard that everything in the room rattled and rang.

Peregrinus wrung his hands in anguish and despair. The lady showed no sign of life. But just as the terrified Peregrinus had managed to find a bottle of eau-de-Cologne and was about to rub the lady's temples with it, she jumped up from the sofa, fresh and cheerful, and cried: 'At last, at last we're alone! At last, O my Peregrinus, I can tell you why I followed you to Lämmerhirt's house and why I could not leave you tonight. Peregrinus! set free the prisoner who is locked up in this room. I know that you are not obliged to do so, that it depends only on your good nature, but I also know your good and faithful heart, and so, my good, my dearest Peregrinus, do set the prisoner free!'

'What prisoner?' asked Peregrinus, astounded. 'Who is supposed to be imprisoned in my house?'

'Yes,' continued the lady, taking Peregrinus's hand and pressing it tenderly to her breast, 'I must confess, only a great and noble spirit surrenders benefits that a kindly fate has conferred on him, and it is true that you must do without many things which you could easily attain if you did not release the prisoner—but remember, Peregrinus, that Aline's entire destiny, her entire life depends upon the possession of the prisoner, and that . . .'

'If you don't want me, my angelic lady, to take all this for a fevered dream, and perhaps go mad on the spot,' interrupted Peregrinus, 'then do tell me whom you are talking about—what prisoner?'

'What?' replied the lady. 'Peregrinus, I don't understand you. Will you deny that he became a prisoner in your hands? Wasn't I there when you bought the hunt and he . . .'.

'Who is *HE*? shouted Peregrinus, quite beside himself, 'I've never seen you before in my life, madame. Who are you, and who is *HE*?'

At this the lady fell at Peregrinus's feet, distraught with sorrow and in floods of tears, and cried: 'Peregrinus, be human, be merciful, give him back to me! give him back to me!' Meanwhile Mr Peregrinus shouted: 'I'm going mad! I'm going crazy!'

Suddenly the lady picked herself up. She seemed much bigger than before, her eyes darted fire, her lips trembled, and she cried with a gesture of fury: 'Ha, barbarian! You haven't got a human heart, you're inexorable, you wish for my death, my destruction, you won't give him back to me! No! Never! Never! Ha, wretch that I am! Lost Lost!' And with these words the lady rushed out of the room, and Peregrinus heard her running downstairs, filling the whole house with shrieks of lamentation, until a door was slammed below.

Then all was silent as the grave.

SECOND ADVENTURE

The Flea-tamer. Sad fate of Princess Gamaheh in Famagusta. The clumsiness of the spirit Thetel, and some remarkable microscopic experiments and amusements. The beautiful Dutchwoman and the strange adventure of young Mr George Pepusch, sometime student at the University of Jena.

At this time there lived in Frankfurt a man who practised a very strange art. He was known as the Flea-tamer, because he had managed, no doubt with immense toil and effort, to give these little creatures some culture and train them in all manner of pleasing tricks.

On a table-top made of the finest white polished marble, the astonished spectator saw fleas pulling little cannon, powder-wagons, and weapon-carriages; others leapt to and fro with guns under their arms, ammunition-pouches on their backs, and swords at their sides. At the artist's word of command they performed the most difficult exercises, and they seemed much more lively and cheerful than real full-scale soldiers, because they marched in the most dainty *entrechats* and leaps, and turned 'about face' in delightful pirouettes. The whole team displayed astonishing aplomb, and their commanding officer seemed also to be a competent *maître de ballet*. Even more wonderful and beautiful, however, were the little golden coaches drawn by four, six, or eight fleas. The coachmen and footmen were rose-beetles of the tiniest species, and almost invisible; the occupants of the coaches were impossible to make out. One could not but recall the fairy Queen Mab and her 'team of little atomies,' which honest Mercutio in Shakespeare's *Romeo and Juliet* describes so well that it is clear how often she has galloped over his nose.

Only by surveying the whole table with the aid of a good magnifying glass could one appreciate the full extent of the flea-tamer's art. For only thus could one perceive the magnificence and daintiness of the equipment, the delicate construction of the weapons, and the neatness of the uniforms, all of which excited the deepest admiration. It seemed impossible to conceive what tools the flea-tamer might have used to make various accessories, such as spurs and buttons, in the correct proportion. By comparison, the task which was generally considered a tailor's masterpiece, consisting of nothing less than supplying a flea with a pair of perfectly fitting riding-breeches (the hardest part of which was taking the customer's measure), seemed quite easy and commonplace.

The flea-tamer's exhibition was immensely popular. All day long his room was filled with inquisitive people who were not deterred by the high cost of entry. In the evening, too, his visitors were numerous, indeed more so than during the day, for he then received people who were not interested in comical oddities but wanted to admire a piece of work which had given the flea-tamer a very different reputation and had earned him the sincere respect of natural scientists. This piece of work was a nocturnal microscope, resembling a magic lantern. Like the solar microscope by day, it lit up the object and reflected it with the utmost sharpness and precision against a whitewashed wall. In addition, the flea-tamer carried on a trade in the finest microscopes that were to be found, and people were happy to pay large sums for them.

It so happened that a young man by the name of George Pepusch (the kind reader will soon make his closer acquaintance) was anxious to visit the flea-tamer late one evening. While still on the stairs he heard the sound of quarrelling, which increased in volume until it turned into furious shrieking and yelling. As Pepusch was about to enter, the door of the flea-tamer's room was thrust violently open and a frenzied throng of people rushed towards him, their faces deadly pale with horror.

'That accursed wizard! That child of Satan! I'll tell the Town Council about him! He should be run out of town, that cheating conjurer!' cried the visitors in wild confusion. Urged on by fear and terror, they did their best to escape from the house as quickly as possible.

A glance into the room immediately showed young Pepusch the cause of the dreadful horror which had driven them away. It was crawling with life, filled by a pullulating mass of the most loathsome creatures. Lice, beetles, spiders, centipedes, all monstrously enlarged, stretched out their snouts and strutted on long hairy legs; hideous ant-lions seized gnats and crushed them with their jagged tongues, while the gnats tried to defend themselves by flapping their long wings; among them coiled sea-anemones, paste-eels, and hundred-armed polyps, and from all sides peeped infusoria with distorted human faces. Pepusch had never beheld anything more disgusting. Just as he was on the point of being overcome by horror, something rough hit him in the face, and he found himself enveloped in a thick cloud of flour. This dispelled his horror, for he knew at once that the rough thing could only be the flea-tamer's round powdered wig; and so it was.

When Pepusch had wiped the powder out of his eyes, the weird and horrible insect population had vanished. The flea-tamer was sitting back in his armchair, quite exhausted.

'Leuwenhoek,'* cried Pepusch, 'do you see now what your goings-on must lead to? You've again had to resort to your vassals to protect you against the crowd! Is that not so?'

'Is that you, my good Pepusch?' asked the flea-tamer in a toneless voice. 'Oh dear! I'm finished, completely finished; I'm done for! Pepusch, I'm beginning to think that you were trying to help me, and that I was wrong to ignore your warnings.'

When Pepusch asked him calmly what had happened, the flea-tamer turned his armchair to the wall, covered his face with his hands, and told Pepusch in a tearful voice to pick up a magnifying glass and inspect the marble surface of the table. Even with the naked eye Pepusch could see that the little coaches, soldiers, and so on were standing stock still, with no life or movement. The trained fleas seemed also to have assumed a different form. With the magnifying glass, however, Pepusch soon discovered that there was not a single flea left, and that what he had taken for fleas were in fact black peppercorns and fruit-pips lodged in the harness and the uniforms.

'I have no idea', began the flea-tamer in tones of melancholy remorse, 'what evil spirit blinded me and prevented me from noticing the desertion of my team until all my visitors had come to the table and equipped themselves to inspect it. You can imagine, Pepusch, how, on seeing themselves deceived, they first muttered darkly and then broke out in a blaze of anger. They charged me with the basest fraud, and as they grew more heated and stopped listening to my apologies, they were about to lay violent hands upon me in order to have their revenge. The only way for me to escape a thrashing was immediately to turn on the big microscope and surround them with creatures of which they were terrified, as the rabble always is.'

'But tell me, Leuwenhoek,' asked Pepusch, 'how was it that your well-trained team, which has shown you such loyalty, could suddenly run away from you without you noticing instantly?'

'Oh, Pepusch!' lamented the flea-tamer, '*he* has left me, *he* to whom I owe my entire command over them, and it is *he* whose wicked treachery I blame for my blindness and all my misfortune!'

'Did I not warn you long ago', replied Pepusch, 'not to rely on artifices which I know you cannot accomplish without possessing the Master? And you know now how precarious this possession is, despite all your efforts.' Pepusch further declared that he was at a loss to understand how the flea-tamer's life could be so devastated by abandoning these artifices; after all, the invention of the nocturnal microscope and his dexterity in making microscopic lenses had long since assured his position. The flea-tamer, however, insisted that other secrets were concealed in these artifices, and that he could not abandon them without abandoning himself and his entire existence.

'But where is Dörtje Elwerdink?' asked Pepusch, interrupting the flea-tamer.

'Where is she?' screeched the flea-tamer, wringing his hands. 'Where is Dörtje Elwerdink? She's gone, gone no one knows where—disappeared. Strike me dead on the spot, Pepusch, for I can see your wrath and fury gathering. Give me a speedy end!'

'You see now', said Pepusch, scowling, 'the result of your folly and your silly behaviour. Who gave you the right to lock poor Dörtje up like a slave and then to display her in all her finery, like a natural curiosity, solely in order to attract visitors? Why did you do violence to her affections by forbidding her to marry me, though you could not help seeing how dearly we loved each other? So she's run away, has she? Very well, at least she's no longer in your power, and although at this moment I have no idea either where to look for her, I'm certain that I shall find her. There, Leuwenhoek, put on your wig and resign yourself to your fate; that's the best and most sensible thing you can do now.'

The flea-tamer held his wig on his bald head with his left hand and seized Pepusch's arm with his right. 'Pepusch,' he said, 'you are my true friend; for you are the only person in the whole city of Frankfurt who knows that I have been lying buried in the old church at Delft since the year 1725, and yet you have never given me away, even when you were angry with me on account of Dörtje Elwerdink. Sometimes I myself can't quite grasp that I am really the Anton van Leuwenhoek who was buried in Delft, but when I look at my work and recall my life, I can't help believing it, and so I am very glad not to have the subject discussed. I realize now, my dear Pepusch, that I acted wrongly in the case of Dörtje Elwerdink, though in a quite different way than the one you probably mean. That's to say, I was right to dismiss your courtship as a foolish and futile ambition, but I was wrong in being less than completely frank with you, in not telling you just how matters stand with Dörtje Elwerdink. You would then have realized how praiseworthy it was to dissuade you from ambitions whose fulfilment could only have been disastrous. Sit down, Pepusch, and let me tell you a wondrous story!'

'That won't surprise me,' replied Pepusch with a venomous glance, taking a seat on a padded armchair opposite the flea-tamer.

'Pepusch, my dear friend,' began the flea-tamer, 'since you have a thorough knowledge of history, you are doubtless aware that King Sekakis* lived for many years on intimate terms with the Flower Queen, and that the fair and charming Princess Gamaheh was the offspring of their love. It is less well known, and even I cannot tell you, how Princess Gamaheh arrived at Famagusta.* Many people maintain, with good reason, that the Princess was to hide in Famagusta from the loathsome Leech Prince, the sworn enemy of the Flower Queen.

'Enough! It happened one day in Famagusta that the Princess was walking in the refreshing cool of the evening and found herself in a dark and delightful grove of cypresses. Allured by the pleasant sighing of the evening breeze, the murmuring of the brook, and the melodious chirruping of the birds, the Princess stretched herself out in the soft fragrant moss and soon fell into a deep slumber. But the very enemy whom she wanted to escape, the hideous Leech Prince, raised his head from the muddy water, caught sight of the Princess, and fell so madly in love with the sleeping beauty that he could not resist the desire to kiss her. He crept softly towards her and kissed her behind her left ear. I expect you know, Pepusch, that any lady whom the Leech Prince presumes to kiss is doomed, for he is the worst blood-sucker in the world. And so it befell that the Leech Prince went on kissing the poor Princess until all life had fled from her. He then fell back into the moss, drunk and surfeited, and had to be taken home by his servants, who hastily slithered up out of the mud. It was in vain for the Mandrake to struggle out of the earth and lay itself on the wound where the malicious Leech Prince had kissed the Princess; and when the Mandrake uttered a doleful cry, it was in vain for all the flowers to rise and join in the sorrowful lament!

'However, the spirit Thetel happened to pass that way, and he too was deeply moved by Gamaheh's beauty and her unhappy death. He took the Princess in his arms, pressed her to his breast, and struggled to breathe renewed life into her, but she did not awake from her sleep of death. Then the spirit Thetel caught sight of the abominable Leech Prince, who was so heavy when drunk that his servants had been unable to transport him to his palace. Thetel was incensed and threw a fistful of crystal salt upon the body of his hideous foe, so that the Leech Prince promptly voided forth all the crimson ichor he had sucked out of Princess Gamaheh and then, with many contortions and grimaces, miserably gave up the ghost. But all the nearby flowers dipped their garments in the ichor in memory of the murdered Princess and dyed them a magnificent shade of red that no painter on earth can emulate. You know, Pepusch, that the most beautiful red carnations, belladonna lilies, and gilly-flowers come from that very grove where the Leech Prince kissed the fair Gamaheh to death.

'Thetel was about to hasten away, since he still had much to do in Samarkand before nightfall, but on casting another look at the Princess he stopped as though spellbound and contemplated her with heartfelt sorrow. Suddenly an idea occurred to him. Instead of proceeding on his way, he took the Princess in his arms and soared high into the air.

'Just then two wise men, one of whom, let it be admitted, was myself, were observing the stars from the gallery of a lofty tower. High above their heads they saw the spirit Thetel with the Princess Gamaheh, and at that moment one of them—but stop! never mind that for the present! Both these Magi recognized Thetel, but not the Princess, and they wore themselves out in all manner of conjectures about the significance of the phenomenon, without managing to arrive at any certain or even probable conclusion. Soon afterwards, however, the unhappy fate of Princess Gamaheh became generally known in Famagusta, and the Magi were then able to explain the appearance of the spirit Thetel with the girl in his arms. They both surmised that Thetel must have found some way of restoring the Princess to life, and resolved to make enquiries in Samarkand, towards which, according to their observations, he was evidently flying. In Samarkand, however, nothing was said about the Princess; nobody knew anything.

'Many years had passed, and the two Magi had quarrelled, for learned men are more ready to quarrel, the more learned they are. Only a solidly established habit ensured that they still shared their most important discoveries. (You have not forgotten, Pepusch, that I myself am one of these Magi.) I was not a little astonished when my colleague communicated to me the most wonderful and blessed tidings, concerning the Princess Gamaheh, that anyone could possibly have imagined. This was the essence of the matter. A scholarly acquaintance in Samarkand had sent my colleague the finest and rarest tulips, as perfectly fresh as though they had just been cut from the stem. He was principally concerned with the microscopic study of their internal organs, especially of the pollen. He therefore dissected a beautiful lilac and yellow tulip, and discovered inside the calyx a tiny grain of alien matter which caught his attention in a singular fashion. How great was his astonishment when, on applying the magnifying glass, he clearly perceived that the tiny grain was none other than Princess Gamaheh, who was reposing on the pollen of the tulip's calyx and seemed to be sleeping calmly and peacefully.

'Notwithstanding the immense distance separating me from my colleague, I instantly set out and hastened to join him. He had set aside all his investigations in order to give me the pleasure of seeing his discovery in its pristine form; fearing too, no doubt, that if he did not ask for advice he might do some damage. I soon confirmed the entire accuracy of my colleague's observation and shared his conviction that it must be possible to arouse the Princess from her slumbers and restore her to her previous form. The sublime spirit that dwells within us soon guided us to the proper remedy. Since you know very little, indeed virtually nothing, about our art, Pepusch, it would be pointless to describe to you the diverse operations that we performed in order to achieve our purpose. Suffice it to say that the adroit application of various glasses, mostly prepared by myself, enabled us not only to extract the Princess unharmed from the pollen, but to assist her growth in such a way that she soon regained her natural size. Admittedly, she was still devoid of life, and the possibility of restoring this to her depended on the last and most difficult operation. We reflected her image by means of one of Cuff's splendid solar microscopes* and adroitly detached this image from the whitewashed wall, without any damage being done. No sooner was the image floating free than it entered the glass like a flash of lightning and broke it into a thousand pieces. The Princess stood before us, alive and well. We gave a joyful cheer, but our horror was all the greater when we noticed that the circulation of her blood was blocked at the place where the Leech Prince had kissed her. Just as she was about to collapse in a faint, we noticed a small black dot appearing and disappearing with equal rapidity at that very place, behind her left ear. The blockage ceased at once, the Princess recovered, and our work was accomplished.

'Each of us, my colleague and myself, knew full well the inestimable value of possessing the Princess, and each sought possession of her by maintaining that his claim was superior to the other's. My colleague alleged that the tulip in whose calyx he had found the Princess was his property, and that he had first made the discovery and then informed me of it, so that I was no more than an assistant who could not expect his labours to be rewarded by the product of the work in which he had helped. I, however, pointed out that the last and most difficult operation, which restored the Princess to life, had been devised by me, and that my colleague had merely helped to carry it out; so that, whatever proprietorial claims he might have had on the embryo amid the pollen, the living person must belong to me. After quarrelling for several hours and shouting ourselves hoarse, we arrived at a compromise. My colleague yielded the Princess to me, and in return I gave him a mysterious and very important glass. But that very glass is the cause of our present antagonism. My colleague, you see, maintains that I fraudulently failed to deliver the glass; but that is a barefaced lie, and while I know that he mislaid the glass as soon as he received it, I can say in all conscience that I am not to blame. Indeed I can't understand how he could mislay the glass, for it is not all that small: it must be at least one-eighth the size of a grain of gunpowder.

'You see, Pepusch, I have now taken you entirely into my confidence. Now you know that Dörtje Elwerdink is none other than the reanimated Princess Gamaheh, and you see that a simple young man like you could never aspire to such an elevated and mystical . . .'

'Stop,' interrupted George Pepusch, looking at the flea-tamer with rather a Satanic grin; 'one confidence deserves another, so I for my part will let you into a secret. All that you have told me was already known to me, much more fully, long before you knew it. I cannot express my astonishment at your stupidity and your silly vanity. Let me tell you something that you would have realized long ago, if your science were not so helpless in everything except the polishing of glasses. Let me tell you that I am myself the thistle Zeherit, which was standing on the spot where Princess Gamaheh laid her head, and about which you chose to say nothing whatever.'

'Pepusch,' cried the flea-tamer, 'are you in your right mind? The thistle Zeherit blooms far away in India, in the beautiful valley, surrounded by lofty mountains, where the wisest Magi on earth sometimes assemble. Archivist Lindhorst is the best person to inform you about it. And you, whom I have seen in your short jacket running to the schoolmaster, you whom I have known for years as a Jena student, turned thin and yellow from too much studying on an empty stomach, you claim to be the thistle Zeherit? Go and pull someone else's leg, but don't bother me with your tale.'

'What a wise man you are, Leuwenhoek,' said Pepusch, laughing. 'Now, you can think what you like about me, but don't be so silly as to deny that when the thistle Zeherit felt the sweet breath of Princess Gamaheh, he promptly blossomed in ardent love and yearning, and that when he touched her temples, the lovely Princess fell into sweet dreams of love. The thistle noticed the Leech Prince too late, or else he would have killed the Prince on the spot with his prickles. But he would have succeeded in restoring the Princess to life with the help of the Mandrake, had not the lubberly spirit Thetel blundered along and made a clumsy attempt to rescue her. It is true that the infuriated Thetel put his hand in the salt-cellar which he generally carries on his belt when travelling, as Pantagruel* did the bark full of spices, and threw a good handful of salt at the Leech Prince; but it isn't true that this killed the Prince. All the salt fell in the mud, not a single grain struck the Leech Prince, who was killed by the thistle Zeherit with his prickles. Thus the thistle avenged the Princess's death but condemned himself to death in turn. It is all the fault of the spirit Thetel, who meddled with something that did not concern him, that the Princess had to lie for so long in a flower-sleep; the thistle Zeherit awoke much sooner. For their deaths were nothing but the stupor of flower-sleep, from which they were restored to life, albeit in different forms. Your gross mistake would become yet grosser if you supposed that Princess Gamaheh looked exactly as Dörtje Elwerdink now does, and that it was you who restored her to life. My dear Leuwenhoek, you were in the same situation as the clumsy servant in the story of the Three Oranges:* he released two maidens from the oranges without making sure beforehand that he was able to keep them alive, so that they perished miserably before his eyes. It was not you, but *he* who has run away from you and whose loss you so much regret and bemoan, it was he who completed the work which you began so clumsily.'

'Ha!' shouted the flea-tamer, quite beside himself, 'ha! I suspected as much! But you, Pepusch, to whom I have shown so much kindness, I now see plainly that you are my worst and bitterest enemy. Instead of aiding and comforting me in my misfortune, you spin me a lot of cock-and-bull stories.'

'Cock-and-bull stories, are they? Have it your own way,' shouted Pepusch angrily, 'you'll regret your folly when it's too late, you conceited mountebank! I'm going to look for Dörtje Elwerdink. But I'll make sure first that you don't annoy honest people . . .'

Pepusch reached for the screw which set in motion all the microscopic machinery.

'Kill me on the spot!' screeched the flea-tamer; but at that moment all the machinery collapsed with a crash, and the flea-tamer fell to the floor in a faint.

'How does it come about', said George Pepusch to himself, as he was walking along the street, 'that someone who has a fine warm room and a comfortable bed roams the streets at night amid wind and rain? Because he has forgotten his latchkey and because he is pursued by love and foolish desire.' He was obliged to supply this answer to his own question, for all his behaviour now struck him as foolish. He recalled the moment when he first saw Dörtje Elwerdink. Several years earlier the flea-tamer had displayed his tricks in Berlin and attracted a considerable number of visitors as long as the show retained its novelty. Soon, however, people had seen enough of the trained and drilled fleas. Although they had initially talked of unfathomable skill and magic, they now no longer considered the clothing, harness, saddles, and weapons of these tiny people worthy of much admiration, and the flea-tamer seemed to be entirely forgotten. Soon, however, word spread that a niece of the flea-tamer's, who had not yet been seen in public, now attended the performances. This niece was said to be a beautiful, charming girl dressed in indescribable finery. The fickle *beau monde* of modern young gentlemen, the skilful conductors who set society's tone, flocked to see her; and since the *beau monde* only recognizes extremes, the flea-tamer's niece aroused unprecedented wonderment. Soon it was the done thing to visit the flea-tamer; anyone who had not seen his niece was hopelessly out of fashion;

and so the man's fortunes were restored. What is more, nobody could get used to the name Dörtje, and since the magnificent Bethmann* was just then displaying all her sex's dignified charm, ravishing grace, and feminine tenderness in the role of the Queen of Golconda, and seemed to embody the unutterable magic with which a woman can enchant all who see her, the Dutchwoman was known as 'Aline'.

When George Pepusch arrived in Berlin, Leuwenhoek's beautiful niece was the talk of the town. Hence, at the dinner table in the hotel where Pepusch put up, scarcely anything else was spoken of but the charming little miracle who enchanted all the men, old and young, and even the women. Pepusch was urged to join in the latest Berlin fashion by seeing the beautiful Dutchwoman. Pepusch had a melancholy and irritable temperament; in every pleasure he was too conscious of the bitter aftertaste which comes, indeed, from the black Stygian brook that runs through the whole of our life. This made him grim, introverted, and often unjust to people around him. You may imagine, therefore, that Pepusch was not disposed to go running after pretty girls. Nevertheless, he went to the flea-tamer's, less for the sake of the dangerous miracle than to confirm his preconceived opinion that here, as so often in life, only a strange delusion was at work. He found the Dutchwoman very pretty, charming, and pleasing, but as he contemplated her he could not but smirk at his own sagacity, which had enabled him to guess that the heads this little person had turned must have been decidedly unsteady to start with.

This beauty had a perfect command of the easy, natural tone which demonstrates the finest social cultivation. With that pleasing coquetry that enables one to hold out one's hand familiarly to someone while discouraging him from seizing it, the gracious little thing contrived to attract admirers from all sides 'and also to keep them within the bounds of the most delicate respect.

No one paid any attention to the stranger Pepusch, and he found ample leisure to observe the behaviour and the character of this beautiful girl. The longer he looked into her lovely little face, however, the more there stirred a faint memory in the deepest recesses of his mind. He felt he had seen the Dutchwoman somewhere before, but in quite different surroundings and differently dressed; likewise, he felt that at that time he too had had a quite different form. Although he struggled in vain to clarify these memories, the conviction that he had seen this little person somewhere before grew steadily in strength. He blushed when at last someone nudged him and whispered: 'The lightning has struck you too, hasn't it, my philosophical friend?' It was his neighbour from the dinner table in the inn, to whom he had declared that the general ecstasy must be a strange madness which would vanish as quickly as it had arisen. Pepusch perceived that while he had been staring fixedly at the little beauty the room had gradually emptied, so that the last visitors were just leaving. Only now did the Dutchwoman appear to notice him; she greeted him in a friendly and charming fashion.

Pepusch could not free himself from his obsession with the Dutchwoman. Lying awake at night, he tormented himself in order to trace that memory, but all was in vain. He thought, quite rightly, that only the sight of the fair one could put him on the correct track, and so the very next day and every day after that he did not fail to make his way to the flea-tamer's house and stare at pretty Dörtje Elwerdink for two or three hours.

If a man cannot stop thinking about an attractive woman who has caught his attention in some manner, he has taken the first step to love; and so it came to pass that when Pepusch thought he was only trying to recall a dim memory, he was already head over heels in love with the beautiful Dutchwoman.

Nobody now troubled about the fleas, over which the Dutchwoman's irresistible attraction had won a brilliant victory. The flea-tamer himself felt that with his fleas he was playing rather a foolish part. He therefore locked up his team for the time being and skilfully remodelled his show, assigning the leading role to his beautiful niece.

The flea-tamer had the happy idea of organizing soirées, at which places could be reserved for a considerable sum. In these, the flea-tamer first displayed some pleasing optical tricks, then left his niece to entertain the company. The fair one revealed her social talents to the full, and exploited the slightest pause in the conversation to reanimate the company by singing and playing the guitar. Her voice was not strong, her technique was far from overwhelming and indeed often violated the rules, but the sweetness, clarity, and distinctness of her singing perfectly matched her gracious personality; and when she allowed her languishing gaze to shine upon the audience from under her silky black eyelashes like moist beams of moonlight, everyone present felt a tug at his heart-strings, and even the most stubborn of pedants refrained from criticism.

In these soirées Pepusch zealously pursued his studies: that is to say, he stared at the Dutchwoman for two hours, and then left the room with the others.

Once he was standing closer to the Dutchwoman than usual and distinctly heard her say to a young man: 'Tell me, who is the lifeless ghost who stares at me every evening and then disappears without a sound?'

Pepusch, feeling deeply hurt, raged and stormed around his room, behaving so like a madman that none of his friends would have recognized him. He swore by all the gods that he would never see the ill-natured Dutchwoman again, but the following evening he did not fail to appear in Leuwenhoek's room and gape at the fair Dörtje more fixedly, if anything, than before. On the stairs he was alarmed to find himself going up there, and quickly made the wise resolution to keep his distance from the seductive being. He carried out this resolution by skulking in a corner of the room; but his attempt to lower his eyes failed completely, and, as has been said, he gazed into the Dutchwoman's eyes even more fixedly than before.

He himself could not tell how Dörtje Elwerdink suddenly came to be standing just beside him in his corner.

She addressed him graciously in a soft voice like a sweetly whispered melody: 'I don't remember seeing you anywhere before, sir, except here in Berlin, and yet your features, and everything about you, seem very familiar. I feel as though we had been friends long, long ago, but in a very distant land and under strange circumstances quite different from our present ones. I beg you, sir, to dispel my uncertainty, and unless I am deceived by a chance resemblance, let us renew the friendship which I can dimly remember, like a beautiful dream.'

Mr George Pepusch was strangely affected by the beautiful Dutchwoman's charming words. His heart beat faster, and his face blushed fiery red, yet he shuddered in every limb as though with fever. Even if this meant only that Mr Pepusch was over his ears in love with the Dutchwoman, there was an additional reason for the confusion which deprived him of speech and almost of consciousness. As soon as Dörtje Elwerdink said that she thought she had known him long before, he felt as though another image had been inserted into his mind, as in a magic lantern; he glimpsed a distant time lying far back before his first taste of his mother's milk, a time in which both he and Dörtje Elwerdink had lived and moved. Enough! At that moment there first flashed upon his mind an idea which was to become clear and firm only after prolonged meditation; and this idea was nothing less than the conviction that Dörtje Elwerdink was Princess Gamaheh, King Sekakis's daughter, whom he had loved as a green youth, when he was still the thistle Zeherit. It was a good thing that he did not tell other people about this idea, or else he might have been taken for a lunatic and locked up; though the *idée fixe* of a semi-lunatic may often be nothing but the irony of a state of being that preceded the present.

'But, good heavens, sir, you seem to have lost your tongue!' said the little Dutchwoman, touching George's chest with her dainty little fingers. From the tips of her fingers an electric current passed into George's heart, and awoke him from his stupor. In his ecstasy he seized her hand, covered it with burning kisses, and exclaimed: 'Heavenly, divine being'—and so forth. The kind reader may easily imagine what other exclamations Mr George Pepusch uttered at this moment.

Suffice it to say that the little Dutchwoman responded to George's declarations of love just as he desired, and that the fateful minute in a corner of Leuwenhoek's room gave birth to a love affair that transported the good Mr George Pepusch first into heaven and then, for a change, to hell. For, since Pepusch was of a melancholy temperament and also surly and suspicious, it was inevitable that Dörtje's behaviour should often give rise to fits of jealousy. These very fits of jealousy, however, provoked Dörtje's somewhat mischievous sense of humour, and she took pleasure in subjecting poor Mr George Pepusch to ingenious torments. But as everything can be taken only so far, Pepusch's long-restrained anger finally burst out. Once he was talking about the wondrous time in which he, as the thistle Zeherit, had so tenderly loved the beautiful Dutchwoman, who was then the daughter of King Sekakis. With all the enthusiasm of tender love he recalled that their relationship at that time, and his combat with the Leech Prince, had given him an unchallenge-able right to Dörtje's hand. Dörtje Elwerdink declared that she distinctly remembered that time and their relationship, and that the recollection had first dawned on her soul when Pepusch had looked at her with the thistle's gaze. The little person spoke so charmingly about these wondrous things, she talked with such enthusiasm about her love for the thistle Zeherit, whose destiny it was to study in Jena and then find Princess Gamaheh once more in Berlin, that Mr George Pepusch thought himself in the Eldorado of rapture. The lovers were standing at the window, and Dörtje suffered the lovelorn George to put his arm round her. Their dreamy conversation about the wonders of Famagusta turned into an exchange of sweet nothings, and they were billing and cooing in this intimate position, when a hand-some Hussar officer in a gleaming new uniform happened to walk past and give a friendly greeting to Dörtje, whom he knew from the soirées. Dörtje's eyes were half shut and her little head was turned away from the street; one would have thought it impossible for her to see the officer; but how potent is the magic of a gleaming new uniform! Probably alerted by the suggestive clattering of the officer's sword against the cobblestones, Dörtje opened her eyes wide, slipped from George's arm, threw open the window, blew the officer a kiss, and followed him with her gaze until he had disappeared round the corner.

'Gamaheh,' cried the thistle Zeherit, beside himself, 'what's this? Are you making fun of me? Is that the loyalty you swore to your thistle?'

Dörtje spun round on her heels, uttered a peal of laughter, and cried: 'Be off with you, George! If I'm the daughter of good old King Sekakis and you're the thistle Zeherit, then that charming officer is the spirit Thetel, whom I much prefer to a dreary prickly thistle.' With these words the Dutchwoman ran out of the door, but George Pepusch, as may be imagined, instantly fell into a fury of despair and rushed wildly down the stairs and out of the house as though pursued by a thousand devils.

As luck would have it, George met a friend who was sitting in a post-chaise and about to drive away. 'Stop, I'm coming with you!' cried the thistle Zeherit. He dashed home, pulled on his overcoat, thrust some money into his pockets, gave the key to his landlady, took his seat in the coach and drove away with his friend.

Despite this hostile parting, his love for the beautiful Dutchwoman was by no means extinguished in George's heart. Nor could he persuade himself to abandon the just claims on Gamaheh's hand and heart, which, as the thistle Zeherit, he considered rightfully his. He therefore renewed his claims when he again met Leuwenhoek several years later in the Hague, and the kind reader has already learnt how zealously he pursued his claims in Frankfurt.

Mr George Pepusch was running through the dark lanes of Frankfurt, quite inconsolable, when his attention was suddenly caught by the unusual brightness of a flickering light coming through a crack in a shutter on the ground floor of a handsome house. Thinking the room inside must be on fire, he seized the railings and pulled himself up in order to look in. What he beheld filled him with boundless amazement.

. A bright, cheerful fire was blazing in the fireplace right opposite the window. In a big, old-fashioned armchair before the fire sat, or rather lay, the beautiful Dutchwoman, as finely dressed as an angel. She seemed to be dozing, while a very old, withered man was kneeling in front of the fire and peeping through his spectacles into a pot where some brew was evidently boiling. As Pepusch tried to raise himself further in order to have a better view of the group, he felt someone seizing him by the legs and pulling him forcibly to the ground. A gruff voice cried: 'Look at this villain, what does he think he's up to? It's the clink for you, matey!' It was the night-watchman, who had seen George climbing up to the window, and naturally supposed that he wanted to burgle the house. Despite his protestations, Mr George Pepusch was dragged away by the watchman, whom the patrol hastened to assist, and thus his nocturnal ramble ended cheerfully in the police-station.

THIRD ADVENTURE

Appearance of a tiny monster. Further elucidation of the fortunes of Princess Gamaheh. Mr Peregrinus Tyss enters into a remarkable alliance, and the identity of the old gentleman who lodges in his house is revealed. Wonderful effect of a fairly small microscopic glass. Unexpected arrest of the hero of the story.

Anyone who has had such experiences on a single evening as Mr Peregrinus Tyss had had, anyone in such a mood as his, cannot possibly sleep well. Mr Peregrinus tossed and turned restlessly on his bed, and every time he passed into the delirious state of consciousness that precedes sleep, he again had the lovely little being in his arms and felt ardent kisses burning on his lips. He then started up and fancied he could hear Aline's delightful voice while wide awake. In the fervour of his yearning he wished that she might not have fled, yet he feared also that she might enter there and then and entangle him inextricably. This conflict of opposing emotions constricted his heart, yet filled it at the same time with a delicious agitation that he had never before experienced.

'Don't go to sleep, Peregrinus, don't go to sleep, noble sir! I must have a word with you at once!' whispered a voice close to Peregrinus. It kept repeating: 'Don't go to sleep!' until he finally opened his eyes, which he had only closed in order to see the lovely Aline more distinctly.

In the light of his bedside lamp he perceived a tiny monster, barely six inches long, sitting on his white coverlet. At first he was terrified, but then he courageously stretched out his hand in order to see whether his imagination was deceiving him. At once, however, the tiny monster vanished without a trace.

There may be no need for a detailed portrayal of the fair Aline, Dörtje Elwerdink, or Princess Gamaheh (for the kind reader has long been aware that these are one and the same person, seemingly split into three), but it is essential to give a minute description of the tiny monster that was sitting on the coverlet and causing Mr Peregrinus some terror.

As we have said, the creature was scarcely six inches long. In its bird-like head were a pair of gleaming round eyes; from its beak, which resembled a sparrow's, there projected a long pointed thing like a slender rapier, and just above its beak two horns grew out of its forehead. Its neck at first, just below its head, resembled that of a bird, but grew fatter and fatter so that it developed continuously into a clumsy body that was shaped somewhat like a hazel-nut and seemed to be covered with dark brown scales, like the armadillo. Its strangest and most extraordinary feature, however, was the construction of its arms and legs. The former had two joints and grew out of the creature's cheeks, close to its beak. Immediately below these arms were a pair of feet and then another pair, both with two joints like the arms. These latter feet seemed to be the ones on which the creature principally relied, for not only were they perceptibly longer and stronger than the others, but on them the creature wore very beautiful golden boots with diamond spurs.

Since, as we said, the tiny monster vanished without a trace the moment Peregrinus stretched out his hand towards it, he would undoubtedly have dismissed it as an illusion produced by his overexcited senses, if a little voice had not become audible from a corner of the bed, uttering the following words.

'Good heavens, Peregrinus Tyss, have I misjudged you? You treated me yesterday with such nobility, and now that I want to show you how grateful I am, you stretch out a murderous hand towards me? But perhaps you were put off by my shape, and I did wrong in showing myself to you with the aid of the microscope in order to make sure you would see me—something which isn't as easy as you might think. I'm still sitting on your white coverlet, as I did before, and yet you can't see any sign of me. Don't take it amiss, Peregrinus, but your visual nerves are really rather too coarse for my slender build. Promise me, however, that I will be safe with you and that you will do nothing to harm me, and I'll come closer and tell you many things which you will not be sorry to learn.'

'Tell me,' Peregrinus Tyss answered the voice, 'tell me first of all who you are, my good unknown friend, and the rest will take care of itself. I can assure you at the outset that it is not in my nature to do anyone any harm, and that I will continue to treat you nobly, even though I can't understand at present how I am supposed to have demonstrated my nobility to you. Retain your incognito, however, for your appearance is not exactly charming.'

'You are a noble man, Peregrinus Tyss,' continued the voice, after the sound of throat-clearing, 'I am glad to repeat it, but you are a novice in science, and rather inexperienced in general, or else you would have recognized me at a glance. If I wanted, I could talk big and say that I am one of the mightiest of all kings, and rule over many, many millions. Because of my innate modesty, however, and because the word "king" is not really quite suitable, I'll refrain. You see, the nation which I have the honour to lead lives under a republican constitution. The business of government is performed by a senate which is limited to 45,999 members, for ease of voting; and since the leader of this senate must have attained mastery in all things, he bears the title of Master. I'll now reveal, without further ado, that I who am speaking to you, although you cannot see me, am none other than Master Flea. I have not the slightest doubt that you know my nation, worthy sir, for you are sure to have refreshed and invigorated many of my people with your own blood. You must therefore be aware that my nation is animated by an indomitable love of freedom; it consists entirely of jumped-up fellows who escape from any regular order by continually hopping about. You will realize, Mr Peregrinus, what a talent it requires to be master of such people, and therefore be suitably in awe of me. Give me your assurance of this, Mr Peregrinus, before I continue.'

For a few minutes Mr Peregrinus Tyss felt as though a huge mill-wheel, driven by roaring waves, were turning round and round in his head. Then it calmed down and he bethought himself that the appearance of the strange lady in Lämmerhirt's house was just as wonderful as what was happening now, and that the latter might be the proper continuation of the strange story in which he was caught up.

Mr Peregrinus declared that he held Master Flea in the highest esteem on account of his unusual gifts, and that the desire to hear more from him was heightened by his melodious voice and a certain delicacy in his speech which matched his dainty physique.

'I am most grateful to you, my good Mr Tyss,' went on Master
Flea, 'for your amiable disposition, and I hope to prove that you
have not misjudged me. For you to understand the service you
have done me, my good friend, I must tell you the entire story
of my life. Listen then! My father was the illustrious—but wait!
I've just remembered that readers and listeners are now notably
deficient in the admirable gift of patience, and that the minute
biographies that used to be popular are now detested. Instead
of giving a detailed account, therefore, I shall merely allude in
a casual and episodic fashion to those matters directly relevant
to my presence in your house. Since I am Master Flea, you
cannot fail to discern in me, my dear Mr Peregrinus, a man of
the most comprehensive erudition, profoundly versed in all
branches of learning. However, you cannot judge my learning
by your standards, since you are unacquainted with the wondrous world which I and my people inhabit. How astonished
you would be if your eyes could be opened to perceive this
world; you would think it a strange and incomprehensible
realm of magic. For that very reason you may not be surprised
if everything originating from that world appears to you like a
bewildering fairy-tale dreamt up by an idle brain. Don't let that
put you off, however, but take my word for it.

'My people, as you see, are much superior to you human
beings in many things, such as understanding the secrets of
nature, strength, and agility—both mental and physical agility.
But we too have powerful emotions, and, as with you, these are
the source of much misfortune, and sometimes of catastrophe.
Thus I was loved, indeed worshipped, by my people; my mastery could have brought me to the highest pitch of happiness,
had I not been blinded by an unhappy passion for a person who
had me entirely under her sway, yet could never become my
wife. Our race is indeed accused of harbouring a particular
preference for the fair sex which often goes beyond the bounds
of modesty. There may be something in this accusation, but on
the other hand everybody knows . . . Stop! Without more ado:
I beheld King Sekakis's daughter, the fair Gamaheh, and fell so
frantically in love with her on the spot that I forgot about my
people, about myself, and lived only in the bliss of hopping
about on the fairest of throats, the fairest of bosoms, and tick-

ling the gracious maiden with my sweet kisses. She often tried to catch me with her rosy fingers, but never succeeded. I took this for the charming caresses, the sweet toying of happy love! How foolish is the mind of a lover, even if he be Master Flea. Suffice it to say that poor Gamaheh was attacked by the hideous Leech Prince, who kissed her to death; but I could have rescued my beloved, if a conceited simpleton and a clumsy lout had not put their oar in and spoiled everything. The simpleton was the thistle Zeherit and the lout was the spirit Thetel. As Thetel rose into the air with the sleeping Princess, I clung tightly to the Brussels lace which she had round her neck, and so accompanied Gamaheh faithfully on her journey, without being noticed by the spirit. We happened to fly over two Magi, who were watching the stars from a lofty tower. One of these Magi focused his telescope on me so sharply that I was almost dazzled by the gleam of the magical instrument. I grew dizzy, my efforts to hold tight were in vain, I fell haplessly down from this monstrous height, and landed right on the nose of the Magus who had been observing us. My life was saved only by my light weight and my exceptional agility.

'While I was still too stunned to hop to safety from the Magus's nose, this fiend, the treacherous Leuwenhoek (*he* was the Magus), skilfully caught me between his fingers and promptly placed me in one of Russwurm's Universal Microscopes. Although it was night-time and he was therefore obliged to light the lamp, he was too practised an observer, and too well versed in science, not to recognize me instantly as Master Flea. Delighted that a fortunate chance had put this distinguished captive in his power, he resolved to exploit it to the full and bound me, wretch that I was, in chains. That was the beginning of an agonizing captivity from which I was freed only yesterday morning by you, Mr Peregrinus Tyss. The possession of me gave the vile Leuwenhoek complete power over my vassals. He soon gathered swarms of them around him and with barbarous severity imposed on us what he was pleased to call culture. This soon deprived us of all our freedom, all our enjoyment of life. As regards scholarly studies, and sciences and arts in general, Leuwenhoek soon found, to his surprise and annoyance, that we were almost more learned than he. But the

higher culture that he imposed on us consisted mainly in forcing us to *be* something, to *represent* something. And this *being*
and *representing* something brought with it a number of new and
previously unknown desires which we had to satisfy in the sweat
of our brows. The cruel Leuwenhoek turned us into statesmen,
soldiers, professors, and I don't know what else. These had to
march about in the costumes appropriate to their stations, to
carry weapons, and so on. Hence there came to be tailors,
shoemakers, hairdressers, embroiderers, button-makers, ar-
mourers, belt-makers, sword-makers, wheelwrights, and a host
of other specialists among us, working only to create superflu-
ous and pernicious luxuries. Worst of all, in displaying us to
his visitors as cultured people and pocketing the proceeds,
Leuwenhoek had only his personal advantage in mind. Moreover, he was given credit for all the culture we had acquired and
received praise that by rights was ours alone. Leuwenhoek was
well aware that if he lost me his command over my people
would be at an end, and so he cast even stronger spells upon me
and made my unhappy captivity even more agonizing. I
thought of the fair Gamaheh with ardent yearning and medit-
ated how I might learn news of her fate. But the solution, which
defeated even the keenest intellect, was supplied by a fortunate
accident.

'Old Swammerdamm,* the friend and associate of my Magus,
had discovered Princess Gamaheh amid the pollen of a tulip and
informed his friend of this discovery. By a method which I shall
refrain from describing, my dear Mr Peregrinus Tyss, since it
would not mean much to you, the gentleman succeeded in
restoring the Princess's natural form, and bringing her back to
life. In the long run, however, both these wiseacres were just
such clumsy louts as the spirit Thetel and the thistle Zeherit.
In their zeal, you see, they had overlooked the most important
part, and so at the very moment when Princess Gamaheh was
restored to life, she was about to drop down dead once more. I
alone knew what the matter was; my love for the fair Gamaheh,
which had flared up in my breast more strongly than ever, gave
me a giant's strength; I broke my chains, I leapt onto the fair
one's shoulder in one mighty bound, and one small bite was
enough to set her blood flowing. She was alive! I must however

tell you, Mr Peregrinus Tyss, that this bite must be repeated if the Princess is to continue blooming in youth and beauty; otherwise she would shrivel up in a few months and turn into a withered old hag. Hence, as you will realize, she cannot do without me, and only her fear of losing me can explain the black ingratitude with which Gamaheh rewarded my love. For she delivered me on the spot to my hateful tormentor, Leuwenhoek, who put me in heavier chains than I had ever worn before. However, this brought about his own downfall.

'Despite the vigilance of old Leuwenhoek and the fair Gamaheh, I eventually succeeded in fleeing my prison when their backs were turned. Although my heavy riding-boots, which I had no time to remove from my feet, greatly hampered my escape, I arrived safely in the toy-shop where you bought your goods. It was not long before Gamaheh, to my consternation, entered the shop. I thought I was lost; you alone could rescue me, noble Mr Peregrinus; I complained softly of my peril, and you were kind enough to open a box; I swiftly hopped inside, and you then took the box with you just as quickly; Gamaheh sought me in vain, and it was only much later that she found out how and where I had fled. As soon as I was at liberty, Leuwenhoek lost his power over my people. All regained their freedom, made their escape, and left peppercorns, fruit-pips, and so forth, in their clothes, as an insult to the tyrant. Let me thank you cordially once more, my good and noble Mr Peregrinus, for your extreme kindness towards me, which I appreciate as no one else can. Permit me, as a free man, to spend a little time in your company; you can scarcely imagine how useful I can be to you in numerous matters that concern you deeply. It might indeed be thought dangerous for you to fall violently in love with that lovely being . . .'

'What are you saying, Master?' asked Peregrinus, interrupting his invisible guest. '*Me? Me*, violently in love?'

'Exactly so', went on Master Flea. 'Imagine my fear, my terror, when you came in yesterday with the Princess in your arms, inflamed by passion, and when she employed all the feminine wiles, in which she is unfortunately most accomplished, in order to persuade you to hand me over! But it was only then that I realized the full extent of your magnanimity, when you remained steadfast and skilfully pretended to be unaware of my presence and unable to make out what the Princess wanted.'

'That was actually the case', interrupted Peregrinus once more. 'You're giving me credit, my dear Master Flea, for things I never even suspected. In the shop where I bought the toys I noticed neither you nor the pretty woman who looked for me in Lämmerhirt's house and whom you are pleased to call by the strange name of Princess Gamaheh. I had no inkling that the boxes I took with me, in which I thought there were lead soldiers and huntsmen, included an empty one in which you were sitting; and how on earth was I to guess that *you* were the captive whom the charming little girl demanded so fervently? Be reasonable, Master Flea, and don't imagine things of which I have not the least notion.'

'You are trying', replied Master Flea, 'to evade my gratitude, and very skilfully too, my good Mr Peregrinus! And this, to my great relief, offers further proof of your selfless character. Allow me to tell you, noble sir, that the efforts of Leuwenhoek and Gamaheh to recapture me will remain futile as long as you grant me your protection. You would have to hand me over voluntarily to my tormentors; any other means would be fruitless. Mr Peregrinus Tyss, you are in love!'

'Oh, don't say such things!' broke in Peregrinus. 'Don't use the word love for a moment of foolish passion which is already over!' Mr Peregrinus felt the blood mounting to his face and giving him the lie. He crept under the coverlet.

'It is not in the least surprising', continued Master Flea, 'that you too should have been unable to resist the wonderful charms of Princess Gamaheh, especially as she employed many perilous arts to entrap you. The storm is not yet past. There are many spells available to other delightful women who happen not to be Princess Gamaheh, and the malicious little thing will use these to ensnare you in her amorous toils. She will try to gain such entire power over you that you will live only for her and her desires, and then—alas for me! It will depend whether your nobility is strong enough to conquer your passion; whether you will choose to satisfy Gamaheh's desires by plunging not only your protégé, but the entire wretched people whom you have freed from base servitude, into renewed misery; or whether you will resist the evil and deceitful wiles of the temptress and thus establish the happiness of myself and my people. Oh, if only you would promise me the latter—if only you could!'

'Master,' replied Mr Peregrinus, removing the coverlet from his face, 'my dear Master, you are right, nothing is more dangerous than the allure of women; they are all deceitful and malicious, they play with us as cats do with mice, and our tenderest efforts earn us nothing but mockery and scorn. That is why I used to perspire with mortal terror as soon as a female approached, and I really think there must be something special about the fair Aline or, if you prefer, Princess Gamaheh, even though what you have told me is too much for my simple common sense and makes me feel as though I were having a wild dream or reading the Arabian Nights. But, be that as it may, you have put yourself under my protection, my dear Master, and nothing shall induce me to hand you over to your enemies. I never want to see that seductive wench again. I give you my solemn promise, and would give you my hand as well, if you yourself had one to return the honest pressure of mine'. With these words Mr Peregrinus stretched out his arm over the coverlet.

'Now I feel comforted,' said his invisible guest; 'I'm quite easy in my mind. Even if I have no hand to give you, allow me at least to bite your right thumb, partly to demonstrate my heartfelt joy, and partly to cement our alliance.'

At that moment Mr Peregrinus felt the thumb of his right hand being bitten so painfully that the biter could only be the Master of all the fleas.

'You bite', cried Peregrinus, 'like a little devil.'

'Take that', replied Master Flea, 'as a clear sign of my honest character. But it is only fair that as a token of my gratitude I should give you a present which is one of the most extraordinary things that art has ever produced. It is a microscope made by a very skilled and ingenious optician of my nation, when he was still in Leuwenhoek's service. You will think the instrument rather too delicate, for it is actually one hundred and twenty times smaller than a grain of sand, but the manner of its use means that it cannot be particularly large. You see, if I place the glass in the pupil of your left eye, that eye functions like a microscope. You'll be surprised by its effect, and so I'll say no more about it for the present, but simply ask for your permission to undertake the operation whenever I think that a microscope in your eye would be of service to you. And now sleep well, Mr Peregrinus; you still need some rest.'

Peregrinus did indeed fall asleep and did not wake until it was broad daylight.

He heard the familiar scraping of old Aline's broom as she swept out the next room. A small child with some misdeed on its conscience cannot fear its mother's rod so much as Mr Peregrinus feared the old woman's reproaches. At last old Aline tip-toed in with the coffee. Mr Peregrinus squinted through the bed-curtains, which he had drawn, and was not a little surprised at the bright and sunny countenance that the old woman displayed.

'Are you still asleep, dear Mr Tyss?' asked the old woman, in the sweetest tone that her throat was capable of.

Peregrinus, taking heart, replied in an equally cordial fashion: 'No, dear Aline; just put my breakfast down on the table, I'll be out of bed in a minute.'

When Peregrinus got up, it seemed to him as though the breath of the charming creature that had lain in his arms were wafting through the room. He felt at ease, yet also fearful; he would have given anything to know what had become of the amorous mystery, for, like the mystery itself, the delightful being had appeared only to vanish.

While Mr Peregrinus tried vainly to drink his coffee and enjoy his white bread, every bite of which came close to choking him, the old woman came in and busied herself with this and that, murmuring as she did so: 'Amazing! Incredible! The things that happen! Who would ever have thought it!'

Unable to control the beating of his heart, Peregrinus asked: 'What's amazing, dear Aline?'

'All sorts of things!' replied the old woman with a mischievous smile, as she went on tidying the room.

Poor Peregrinus felt his heart would burst, and he involuntarily cried in a tone of agonized yearning: 'Oh, Aline!'

'Yes, Mr Tyss, here I am, what's your wish?' said the old woman, planting herself in front of Peregrinus as though awaiting his orders.

Peregrinus stared into the old woman's hideously contorted copper-coloured face, and his timidity yielded to the deep anger with which he was suddenly filled.

'What', he asked in a decidedly gruff tone, 'has become of the strange lady who was here last night? Did you open the front door for her? Did you fetch her a carriage, as I ordered? Was the lady taken home?'

'Open the door?' said the old woman with a horrible grin which was intended to look like a sly smile. 'Fetch a carriage? Take her home? There was no need! The beautiful lady, the pretty little pet, stayed here in your house. She's still here, and I don't suppose she'll be leaving for some time.'

Peregrinus started up with a shock of pleasure. The old woman now told him the following story.

As the lady sprang down the stairs in a most breath-taking fashion, old Mr Swammer was standing in the doorway of his ground-floor room with a huge candelabrum in his hand. With much bowing and scraping, which was by no means characteristic of him, the old gentleman invited the lady into his room. She tripped inside without demur, and Mr Swammer then locked and barred the door.

Old Aline thought it extremely strange that Mr Swammer, normally a recluse, should behave in this way, so she could hardly do otherwise than listen at his door and peep through the keyhole. She saw Mr Swammer standing in the middle of the room and addressing the lady so persuasively and wisely that she herself, old Aline, had tears in her eyes, even though she could not understand a single word, since Mr Swammer was speaking in a foreign tongue. She could only suppose that Mr Swammer was endeavouring to recall the lady to a virtuous and God-fearing way of life, for he grew more and more animated, until the lady fell on her knees and humbly and tearfully kissed his hand. Mr Swammer now raised her up with great kindness, bent down to kiss her on the forehead, and led her to an armchair. He then set to work lighting a fire, fetching spices, and, so far as Aline could make out, preparing mulled wine. At this point, unfortunately, old Aline took some snuff and sneezed loudly. Thereupon Mr Swammer stretched out his arm towards the door and cried in a terrible voice that pierced her to the marrow: 'Get thee gone, Satan, thou eavesdropper!' Old Aline trembled in every limb and felt altogether crushed. How she got upstairs and into bed was more than she could tell. When she opened her eyes the next morning, she thought she was seeing a ghost. For in front of her bed she beheld Mr Swammer, wearing a beautiful sable coat with braiding and tassels, with his hat on his head and his stick in his hand.

'Good Mrs Aline,' said Mr Swammer, 'I must go out on important business and shall probably not return for several hours. Take care that there is no noise in the hallway outside my room, and that nobody tries to force his way into my chamber. A noble lady—to tell you the truth, a rich and wonderfully beautiful foreign princess—has taken refuge with me. In the past, at the court of her royal father, I was her tutor, and therefore she trusts me and I must and will protect her against all evil assaults. I am telling you this, Mrs Aline, so that you may show her the deference due to her station. If Mr Tyss permits, she will require you to wait on her, and you shall be royally rewarded, good Mrs Aline, provided you keep your mouth shut and tell nobody where the Princess is living.'

Having said this, Mr Swammer promptly departed.

After hearing this story, Mr Peregrinus Tyss asked the old woman whether she did not find it odd that the lady whom, as he could again assure her, he had met in the house of the bookbinder Lämmerhirt in Kalbach Lane, should be a princess and have taken refuge with old Mr Swammer. The old woman declared that she trusted Mr Swammer's words more than her own eyes, and was therefore convinced either that everything that had occurred in Lämmerhirt's house or in Peregrinus's room must be a magical illusion, or else that the fear and confusion of her flight had induced the Princess to behave in such an eccentric fashion. 'In any case,' added Aline, 'I expect I'll soon hear the whole story from the Princess herself.'

'But', went on Mr Peregrinus, really wishing only to prolong the conversation about the lady, 'what has become of your suspicions? What about the low opinion you had of the lady yesterday?'

'Oh,' replied the old woman, chuckling, 'that's all over and done with. You only have to look properly at the dear lady to see that she's a noble princess, and as beautiful into the bargain as only a princess could be. After Mr Swammer had gone, I couldn't help looking to see what the good lady was doing, and I took a peep through the keyhole. There she lay, stretched out on the sofa, with her angelic little head resting on her hand, and her black curls peeping between her lily-white fingers, which looked very pretty. And the lady was dressed all in silver taffeta, so that you could see her dainty bosom and her round little arms gleaming through it. On her little feet she had golden slippers. One of them had come off, and you could see that she hadn't any stockings on; her bare foot was peeping out from under her dress, and she was playing with her toes, and a very nice sight it was too. But I'm sure the lady is still lying on the sofa, just as she was earlier, and if you will take the trouble, dear Mr Tyss, to go to the key-hole, then . . .'

'What are you saying,' interrupted Peregrinus vehemently, 'what are you saying! Am I to abandon myself to the tempting vision that might lead me into all manner of folly?'

'Courage, Peregrinus, resist the temptation!' whispered a little voice close to Peregrinus, who recognized it as that of Master Flea.

The old woman gave a mysterious smile, was silent for a few minutes, and then said: 'I'll tell you the whole truth, Mr Peregrinus, about how this looks to me. Whether the strange lady is a princess or not, it's certain that she's noble and rich and that Mr Swammer is looking after her attentively, so he must have known her for a long time. And why did the lady run after you, dear Mr Tyss? I say it's because she's mortally in love with you. After all, love makes people blind and crazy, and it must lead even princesses into strange and reckless goings-on. A gypsy-woman told your dear departed mother that you would one day reach happiness through marriage, just when you least expected it. That's going to come true!'

And now the old woman again began to describe the lady's charms.

You can imagine how Peregrinus felt with all these ideas being forced on him. 'Be quiet,' he burst out eventually, 'don't say any more about these things, Mrs Aline. The lady in love with me! How silly, how senseless!'

'Hm,' said the old woman, 'if that weren't so, the lady wouldn't have sighed so miserably; she wouldn't have cried so wretchedly: "No, my dear Peregrinus, my sweet friend, you won't, you can't be cruel to me! I'll see you again and enjoy all the happiness of heaven!" And she's made a new man of our old Mr Swammer. Has he ever given me a single penny, except for a thaler at Christmas? And now look at this beautiful gleaming Carolina thaler! He gave it to me this morning with a kind smile, the like of which I've never seen in him, as a consideration in return for the services I'm going to do the lady. There's more to this than meets the eye. I shouldn't wonder if Mr Swammer will end up playing the matchmaker on your behalf, Mr Tyss!'

The old woman launched into yet another enthusiastic description of the lady's beauty and charm, which sounded strange coming from the lips of a withered old crone, until Peregrinus, all on fire with excitement, leapt up and cried like a madman: 'I don't care what happens—down to the keyhole!' It was in vain for Master Flea, who had leapt on to the neckerchief of the lovelorn Peregrinus and hidden in the corner of a fold, to issue warnings; Peregrinus did not hear his voice, and Master Flea learnt what he should already have known: that the most stubborn people may be brought round, but not a lover.

The lady was indeed still lying on the sofa, just as the old woman had described, and Peregrinus concluded that no human language could suffice to express the heavenly magic that enwrapped her lovely figure. Her dress, real taffeta with strange embroidery in many colours, was very fanciful, and might well have been the négligé which Princess Gamaheh was wearing in Famagusta when the malicious Leech Prince kissed her to death. At any rate, the dress was so charming and likewise so exceedingly unusual, that it could not have been dreamt up even by a theatrical costumer of genius or by the sublimest of milliners.

'Yes, it is she, it is Princess Gamaheh!' murmured Peregrinus, trembling with sweet bliss and thirsting with desire. But, when the fair lady sighed: 'Peregrinus, my Peregrinus!', Mr Peregrinus Tyss was gripped by the full madness of passion, and only an unspeakable fear that robbed him of his resolution restrained him from breaking down the door by force and throwing himself at the feet of the angelic being.

The kind reader already knows the nature of little Dörtje Elwerdink's enchanting charms and more than earthly beauty. The editor can assure you that he too, after peeping through the keyhole and espying the little lady in her fanciful taffeta dress, could say only that Dörtje Elwerdink was an altogether delightful and charming little poppet. Since, however, the first person that a young man falls in love with is always a supernatural being, an angel without a peer on earth, let us permit Mr Peregrinus to imagine that Dörtje Elwerdink was such a magical, supernatural being.

'Pull yourself together and think of your promise, worthy Mr Peregrinus Tyss. You never wanted to see the temptress Gamaheh again, and look at you now! I could insert the microscope into your eye, but even without it you ought to perceive that the malicious little thing has long since observed you and that all her actions are an artful deception intended to entice you. Take my word for it! I'm only trying to help you!' Thus did Master Flea whisper from the fold of Peregrinus's neckerchief; but whatever timorous doubts might arise in Peregrinus's mind, he still could not tear himself away from the enchanting sight of Dörtje, who, pretending to think herself unobserved, took full advantage of the situation and drove poor Peregrinus almost out of his wits by changing from one seductive posture to another.

Mr Peregrinus Tyss might still be standing at the door of that fateful chamber, if there had not come a loud ring at the bell and a cry from the old woman, warning him that Mr Swammer was returning. Peregrinus flew up the stairs and into his room. Here he abandoned himself entirely to amorous thoughts; but these very thoughts recalled the doubts which Master Flea's admonitions had excited. Peregrinus had indeed had a flea in his ear, and he fell into all manner of disquieting cogitations.

'Am I not compelled,' he thought, 'to believe that that gracious being is in very truth Princess Gamaheh, the daughter of a mighty king? But if that is so, I must consider it folly and madness to wish to possess such a lofty personage. And then, she herself demanded the release of a captive on whom her life depended, and since this agrees exactly with what Master Flea told me, I can scarcely doubt that all the actions that I thought revealed her love for me may only be a device for subjecting me entirely to her will. And yet! To leave her, to lose her, would be hell and death!'

Mr Peregrinus Tyss was roused from these painful reflections by a gentle and unassuming knocking at his door.

The person who entered was none other than Mr Peregrinus's lodger. Old Mr Swammer, previously a withered and surly recluse, seemed suddenly to have grown twenty years younger. His forehead was smooth, his eyes were lively, his mouth had a friendly smile; instead of his ugly black wig he was wearing his own white hair, and instead of his dark-grey overcoat he had on a beautiful sable coat, as Mrs Aline had described.

Mr Swammer advanced towards Peregrinus with a cheerful, indeed joyful expression that was wholly uncharacteristic of him. 'I have no desire', said he, 'to divert my kind landlord from his business; my duty as a tenant, however, compels me to inform you this very morning that last night I was obliged to give shelter to a helpless female who wanted to escape from the tyranny of her cruel uncle. She will therefore be spending some time in this house, provided that my kind landlord grants the permission which I hereby request.'

Peregrinus could not help asking who the helpless female was, without thinking that this was indeed the most serviceable question he could ask in order to pursue the strange secret.

'It is only right and proper', replied Mr Swammer, 'that the landlord should know whom he is harbouring in his house. Allow me therefore to inform you, my esteemed Mr Tyss, that the girl who has taken refuge with me is none other than the pretty Dutchwoman Dörtje Elwerdink, the niece of the famous Leuwenhoek, who, as you know, displays remarkable microscopic feats in this town. Leuwenhoek has hitherto been an intimate friend of mine, but I must confess that he is a hard man and has brutally maltreated poor Dörtje, who moreover is my godchild. A violent scene that occurred yesterday evening forced the girl to take flight, and it would seem natural for her to seek help and comfort at my hands.'

'Dörtje Elwerdink,' said Peregrinus, half in a reverie, 'Leuwenhoek! Perhaps a descendant of the scientist Anton van

Leuwenhoek, who made the famous microscopes?'

'One could hardly describe our Leuwenhoek as a descendant of that famous man,' replied Mr Swammer with a smile, 'since he himself is that famous man, and it is only a fable that he was buried in Delft almost a hundred years ago. You must believe me, my good Mr Tyss; otherwise you might doubt that although I now call myself Swammer, for the sake of brevity, and in order not to have to explain the subject of my researches to every inquisitive fool, I am the famous Swammerdamm. Everyone claims that I died in 1680, but you can see, worthy Mr Tyss, that I am standing before you alive and well, and with the help of my *Biblia naturae* I can prove to even the simplest intellect that *I* am *myself*. You believe what I say, my good Mr Tyss?'

'Recently,' said Peregrinus in a tone that revealed his confusion of mind, 'so many wondrous things have happened to me that I should doubt them eternally, if they were not all clearly apparent to my senses. But now I believe everything, however weird and wonderful it may be! Perhaps you are the deceased Johann Swammerdamm, and, being a *revenant*, you know more than ordinary people do; but concerning the flight of Dörtje Elwerdink, or Princess Gamaheh, or whatever the lady may call herself, you are completely mistaken. Let me tell you what happened.'

Peregrinus then quite calmly recounted his adventure with the lady, from her entry into Lämmerhirt's parlour to her reception in Mr Swammer's room.

'It seems to me', said Mr Swammer, when Peregrinus had finished, 'that everything you have been kind enough to tell me is nothing but a remarkable though very agreeable dream. I shall not enquire further into the matter, however, but shall ask you for your friendship, of which I may stand in dire need. Forget my surly behaviour, and let us become better acquainted. Your father was a man of discernment, and my closest friend, but in learning, profundity of intellect, maturity of judgement, and a correct and experienced understanding of life, the son is far superior to the father. You have no idea how highly I regard you, my dear and esteemed Mr Tyss . . .'

'Now's the time', whispered Master Flea, and at that moment

Peregrinus felt a slight and transient pain in the pupil of his left eye. He knew that Master Flea had inserted the microscopic glass into his eye, but truly he could never have suspected what effects the glass would have. Behind the cornea of Mr Swammer's eyes he perceived strange nerves branching off, and he could follow their ramifications deep into the brain and recognize Swammer's thoughts. These ran more or less as follows.

'I never thought I'd get off so easily; I expected to be asked a lot more questions. The old man wasn't particularly bright, and I never thought much of him, but his son's wits are still more addled, and full of childish folly. Why, the simpleton has told me the whole story of the Princess, and it didn't occur to him that she would already have told me everything, since my treatment of her makes it obvious that we must have had a close relationship in the past. There's nothing else for it, though; I must butter him up, because I need his help. He's naïve enough to believe every word I say, and his simple-minded good nature will make him go to a great deal of trouble on my behalf; but he won't get any thanks for it, except that when all is happily over and Gamaheh is mine again, I'll have a good laugh at him behind his back.'

'Why,' said Mr Swammer, advancing close to Mr Peregrinus, 'I thought I saw a flea sitting on your neckerchief, my good Mr Tyss!' His thoughts, however, ran: 'Damn and blast it, that really was Master Flea! It would be a confounded nuisance if Gamaheh were right after all.'

Peregrinus stepped quickly back, assuring his guest that he had no objection to fleas.

'Then,' said Mr Swammer, with a low bow, 'permit me to take my leave of you, as your most humble servant, my dear and most esteemed Mr Tyss.'

His thoughts ran: 'I wish Satan, with his horns and tail, would gobble you up, you confounded wretch!'

While Peregrinus remained speechless with astonishment, Master Flea removed the glass from his pupil and said: 'Now, dear Mr Peregrinus, you have seen the wondrous effect of this instrument, which I dare say has not its like in the whole world; and you will realize what supreme power it could give you over other people, if their innermost thoughts were exposed to your gaze. However, if you were always to carry the glass in your eye, the constant perception of their thoughts would send you into deep depression, for the insult you have just received would be repeated only too often. When you leave your house, I will always be with you, either in your neckerchief, or your jabot, or in some other suitable and comfortable place. If you want to know the thoughts of the person speaking to you, you have only to snap your fingers and the glass will instantly be in your eye.'

Understanding how immeasurably useful this gift would be, Mr Peregrinus Tyss was about to utter his fervent gratitude, when two representatives of the Town Council entered and informed him that he had been charged with a serious crime, and that the immediate consequence of the charge must be his arrest and the confiscation of his papers.

Mr Peregrinus swore by all that was sacred that he was unaware of having committed the slightest crime. One of the Council representatives said with a smile that his complete innocence might be revealed within a few hours, but that until then he must submit to the orders of higher authority.

What could Mr Peregrinus do but climb into the carriage and let himself be transported to prison?

You can imagine how he felt as he passed Mr Swammer's room.

Master Flea was sitting in the captive's neckerchief.

FOURTH ADVENTURE

*An unexpected encounter between two friends. Counsellor Knarrpanti
and his principles of criminal justice. Unrequited love drives the
thistle Zeherit to despair. An optical duel between two Magi. Princess Gamaheh's trance-like condition. The dream-thoughts. Dörtje
Elwerdink almost tells the truth, and the thistle Zeherit runs off
with Princess Gamaheh.*

It did not take long to clear up the mistake made by the
watchman in arresting Mr Pepusch on suspicion of burglary.
Meanwhile, however, the authorities claimed to have noticed
some irregularities in his passport documents; for this reason he
was requested to provide some resident of Frankfurt to vouch
for his good reputation, and in the mean time to stay in the
Mayor's official premises.

Mr George Pepusch was now sitting in a pleasant room,
pondering whom in Frankfurt he could ask to vouch for him.
He had been away for so long that he could not but fear that
even his previous close acquaintances might have forgotten him,
and he had no other addresses to turn to.

He looked out of the window in deep gloom and began to
curse his fate out loud. Just then another window, next to his,
was opened, and a voice cried: 'What? Are my eyes deceiving
me? Is that you, George?' Mr Pepusch was most astonished to
see the friend with whom he had been on the most intimate
terms during his stay in Madras.

'Damn it,' said Mr Pepusch, 'how can one be so forgetful, as
if one hadn't a brain in one's head! I knew quite well that you'd
docked safely in your home port. I heard amazing things in
Hamburg about your strange way of life, and yet once I'd
arrived here I never thought of looking you up. But anyone with
such worries as mine . . . Well, how fortunate that chance has
brought us together. I'm under arrest, as you see, but you can
have me set free in a jiffy, if you'll vouch for the fact that I'm
the George Pepusch whom you've known for many years, and
not a villain or a burglar!'

'I'm the ideal person to vouch for you at present, and no mistake,' cried Mr Peregrinus Tyss, 'for I myself have been arrested for a serious crime, though I don't know what it is, and haven't the least inkling of it.'

However, it may be advisable to interrupt the conversation between the two friends, who had met again in a way they little expected, and to tell the gentle reader what was behind the arrest of Mr Peregrinus Tyss. It is hard, perhaps impossible, to describe how rumours originate; they are like the wind, which bloweth where it listeth. In this way a rumour had spread through the town to the effect that on Christmas Eve a lady of the highest rank had been inexplicably abducted from a large gathering in the house of a wealthy banker. Everyone was talking about it, mentioning the banker by name, and complaining loudly that the police could hardly be very vigilant if such an act of violence could be performed so boldly. The Town Council had no choice but to institute enquiries, and all the guests who had been at the banker's house on Christmas Eve were interrogated. Each one declared that he had heard how a noble lady had been abducted from the gathering, and the banker expressed his deep regret that such a crime had occurred in his house. Yet nobody was able to name the abducted lady, and when the banker handed over his guest list, not a single one of the ladies present was found to be missing. As this proved likewise to be the case with all the women and girls, whether native or foreign, in the entire town, the Council naturally considered the rumour to be without foundation and declared the matter closed.

At that point a strange man, strange both in his clothing and in his whole demeanour, appeared before the Town Council. He said that he was a Privy Aulic Counsellor, and that his name was Knarrpanti. He then produced from his pocket a paper with a large seal and handed it over with a civil bow. His expression clearly conveyed how surprised the Council would be by the exalted station which he, Privy Aulic Counsellor Knarrpanti, occupied, and by the important task which had been assigned to him, and what respect the Council would now accord him.

Knarrpanti was a very important man, the 'factotum' at the court of a petty prince whose name the editor cannot recall;

suffice it to say that this prince was perennially hard up and that of all the institutions of government known to him from history, his favourite was the secret State Inquisition which was formerly held in Venice. Some time before, this prince had happened to lose one of his princesses, nobody quite knew how. Knarrpanti was then in Frankfurt trying to borrow some money on his employer's behalf. When the rumour concerning the abduction of the noble lady reached his ears, Knarrpanti promptly wrote to the prince, saying that he had succeeded in his efforts to trace the lost princess. Thereupon he was promptly assigned the task of pursuing the abductor and using every possible means to find the princess and lay hands upon her, cost what it might. This assignment was accompanied by a polite letter to the Town Council, requesting it to afford Privy Aulic Counsellor Knarrpanti every possible assistance in his enquiries, and to arrest and try the abductor when Knarrpanti should demand it. This letter was the very paper which Knarrpanti handed to the Council during the public audience, and which he expected to produce such a dramatic effect.

The Council replied that the rumour concerning the supposed abduction of a noble lady had been shown to be without foundation; on the contrary, it had been definitively established that nobody at all had been abducted. There could therefore be no question of discovering an abductor, and since Privy Aulic Counsellor Knarrpanti had no need to conduct further enquiries, he would presumably not require assistance.

Knarrpanti listened to all this with a self-satisfied smile, and assured the Council that his exceptional sagacity had already succeeded in identifying the culprit. On being reminded that there could only be a culprit if a crime had been committed, Knarrpanti observed that once the culprit had been identified, the crime would follow automatically. Even if the principal charge could not be proved, owing to the obduracy of the accused, only a shallow and superficial judge would be incapable of introducing issues into the enquiry which would blemish the accused somehow and justify his arrest. Therefore, Knarrpanti concluded, he must now urgently request the prompt arrest of the abductor of his princess, and this abductor was none other than Mr Peregrinus Tyss, who had long been known to him as a highly suspicious character, and whose papers he wanted to be confiscated forthwith.

The Council was astonished that a quiet and blameless citizen should be so impudently charged with a crime, and rejected Knarrpanti's request with indignation.

Knarrpanti lost not a jot of his composure. With the odious insolence that was characteristic of him, he assured the Council that if he were asked to provide grounds for his charge, he could do so with the utmost ease. He would summon two witnesses, he continued, to testify that on Christmas Eve Mr Peregrinus Tyss had forcibly dragged a smartly dressed girl into his house.

Intending to demonstrate the full absurdity of this claim rather than to investigate the matter seriously, the Council resolved to hear evidence from the two witnesses cited. One was a neighbour of Mr Peregrinus Tyss, who happened just to be entering his house on that fateful Christmas Eve; the other was the night-watchman. Both had observed Peregrinus from a distance as he carried the mysterious lady indoors, and they concurred in affirming that Mr Tyss had indeed taken a smartly dressed lady into his house. They both claimed also to have observed the lady struggling to free herself and making a great outcry. Asked why they had not hastened to help the unfortunate female, they replied that it had never occurred to them.

The testimony of these witnesses caused the Council no small degree of embarrassment, for Mr Peregrinus did indeed appear to have committed the offence with which he was charged. Knarrpanti spoke like a Cicero, proving that the fact that no lady was missing had no bearing on the matter, since the lady might have escaped from Peregrinus's house and now be keeping silent about the whole incident simply out of embarrassment. The lady's identity, along with other crimes that Mr Tyss might have committed in his perilous amatory intrigues, would doubtless be revealed by the culprit's papers, and so, continued Knarrpanti, he appealed to the Council's love of justice, which would doubtless ensure that no accursed misdeed would go unpunished. The Council resolved for the present to grant the application from the worthy Privy Aulic Counsellor, and so it came about that poor Mr Peregrinus Tyss was suddenly arrested and his papers were confiscated.

Let us now return to the two friends who had just stuck their heads out of neighbouring windows of their prison.

Peregrinus told his friend in great detail how on returning to Frankfurt he found himself an orphan, and how he had since lived in entire seclusion, absorbed in his memories of the past, and leading a lonely and joyless existence amidst the bustle of the town.

'Oh yes,' replied Pepusch in a surly tone, 'I've heard about this. People have told me about the tomfoolery you get up to in order to spend your life in childish day-dreams. You want a reputation for child-like merriment, and so you scorn the rightful claims of life and human society. You give imaginary family dinners, and then feed the poor on the delicacies and the costly wines that you have served up to the dead. You buy your own Christmas presents and behave like a child, but then you give poor children the presents, although they are the sort of thing normally given to spoiled brats in the houses of wealthy parents. But you never reflect that it's a poor kind of charity to tickle the palates of poor people and make them feel their misery twice as bitterly afterwards, when their pangs of hunger force them to chew scraps that many a pampered lap-dog would turn up his nose at. Oh, how I detest this Lady Bountiful behaviour when I think that what you give away on a single day would suffice to keep them in moderate comfort for months on end! You load poor people's children with gleaming toys, but you don't reflect that a painted wooden sword, a rag doll, a cuckoo, a trifling titbit, given them by their father or mother, would give them just as much pleasure, if not more. But they devour your damned marzipan until it makes them sick, and their knowledge of glittering gifts which are afterwards denied to them plants the seed of discontent and anger in their souls. You are rich and healthy, and yet you shun all human contact and frustrate the friendly advances of people who wish you well. I'm willing to believe that you were shattered by your parents' death, but if everyone who suffers a painful loss were to crawl into his shell, then, devil take it, the world would be like a morgue, and I wouldn't want to live in it. But do you realize, old son, that you are governed by the most stubborn selfishness, concealed behind a silly shyness? I tell you, Peregrinus, if you don't change your way of life and give up this hopeless way of managing your affairs, I shan't respect you, and I shan't be your friend any longer!'

Peregrinus snapped his fingers, and Master Flea promptly inserted the microscopic glass into his eye.

The wrathful Pepusch's thoughts ran as follows: 'Isn't it a crying shame that such a good-hearted and intelligent fellow can go so badly astray, and risk all his better energies becoming completely paralysed? But there's no doubt that his soft and melancholy character was unable to stand the blow of losing his parents, and that he tried to console himself with an occupation which is close to madness. He's lost unless I can save him. I'll speak to him severely, and portray his folly in harsh colours, just because I do think so highly of him, and because I am and will remain his true friend.'

From these thoughts, Peregrinus realized that in the surly Pepusch he had again found his old friend unchanged.

'George,' said Peregrinus, when Master Flea had once more removed the microscopic glass from his eye, 'I don't want to wrangle with you about the features of my way of life which you criticize, for I know that you are very well disposed towards me. But I must tell you that it makes my breast swell with pleasure if I can give poor people a day of happiness, and if this is odious selfishness—even though I think of nobody less than of myself—then at least my error is unconscious. These are the flowers in my life; the rest of it seems to me like a dismal barren field full of thistles.'

'What are you saying about thistles?' exclaimed George Pepusch violently. 'Why do you despise thistles and oppose them to flowers? Are you so ignorant of natural history as not to know that the most magnificent flower in existence is none other than the blossom of a thistle? I mean the Cactus grandiflorus. And isn't the thistle Zeherit the most beautiful cactus under the sun? Peregrinus, I've kept this secret from you for a long time, or rather I've had to keep it secret, because I wasn't sure about it myself; but let me tell you now that I am myself the thistle Zeherit and I shall never renounce my claims to the hand of the lovely, heavenly Princess Gamaheh, the daughter of noble King Sekakis. I found her, but at that very moment demonic watchmen and guards seized me and dragged me off to prison.'

'What,' cried Peregrinus, almost paralysed with amazement, 'are you too, George, involved in this incredible story?'

'What story?' asked Pepusch.

Peregrinus had no scruples about telling his friend, as he had told Mr Swammer, all the events that had occurred in Lämmer-hirt's house and then in his own house. He did not even conceal the appearance of Master Flea, though, as you may imagine, he kept quiet about his possession of the mysterious glass.

George's eyes blazed; he bit his lip, struck his forehead, and when Peregrinus had finished, he cried in fury: 'That vile, faithless hussy! That traitress!' To heighten the self-inflicted torment of despairing love by savouring every drop in the poisoned chalice that Peregrinus had unsuspectingly handed him, he made his friend repeat every detail, however slight, of Dörtje's conduct. While listening, he muttered: 'In his arms—on his breast—ardent kisses . . .' He then sprang back from the window and ran round the room, gesticulating like a madman. It was in vain for Peregrinus to assure him that he would learn more consoling information if he would only go on listening; Pepusch would not stop ranting and raving.

The room was unlocked, and a representative of the Council informed Mr Peregrinus Tyss that in the absence of legal grounds for his continued detention he was free to return home.

The first thing Peregrinus did with his newly won freedom was to come forward as a character witness for the captive George Pepusch. He attested that this was indeed the George Pepusch with whom he had lived in close friendship in Madras and who was known to him as a man of property and blameless reputation. About the thistle Zeherit, the most beautiful of all torch-thistles, Peregrinus had the sense to say nothing, since he realized that under the circumstances this might have done his friend more harm than good.

Master Flea let loose a torrent of instructive philosophical observations, the general drift of which was that the thistle Zeherit, though rough and uncouth in manner, was thoroughly humane and intelligent, but had always been a little too over-bearing. 'After all,' he added, 'the thistle was really quite right to criticize your way of life, Mr Peregrinus, even if his language was rather too harsh. For my part, I would seriously advise you to mingle with the world.

'Believe me, Mr Peregrinus,' continued Master Flea, 'you will gain a great deal by emerging from your solitude. For one thing, you need no longer worry about appearing shy and ill-at-ease, since with the mysterious glass in your eye you can have perfect knowledge of people's thoughts, and it is therefore quite impossible that you should ever fail to strike the right note. You can appear before the highest dignitaries with unruffled self-assurance, since their innermost thoughts will be plain to you. If you move freely in the world, your blood will flow more easily, you will no longer be absorbed in melancholy brooding, and, best of all, your brain will be filled with colourful thoughts and ideas; the image of the beautiful Gamaheh will lose some of its radiance, and you will soon be better able to keep your promise to me.'

Mr Peregrinus was aware that both George Pepusch and Master Flea were anxious for his welfare, and he resolved to follow their wise advice. But as soon as he heard the dulcet tones of his fair beloved, who often sang and played music, he could not imagine the possibility of leaving the house, which had become a paradise for him.

Finally he forced himself to take part in a public promenade. Master Flea inserted the glass in his eye and seated himself in Peregrinus's jabot, where he rocked gently to and fro.

'Have I the rare pleasure of seeing my dear, good Mr Tyss once more? My dear fellow, you are practically a stranger, and yet everyone longs for your company. Let's go into some hostelry and drink a bottle of wine, so that I may wish good health to my bosom friend. How delighted I am to see you!' This greeting came from a young man whom Peregrinus had scarcely met more than two or three times. The young man's thoughts were as follows: 'So that misanthropic idiot is showing his face again? I've got to butter him up, because I want to borrow money from him. I hope to God he won't accept my invitation—I haven't got a penny, and none of the innkeepers will give me any more tick.'

Two elegantly dressed girls virtually blocked Peregrinus's path. They were sisters, and distant relatives of his.

'Why, cousin,' exclaimed one of them, laughing, 'fancy meeting you! It's horrid of you to lock yourself up and never see a soul. You'd never believe how fond Mummy is of you, because you're such a clever fellow. Do promise to call on us soon. There! Kiss my hand!' Meanwhile, she was thinking: 'What on earth is this? Whatever has got into my cousin? I wanted to give him the fright of his life. He used to run away from me and from every other female, and now he's stopping, and looking me in the face in such a strange way, and kissing my hand without the least shyness! He's not in love with me, is he? That's all I need! Mother says he's not quite all there. Never mind, I'll take him; a man who's a bit soft in the head is the best of all, so long as he's rich, like my cousin.'

Her sister, with downcast eyes and blushing cheeks, only whispered: 'Yes, do call on us as soon as you can, dear cousin!' She was thinking: 'My cousin's a really handsome man; I don't understand why Mother can't stand him, and says he's silly and tiresome. If he visits us he'll fall in love with me, for I'm the most beautiful girl in the whole of Frankfurt. I'll take him, because I want to marry someone rich, so that I can lie in bed till eleven o'clock and wear more expensive shawls than Mrs von Carsner.'

A doctor who was driving past halted his carriage on spying Peregrinus and called out of the door: 'Good morning, my dear Tyss! You look as fit as a fiddle! May heaven preserve your health! But if anything happens to you, remember me, your late father's old friend. If anyone is as robust as you, I can have them on their feet again in no time! Bye!' He was thinking: 'I believe that fellow keeps healthy just to save money! But he's looking so pale and disturbed that he must have something wrong with him at last. Well, if I ever get my hands on him, he won't leave his bed again in a hurry; he'll pay dearly for his stubborn good health.'

'A very good morning to you, your honour,' cried an old merchant a moment later; 'see how I'm run off my feet, and how hard I have to toil for the sake of business. How wise you are to have given up business, though with your gifts you couldn't have failed to become twice as rich as your worthy father.' What he thought was: 'If he'd only do business, that muddle-headed simpleton would soon lose his whole fortune in speculations, and that would be a real treat. His old dad took pleasure in mercilessly ruining other people who only wanted to help themselves by a little bit of bankruptcy; he'd turn in his grave.'

Peregrinus encountered many more such gross discrepancies between words and thoughts. His replies were always more attuned to what people were thinking than to what they had said, and so it was inevitable that, after he had penetrated their minds, people did not know what to make of him. Finally Peregrinus felt tired and dazed. He snapped his fingers, and the glass promptly disappeared from the pupil of his left eye.

On entering his house, Peregrinus was surprised by a strange spectacle. A man was standing in the middle of the hallway and looking fixedly through a strangely shaped glass at the door of Mr Swammer's room. Iridescent rings of sunlight were playing upon the door and coalescing in a single fiery point which seemed to penetrate through the door. When this happened, a dull moaning, interrupted by cries of pain, could be heard, apparently from inside the room. To his horror, Peregrinus thought he recognized Gamaheh's voice.

'What do you want? What are you up to?' demanded Peregrinus. The man really seemed to be practising devilish arts, for as the iridescent rings moved more quickly and grew more fiery, so the point penetrated the door with more intensity, and the moans from inside the room sounded more agonized.

'Ah,' said the man, bundling his glasses together and hastily putting them in his pocket, 'just look, it's the landlord! Forgive me, my dear Mr Tyss, for operating here without your kind permission. But I did call on you to ask for permission, and the good, kindly Aline told me you had gone out. The matter down here brooked no delay.'

'What matter?' asked Peregrinus, rather roughly, 'what matter down here is it that brooks no delay?'

'Don't you know, my worthy Mr Tyss,' went on the man with a repulsive leer, 'that my ill-behaved niece, Dörtje Elwerdink, has run away from me? After all, you were arrested as her abductor, although quite unjustly, and if it should be necessary I shall be very glad to testify to your entire innocence. It wasn't to you but to Mr Swammerdamm, my former friend and now my enemy, that the faithless Dörtje fled. She's sitting in this room, I know she is, and what's more, she's alone, for Mr Swammerdamm has gone out. I can't get in, as the door is firmly locked and bolted, and I am much too good-natured to resort to force. I have therefore taken the liberty to torment the girl somewhat with my optical instrument of torture, so that she will realize that, although she may fancy herself a princess, I am her lord and master.'

'You may be the Devil, sir,' shouted Peregrinus in a towering rage, 'but not the lord and master of the lovely, heavenly Gamaheh. Get out of the house! Practise your Satanic arts wherever you want, but you won't succeed here, I'll make sure of that!'

'Don't get so excited, my dear Mr Tyss,' said Leuwenhoek; 'I'm an innocent man, and I only want to do good. You don't know who you're defending. It's a little monster, a little basilisk, that's sitting in that room in the shape of a lovely woman. Perhaps it was all right for her to flee if she disliked staying with my humble self; but should the traitress be allowed to rob me of my finest treasure, the best friend of my soul, without whom I can't live, can't survive? Should she have abducted Master Flea? You won't understand what I'm referring to, my good sir, but . . .'

At this point Master Flea, who had jumped up from Mr Peregrinus's jabot and assumed a safer and more comfortable seat in his neckerchief, could not restrain himself from uttering a shrill peal of mocking laughter.

'Ha!' cried Leuwenhoek, as though he had received a sudden fright, 'ha! what was that? Can it be possible? Yes, in this very place! Allow me, won't you, my esteemed Mr Peregrinus . . .'

With these words Leuwenhoek stretched out his arm, approached close to Mr Peregrinus, and tried to reach for his neckerchief.

Peregrinus, however, adroitly stepped aside, took a firm grip of him, and dragged him to the front door, intending to throw him out without further ado. Just as Peregrinus and Leuwenhoek, who was wearing himself out in futile protestations, had reached the door, it was opened from outside and in stormed George Pepusch, followed by Mr Swammerdamm.

As soon as Leuwenhoek caught sight of his enemy Swammerdamm, he tore himself free in a supreme exertion of his remaining strength, sprang back, and planted himself with his back to the door of the fateful room where the fair Dörtje was imprisoned. Perceiving this, Swammerdamm drew a small telescope from his pocket, extended it to its full length, and assailed his enemy with a loud cry of: 'Draw, you scoundrel, if you have the courage!'

Leuwenhoek promptly had a similar instrument in his hand, likewise extended it, and shouted: 'Come on, I'll fight you, and you'll soon feel my power!' The two put the telescopes to their eyes and fell upon each other furiously with sharp and murderous strokes, lengthening and shortening their weapons by pulling the extensions in and out. There were feints, parries, turns, in a word all the tricks of the fencer, and they seemed to grow ever more infuriated. If one of them was hit, he screamed, leapt into the air, and performed the most wonderful caprioles, and the most beautiful *entrechats* and pirouettes, like the best solo dancer in the Paris ballet, until the other focused the shortened telescope on him. If the same thing happened to the other, he behaved similarly. Thus they alternately displayed the boldest leaps, the wildest gestures, the most furious outcry; the sweat was dripping from their foreheads, their bloodshot eyes were protruding from their heads, and since no cause for their St Vitus dance was visible, save that they looked through the telescopes in turn, one was obliged to conclude that they were lunatics escaped from the madhouse. For the rest, the duel was a most pleasing sight.

Eventually Mr Swammerdamm succeeded in forcing the evil Leuwenhoek out of his position in front of the door, which he had maintained with obstinate valour, and to transfer the combat to the back of the hallway.

George Pepusch saw his chance, pushed open the door, which was neither locked nor bolted, and slipped into the room. A second later he rushed out again, shouted: 'She's gone, gone!', and sped out of the house like lightning. Both Leuwenhoek and Swammerdamm had struck each other severe blows, for both were hopping and dancing about wildly and, with their howling and shrieking, making a music that seemed like the lamentation of damned souls in hell.

Peregrinus had no idea what to do to separate the furious combatants and put an end to a scene that was as ridiculous as it was horrifying. Finally both duellists noticed that the door of the room was wide open. They forgot their duel and their pain, pocketed their fatal weapons, and rushed into the room.

Mr Peregrinus was deeply distressed at the flight of the lovely Gamaheh from his house, and he wished that the abominable Leuwenhoek were in hell. Just then the voice of Aline became audible on the stairs. She was laughing loudly and calling repeatedly: 'The things that happen! Amazing, incredible, who would ever have dreamt it!'

'What incredible things have happened now?' asked Peregrinus in a small voice.

'Oh, dear Mr Tyss,' called the old woman, 'do come up here quickly, just go into your room.'

The old woman opened the door of his chamber with a mischievous chuckle. As he entered—wonderful to relate! blissful to behold!—the lovely Dörtje Elwerdink tripped towards him, dressed in the seductive taffeta dress that he had seen her wearing in Mr Swammer's room. 'At last! At last I see you again, my sweet friend,' lisped the little beauty, nestling up to Peregrinus so adeptly that, despite all his good resolutions, he could not help enfolding her in the tenderest of embraces. He almost fainted with pleasure and amorous delight.

No doubt it is a frequent experience for someone in the utmost rapture of supreme bliss to bump against something with his nose and, suddenly awakened by earthly pain, fall from the seventh heaven into ordinary life. This is just what happened to Mr Peregrinus. For as he bent down to kiss Dörtje's delicious lips, his not inconsiderable nose collided in a horribly painful manner with the sparkling diadem that she was wearing in her dark curls. The severe pain of contact with the jewels, which were cut in an angular shape, brought him sufficiently to his senses so that he observed the diadem. The diadem, however, reminded him of Princess Gamaheh, and this naturally recalled everything Master Flea had said about the temptress. He bethought himself that a princess, the daughter of a mighty king, could not care about his love, and that all her amorous behaviour must be artful hypocrisy, by which the traitress wanted to regain the magical flea. As he considered this, an ice-cold jet shot through his heart, and if it did not completely extinguish the flames of love, it at least damped them down.

Peregrinus extricated himself gently from Dörtje's amorous embrace and said in a low voice and with downcast eyes: 'Heavens above! You are the daughter of the mighty King Sekakis, the high, beautiful, and magnificent Princess Gamaheh! I ask your pardon, Princess, if an emotion I could not resist led me into folly and madness. But you, Your Royal Highness . . .'

'What are you saying, my dear friend?' interrupted Dörtje Elwerdink. 'Me, the daughter of a mighty king? Me, a princess? Why, I'm your Aline, and you will love me to distraction if you—but what's the matter with me? Aline, Queen of Golconda? She's in your house already; I've spoken to her. A dear good woman, but she's grown old, and isn't nearly so pretty as she was when she got married to a French general! Oh dear! Perhaps I'm not the right person, perhaps I never reigned in Golconda? Oh dear!'

Dörtje had closed her eyes and was becoming unsteady on her feet. Peregrinus placed her on the sofa.

'Gamaheh,' she continued, as though in a trance, 'Gamaheh, did you say? Gamaheh, the daughter of King Sekakis? Yes, I remember, in Famagusta! I was really a beautiful tulip—but no, even then I felt yearning and love in my heart—not another word!'

The girl fell silent and seemed ready to go to sleep. Peregrinus undertook the perilous venture of putting her in a more comfortable position. But, as soon as he gently embraced the lovely female, a concealed pin pricked him very hard in the finger. As was his habit, he snapped his fingers. Master Flea, however, mistook this for the signal agreed between them, and promptly placed the microscopic glass in his pupil.

Behind the cornea, as usual, Peregrinus perceived the strange network of nerves and veins receding into the depths of the brain. But this network was interwoven with gleaming silver threads, at least a hundred times thinner than those of the finest spider's web, and these threads, which seemed endless, as they twined out of the brain into some entity invisible even with the aid of the microscope, were perhaps thoughts of a sublimer kind, while the others were of a sort easier to grasp. Peregrinus perceived a colourful medley of flowers assuming human shape, and human beings that melted into the earth and then gleamed forth as stones and metals. Among them moved all manner of strange animals, incessantly changing their shapes and speaking in wondrous languages. None of these phenomena matched the others, and the timorous lament of heart-rending melancholy that rang through the air seemed to express the dissonance among them. Yet this very dissonance added new splendour to the deep underlying harmony that triumphantly broke through, uniting all apparent discords in an eternity of unutterable pleasure.

'Don't let this confuse you, good Mr Peregrinus,' whispered Master Flea, 'what you behold are dream-thoughts. If there's anything more to them, this is hardly the time to investigate it. Call the little temptress by her real name and ask her any questions you want.'

Since the girl had various names, you might think that Peregrinus would have found it difficult to choose the right one. However, Peregrinus cried without pausing to think: 'Dörtje Elwerdink! my dear, lovely girl, might it be true? Is it possible that you might really love me?'

Dörtje instantly awoke from her trance-like state, opened her eyes, and said with a radiant look: 'What makes you doubt me, my Peregrinus? Could a girl do what I have done if her heart were not filled by the most ardent love? Peregrinus, I love you as I love nobody else, and if you will be mine, I'll be yours with all my soul, and I'll stay with you because I can't leave you, not just because I want to escape from my uncle's tyranny.'

The silver threads had vanished and Dörtje's normal thoughts went as follows: 'How did it happen? First I pretended to love him, simply in order to get Master Flea back for myself and Leuwenhoek, and now I really am fond of him. I've been caught in my own snare. I hardly think about Master Flea anymore; I'd like to be attached for ever to him, for he seems nicer than any man I've ever seen.'

You may imagine how these thoughts inflamed all the blissful delight in Peregrinus's heart. He fell on his knees before the lovely Dörtje, covered her delicate hands with a thousand ardent kisses, called her his joy, his heaven, his entire happiness.

'Now,' lisped Dörtje, pulling him gently to her side, 'now, my precious, you won't refuse me a wish on which your beloved's peace of mind, in fact her whole existence, depends.'

'Ask for anything you want, my sweet life,' replied Peregrinus, 'your slightest wish is my command. There is nothing in the world so precious to me that I would not surrender it joyfully for you and your love.'

'Alas!' whispered Master Flea. 'Who would have thought that the treacherous creature would triumph? I'm done for!'

'Listen, then,' continued Dörtje, having enthusiastically returned the ardent kisses that Peregrinus had planted on her lips, 'listen, I know how the . . .'

The door burst open and in came Mr George Pepusch.

'Zeherit!' shrieked Dörtje in apparent despair, and she sank back unconscious on to the sofa.

The thistle Zeherit, however, dashed over to Princess Gamaheh, took her in his arms, and sped away with her like lightning.

Master Flea was saved for the present.

FIFTH ADVENTURE

*The remarkable legal proceedings conducted by Privy Aulic Counsel-
lor Knarrpanti, and his wise and judicious behaviour. The thoughts
of young poetic enthusiasts and literary ladies. Peregrinus's reflections on his life, and the erudition and good sense of Master Flea.
The unusual virtue and steadfastness of Mr Tyss. Unexpected
conclusion of a potentially tragic scene.*

The gentle reader will remember that Mr Peregrinus Tyss's
papers had been confiscated in order to ascertain further par-
ticulars about a deed which had never been committed. Both
the Council representative and Privy Aulic Counsellor Knarrpanti had minutely examined every piece of writing, every
letter, every scrap of paper (not excluding laundry-lists and
shopping-lists) that they had found, but had arrived at diamet-
rically opposed views concerning the result of their enquiries.

The representative asserted that the papers contained not a
single word that might refer to a crime such as Peregrinus was
charged with committing. The penetrating gaze of the hawk-
eyed Privy Aulic Counsellor Knarrpanti, on the other hand, had
found a great deal in Mr Peregrinus Tyss's papers that showed
him to be a highly dangerous individual. Formerly, as a young
man, Peregrinus had kept a diary; and this diary contained a
host of incriminating entries which not only cast a very unfavourable light on his attitude to the abduction of young
females, but proved beyond a peradventure that he had committed this crime on numerous occasions.

Thus one entry ran: 'Abduction is a fine and splendid thing!'
Another: 'But I have now conquered the fairest of all!' Another:
'I have carried off Mariane, Philine, and Mignon!'* Another:
'I enjoy these abductions.' Another: 'Julia was to be abducted,
it could not be otherwise, and I performed it by causing masked
men to attack her and drag her away as she was walking by
herself in the woods.'

In addition to these conclusive diary entries, a letter from a
friend was discovered which contained the incriminating words:

'I would therefore ask you to take Friderike away from him whenever you can.'

All the words cited, and a hundred other phrases containing the words 'abduct', 'conquer', or 'carry off', had not only been heavily underlined with a red pencil by the wise Knarrpanti, but he had also copied them on to a separate sheet of paper, which looked very pretty. This last piece of work seemed to cause him especial pleasure.

'Now do you see, my respected colleague?' said Knarrpanti to the Council representative; 'did I not tell you as much? That Peregrinus Tyss is an abominable villain, a veritable Don Juan. Who knows what has become of the unfortunate victims of his murderous lust, Mariane, Philine, and all the rest. It was high time to put a stop to these terrible goings-on, otherwise this dangerous character might have caused untold suffering to the good town of Frankfurt with his intrigues and his abductions. What crimes he has already committed, by his own admission! Look at this passage, my dear colleague, and judge for yourself how Peregrinus advertises his foul intentions.'

The passage from the diary to which the wise Privy Aulic Counsellor Knarrpanti drew the representative's attention ran as follows: 'Today I only killed time.' The word 'killed' was underlined three times, and Knarrpanti asked whether anyone could reveal his criminal inclinations more clearly than by regretting that on a given day he had killed nothing but time!

The representative repeated his view that Mr Peregrinus Tyss's papers had not disclosed the slightest trace of any crime. Knarrpanti shook his head incredulously, and the representative asked him to listen once more to the passages which he had extracted as being suspicious, only this time in their proper context.

The gentle reader will soon be entirely persuaded of Knarrpanti's sublime cunning.

The representative opened the incriminating diary and read: 'Today I saw Mozart's *Abduction from the Seraglio* for the twentieth time, with as much delight as ever. The *Abduction* is a fine and splendid thing!' Again: 'Full many a flower | Adorns this sweet bower, | But I have now conquered | The fairest of all!' Again: 'I have carried off Mariane, Philine, and Mignon, for he was too deeply absorbed in these characters; he was talking wildly about the old harpist and quarrelling with Jarno. *Wilhelm Meister* is not a book for somebody who is recovering from a nervous breakdown.' Again: 'Jünger's *Abduction** is a pleasant comedy. I enjoy these abductions, because they breathe special life into the plot.' Again: 'As I had thought too little about the plot, I found myself in difficulties. Julia was to be abducted, it could not be otherwise, and I performed it by causing masked men to attack her and drag her away as she was walking by herself in the woods. I was very pleased with this new idea and developed it at great length. All things considered, this tragedy was quite amusing as the work of an enthusiastic boy, and I am sorry I threw it in the fire.' The letter ran: 'Do you really meet Friderike in society so often, you lucky man? I expect Moritz won't let anyone near her and claims all her attention for himself. I would therefore ask you to take Friderike away from him whenever you can.'

Knarrpanti insisted that even the context made things no better, since it was an artful device of criminals to state their intentions in a veiled manner which at first glance might seem quite trivial and innocent. As particular evidence of such artfulness, the ingenious Knarrpanti drew the representative's attention to a phrase in Peregrinus's diary about the '*se*cond pro*duction*' of a play. Knarrpanti prided himself not a little on the sagacity with which he had instantly discovered that the word 'seduction' had been divided into two words, in order to divert attention and suspicion.

The Council still refused to authorize further proceedings against the accused Peregrinus Tyss, and the legal experts employed a term which may be cited here because it looks so curious in the tale of Master Flea; and although fairy-tales are properly embellished with marvels, mere curiosities may add a pleasing flourish, and are not to be despised. They said (the legal experts, that is) that there was no *Corpus delicti*;* the wise Counsellor Knarrpanti, however, insisted that he didn't give a tinker's curse about the *delictum* if he could get his hands on a *Corpus*, and the *Corpus* was the dangerous rapist and murderer Mr Peregrinus Tyss. The editor requests the kind reader who happens not to be a legal expert, and more particularly the fair female reader, to ask some young jurisprude to explain this passage to them. The aforementioned jurisprude will instantly strike a dramatic pose and begin: 'In legal terminology . . .', etc., etc.

The representative considered that the only matter on which Mr Peregrinus Tyss should be interrogated was the nocturnal incident mentioned by the witnesses.

Peregrinus was not a little embarrassed when the representative asked him what had taken place. He felt that if he were to stick closely to the truth, that in itself would make the whole story sound like a falsehood, or at least highly improbable. He therefore thought it advisable to remain silent and to protect himself by saying that, not being charged with any specific crime, he did not consider himself obliged to answer questions about individual events in his life.

Knarrpanti was jubilant over this declaration by the accused, finding in it confirmation of all his suspicions. He told the representative fairly bluntly that the latter had no idea how to handle the matter, and the representative had wit enough to see that an interrogation conducted by Knarrpanti himself would do Peregrinus no harm and might decisively benefit him.

The sharp-witted Knarrpanti had prepared over a hundred questions with which he assailed Peregrinus. Some of them were indeed not easy to answer. Their principal purpose was to discover what Peregrinus had been *thinking*, not only in general throughout his entire life, but also on this and that particular occasion, as for example when writing the suspicious words in his papers. Thinking, according to Knarrpanti, was in itself a dangerous undertaking, and all the more so when performed by dangerous individuals.

There were also such incriminating questions as these: 'Who was the elderly man with close-cropped hair, wearing a blue overcoat, with whom you discussed the best method of cooking Rhine salmon while having lunch in a restaurant on 24 March last year?' Or: 'Do you yourself not realize that all the mysterious passages in your papers arouse the justified suspicion that what you refrained from writing down might have been much more damning, and might indeed have contained a complete confession of your crime?'

This form of enquiry, and indeed Privy Aulic Counsellor Knarrpanti himself, struck Peregrinus as so peculiar that he was curious to read the thoughts of the jesuitical hair-splitter. He snapped his fingers, and Master Flea quickly inserted the microscopic glass in his pupil.

Knarrpanti's thoughts went more or less like this: 'I don't believe for a moment that this young man abducted our Princess; in fact he couldn't have, for she ran off several years ago with a strolling actor. But I could not neglect the opportunity of advancing my own career by causing a sensation. My little employer was beginning to ignore me and people at court were calling me a tedious day-dreamer; indeed they often thought I was silly and boring, just because none of them could match my intellect and taste, and none was so good as I was at currying favour with the Prince by doing little jobs for him. Didn't I help his groom of the bedchamber to polish his boots? The business of the abduction was like a gift from heaven. The news that I was on the track of the runaway Princess suddenly restored the reputation that I had almost lost. Now people again think me judicious, wise, adroit, and, above all, so loyally devoted to the Prince that I may well be called a pillar of the state, on whom its entire well-being depends.

'Nothing can or will come of this matter, since there's no way of pinning the Princess's abduction on this man, but that's neither here nor there. For that very reason, I'll torment the young man as much as I can with a cross-fire of awkward questions. The more I do so, the more people will praise my dedication to this matter and my active commitment to the good of my employer. All I need do is make the young man impatient and extort a few snappish answers from him. I'll mark them with a red pencil, add a few comments, and before you know where you are, the young man will be shown in a bad light, and a lot of ill-feeling will arise which will harm him and even turn quiet, impartial people, like the Council representative, against him. What a skill it is to make the most trivial matter seem important and derive ill-feeling from it! I was born with this skill, and thanks to it I can dispose of my enemies and feather my own nest. I can hardly keep a straight face when I see how the Council thinks I really want to get at the truth, when all the time I'm only concerned about Number One and just see this whole business as a means of impressing my employer and getting all the applause and money I can. Even if nothing comes of this, nobody will say my efforts were pointless; they'll say that I was probably right all along, and that my precautions ensured that the villainous Peregrinus Tyss didn't abduct the Princess who had been abducted already.'

Since Peregrinus was thus able to read the thoughts of the sublime Aulic Counsellor, he naturally maintained a suitable composure, and instead of becoming uneasy, as Knarrpanti hoped, he managed by his skilful replies to make Knarrpanti's ingenuity look ridiculous. The Council representative seemed to enjoy the spectacle. After Knarrpanti had concluded his interminable interrogation, mainly because he was out of breath, Peregrinus, without being asked, told the representative briefly that the young lady whom he had taken into his house on that Christmas Eve, at her own request, was none other than the niece of the optical artist Leuwenhoek, Dörtje Elwerdink by name, and that she was now staying with her godfather, Mr Swammer, who was a lodger in Peregrinus's house.

This declaration was found to be correct, and the strange trial for abduction was brought to a close.

Knarrpanti indeed urged that more hearings should be conducted, and read his ingeniously composed minutes of the proceedings aloud to the Council; this masterpiece, however, elicited a universal roar of laughter. It was judged advisable for Privy Aulic Counsellor Knarrpanti to leave Frankfurt and to bring this admirable document to his employer as the result of his labours and as proof of his sagacity and his unwearying devotion to duty. The strange trial became the talk of the town, and the illustrious Knarrpanti, to his considerable annoyance, observed that people held their noses with every sign of loathing and disgust when he walked past, and got up and left when he entered a restaurant. Before long he sneaked away from the town. Thus Knarrpanti was obliged to retire in disgrace from the field on which he had hoped to gather laurels.

The events that have been compressed into a short narrative in fact occupied a number of days, for one can hardly suppose that Knarrpanti was able to compile a sizeable folio volume in a short time, and the minutes of the proceedings resembled just such a volume.

Peregrinus was greatly vexed by the pestering to which Knarrpanti daily subjected him and by the latter's silly and arrogant behaviour. His feelings were heightened by his continuing uncertainty about the fate of the fair Dörtje. As the kind reader learnt at the end of the Fourth Adventure, George Pepusch had torn Dörtje from the arms of the lovelorn Peregrinus with lightning speed, leaving the latter petrified with surprise and shock. When Peregrinus finally regained his senses, jumped up, and set off in pursuit of the kidnapper, the entire house was silent as the grave. In response to repeated loud calls, old Aline shuffled along from the most distant room in the house, and declared that she had been completely unaware of the incident.

The loss of Dörtje drove Peregrinus almost out of his wits. Master Flea, however, offered some words of comfort. 'You don't know,' said he in a tone that would have heartened even someone in the depths of despair, 'you don't know, dear Mr Peregrinus Tyss, whether the fair Dörtje Elwerdink has left your house at all. So far as I can judge these things, she isn't far away; I seem to sense her presence. But if you will trust me and follow my friendly advice, then leave the fair Dörtje to her fate. She's a fickle little thing, believe you me. Perhaps, as you told me, she really has become fond of you, but how long will it be before she plunges you into such grief and sorrow that you risk losing your reason, like the thistle Zeherit? I tell you again, give up your solitary life. You'll feel much better if you do. If you knew any other girls, you'd hardly think Dörtje the most beautiful of all; and if you had made advances to any other woman, you wouldn't think that Dörtje was the only one who could love you. Come, come, Peregrinus, a bit more experience will teach you better. You're a good-looking man, and I wouldn't have to be as intelligent and perceptive as Master Flea is, to foresee that you'll enjoy happiness through love in a quite different way than you now imagine.'

By visiting public places, Peregrinus had already made some headway, and he now found it less difficult to attend the parties which he had formerly shunned. On these occasions Master Flea did him admirable services with the microscopic glass, and it is said that at this period Peregrinus kept a diary in which he noted down the strangest and most entertaining discrepancies between words and thoughts, such as he encountered daily. The editor of the strange tale *Master Flea* may find the opportunity in future to publish excerpts from this diary that deserve a wider audience; here, however, they would only impede the progress of the narrative and hence be unwelcome to the kind reader. It can be said, though, that many polite phrases proved to be firmly attached to certain corresponding thoughts: e.g. 'I'd appreciate your friendly advice' means 'He's silly enough to believe that I want his advice about something I've decided long ago, and that will tickle his vanity!' while 'I trust you completely' means 'I've known all along that you were a scoundrel', and so forth.

It may finally be remarked that as a result of his observations through the microscope Peregrinus suffered great embarrassment from many people. These people were the young men who were constantly being carried away by rapturous enthusiasm and letting loose torrents of sonorous clichés. The most profound and sonorous among them were young poets, brimming over with imagination and genius, who had to endure a great deal of adulation, especially from ladies. There were also literary women, who knew all the depths of sublunary existence, as the phrase goes, like the backs of their hands; they also held penetrating philosophical views on the constitution of society, and could deliver these in eloquent language, like an Easter sermon. If Peregrinus had been astonished to see the silver threads in Gamaheh's brain twining into an invisible region, he was no less amazed at what he beheld in the brains of the people just mentioned. He saw the strange network of veins and nerves, but noticed also that when these people talked with exceptional eloquence about art and learning and the main currents of intellectual life, their veins and nerves did not penetrate into the recesses of their brains, but curved back, so that it was impossible to discern their thoughts with any clarity. He communicated this observation to Master Flea, who was sitting as usual in a fold of his neckerchief. Master Flea remarked that what Peregrinus had mistaken for thoughts were nothing more than words, vainly endeavouring to become thoughts.

While Peregrinus amused himself socially in diverse ways, his faithful companion, Master Flea, relaxed the gravity of his demeanour and showed himself to be a voluptuary, a rogue, and an *aimable roué*. That is to say, whenever he saw a female's comely throat or white neck, he could not resist seizing the first opportunity to emerge from his hiding-place and leap on to the tempting spot, where he managed adroitly to evade pursuit by the sufferer's fingers. This manœuvre served two purposes. For one thing, he enjoyed it; for another, he wanted to attract Peregrinus's gaze to beauties who might obscure Dörtje's image. This, however, seemed to be entirely lost labour, for not one of the ladies whom Peregrinus approached confidently and without any timidity seemed as pretty and charming as his little Princess. Another reason why his love for Dörtje was so firm was that he found nobody else whose flattering words so closely corresponded to her thoughts as in Dörtje's case. He felt unable to leave her, and frankly declared as much. Master Flea felt no little alarm.

One day Peregrinus noticed that old Aline was grinning mischievously to herself, taking snuff more frequently than usual, clearing her throat, muttering indistinctly, and, in a word, behaving altogether as though she had something on her mind and wanted to communicate it. To every question, however, she replied: 'Yes! there's no telling—we'll just have to wait and see!' whether these phrases were suitable or not. In the end Peregrinus cried impatiently: 'Spit it out, Aline, and tell me what's up now, instead of creeping about with a mysterious look on your face.'

'Oh,' cried the old woman, clapping her withered hands, 'oh, the pretty darling moppet, the dainty little thing!'

'Who are you talking about?' interrupted Peregrinus crossly.

'Why,' said Aline, chuckling, 'who should I be talking about, but our dear Princess down in Mr Swammer's room, your dear fiancée, Mr Tyss.'

'Woman,' burst out Peregrinus, 'unhappy woman, she's here, here in this house, and you haven't told me till now?'

'Where else,' replied the old woman, with her cheerful composure undiminished, 'where else would the Princess be, but here, where she's found her mother.'

'What?' cried Peregrinus. 'What are you saying, Aline?'

'Yes,' said the old woman, lifting her head, 'Aline is my real name, and who knows what else will come to light soon, before your wedding.'

Although Peregrinus implored her to speak, by all the angels and devils, the old woman paid not the slightest heed to his impatience, but settled herself slowly in an armchair, produced her snuff-box, took a large pinch of snuff, and then demonstrated long-windedly and in great detail that there was no greater or more harmful failing than impatience.

'Above all else, my lad,' said she, 'you must keep your cool, for otherwise you risk losing everything at the moment when you think you've gained it. Before I tell you a single word, you must sit down like a good child and not interrupt my story, as you value your life.'

What could Peregrinus do but obey the old woman? And as soon as he had sat down, she recounted things that were indeed strange and wondrous to hear.

According to the old woman's story, the two gentlemen, that is Swammerdamm and Leuwenhoek, went on fighting inside the room, making a terrible uproar. After that they fell silent, but a dull groaning sound caused her to fear that one of them was mortally wounded. On peeping inquisitively through the keyhole, however, she beheld something quite different from what she had expected. Swammerdamm and Leuwenhoek had got hold of George Pepusch and were stroking and rubbing him with their hands in such a way that he kept growing thinner, and emitted the groans which the old woman had heard. At last, when Pepusch had become as thin as the stalk of a thistle, they tried to push him through the keyhole. Half of poor Pepusch's body was already hanging into the hallway when the old woman took flight in terror. Soon afterwards the old woman heard a loud peal of laughter and saw Pepusch, in his natural shape, being peacefully led out of the house by the two Magi. The fair Dörtje was standing in the doorway of the room, beckoning the old woman to enter. She wanted to dress herself up and needed the old woman's help.

The old woman could not say enough about the vast quantity of dresses which Dörtje fetched from various old wardrobes and

displayed to her, each of them richer and more magnificent than
the last. The old woman further assured Peregrinus that only
an Indian princess could own such jewellery as Dörtje had; her
eyes were still hurting from being dazzled by its brilliance.

The old woman then related how she had said this and that
while helping the darling moppet to dress, how she had recalled
the late Mr Tyss senior and the fine life that had formerly gone
on in the house, and how she had ended up by remembering
her own deceased relatives.

'You know, Mr Tyss,' said the old woman, 'that there's no one
I care for more than my late aunt, who was married to a calico-
printer. She had been in Mainz, and also, I think, in India, and
she could pray and sing in French. If I have my aunt to thank
for my un-Christian name Aline, I'll willingly forgive her in
the grave, for it's from her that I learnt good manners, proper
behaviour, and the art of using the right words. When I had
told her a good deal about my aunt, the little Princess asked
me about my parents, my grandparents, and so on through the
rest of my family. I poured out my heart to her, and told her
without reserve that my mother was almost as beautiful as I am,
though my nose is superior to hers; it comes from my father's
side, and its shape has been traditional in our family from time
immemorial. Then I got talking about the fair where I waltzed
with Sergeant Häberpiep, wearing my sky-blue stockings with
red gussets. Well! God knows, we are all of us poor sinners.
But, Mr Tyss, if only you had seen for yourself how the little
Princess, after laughing and chuckling fit to gladden your heart,
grew quieter and quieter, and gazed at me with such a strange
look that I really felt quite queer. And just think, Mr Tyss,
suddenly, before I knew what was happening, the little Princess
is kneeling before me and trying to kiss my hand and calling:
"Yes, it's you, I didn't realize it before, it's you yourself!" And
when I ask in astonishment what she means . . .'

The old woman paused, and when Peregrinus urged her to
continue, she took a large pinch of snuff in a grave and thoughtful manner and said: 'You'll learn soon enough, lad, what happened next. There's a time for everything!'

As Peregrinus was about to press the old woman harder to
tell him more, she uttered a piercing laugh. Peregrinus ad-

monished her, with a frown, that his room was no place for tomfoolery. But the old woman, sitting with arms akimbo, seemed in danger of suffocating. The fiery red of her complexion changed into a pleasing cherry colour, and Peregrinus was on the point of pouring a full glass of water over her face, when she regained her breath and was again able to speak. 'It's wrong', said she, 'to laugh at the foolish little thing. No, there's no such love on earth any more! Just think, Mr Tyss . . .' The old woman burst out laughing again, and Peregrinus's patience was almost at an end. Finally he managed with much effort to extract the information that the little Princess was under the illusion that he, Mr Peregrinus Tyss, was bent on marrying the old woman, and that she, the old woman, had had to give her a solemn promise to reject his suit.

Peregrinus felt as though he were entangled in evil witchcraft, and he had such an uncanny sensation that even honest old Aline seemed like a ghostly being whom he should flee from as quickly as possible.

The old woman would not let him go, on the grounds that she wanted quickly to tell him a secret concerning the little Princess.

'It's now certain', said the old woman in a confidential tone, 'that the glittering star of happiness is shining on you, dear Mr Peregrinus, but it's up to you to keep the star favourable. When I told the little thing that you were incredibly enamoured of her and had no thought of marrying me, she said that she would only be convinced, and would only give you her fair hand in marriage, if you would grant her a wish that she has long carried in the depths of her heart. She says that you have taken a pretty little black boy into your service, who had run away from her; I said that wasn't so, but she claims that the boy is so tiny that he can live in a nutshell. Now this boy . . .'

'Not on your life', burst out Peregrinus, who had long since perceived what the old woman was getting at. He stormed out of the room and out of the house.

It is an old-established custom for the hero of a story, when overcome by violent emotion, to run out into the forest, or at least to some solitary glade. This custom is a good one, because it prevails in real life. Mr Peregrinus Tyss therefore had no alternative but to run in a straight line from his house on the Horsemarket until he had left the town behind him and reached a nearby glade. And since a glade in a romantic tale must not be deficient in rustling leaves, the sighing and whispering of the evening breeze, murmuring springs, babbling brooks, etc., you may suppose that Peregrinus found all these in his retreat. He sat down on a mossy stone half-covered by the clear brook whose waves were rippling and splashing at his feet. Reflecting on the strange adventure he had just experienced, he firmly resolved to seek and find the clue which should show him how to escape from this labyrinth of extraordinary riddles.

Perhaps the regular whispering of the bushes, the monotonous murmuring of the water, the steady clatter of a distant mill, can form the ground-note which help one to control and organize one's thoughts, so that instead of rushing aloud without rhythm or beat, they become a distinct melody. And so, after spending some time in this charming spot, Peregrinus began to contemplate his experiences more calmly.

'Indeed,' said Peregrinus to himself, 'a writer of fantastic fairy-tales could not invent wilder or more bewildering events than those I have experienced in the small space of a few days. Charm, delight, and love itself visit the solitary misogynist, and a glance and a word are sufficient to fill his bosom with the flames whose torture he shunned before he knew it! But the time and place, and the whole appearance of the strange seductive being, are so mysterious that the intervention of a strange magic spell seems visibly apparent. Before long a tiny animal, which is normally despised, displays learning, intelligence, and a wondrous magical power. And this animal talks about things that are incomprehensible to our normal way of thinking, as though they were the constantly repeated stuff of everyday life behind the meat-dish and the winebottle.

'Have I come too close to the revolving wheel driven by dark unknown powers, and has it caught me up in its revolutions? Would one not expect that certain things, when they enter one's life, would drive one out of one's mind? And yet I feel perfectly well; I no longer find it remarkable that a king of the fleas should have put himself in my care and, in return, confided a secret to me that discloses people's inmost thoughts and raises me above life's deceits. But where will, where can all this lead? What if the flea's extraordinary mask concealed an evil demon that wanted to lead me to my doom, and to rob me by foul means of all the happy love that might be mine if I possessed Dörtje? Would it not be better to dispose of the tiny monster forthwith?'

'That,' put in Master Flea, interrupting Peregrinus's self-communings, 'that wasn't a nice idea at all, Mr Peregrinus Tyss! Do you think the secret I confided to you is a trivial one? Can't you regard this gift as the clearest token of my sincere friendship? Shame on you for being so mistrustful! You are surprised by the intelligence and the mental powers of a tiny animal which is normally despised, but, with respect, that reveals the limitations of your scientific education. Concerning the intellectual and self-determining soul of animals, I wish you had read the Greek Philo,* or at least the treatise of Hieronymus Rorarius,* *That Brute Beasts Employ Their Reason Better than Man*, or his *Oration on Behalf of Mice*. Or that you knew what Lipsius* and the great Leibniz* thought about the intellectual powers of animals, or that you were acquainted with what the learned and profound Rabbi Maimonides* says about animals' souls. If you did, you would scarcely consider me an evil demon on account of my intelligence, or suppose that intellectual power must correspond to bodily extension. I suspect that you incline to the ingenious opinion of the Spanish physician Gomez Pereira,* who thinks animals nothing more than artificial machines moving automatically without the power of thought or free will. But no, don't let me think you as foolish as that, my good Mr Peregrinus Tyss; I prefer to believe that my humble person has long since taught you to know better.

'Nor do I quite see what you mean by wonders, my excellent Mr Peregrinus, or how you contrive to divide phenomena into the wondrous and the non-wondrous, since the reality they manifest is the same as ourselves, and we and they determine each other reciprocally. If you wonder at something because it has not yet happened to you, or because you think you cannot perceive the connection of cause and effect, that simply shows that your powers of perception are limited by the deficiencies of your vision. Whether your vision is naturally deficient, or sicklied o'er with the pale cast of thought, I cannot say. But, with respect, Mr Tyss, the most comical aspect of the matter is that you are trying to divide yourself into two parts, one of which perceives what you call wonders and readily believes in them, while the other wonders at this perception and this belief. Has it ever occurred to you that you believe in the images of your dreams?'

'I beg you, my dear fellow,' said Peregrinus, interrupting the tiny orator, 'how can you talk about dreams? These arise merely from some disorder in our physical or mental organization.'

On hearing these words of Mr Peregrinus Tyss, Master Flea uttered a shrill peal of mocking laughter.

'Poor Mr Tyss,' he said to the somewhat dismayed Peregrinus, 'is your mind so little enlightened that you do not realize how silly such opinions are? Ever since chaos gathered into plastic material—which must be quite a while ago—the World Spirit* has used this material to shape everything that exists, including dreams and their images. These images are sketches of what was or what may yet be; the spirit draws them rapidly for its own pleasure, when the tyrant called the body has released it from its slavery. But this is neither the time nor the place to refute your views and teach you more correct ones; besides, it might be pointless. There is just one more thing that I want to reveal to you.'

'Speak or be silent, dear Master,' exclaimed Peregrinus, 'do whatever you think fit, for I see well enough that, despite your smallness, you have infinitely more intelligence and knowledge. You force me to place absolute confidence in you, although I don't always understand your flowery language.'

'Let me tell you, then,' continued Master Flea, 'that you are involved in the story of Princess Gamaheh, in a very special way. Swammerdamm and Leuwenhoek, the thistle Zeherit, and the Leech Prince, not to mention the spirit Thetel, are all striving for the possession of the beautiful Princess, and I myself must confess that my old love has unfortunately revived and I could be fool enough to share my rule with the fair traitress. But you, you, Mr Peregrinus, are the principal person: the beautiful Gamaheh can be nobody's without your consent. The full truth of the matter is not known to me, and if you want to learn it you must talk to Leuwenhoek, who has found it all out and will doubtless let a good deal slip, if you take the trouble to interrogate him properly.'

Master Flea was about to continue his speech, when somebody burst out of the bushes and rushed frantically at Peregrinus.

'Ha!' shouted George Pepusch (for it was he) with gestures of rage; 'ha! faithless, treacherous friend! Have I caught you? Have I caught you at the fateful moment? Up then, run me through the heart, or fall at my hands!'

With these words Pepusch pulled a pair of pistols from his pocket, handed one to Peregrinus, and struck an appropriate pose with the other, crying: 'Fire, base poltroon!'

Peregrinus took up his position, but declared that nothing would force him into the utter madness of fighting a duel with his only friend without the least inkling of the cause. At all events, he added, he would never be the first to attack his friend with murderous intent.

Pepusch gave a peal of wild laughter, and in the same instant the bullet from the pistol which Pepusch had fired went through Peregrinus's hat. Without picking up his hat, which had fallen to the ground, Peregrinus stared at his friend in complete silence. Pepusch came within a few steps of Peregrinus and muttered dully: 'Fire!'

Peregrinus quickly fired his pistol into the air.

Howling like a madman, George Pepusch fell on the breast of his friend and shouted in heart-rending tones: 'She's dying, she's dying of love for you, you wretch! Hurry—save her—you can do it! Save her for yourself, and let me perish in frantic despair!'

Pepusch sped away so fast that Peregrinus immediately lost sight of him.

Peregrinus was alarmed by the thought that his friend's furious behaviour must have been caused by some terrible calamity which had befallen the lovely Dörtje. He hastened back to the town.

As he entered his house, the old woman approached him, lamenting loudly that the poor beautiful Princess had suddenly fallen violently ill and was sure to die. She said that Mr Swammer had just gone to fetch the most famous doctor in Frankfurt.

Peregrinus, with death in his heart, crept into Mr Swammer's room, which the old woman had opened for him. There was Dörtje, pale and motionless as a corpse, lying on the sofa, and it was not until he had knelt down and bent over her that Peregrinus could feel her faint breathing. When he grasped the poor girl's ice-cold hand, a painful smile played around her pallid lips, and she whispered: 'Are you there, my sweet friend? Have you come for another look at someone who loves you inexpressibly—and who is dying, just because she can't breathe without you!'

Consumed by the bitterest sorrow, Peregrinus assured her repeatedly of his tender love and again said that there was nothing in the world so dear to him that he would not surrender it for her sake. His words turned into kisses, but in these kisses words, like the breath of love, became audible.

These words were roughly as follows: 'You know, my Peregrinus, how much I love you. I can be yours, you can be mine, I can be restored to health on the spot, you will see me flourishing in youthful freshness like a flower raising its bowed head refreshed by the dew—but—give me the captive, my dear, beloved Peregrinus, or else you will see me perish in unspeakable torments before your eyes! Peregrinus—I can't—it's all over . . .'

As she uttered these words, Dörtje, who had been half sitting up, sank back into the pillows. Her bosom heaved as though in the agony of death, her lips turned blue, her eyes seemed to be glazing over. Frantic with terror, Peregrinus reached for his neckerchief, but Master Flea himself leapt on to Dörtje's white throat, crying in a tone of deep sorrow: 'I'm done for!'

Peregrinus stretched out his hand to grasp the Master. Suddenly, however, an invisible force seemed to be restraining his arm, and quite different thoughts went through his mind.

'What's this?' he thought. 'Just because you're a weakling who yields to mad passion, whose madly inflamed desire makes him believe what can only be lies and deceit, are you going to betray the person whom you have promised to protect? Because of your passion, are you going to condemn a free and inoffensive small nation to the fetters of everlasting slavery, and impose irremediable ruin on the friend who has proved to be the only one whose words match his thoughts? No! No! Be a man, Peregrinus! Better die than be a traitor!'

'Give—me—the captive—I'm dying!' gasped Dörtje in expiring tones.

'No,' cried Peregrinus, embracing her in an agony of despair, 'no, never! But let me die with you!'

At that moment a loud harmonious sound was heard, like the ringing of little silver bells. Dörtje, with a fresh rosy glow suddenly on her lips and cheeks, sprang up from the sofa, burst into convulsive laughter, and skipped about the room, as though she had been bitten by a tarantula.

Peregrinus watched this uncanny spectacle in terror, and so did the doctor, who was standing as if petrified in the doorway and blocking the entrance to Mr Swammer, who was just behind him.

SIXTH ADVENTURE

Strange behaviour of some travelling jugglers in an inn, with no lack of beatings. The tragic story of a little tailor from Sachsen-hausen. How George Pepusch astonished respectable people. The horoscope. A pleasant combat between well-known persons in Leuwenhoek's room.

All the passers-by stopped, craned their necks, and peeped through the window into the inn parlour. The crowd grew thicker by the minute, thronging and jostling more and more roughly, and uttering a wild medley of laughter, howls, and cries of jubilation. This uproar was caused by two strangers who had appeared in the parlour. Not only was their appearance, their dress, in short, everything about them, quite outlandish, in a way that was at once repellent and ridiculous, but they were performing extraordinary tricks such as no one had ever seen before. One of them, an elderly man horribly streaked with dirt, was wearing a long and very tight-fitting overcoat of some dull black, shiny material. He was able first to make himself long and thin, then to shrink into a short fat fellow, and it was strange to see how in doing this he writhed like a smooth worm. The other had his hair elaborately dressed and was wearing a colourful silk coat and matching knee-breeches with large silver buckles, like a *petit maître* from the latter half of the eighteenth century. He repeatedly flew up to the parlour ceiling and then gently descended, cheerfully trilling discordant songs in a completely unknown language.

According to the landlord, both of them, in quick succession, had come into the parlour like sensible and well-behaved people and asked for wine. Then they looked each other more and more keenly in the face and began to converse. Although none of the guests could understand their language, their tone and their gestures showed that they were engaged in a quarrel which was growing more violent by the minute. Suddenly they transformed themselves into their present guise and began the wild antics which were drawing more and more spectators to the scene.

'That fellow who is flying up and down so prettily,' cried one of the onlookers, 'isn't he the clock-maker Degen from Vienna, who invented a flying-machine and keeps tumbling down from the air and landing on his nose?'

'No, no,' replied another, 'he isn't the flying Degen. I'd sooner believe that he was the little tailor of Sachsenhausen, if I didn't know that the poor creature had been burnt.'

I wonder whether the kind reader knows the story of the little tailor of Sachsenhausen? Here it is:

THE STORY OF THE LITTLE TAILOR OF SACHSENHAUSEN

One Sunday a good, pious little tailor of Sachsenhausen happened to be coming out of church, dressed up to the nines, with his dear wife. The air was raw, and the tailor had had no supper the night before, except half a soft-boiled egg and a gherkin. So he felt quite faint and miserable, especially as he had sung lustily in church, and he wanted nothing so much as a little glass of schnapps. He had worked hard all the week and been kind to his dear wife, for he had made her a smart petticoat out of the scraps of material that had fallen under his bench. So his dear wife agreed that the little tailor should call on the apothecary and warm himself with a good glass of schnapps. Off he went and asked for some schnapps.

The apothecary was out, and his assistants had gone out as well, leaving only a clumsy apprentice lad; and this lad mistakenly took the wrong bottle down off the shelf. What the bottle contained was not schnapps, but inflammable gas, such as they fill balloons with. The apprentice lad poured out a glass of this, and the little tailor promptly raised it to his lips and gulped down the hot air, thinking it a refreshing draught. No sooner had he swallowed it than he had a very funny feeling, just as if wings had sprouted from his shoulders or as if people were playing ball with him. For he found himself rising and falling, right there in the apothecary's shop, and higher each time. 'O jiminy,' he cried, 'what a nimble dancer I've become all of a sudden!' But the apprentice lad was gaping in surprise. Now it happened that somebody opened the door in a hurry, so that the window opposite flew open. A strong draught of air blew through the shop and seized the little tailor, and away he went like the wind, through the open window, into the sky; and nobody ever saw him again.

After some time had passed, the people of Sachsenhausen one evening saw a ball of fire, high in the air, which lit up the whole district with its dazzling light and then went out and fell to the earth. They all wanted to know what had fallen down, and ran to the spot, but they found only a little heap of ash, and beside it the tongue of a shoe-buckle, a piece of lemon-yellow satin with coloured flowers on it, and a black thing that looked almost like the horn knob of a walking-stick. They all racked their brains to think how such things could fall from the sky in a ball of fire. Then the dear wife of the vanished tailor came along, and when she saw the things that had been found, she wrung her hands in a most sorrowful manner and shrieked: 'Misery me, that's the tongue of my dear husband's shoe-buckle; misery me, that's my dear husband's best waistcoat; misery me, that's the knob of my dear husband's walking-stick!' A great scholar explained that the knob wasn't a knob at all, but a meteor or a stray planet. But in this way it became known to the people of Sachsenhausen, and to all the world besides, that the poor little tailor, whom the apothecary's apprentice had given inflammable gas instead of schnapps, had been burnt up in the sky and fallen to the earth as a meteor or a stray planet.

HERE ENDS THE STORY OF THE
LITTLE TAILOR OF SACHSENHAUSEN.

The waiter finally lost patience with the extraordinary stranger who would not stop growing and shrinking, instead of paying any attention to him, and held the bottle of Burgundy that the stranger had ordered under his nose. Thereupon the stranger began sucking at the bottle and did not pause until he had swallowed the last drop. He then collapsed into the armchair as though in a faint, and could only make feeble movements.

The guests were astonished to see how he kept swelling up while drinking, so that he now seemed fat and shapeless. The other seemed to have done enough flying, and was about to sit down, panting, and quite out of breath; but when he noticed that his antagonist was lying there half-dead, he rushed over to him and began pummelling him brutally with his fists.

The landlord pulled him back, threatening to throw him out there and then if he would not be quiet. If they wanted to show off their conjuring tricks, they could do so without quarrelling and fighting, like riff-raff.

The flying man seemed offended at being taken for a conjurer. He declared that he was far from being a common juggler who performed mere tricks. Formerly, he said, he had been the *maître de ballet* at the theatre of an illustrious king; he was now a self-employed *bel esprit* and was called Legénie, as befitted his profession. If his righteous anger with the damnable fellow had made him leap somewhat higher than was right and proper, that was his own business and concerned nobody else.

The landlord remarked that that was no reason to beat somebody up.

'You don't know this crafty, malicious fellow', rejoined the *bel esprit*; 'if you did, you'd feel that he thoroughly deserved a good beating. He used to be a customs officer in the French service, but he makes his living now from blood-letting, cupping, and shaving, and calls himself Monsieur Le Ech. He's a clumsy, greedy lubber, and he makes a nuisance of himself wherever he goes. Not only does this good-for-nothing rogue drink up my wine in front of my eyes, whenever we meet, as he has just done; but the villain is planning nothing less than to grab the beautiful bride whom I am going to fetch home from Frankfurt.'

The customs officer had heard everything the *bel esprit* had said; he now gave him a flashing glance from his little eyes, which seemed to emit poisonous fire, and said to the landlord: 'You mustn't believe a single word, landlord, that this gallows-bird, this worthless coxcomb, has been gabbling. A fine *maître de ballet*, forsooth, who breaks the legs of the delicate ballerinas with his elephant's feet! When he did a pirouette, he knocked out one of the grinders from the jaw of the director, who was standing in the wings, and kicked the opera-glass away from his eye! And his verses have feet as clumsy as his own; they stagger to and fro like drunkards, and crush the ideas to pulp. And just because he sometimes flutters clumsily through the air, like a bad-tempered gander, this conceited clown thinks that the fairest must be his bride.'

The *bel esprit* cried: 'You spiteful limb of Satan, you'll feel the gander's beak!' and was about to attack the customs officer in renewed fury; the landlord, however, seized him from behind in a pair of strong arms and threw him out of the window, to the inexpressible jubilation of the assembled crowd.

As soon as the *bel esprit* had been sent packing, Monsieur Le Ech resumed the simple and respectable appearance which he had had on entering the inn. The people outside thought him a different person from the one who had performed such contortions, and gradually dispersed. The customs officer thanked the landlord with the utmost civility for helping him to deal with the *bel esprit*, and offered to display his gratitude by shaving the landlord, free, gratis, and for nothing, in such an easy and pleasant manner as he had never known in his life. The landlord stroked his beard and thought that the hairs were long and prickly, and so he agreed to Monsieur Le Ech's suggestion. The customs officer began the operation with a light and practised hand, but suddenly he gave the landlord such a savage cut in the nose that a torrent of blood gushed out. Taking this for spiteful malice, the landlord sprang up in a rage and seized the customs officer, who shot out of the door as quickly and nimbly as the *bel esprit* had shot through the window. Soon afterwards an uproar broke out in the hallway; scarcely taking the time to wrap up his injured nose, the landlord rushed out to see what devil was stirring up trouble this time.

To his considerable astonishment, he saw a young man who had seized the *bel esprit* in one hand and the customs officer in the other and was shrieking furiously, while his burning eyes rolled wildly: 'Ha, brood of Satan, you shan't stand in my way, you shan't rob me of my Gamaheh!'

Meanwhile the *bel esprit* and the customs officer were screeching: 'A madman—save us, save us, landlord! He wants to murder us—he's mistaken us for someone else!'

'Why,' cried the landlord, 'what on earth are you doing, my dear Mr Pepusch? Have these extraordinary people offended you? Isn't it a case of mistaken identity? This is the *maître de ballet*, Mr Legénie, and this is the customs officer, Monsieur Le Ech.'

'Mr Legénie? Monsieur Le Ech?' repeated Pepusch in a toneless voice. He seemed to be awaking from a dream and gradually realizing where he was. Meanwhile two respectable townsmen who also knew Mr George Pepusch had emerged from the parlour and were urging him to remain calm and let the queer strangers go.

Pepusch again repeated: 'Mr Legénie? Monsieur Le Ech?' and feebly lowered his arms. Once released, the two sped away like the wind, and several people in the street claimed to have seen the *bel esprit* flying away over the roof of the house opposite, while the barber vanished into the muddy puddle that had gathered among the stones just in front of the door.

As Pepusch still looked distraught, the townsmen pressed him to enter the parlour and drink a bottle of real Niersteiner wine with them. Pepusch agreed, and seemed to quaff the noble wine with enjoyment and appetite, though he was still mute, saying not a word in reply to his companions' remarks. At last his features assumed a more cheerful look and he said perfectly affably: 'My dear people and friendly companions, you were quite right to prevent me from killing those wretches on the spot when I had them in my power. But you do not know what menacing creatures had concealed themselves behind these extraordinary masks.'

Pepusch paused, and you may imagine the intense curiosity with which the townsmen pricked up their ears, wondering what Pepusch would now reveal to them. The landlord, too, had come closer, and all three, the two townsmen and the landlord, put their heads close together, bent over the table with folded arms, and held their breath, so as not to miss a single sound from Pepusch's lips.

'You see,' continued Mr George Pepusch in a low and solemn voice, 'you see, good people, the person you call the *maître de ballet* Legénie is none other than the malicious and clumsy spirit Thetel, while the person you take for the customs officer Le Ech is the abominable blood-sucker, the hideous Leech Prince. They are both in love with Princess Gamaheh, who, as you doubtless know, is the beautiful and glorious daughter of the mighty King Sekakis, and are here in order to entice her away from the thistle Zeherit. This is the silliest absurdity, and could only find lodging in an idiot's brain, for besides the thistle Zeherit there is only one being in the whole world to whom the fair Gamaheh could belong, and this being is unlikely to win a combat with the thistle Zeherit. For soon, at midnight, the thistle will bloom in all its strength and magnificence, and it is in love and death together that the higher life will dawn. I myself, however, am the thistle Zeherit, and for that reason you cannot blame me, good people, if I am enraged against those traitors and indeed take the whole business very much to heart.'

His companions opened their eyes wide and gaped at Pepusch, speechless and open-mouthed. You could have knocked them down with a feather, as the saying goes.

Pepusch gulped down a large goblet of wine and then said, turning to the landlord: 'Yes, yes, landlord, you'll soon see this for yourself; I shall soon flower as a *Cactus grandiflorus*, and the whole district will reek of vanilla, take my word for it.'

The landlord could only say stupidly: 'That would be a turn-up for the book!' The other two men, however, exchanged worried glances, and one of them took George's hand and said with an ambiguous smile: 'You seem a little disturbed, dear Mr Pepusch; how would it be if you took a glass of water . . .'.

'Not one drop,' interrupted Pepusch, cutting short this well-intentioned advice; 'did anyone ever pour water on boiling oil without increasing the fury of the flames? You think I'm disturbed, do you? I may well be, and I defy the Devil to stay calm if he has just fought a duel with his dearest friend, as I have, and then blown his own brains out! Here! I'll deliver the murder weapons into your hands, now that it's all over.'

Pepusch pulled a pair of pistols from his pocket; the landlord started back, but the two townsmen reached for them and, as soon as they had the murder weapons in their hands, burst out laughing immoderately. The pistols were made of wood; they were children's toys from the Christmas market.

Pepusch seemed not to perceive what was going on around him; he sat plunged in thought, exclaiming repeatedly: 'If only I could find him, if only I could find him!'

The landlord plucked up his courage and asked mildly: 'Whom do you mean, my good Mr Pepusch, whom cannot you find?'

'If you know anyone,' said Pepusch solemnly, looking the landlord keenly in the eye, 'if you know anyone whose power and wondrous strength can be compared to that of King Sekakis, then tell me his name and I'll kiss your feet! But in any case I wanted to ask you if you know anyone who knows Mr Peregrinus Tyss, and can tell me where I can find him at this moment?'

'There,' replied the landlord with a friendly chuckle, 'there I can help you, honoured Mr Pepusch, and I can inform you that the good Mr Tyss was here only an hour ago, drinking a glass of Würzburger wine. He was very thoughtful, and when I merely mentioned the news from the Stock Exchange, he suddenly exclaimed: "Yes, sweet Gamaheh! I have renounced you! Be happy in the arms of my George!" Then a very odd, piping voice said: "Let's go to Leuwenhoek and look at the horoscope!" Mr Tyss promptly emptied his glass in all possible haste and dashed away, along with the disembodied voice; I expect that both of them, the voice and Mr Tyss, have gone to Leuwenhoek, who is weeping and wailing because all his trained fleas are dead.'

Thereupon George sprang to his feet in a fury, seized the landlord by the throat, and shrieked: 'Scoundrelly messenger of the Leech, what are you saying? Renounced? Renounced her? Gamaheh—Peregrinus—Sekakis?'

The landlord's story accorded perfectly with the truth: he had overheard Master Flea's shrill silvery tones inviting Mr Peregrinus Tyss to go to the microscopist Leuwenhoek, and the kind reader already knows what their purpose was. Peregrinus did indeed betake himself thither.

Leuwenhoek received Peregrinus with a repulsively unctuous display of friendship and with the servile compliments which convey an enforced and reluctant acknowledgement of superiority. Since, however, Peregrinus had the microscopic glass in his pupil, all his friendliness and servility did Mr Anton van Leuwenhoek no good at all; on the contrary, Peregrinus instantly discerned the ill-humour, indeed hatred, which filled the soul of the microscopist.

While Leuwenhoek was declaring what an honour and pleasure Mr Tyss's visit was for him, his thoughts ran like this: 'I wish that Satan, with his horns and tail, would hurl you ten thousand fathoms deep into the abyss, but I must behave towards you in a friendly and obsequious manner, since the accursed conjunction of the planets has put me in your power and, in a way, my entire existence depends on you. But I may be able to outwit you, for despite your distinguished ancestry you're a dunderhead. You think the beautiful Dörtje Elwerdink loves you, and perhaps you even want to marry her? I'm the best person you can turn to, for despite the power that dwells in you you'll fall under my control without realizing it, and I'll do everything I can to destroy you and get hold both of Dörtje and of Master Flea.'

Naturally Peregrinus adjusted his behaviour in accordance with these thoughts and took care not to say even a word about the beautiful Dörtje; instead he pretended to have come in order to inspect Mr van Leuwenhoek's collection of natural curiosities.

While Leuwenhoek was opening his big cupboards, Master Flea said very softly in Peregrinus's ear that his (Peregrinus's) horoscope was lying on the table by the window. Peregrinus approached cautiously and looked keenly at the horoscope. He saw all manner of lines in mystical criss-cross patterns, and other wondrous signs; but as he was entirely ignorant of astrology, it all remained indistinct and confusing, no matter how keenly he looked at it. Strangely enough, he could not help recognizing the shining red spot in the middle of the board on which the horoscope was drawn as himself. The longer he gazed at the spot, the more clearly it assumed the shape of a heart, and the more fiery red it became; but its sparkling seemed due only to the web woven around it.

Peregrinus clearly perceived that Leuwenhoek was trying to distract him from the horoscope, and sensibly resolved to ask his friendly foe straight out about the meaning of the mysterious board, since he was in no danger of being lied to.

Leuwenhoek declared with a spiteful grin that nothing could give him greater pleasure than to explain to his highly esteemed friend the signs on the board, which he had drawn with the aid of his slender knowledge of such matters. What he thought was: 'Ho, ho! so that's what you're after, you smart fellow? Master Flea hasn't given you bad advice, forsooth! I myself, by explaining the mysterious board, am to give you some help, as far as the magic power of your worthy self is concerned? I could tell you a pack of lies, but what would be the point, for even if I tell you the truth you won't understand the first thing about it, but will still be as stupid as before. So, to save myself the trouble of making something up, I'll tell you as much as I see fit about the signs on the board.'

Peregrinus now knew that although he would not learn everything, he would at least not be lied to.

Leuwenhoek placed the board on a stand resembling an artist's easel, which he moved from a corner of the room into the centre. Both Leuwenhoek and Peregrinus sat down in front of the board and contemplated it in silence.

'You may not suspect, Peregrinus Tyss,' began Leuwenhoek at last with some solemnity, 'that these strokes and signs on the board, which you are looking at so attentively, are your own horoscope, which I have drawn with the aid of the mysterious art of astrology and under the favourable influence of the constellations. "How can you be so presumptuous? How dare you enquire into the twists and turns of my life and try to disclose my destiny?" You might ask me these questions, Peregrinus, and you would have every right to do so, if I were not able instantly to demonstrate my spiritual vocation for this art. I don't know if you ever happened to meet the famous Rabbi Isaac Ben Harravad,* or if you have at least heard of him. Along with other profound secrets, Rabbi Harravad possessed the rare gift of discerning from people's faces whether their souls had previously inhabited another body or were entirely fresh and new. When I was still very young, the old rabbi died of indigestion, in consequence of eating a tasty dish made with garlic. The Jews ran off so fast with the corpse that the departed Rabbi had not time to gather up and take with him all the learning and abilities which his illness had dispersed. They were shared out among his laughing heirs; I, however, had snatched away the wondrous gift of spiritual insight at the very moment when it was poised on the point of the sword which the Angel of Death had placed against the old Rabbi's breast. Thus this wondrous gift has passed to me, and, like Rabbi Isaac Ben Harravad, I can discern from a person's face whether or not his soul has previously inhabited another body. When I first beheld your countenance, Peregrinus Tyss, it aroused in me the strangest doubts and scruples. I was *certain* that your soul had had a long previous existence, and yet the forms it had assumed before your present life remained entirely obscure. I was obliged to have recourse to the stars, and to draw your horoscope, in order to solve the mystery.'

'And', said Peregrinus, interrupting the flea-tamer, 'did you find out anything, Mr Leuwenhoek?'

'Indeed I did,' rejoined Leuwenhoek, adopting a yet more solemn tone, 'indeed I did! I perceived that the psychic principle at present animating the personable body of my worthy friend Mr Peregrinus Tyss existed long before, albeit only as an idea without consciousness of material form. Look, Mr Peregrinus; observe carefully the red spot in the middle of the board. Not only is that you yourself; the spot is also the shape which, long ago, your psychic principle was unable to bring to consciousness. You were lying in the depths of the earth in the form of a radiant carbuncle, but stretched out above you, on the green surface of the ground, the lovely Gamaheh was slumbering, and this absence of consciousness caused her material form to dissolve. Your life has been intersected by strange lines and alien constellations ever since the moment when the idea assumed material form and became Mr Peregrinus Tyss. You are the unwitting possessor of a talisman, and this talisman is the red carbuncle; it may be that King Sekakis wore it as a jewel in his crown, or that in some manner he was himself the carbuncle; enough—you now possess it, but a certain event must supervene if its dormant power is to be awakened, and once the power of your talisman awakes, then it will decide the fate of an unhappy person who hitherto has led a toilsome illusory life suspended between fear and tremulous hope. Ah! an illusory life was all that the profoundest magical art could provide for the sweet Gamaheh, once the talisman and its effects had been taken from us! You alone killed her, and you alone can breathe life into her, once the carbuncle is again glowing in your breast!'

'And,' interrupted Peregrinus again, 'and the event by which the power of the talisman is to be awakened, can you explain that to me, Mr Leuwenhoek?'

The flea-tamer goggled at Peregrinus with eyes like saucers, looking just like somebody in the grip of sudden and extreme embarrassment who is at a loss what to say. He was thinking: 'Damn it, what on earth made me say so much more than I intended? I should at least have kept my mouth shut about the talisman which the fortunate rascal carries in his body, and which can give him enough power over us to make us all dance to his tune! And now he wants me to tell him the event which will awaken the power of his talisman! How can I possibly admit that I myself don't know what it is? That all my skill has failed to untie the knot in which all the lines meet; that when I contemplate the sidereal sign which dominates the horoscope, I feel absolutely miserable, and my venerable head feels like a milliner's painted block made of base cardboard? Nothing shall extort such a confession from me; why, it would degrade me, and give him weapons to use against me. I'll spin this feather-brained smart alec some yarn that will scare him out of his wits and prevent him from asking me any more questions.'

'My dear fellow,' said the flea-tamer, assuming an expression of concern, 'my dearest Mr Tyss, don't ask me to say anything about this event. You know that the horoscope gives us clear and full information about the commencement of certain developments; but the wisdom of the Eternal Power has decreed that, when danger threatens, the final outcome shall always remain obscure, and only doubtful hints concerning it are possible and permissible. My good Mr Tyss, I am far too attached to you, as a good, admirable person who is very close to my heart, to cause you premature unease and alarm; otherwise I would tell you that the event which might make you conscious of your power could simultaneously destroy the present form of your being amid the most hideous torments that hell has to offer. But no! I'll keep that from you too, and now not another word about the horoscope. Don't be afraid, my good Mr Tyss, although things are looking very black and with all my learning I can hardly discern any prospect that this adventure will turn out well. Perhaps an unforeseen constellation, which is still beyond the scope of observation, may rescue you from this deadly danger.'

Peregrinus was astonished by Leuwenhoek's spiteful dishonesty, but he was so hugely entertained by the whole situation, and by his relation to the unwitting and suspecting Leuwenhoek, that he could not help bursting into a roar of laughter.

'What are you laughing at so heartily, my most estimable Mr Tyss?' asked the flea-tamer, somewhat taken aback.

'You are very clever, Mr Leuwenhoek,' replied Peregrinus, still laughing, 'to conceal this menacing event from me, out of pure thoughtfulness. For besides being too great a friend to alarm or frighten me, you have another compelling reason, and that is that you yourself don't know the first thing about this event. All your efforts to untie the intricate knot were in vain; all your astrology isn't worth twopence; and if Master Flea had not fallen unconscious on to your nose, all your arts would be in deep trouble.'

Rage inflamed Leuwenhoek's visage, he clenched his fists, he ground his teeth, he shook and trembled so hard that he would have fallen off his chair if Peregrinus had not seized him by the arm as firmly as George Pepusch seized the unhappy landlord by the throat. This landlord succeeded in freeing himself by leaping nimbly to one side. Thereupon Pepusch dashed out of the door and entered Leuwenhoek's room at the very moment when Peregrinus was holding him tightly in his chair and he was muttering wrathfully between his teeth: 'Curse you, Swammerdamm, is this *your* doing?'

As soon as Peregrinus caught sight of his friend Pepusch, he let go of the flea-tamer, went over to his friend, and asked in alarm whether he had cast off the dreadful mood that had seized upon him with such fatal force.

Pepusch seemed moved almost to tears; he declared that in all his life he had never committed so many senseless follies as on that day. The worst of them was, he said, that after blowing his brains out in the woods, he had gone into an inn—he didn't know where, perhaps Protzler's, the Swan, the Willow Court, or wherever—told some good-natured people about supernatural matters, and made a murderous attempt to throttle the landlord, just because the latter's disjointed remarks seemed to indicate that the happiest event that could ever befall him (Pepusch) had occurred. All his misadventures, he continued, would shortly reach their climax, for it was only too certain that the people had taken his words and actions for an outbreak of the most violent madness, and he must fear that instead of enjoying the fruits of the happy event, he would be confined in a lunatic asylum. Pepusch then mentioned what the landlord had let fall concerning Peregrinus's actions and words, and asked, blushing bright red and with downcast eyes, whether such a sacrifice, such a renunciation for the sake of an unfortunate friend, as he suspected, was possible or even conceivable at the present time, when heroism had vanished from the earth.

Peregrinus's spirits revived when his friend uttered these words, and he declared fervently that he for his part had no wish to injure his tried and tested friend in the slightest, and that he solemnly renounced all claims to Dörtje Elwerdink's hand and heart, gladly forgoing the paradise which had indeed smiled upon him in a seductive and brilliant light.

'And it was you,' cried Pepusch, clasping his friend to his breast, 'it was you that I tried to murder, and because I didn't trust you, I shot myself! Oh, what madness! Oh, the wild turmoil of a diseased mind!'

'I beg you, George,' interrupted Peregrinus, 'please calm down. You talk about shooting yourself dead, yet here you are, alive and well! What rhyme or reason is there in this?'

'You're right,' replied Pepusch, 'I'm sure I couldn't talk to you so sensibly as I am doing if I really had blown my brains out. Besides, the people in the inn said that my pistols weren't particularly serious weapons, and that they were made of wood, not iron, and hence were only children's toys; so perhaps both our duel and my suicide were nothing but a pleasant irony. Isn't it just as though we had exchanged roles, so that I began play-acting and performing stupid infantile pranks at the very moment when you were leaving your childish fantasy-world and entering real life? But be that as it may, I've got to be sure of your nobility and my happiness, and I've no doubt that will dispel all the mists that are obscuring my gaze, or perhaps deceiving me with delusive mirages. Come, my Peregrinus, accompany me to the lovely Dörtje Elwerdink; I'll receive my sweet bride from your hands.'

Pepusch took his friend by the arm and was about to hasten away with him; but the journey they intended proved unnecessary. For the door opened, and in stepped Dörtje Elwerdink, beautiful and charming as an angel, followed, however, by old

Mr Swammer. Leuwenhoek had been standing mute and motionless all this while, only casting enraged glances at Pepusch
and Peregrinus alternately, but he no sooner caught sight of old
Swammerdamm than he seemed to have received an electric
shock. He stretched his clenched fists towards him and uttered
a piercing shriek of fury: 'Ha! have you come to mock me, you
deceitful old monster? You won't succeed. Defend yourself!
Your last hour has struck!'

Swammerdamm recoiled several paces and, as Leuwenhoek
was already assailing him with a telescope, he drew the same
weapon in his own defence. The duel that had flared up in
Mr Peregrinus Tyss's house seemed about to begin afresh.

George Pepusch threw himself between the combatants; with
his left hand he adroitly knocked aside a murderous flash from
Leuwenhoek, which would have floored his opponent, while
with his right he pushed down the weapon that Swammerdamm
had just pulled out ready for battle, so that it could not wound
Leuwenhoek. Pepusch then declared in a loud voice that he
would not permit any quarrel or dangerous combat between
Leuwenhoek and Swammerdamm until he had learned the full
cause of their dispute. Peregrinus found his friend's conduct so
sensible that he did not hesitate likewise to step between the
combatants and utter the same declaration as Pepusch. Leuwenhoek and Swammerdamm were compelled to yield to the third
parties.

Swammerdamm, moreover, asserted that he had not come
with any hostile intentions, but only in order to reach an amic-
able agreement with Leuwenhoek in respect of Dörtje Elwerdink and thus put an end to a feud which for far too long had
divided two complementary principles, whose combined researches alone could plumb the deepest well-springs of science.
While saying this, he smiled at Mr Peregrinus Tyss and added
that he ventured to hope that Peregrinus would mediate between them, since it was to his arms that Dörtje had fled.

Leuwenhoek, on the other hand, declared that while the possession of Dörtje was indeed the bone of contention, he had just
discovered a new ruse on the part of his unworthy colleague.
Not only did Swammerdamm claim not to possess a certain
microscope, which he had received as an indemnity on a certain

occasion, in order to renew his unwarranted claims to Dörtje, but he had also given this microscope to somebody else, in order to subject him, Leuwenhoek, to yet more fear and torment. Swammerdamm, however, swore solemn oaths that he had never received the microscope and had good cause for believing that Leuwenhoek had withheld it out of malice.

'The fools,' whispered Master Flea softly to Peregrinus, 'the fools, they're talking about the microscope in your eye. You know I was present when Swammerdamm and Leuwenhoek concluded a peace agreement about the possession of Princess Gamaheh. Swammerdamm did in fact receive the microscopic glass from Leuwenhoek, but as he was about to insert it in the pupil of his left eye, I snatched it away, because it was *my* rightful property, not Leuwenhoek's. Tell them straight out, Mr Peregrinus, that you have this treasure.'

Peregrinus did not hesitate to announce forthwith that *he* possessed the microscopic glass that Swammerdamm should have received, but had not, from Leuwenhoek. Consequently, he declared, their treaty had not been put into practice, and at present neither Leuwenhoek nor Swammerdamm had the absolute right to regard Dörtje Elwerdink as his foster-daughter.

After a great deal of argument, both parties to the dispute agreed that Mr Peregrinus Tyss should take Dörtje Elwerdink, who loved him dearly, as his lawful wife, and should then decide after seven months which of the two microscopists was the more desirable as a foster-father and father-in-law.

Although Dörtje Elwerdink looked altogether charming and delightful in the daintiest of costumes, which seemed to have been tailored by cherubs, and although she cast sweet and languishing amorous glances at Mr Peregrinus Tyss, yet Peregrinus, remembering both his protégé and his friend, remained true to his word and again declared that he renounced Dörtje's hand.

The microscopists were considerably taken aback when Peregrinus declared that it was George Pepusch who had the greatest and most justified claims to Dörtje's hand. They opined that at present, at least, Peregrinus had not the power to make such a decision on Dörtje's behalf.

A flood of tears gushed from Dörtje's eyes as she tottered

towards Peregrinus, who caught her in his arms as she was about to sink to the ground half fainting. 'Ungrateful man,' she moaned, 'you're breaking my heart by rejecting me! But that's what you want! Take this parting kiss and let me die.'

Peregrinus bent down, but as his mouth touched Dörtje's, she bit him in the lips so hard that the blood flowed. 'Naughty,' she cried merrily, 'that's the way to punish you! Come to your senses, be good, and take me, and let the other one make as much noise as he likes.' Meanwhile the two microscopists had again fallen into a violent quarrel about goodness knows what. George Pepusch, in despair, threw himself at the fair Dörtje's feet, and cried in a voice that sounded miserable enough to come from the hoarse throat of the unhappiest of lovers: 'Gamaheh! The flame within you is completely extinguished; you no longer remember our marvellous previous existence in Famagusta, our beautiful days in Berlin, our . . .'

'You're such an idiot, George,' cut in Dörtje, laughing, 'with your nonsense about Gamaheh and the thistle Zeherit and all the other things you dreamed up long ago. I used to be fond of you, my friend, and I still am; and even though I like that tall fellow better, I'll take you, if you give me a sacred promise, a solemn oath, that you'll do everything you can to . . .'

She whispered something softly in Pepusch's ear, but Peregrinus thought he heard her mentioning Master Flea.

In the mean time the quarrel between the two microscopists had grown more and more violent; they again seized their weapons, and Peregrinus was labouring to pacify their excited tempers when some new individuals joined the company.

Amid frightful screeching and hideous yelling, the door was pushed open, and in rushed the *bel esprit*, Monsieur Legénie, and the barber Le Ech. They pounced on Dörtje with wild and terrifying gestures, and the barber had already seized her by the shoulder, when Peregrinus forced the hideous enemy away with irresistible strength, practically tying a knot in his flexible body, and squeezing him so tight that he elongated himself into a narrow, pointed shape and roared with pain.

While this was happening to the barber, the two microscopists, who had instantly settled their differences on the appearance of their enemies, were together fighting the *bel esprit* with considerable success. It was of no use whatever for the *bel esprit* to rise to the ceiling once he had received a sound thrashing at floor level. For Leuwenhoek and Swammerdamm seized short, thick cudgels, and each time the *bel esprit* tried to descend, they forced him up again with well-aimed blows upon that part of the anatomy which is best suited to receive them. It was a delightful game of badminton, in which, admittedly, the *bel esprit* was obliged to assume the most exhausting and disagreeable role, that of the shuttlecock.

The battle with the fiendish strangers seemed to terrify little Dörtje out of her wits; she clung to Peregrinus and besought him to remove her from this danger and turmoil. Peregrinus could not refuse, especially since it was clear that his help was not needed on the battlefield; and so he took Dörtje home, that is, to the room occupied by his lodger.

Suffice it to say that as soon as Dörtje found herself alone with Peregrinus, she again practised all her arts of subtle coquetry to lure him into her toils. No matter how clearly Peregrinus remembered that all this was a deception, intended only to restore his protégé to slavery, he became so confused that he did not even think of the microscopic glass, which would have served as an effective antidote.

Master Flea was in renewed danger, but he was once more saved by Mr Swammer, who entered together with George Pepusch. Mr Swammer seemed to be in high good humour, while Pepusch's fiery glare revealed his rage and jealousy. Peregrinus left the room.

With his sore heart filled with the deepest and most bitter vexation, he wandered in gloomy self-absorption through the streets of Frankfurt; he went out of the town gate and beyond, until finally he reached the pleasant spot where the strange adventure with his friend Pepusch had taken place. As he pondered anew his wondrous destiny, the image of little Dörtje came to his mind with more charm, grace, and loveliness than ever. His blood boiled furiously in his veins, his pulse quickened, his heart seemed about to burst with intense desire and yearning. He was only too painfully aware of the magnitude of his sacrifice, with which he thought he had lost all the happiness life had to offer.

Night had fallen when he returned to the town. Unwittingly, perhaps from an unconscious reluctance to return home, he went through many side-streets and ended up in Kalbach Lane. A man with a haversack on his back asked him whether that was where the bookbinder Lämmerhirt lived. Peregrinus looked up and perceived that he was standing outside the tenement in which Lämmerhirt lived; far above his head he could see the brightly lit windows of that industrious man, who was working through the night. The door was opened for the man with the haversack, who entered the house.

Peregrinus's heart smote him when he recalled that in the confusion of the last few weeks he had forgotten to pay the bookbinder Lämmerhirt for sundry pieces of work he had done for him. He resolved to go there first thing the following morning and clear his debts.

SEVENTH ADVENTURE

The malign pursuit instigated jointly by the microscopists, along with their persistent stupidity. New trials for Mr Peregrinus Tyss and new perils for Master Flea. Rosie Lämmerhirt. The decisive dream and the end of the fairy-tale.

Although we have no definite information concerning the outcome of the battle in Leuwenhoek's room, it may safely be assumed that the two microscopists, assisted by young Mr George Pepusch, must have gained an entire victory over their evil adversaries. Otherwise old Swammer could never have been so pleased and friendly on his return as he in fact was. It was with the same glad and cheerful expression that Swammer, or rather Mr Johannes Swammerdamm, entered Mr Peregrinus's room the following morning. Peregrinus was still in bed, engrossed in conversation with his protégé Master Flea.

As soon as he caught sight of Mr Swammerdamm, Peregrinus did not fail to have the microscopic glass inserted in his pupil.

After many long and tedious apologies for calling at such an excessively early hour, Swammerdamm at last sat down close to Peregrinus's bed. He would on no account suffer Peregrinus to get up and put on his dressing-gown.

Using an extraordinary quantity of polite clichés, the old man thanked Peregrinus for the great kindness he had shown him. This kindness consisted not only in receiving him as a lodger in his house, but also in permitting him to enlarge the household by the addition of a young and sometimes rather too boisterous female. Furthermore, however, he could not but consider it the greatest of kindnesses that Peregrinus, at considerable cost to himself, had brought about his (the old man's) reconciliation with his old friend and professional colleague Anton van Leuwenhoek. According to Swammerdamm's account, the hearts of both had been drawn together at the moment when they were attacked by the *bel esprit* and the barber and were obliged to rescue the fair Dörtje Elwerdink from these evil monsters. Very soon afterwards the two had been formally reconciled.

Leuwenhoek had been as quick as Swammerdamm to recognize the favourable influence that Peregrinus had had on them, and the first use they made of their newly cemented alliance was that together they examined the strange and wondrously involved horoscope of Mr Peregrinus Tyss, and tried to interpret as much of it as they could.

'What my friend Anton van Leuwenhoek could not achieve on his own', said Mr Johannes Swammerdamm, 'was accomplished by our combined efforts, and so this experiment was the second which we performed with brilliant success, in the teeth of all obstacles.'

'The silly, short-sighted fool,' whispered Master Flea, who was sitting on the pillow next to Peregrinus's ear, 'he still thinks that he brought Princess Gamaheh back to life. A fine life, forsooth, that the poor thing is compelled to lead by the ineptitude of the stupid microscopists!'

'My dear fellow,' continued Swammerdamm, who had not heard Master Flea's remark, especially as he had been obliged to sneeze violently, 'my most excellent Mr Peregrinus Tyss, you are a person specially singled out by the World-Spirit, one of nature's spoilt darlings; for you possess the most wondrous and powerful talisman, or, to put it in more accurate and scientific terms, the most magnificent *Tsilmenaya* or *Tilsemoht** that ever sprang from the lap of earth, watered by the dew of heaven. It is to the credit of my skill that it was I, and not Leuwenhoek, who established that this fortunate *Tsilmenaya* descends from King Nacrao, who reigned in Egypt long before the Flood. However, the power of the talisman will remain dormant until the advent of a certain constellation whose centre is in your worthy person. Something must and will happen to *you*, my dear Mr Tyss, which will enable you to perceive the awakening of the talisman at the instant when it occurs. Whatever Leuwenhoek may have told you about this most difficult aspect of the horoscope, it is all a pack of lies, for he knew nothing whatever about this aspect until I enlightened him. Indeed, my dear Mr Tyss, the friend of my bosom may have tried to alarm you by talking about some impending catastrophe, for I know that he likes to cause people needless terrors; but trust your lodger, who holds you in high esteem, and who swears, with his hand on his heart, that you have nothing to fear. I should be glad to know, however, whether you are not conscious of possessing the talisman at present, and what you are pleased to think about the whole matter?'

As he uttered these final words, Swammerdamm gave a venomous smile and looked so keenly into Mr Peregrinus's eyes that he seemed to be trying to discern his deepest thoughts; to do this, of course, he was far less well equipped than was Peregrinus, thanks to the microscopic glass. By means of this glass Peregrinus discovered that it was not so much the common struggle against the *bel esprit* and the barber, but rather the mysterious horoscope, that had reconciled the two microscopists. The possession of the mighty talisman was the goal for which both were striving. As regards that mysteriously entwined knot in Peregrinus's horoscope, Swammerdamm was in the same state of perplexity and irritation as Leuwenhoek, but thought that Peregrinus's mind must contain the clue that would lead to the disclosure of the mystery. He was now trying adroitly to extort this clue from his unsuspecting friend so that, with Leuwenhoek's help, he might cheat Peregrinus out of this priceless treasure before the latter had realized its value. Swammerdamm was convinced that Mr Peregrinus Tyss's talisman was similar to the ring owned by the wise King Solomon, and would likewise give its possessor complete mastery over the realm of spirits.

Peregrinus returned like for like. Perceiving that Mr Swammerdamm was trying to pull the wool over his eyes, he pulled the wool over Swammerdamm's eyes. He contrived to reply in such flowery phrases that Swammerdamm could not help fearing that the process of initiation had already begun, and that Peregrinus was about to learn the secret which neither he nor Leuwenhoek had succeeded in discovering.

Swammerdamm lowered his eyes, cleared his throat, and stuttered some unintelligible words. The man was indeed in a very tight corner, and his thoughts kept whirling round in the same circles: 'Confound it, what's this? Is this Peregrinus speaking to me? Am I the wise and learned Swammerdamm, or a donkey?'

Finally, in desperation, he pulled himself together and began:

'But let us speak of something else, my honoured Mr Tyss—
something else, and, as it seems to me, something fine and
gratifying!'

According to what Swammerdamm now related, both he and
Leuwenhoek had been overjoyed to discover the fair Dörtje
Elwerdink's warm affection for Mr Peregrinus Tyss. Although
they had previously held different views, each believing that
Dörtje must stay with *him* and that love or marriage were out
of the question, they had now changed their opinions. For they
thought they could read in Peregrinus's horoscope that he must
inevitably choose the fair and charming Dörtje Elwerdink as his
wedded wife, in order to ensure the greatest benefits for all
future junctures of his life. Neither of them doubted for a
moment that Peregrinus was as ardently in love with the delightful girl, and thus they considered matters settled. Swammerdamm added that Peregrinus was the only person who could
defeat his rivals without the slightest effort, and that even the
most menacing adversaries, such as the *bel esprit* and the barber,
would be unable to oppose him.

From Swammerdamm's thoughts, Peregrinus learnt that the
microscopists genuinely believed that his horoscope had disclosed the unalterable necessity of his marriage to little Dörtje
Elwerdink. They were prepared to yield to this necessity so as
to gain the utmost profit from Dörtje's loss: that is, to capture
Mr Peregrinus Tyss himself, along with his talisman.

Since neither of the two microscopists was able to solve the
horoscope's principal riddle, you may imagine how little confidence Peregrinus could place in their wisdom and learning.
He therefore cared not a jot about the conjuncture which was
alleged to necessitate his marriage to the fair Dörtje, and had
not the slightest difficulty in declaring clearly and firmly that
he had renounced Dörtje's hand in order not to injure his best
and dearest friend, young George Pepusch, whose claims upon
this gracious being were older and stronger, and that nothing
in the world should induce him to break his solemn promise.

Mr Swammerdamm raised the greenish-grey cat-like eyes
which had been lowered to the floor for so long, gave Peregrinus
a broad stare, and smiled like the most cunning of cunning
foxes.

'If,' said he, 'your ties of friendship with George Pepusch are the only scruple which restrains you from yielding to your feelings, then that obstacle has already been removed; for although Pepusch suffers in some measure from madness, he has nevertheless realized that his marriage with Dörtje Elwerdink is contrary to the alignment of the heavenly bodies, and therefore nothing can come of it save misfortune and calamity. He has accordingly withdrawn all his claims to Dörtje's hand, declaring only that she is the fairest of mortals, that she can belong to nobody but his bosom friend Tyss, and that he will defend her with his life against the lubberly *bel esprit* and the blood-thirsty barber.'

An ice-cold stream ran through Peregrinus's veins as he perceived from Swammerdamm's thoughts that all this was true. Overcome by the strangest conflict among his emotions, he fell back among the pillows and closed his eyes.

Mr Swammerdamm urged Peregrinus most insistently to betake himself downstairs and learn the present state of affairs from Dörtje's and George's own lips. He then took his leave in the same long-winded and ceremonious manner as on his arrival.

Master Flea, who all this time had been sitting quietly on the pillow, suddenly leapt on to the tassel of Mr Peregrinus's nightcap. There he rose up on his long hind legs, wrung his hands, stretched them out imploringly to heaven, and cried in a voice that was half-stifled by bitter tears: 'Alas for me, poor wretch! Just when I thought I was secure, I must face the most perilous trial of all! What use is the courage and steadfastness of my noble protector if everything and everyone is leagued against me! I surrender! It's all over!'

'Why are you lamenting like that on top of my nightcap, dear Master?' said Mr Peregrinus in a feeble voice. 'Do you think you are the only person with cause to complain? Am I not also in the most miserable condition possible, devastated through and through, unable to tell what to do or how to direct my thoughts? But never believe, dear Master Flea, that I shall be foolish enough to sail near the rocks, where I might perish along with all my good resolutions and decisions. I shall take good care not to accept Swammerdamm's invitation to see the alluring Dörtje Elwerdink again.'

'As a matter of fact,' replied Master Flea, resuming his old place on the pillow next to Mr Peregrinus Tyss's ear, 'despite the apparent danger to myself, I don't know whether I should not advise you to go down to Swammerdamm straight away. I have a feeling that all the lines of your horoscope are converging with ever-increasing rapidity, and that you yourself are about to enter the red spot. Whatever an obscure destiny may have decided, I perceive that even a Master Flea may not escape its decree, and that it would be both foolish and futile to ask you to save me from it. Go down, see her, take her hand, surrender me to slavery, and, so that all things may follow the will of the stars without intervention from outside, make no use of the microscopic glass.'

'Usually,' said Peregrinus, 'your heart seems stout and your mind firm, Master Flea, and yet now you are so timid and faint-hearted! But however wise you may usually be, and even if Rorarius, the illustrious Nuncio of Pope Clement the Seventh, rated your intelligence far above ours, you do not understand the firmness of man's resolve, or at least you gravely underestimate it. I repeat! I shall not break my solemn promise, and to show you that I am firmly resolved not to see the girl again, I shall now get up and call on the bookbinder Lämmerhirt, as I meant to do yesterday.'

'O Peregrinus,' cried Master Flea, 'man's resolve is a fragile thing, often broken by a passing breeze. What a gulf there is between what one wants and what happens! Many lives consist of nothing but resolve, and many people are so full of resolutions that they do not know what they want. You are resolved never to see Dörtje Elwerdink again, and who can guarantee that it will not happen a moment after you have pronounced your resolution?'

Strangely enough, the event did indeed occur which Master Flea's prophetic soul had foretold.

Peregrinus got up, dressed, and was about to carry out his resolution by going to the bookbinder Lämmerhirt; but as he passed Swammerdamm's room, the door was thrown wide open, and Peregrinus himself could not tell how he suddenly came to be standing arm in arm with Swammerdamm in the middle of the room and right in front of Dörtje Elwerdink. Quite cheerful and unabashed, she blew him a hundred kisses and cried merrily in a voice like the tinkling of silver bells: 'Good morning, Peregrinus, my darling!'

But there was someone else in the room, and that was Mr George Pepusch, who was looking out of the open window and whistling a tune. He now slammed the window shut and turned round. 'Oh, just look,' he exclaimed, as though noticing his friend Peregrinus for the first time, 'you're calling on your fiancée! That's perfectly all right, and any third person would just be in the way. I'll be off at once, but let me tell you first, my good friend Peregrinus, that George Pepusch disdains any gift that his compassionate friend throws him, like alms for a beggar! Confound your self-sacrifice, I don't want to be beholden to you for anything. Take her, the fair Gamaheh, who loves you so dearly, but have a care lest the thistle Zeherit should put down roots and break asunder the walls of your house.'

George's tone and behaviour very much resembled vulgar showing-off, and Peregrinus was deeply displeased to see how entirely Pepusch misinterpreted all his actions. 'It never occurred to me for a moment to stand in your way', he said, without hiding his displeasure; 'the madness of love and jealousy is speaking through your mouth, or else you would consider how innocent I am of all these misdeeds that you have dreamt up in your own mind. Do not ask me to slay the serpent that you nourish in your bosom in order to torture yourself! And let me tell you that when I renounced the fairest thing, perhaps the utmost happiness life has to offer me, I was not throwing *you* a gift or making a sacrifice for *your* benefit. I was compelled to do this by other and higher duties, by an irrevocable promise!'

Pepusch, in savage fury, clenched his fists and raised them against his friend. Thereupon Dörtje leapt between the two and seized Peregrinus by the hand, exclaiming with a laugh: 'Let that stuck-up thistle go his own way; his head is full of nonsense, and, like most thistles, he's stubborn and obstinate and yet doesn't know what he really wants. You're mine and you'll stay mine, my sweet darling Peregrinus!'

With these words Dörtje pulled Peregrinus on to the sofa and seated herself without more ado on his knee. Pepusch chewed his nails for a moment and then rushed wildly out of the door.

Little Dörtje, again wearing her fabulous and seductive dress of silver taffeta, was as charming, as delightful, as ever; Peregrinus felt the electrical heat of her body running through his, and yet from time to time he shivered in an uncanny, icy chill, as though touched by death. For the first time he thought that deep in Dörtje's eyes he could discern something strangely lifeless and rigid, and the tone of her voice, even the rustling of her extraordinary silver taffeta, seemed to reveal an alien being whom he could never trust. He remembered with dismay that on the past occasion when Dörtje had frankly uttered her thoughts she had also been dressed in taffeta; he could not tell why he found the taffeta so disquieting, but the ideas of taffeta and of uncanny goings-on automatically became linked, just as a dream combines the most heterogeneous elements; and one readily declares such things to be senseless if one cannot perceive their deeper interconnections.

Since Peregrinus had no wish to hurt the sweet little thing by voicing suspicions that might be false, he forcibly suppressed his feelings and awaited a favourable moment to disentangle himself and flee the serpent that inhabited Paradise.

'But what's the matter with you today, my sweet friend?' said Dörtje at last. 'You seem so cold, so insensitive! What are you thinking about, my darling?'

'I've got a headache,' replied Peregrinus, as calmly as he possibly could, 'a headache, idle fancies, foolish notions, that's all that troubles me, my dear child. Let me go outside, and it will be over in a few minutes; besides, I have some urgent business.'

'You're only fibbing,' cried Dörtje, hastily jumping up, 'but you're a naughty monkey, and I'll have to teach you manners!'

Peregrinus was glad to find himself out in the street, but Master Flea, in his neckerchief, displayed the most extravagant rapture: he giggled and laughed and struck his fore-hands together so that their clapping was distinctly audible. Peregrinus found the merriment of his tiny protégé rather a nuisance, as it disturbed his thoughts. He asked Master Flea to keep quiet, for some grave people had already cast reproachful glances at him, thinking it was he who was giggling and laughing and playing foolish tricks in the public street.

'Oh, what a fool I was,' cried Master Flea, persisting in his outbursts of unrestrained joy, 'what an idiotic fool, to doubt the victory where not even a struggle was needed. Yes, Peregrinus, there's no question of it: you were victorious at the moment when even the death of your beloved was unable to shake your resolve. Let me rejoice and be merry, for unless I'm greatly mistaken, the bright sun will soon rise and illuminate all mysteries.'

When Peregrinus knocked at Lämmerhirt's door, a gentle female voice called: 'Come in!' He opened the door, and a girl who was alone in the room advanced to meet him and asked him pleasantly whether she could help him in any way.

Let it content the kind reader to be told that the girl was about eighteen years old, that she was tall rather than short, with a slender build and well-shaped limbs, and that she had light-brown hair, dark-blue eyes, and a complexion that seemed woven of lilies and roses. What was even more striking than all this, however, was that the girl's countenance expressed that tender mystery of virginal purity and lofty, heavenly charm, which many old German painters have captured in their portraits.

As soon as Peregrinus looked into the eyes of this lovely maiden, he felt as though a benevolent power had freed him from heavy shackles and he were now meeting the angel of light whose hand would guide him into the realm of unutterable love, bliss, and yearning. Blushing and modestly lowering her eyes before Peregrinus's gaze, the girl repeated her question: 'Can I be of any help to you, sir?'

Peregrinus, with an effort, stammered out: 'Does the bookbinder Lämmerhirt live here?'

When the girl replied that Lämmerhirt did indeed live there but had gone out on errands, Peregrinus rambled incoherently about some bindings he had ordered and some books that Lämmerhirt was to obtain for him. At last he found the thread again and recalled the de luxe edition of Ariosto* which Lämmerhirt had undertaken to bind in red morocco leather with rich gold lettering. At that moment the lovely maiden seemed animated by a spark of electricity: she clapped her hands and exclaimed with tears in her eyes: 'Heavens! You're Mr Tyss!'

She made a movement as though to seize Peregrinus's hand, then stepped quickly back, while a deep sigh seemed to unburden her heavy heart. Then a charming smile overspread the maiden's countenance like the beautiful light of dawn, and she poured out her thanks and good wishes to Peregrinus as the benefactor of her father and mother; not only that, she went on, but his kindness, his gentleness, the way in which he had given presents to all the children last Christmas and spread joy and good cheer among them, had conferred upon them the peace and happiness of heaven. She hastily cleared her father's armchair, which was laden with books, manuscripts, gatherings, and unbound pamphlets, pushed it forward, and, in a charming tone of welcome, invited Peregrinus to sit down. She then fetched out the handsomely bound Ariosto, dusted the morocco volumes gently with a linen cloth, and presented this masterpiece of the bookbinder's art to Peregrinus with a radiant smile, well knowing that he would not fail to appreciate her father's fine work.

Peregrinus took some gold coins from his pocket, and the lovely girl, noticing this, hastily declared that she did not know the cost of the work and therefore could not accept any payment. She hoped, however, that Mr Peregrinus would be good enough to wait a few moments, as her father was sure to be back very soon. Peregrinus felt as though the contemptible metal in his hand were melting into a lump, and he put the coins back in his pocket more quickly than he had taken them out. Once Peregrinus had sat down in Lämmerhirt's roomy armchair, the girl reached for her chair. His instinctive politeness made Mr Peregrinus jump up and try to move the chair for her; it happened, however, that instead of the chair-back he seized the girl's hand, and, as he ventured gently to squeeze this treasure, he thought he felt a barely perceptible answering pressure.

'Kitty, kitty, what are you doing!' With these words the girl turned and picked up from the floor a ball of yarn which the cat had taken between its fore-paws in order to begin weaving a mystic tapestry. With child-like lack of embarrassment she took Peregrinus, who was rapt in heavenly ecstasy, by the arm, guided him to the armchair, and once more asked him to sit down, while she herself took a seat opposite him and picked up some piece of household work.

Peregrinus was being rocked by a gale on a surging sea. 'Oh, Princess!' The word slipped out, he himself could not tell how. The girl gave him a frightened look; he felt as though he had committed an offence against his lovely hostess, and exclaimed in a tone of the gentlest melancholy: 'My dearest, most precious young lady!'

The girl blushed and said with lovely virginal modesty: 'My parents call me Rosie. Call me by that name too, dear Mr Tyss, for I too am among the children to whom you have shown so much kindness and who hold you in such reverence.'

'Rosie!' cried Peregrinus, quite beside himself. He would have liked to prostrate himself at the feet of the lovely maiden, and could scarcely hold himself back.

Continuing tranquilly with her work, Rosie now recounted how, ever since the war had plunged her parents into the direst poverty, she had been looked after by a cousin in a nearby small town, and how this cousin had died a few weeks earlier, whereupon Rosie had returned to her parents.

Peregrinus heard only Rosie's sweet voice, but did not understand much of what she was saying, and he was not quite convinced that it was not all a blissful dream until Lämmerhirt entered the room and gave him a hearty welcome. It was not long before Mrs Lämmerhirt arrived with the children; and as thoughts, impulses, and feelings form a strange colourful tangle in man's unfathomable heart, it happened that, just as his rapture was showing Peregrinus an unsuspected vision of heaven, he suddenly recalled how the peevish Pepusch had criticized him for giving presents to the Lämmerhirt children. He was very pleased to learn, in answer to his enquiries, that the sweets had made none of the children ill, and the friendly solemnity, indeed the pride, with which they looked up at the high glass cabinet containing their glittering toys, showed that they considered the last distribution of presents an extraordinary event that would probably never recur.

So the ill-humoured thistle was quite wrong.

'O Pepusch,' said Peregrinus to himself, 'your distraught and discordant heart has never been touched by a pure ray of genuine love!' Peregrinus meant something more by this than a present of sweets and toys.

Lämmerhirt, a quiet, gentle, peaceable man, looked with visible pleasure at Rosie, who had been bustling in and out, fetching bread and butter, and was now preparing splendid-looking scones for her little brothers and sisters at a small table in the far corner of the room. The merry boys pressed close to their dear sister, and if their pardonable childish appetite made them open their mouths somewhat wider than was strictly necessary, this did not seriously detract from the domestic idyll. Peregrinus was delighted by everything the lovely girl did, without being reminded of Werther's Lotte* and her bread and butter.

Lämmerhirt approached Peregrinus and began talking in low tones about Rosie. He described what a dear, good, sweet-tempered child she was, endowed by heaven with the additional gift of outward beauty, and how he hoped that the lovely child would bring him only joy. What really warmed the cockles of his heart, he added, as a blissful smile overspread his face, was that Rosie wished also to practise the noble art of bookbinding and during the few weeks she had been with him had made uncommon progress in fine and delicate work, so that she was already much more skilful than many a clumsy apprentice-boy, who would waste morocco and gold for years on end and put the letters on askew, making them look like drunken farmers reeling out of the alehouse.

The delighted father then whispered, very confidentially, into Peregrinus's ear: 'I must tell you this, Mr Tyss, I can't help it, otherwise it will weigh too heavily on my heart—did you know that it was *my Rosie* who put the gilt edging on your Ariosto?'

As soon as Peregrinus heard this, he hastily reached for the handsome morocco volumes, as though to take possession of the sacred objects before some malign mischance should snatch them from him. Lämmerhirt took this for a sign that Peregrinus wanted to leave and asked him to be kind enough to spend a few more minutes with his family. This, however, reminded Peregrinus that he must finally tear himself away. He quickly paid the bill, and Lämmerhirt, as usual, took leave of him with a hand-shake; Mrs Lämmerhirt did the same, and so did Rosie! The boys were standing in the doorway, and, not to be lacking in a lover's madness, Peregrinus, as he was leaving, seized the remains of a buttered scone from one of the boys, who was just chewing it, and rushed down the stairs as though running for his life.

'Well, well,' said the little boy, dumbfounded, 'what on earth was that? If Mr Tyss was hungry, he could have told me, and I'd gladly have given him the whole of my scone!'

Mr Peregrinus Tyss went home, step by step, laboriously carrying the heavy quarto volumes under his arms, and savouring each morsel of the buttered scone with a look of ecstasy, as though he were consuming manna from heaven.

'That fellow's gone off his head now, too!' said a passing citizen. One could not blame the man for thinking thus about Peregrinus.

As Peregrinus Tyss entered his house, old Aline came to meet him and gestured, with evident alarm and concern, towards Mr Swammerdamm's room. The door was open, and Peregrinus saw Dörtje Elwerdink sitting rigid in an armchair. Her shrivelled face resembled that of a corpse that has already been lying in its grave. Pepusch, Swammerdamm, and Leuwenhoek were sitting on armchairs in front of her, equally rigid and equally corpse-like. 'What a mad, ghost-like way of carrying on down here!' said the old woman. 'These three unholy people have been sitting like that the whole blessed day, not eating, not drinking, not speaking, and hardly breathing!'

At this sight, which was indeed somewhat grisly, Peregrinus began to feel considerable horror, but as he ascended the stairs the ghostly image was swept away by the surging sea of heavenly dreams in which the enraptured Peregrinus had been swimming ever since his first glimpse of Rosie. Dreams, desires, and blissful hopes easily overflow into the heart of a friend; but what other friend did poor Peregrinus have besides the good and honest-hearted Master Flea? He was now anxious to pour out his whole heart to Master Flea, and to tell him all about Rosie, though it would not have been easy to tell it. But however much Peregrinus called and cajoled, no Master Flea was to be seen; he was up and away. After a more careful search, Peregrinus found in the fold of his neckerchief, where Master Flea had usually taken shelter on excursions, a tiny little box on which were written the following words:

This box contains the microscopic glass for thought-reading. If you look keenly into the box with your left eye, the glass will instantly insert itself in your pupil; if you want to remove it, you need only hold your eye above the box and press your pupil gently, and the glass will fall on to the bottom of the box, I am at work on your behalf, at great risk to myself, but for my dear protector no effort will be spared by

> your most obedient servant,
> MASTER FLEA

A competent professional novel-writer, whose strong hand, furnished with a good quill pen, moulds all human activity according to his pleasure, would now have the ideal opportunity to discourse theoretically upon the vast difference between loving and being in love, and then to use Peregrinus as a concrete instance of this distinction. Much might be said about the sensual urges, the curse of Original Sin, and the heavenly Promethean spark which uses love to create the true spiritual union of the different sexes which forms the real and necessary dualism of nature. And if this Promethean spark should also light the torch of Hymen, a good clear household lamp in whose light you can read, write, knit, and sew, and if a crowd of cheerful progeny should sometimes smear their faces with raspberry jam, just like other children, why, that is the way of things here below. Besides, such heavenly love is an admirable subject for sublime poetry, and the best thing about it is that this love is no mere idle fancy, but really does exist, as many people can attest, who have fared both well and badly with such love.

The kind reader, however, has long since guessed that Mr Peregrinus was only infatuated with little Dörtje, but that at the instant when he glimpsed Rosie Lämmerhirt, the dear, lovely, angelic girl, true heavenly love blazed up brightly within his heart.

The present narrator of this wild and wonderful fairy-tale would, however, earn little gratitude if he were obstinately to follow the parade-ground step of the strutting novelist and fail, at this point, to avoid arousing the tedium that is requisite to any regularly constituted novel. He could easily provoke such tedium by giving a leisurely and reposeful account of each stage that the loving couple, like all loving couples, has to pass through. No, dear reader! let us gallop ahead like stout and sturdy horsemen on courageous racehorses, ignoring whatever lies to left or right, in our haste to attain our goal. Here we are! Sighs, laments, pain, rapture, bliss, all are united in the focal point of the moment when the lovely Rosie, the charming glow of lovely maidenhood on her cheeks, confesses to the overjoyed Peregrinus Tyss that she loves him, indeed more than she can possibly say; she adores him, her life is bound up with his, she thinks only of him and can only be happy with him.

The dark, malignant demon is accustomed to stretch his black claws into the brightest of life's sunlit moments, and to blot out their sunshine by the dark shadow of his ominous nature. So it came about that malign doubts arose within Peregrinus, indeed that an evil suspicion stirred within his breast.

'What's this?' a voice seemed to whisper, 'didn't Dörtje Elwerdink also confess her love for you, and yet wasn't it mere vile self-interest that animated her and made her tempt you to break your promise and betray your best friend, poor Master Flea?'

'I am rich,' thought Peregrinus further; 'it is said that my good-natured behaviour, and a certain frankness that some call simplicity, earns me people's dubious goodwill, and perhaps also that of women; and this one, who is now confessing her love . . .'

He reached hastily for Master Flea's portentous present, drew out the box, and was on the point of opening it to place the microscopic glass in the pupil of his right eye and thus read Rosie's thoughts.

He looked up, and the pure heavenly azure of the loveliest eyes shone into his soul. Rosie, clearly perceiving his inward disturbance, gazed at him in surprise, almost with concern. At that moment a sudden illumination flashed through his mind, and he felt entirely crushed by the mortifying realization of how corrupt his thoughts had become.

'What?' he said to himself, 'do you want to violate the pure sanctuary of this angel with sinful and criminal intent? Do you want to spy out thoughts which can have nothing in common with the base conduct of ordinary souls mired in earthly life? Do you want to mock the very spirit of love, testing him with the accursed arts of uncanny and menacing powers?'

He hastily concealed the box in his pocket, feeling as though he had committed a sin for which he could never, never atone. In an agony of sorrow and pain he prostrated himself at Rosie's feet, much to her alarm, and exclaimed, shedding a flood of tears, that he was an impious and sinful man, unworthy to be loved by a being of such angelic purity as Rosie.

Unable to understand what dark spirit had taken hold of Peregrinus, Rosie knelt down beside him and embraced him, lisping amid her tears: 'For heaven's sake, my beloved Peregrinus, what's the matter with you? What's happened to you? What enemy has come between us? Do come and sit down quietly beside me!'

Peregrinus, unable to move by his own volition, silently allowed Rosie to raise him to his feet.

It was fortunate that the old and rather rickety sofa was laden, as usual, with unbound books, finished bindings, and a vast supply of the tools of the bookbinder's trade, so that Rosie had to clear away a great deal to make room for herself and the contrite Mr Peregrinus Tyss. This gave him time to recover, and his intense pain and heart-rending sorrow were dissolved into the milder feeling that he had indeed done wrong but would be able to atone for it. If his expression had previously resembled that of the despairing sinner on whom the sentence of death has just been irrevocably pronounced, he now looked only somewhat simple-minded. Under these circumstances, however, such an expression invariably augurs well.

When both Rosie and Mr Peregrinus Tyss were seated together on the aforementioned rickety sofa of the honest bookbinder Lämmerhirt, Rosie, with downcast eyes and a bashful smile, began: 'I think I can guess, my beloved, what took possession of your mind so suddenly. Let me confess that people have told me all sorts of extraordinary things about the strange inhabitants of your house. The neighbours—well, you know what neighbours are like, there's nothing they like so much as gossip, even when they don't know what they're talking about—these malicious neighbours have told me that in your house there is a wonderful female, whom many people took for a princess, and whom you yourself carried indoors on Christmas Eve. Old Mr Swammer took her in, saying she was his runaway niece, but this person is supposed to have pursued you with strange wiles. But that's far from being the worst. Just think, my beloved Peregrinus, the old woman directly opposite (you must know her, she's the old woman with the pointed nose who waves so nicely whenever she sees you, and one Sunday when you saw her going to church in her best woollen dress, the brightly coloured one, you said—I can't help laughing whenever I remember it—you said she looked like a bunch of tiger-lilies crossing the street) well, this suspicious old woman has tried to put all sorts of bad ideas about you into my head.

'No matter how nicely she may wave to you, she has always warned me against you, and she goes so far as to claim that Satanic arts go on in your house, and that little Dörtje is none other than a little devil in disguise, who goes about in human form, and a very charming and seductive one, in order to tempt you.

'Peregrinus! my dear, beloved Peregrinus, look me in the eye, and you won't find the least trace of suspicion; I know that your heart is pure, and no word or look from you has ever cast a sombre breath upon the clear, bright mirror of my soul. I believe in you, I believe in the bliss that we shall enjoy when we are tied by a firm bond, as sweet dreams of love and yearning have already foretold! Peregrinus! No matter how dark spirits may have settled your fate, their power will be shattered to pieces by your innocent nature, which is firm and strong in love and unshakeable loyalty.

'What should, what could destroy a love like ours? Banish all your doubts. Our love is the talisman that puts nocturnal phantoms to flight.'

At this moment Rosie seemed to Peregrinus like a higher being, and every word she uttered was like heavenly consolation. An indescribable feeling of the purest bliss engulfed his heart like the sweet and gentle breath of spring. He was no longer the impious and sinful man that he had thought himself; he surmised with rapture that he might deserve the love of the fairest and most angelic of maidens.

The master bookbinder Lämmerhirt now returned with his family from their stroll. Both Peregrinus and the sweet Rosie poured out their hearts, and at nightfall Mr Peregrinus, now happily and blissfully betrothed, left the cramped dwelling of the delighted bookbinder and his good wife, whose joy and rapture made her sob a little more than was strictly necessary.

All the plausible and thoroughly authentic records from which this wondrous tale is taken are in agreement, and the perpetual calendar confirms it, that on the night when Mr Peregrinus came home, happily engaged, the full moon was shining brightly and cheerfully, so that the entire Horsemarket was delightfully decked out in its silvery beams. It seems quite natural that instead of retiring to rest, Mr Peregrinus Tyss should have sat down by the open window, in order to look at the moon and, as is right and proper for lovers, let his thoughts dwell a little longer on his lovely bride.

Although it may reduce Mr Peregrinus Tyss in the estimation of my kind reader, especially of my kind female readers, the truth must be told, and it cannot be concealed that despite his bliss Mr Peregrinus twice yawned so monstrously, and so loudly, that a tipsy market porter who happened to be staggering across the street shouted up to him: 'Hey! You up there in the white nightcap, don't eat me alive!' This was sufficient reason for Mr Peregrinus Tyss to slam the window shut in annoyance, so that the panes rattled. It is even alleged that during this act he exclaimed quite loudly: 'Impudent ruffian!' But this may well not be authentic, since it would seem quite incompatible with his gentle temper and character. Enough! Mr Peregrinus Tyss slammed the window shut and betook himself to rest. His need for sleep, however, seemed to have been satisfied by his monstrous yawn. A succession of thoughts mingled in his brain, and he recalled with particular vividness the danger he had just avoided, when tempted by a dark power to make criminal use of the microscopic glass. Only now, however, did he realize clearly that Master Flea's fateful present, however well intended, was in every way a gift that properly belonged to hell.

'What?' he said to himself. 'If anyone can read his brethren's secret thoughts, will not this fateful gift impose on him the terrible fate of the Wandering Jew, who roamed through the world's colourful tumult without joy, without hope, without sorrow, in dull indifference, the very death's-head of despair, as though he were traversing a dreary and inhospitable wilderness?

'With hope and trust perpetually renewed and perpetually dashed, how can he prevent distrust, foul suspicion, hatred, and vengefulness from taking firm root in his soul and devouring every trace of the truly human principle that is expressed in gentle trust and peaceable good nature? No! your friendly face, your smooth words shall not deceive me, for undeserved hatred of me may lurk deep within your heart; I shall consider you my friend, I shall do you all the good I can, I shall bare my soul to you because it is a relief to do so, and the momentary bitterness if you disappoint me is of small account compared to the joys of a fair departed dream. And even the true friends who genuinely wish me well—how inconstant is man's heart! Cannot an evil conjunction of malign events, a mood of ill-will arising from an injury done by whimsical accident, bring forth temporary enmity even in the souls of these friends?

'And that enmity would be perceived by the unhappy glass, my heart would be filled by dark suspicion, and in the most unjust anger, in mad delusion, I should disown even my true friend, and the deadly poison of evil rancour would eat ever further, into the very roots of life, setting me at odds with all existence here below, and estranging me from myself.

'No! It is a crime, an accursed crime, if, like the fallen angel of light who brought sin into the world, one tries to rival the Eternal Power who reads the souls of mankind because He governs them.

'Away with the ill-omened gift!'

Mr Peregrinus Tyss seized the little box containing the microscopic glass and was about to hurl it with all his strength at his bedroom ceiling.

Suddenly Master Flea, in microscopic form, was sitting on the coverlet in front of Mr Peregrinus Tyss. He was a most pleasing and charming sight, with glittering scales and beautiful polished golden boots. 'Stop!' he cried, 'stop, most honoured sir!

Don't do anything foolish! It would be easier for you to destroy a mote of dust than to move this indestructible little glass even a foot, as long as I am at hand. Besides, although you didn't see me, I hid in the fold of your neckerchief, as usual, when you were at the house of the honest master bookbinder Lämmerhirt, and was a witness of all that took place. I have likewise overheard your edifying soliloquy and learnt many lessons from it.

'First, you have now revealed your heart, purely inspired by true love, in brilliant splendour, like a mighty ray flashing forth from your inmost soul, so that I believe the supreme and decisive moment is approaching.

'Secondly, I have also perceived that with regard to the microscopic glass I was the victim of a grave error. It is true that I have not the pleasure to be a human being like yourself, but only a flea, though no ordinary flea but a fully qualified graduate, on account of my glorious mastership. But believe me, my honoured, tried and tested friend, I nevertheless understand very well the human heart and the ways of human beings, among whom I constantly dwell. Sometimes I find their ways very comical, if not silly; don't take it amiss, honoured sir, I'm speaking only as Master Flea. You are right, my friend, it would be a dreadful thing, and no good could possibly come of it, if one person could gaze into another's brain without so much as a "by your leave"; for the cheerful and untroubled flea, however, the gift of the microscopic glass has no perils.

'You know, my honoured and soon, if destiny permits, happy Mr Peregrinus, that my nation is plucky and light-hearted, indeed given to levity, and one might say that these bold young fellows never look before they leap. Yet I for my part can boast of exceptional worldly wisdom, something in which you sage mortals are commonly deficient. That is to say, I have never done anything at an unsuitable moment. The main purpose of my existence is biting; but I have always bitten at the right time and in the right place. Take that to heart, my true and honest friend!

'I shall now receive from your hands the present intended for you, which neither that deformed monstrosity called Swammerdamm, nor Leuwenhoek, who eats his own heart out in petty jealousy, managed to obtain, and I will preserve it faithfully.

Now, honoured Mr Tyss, surrender yourself to sleep. You will soon fall into a dreamy delirium, in which the great moment will reveal itself. I shall be with you again at the proper time.'

Master Flea disappeared, and the light that had radiated from him faded into the deep dark night of the curtained room.

It came to pass just as Master Flea had said.

Before long Mr Peregrinus Tyss imagined that he was lying on the bank of a purling woodland brook and listening to the murmuring of the wind, the whispering of the bushes, and the humming of innumerable insects that were buzzing around him. Then he seemed to hear strange voices, with ever-increasing distinctness, so that finally Peregrinus thought he could make out words. But all that reached his ears was a confused and bewildering sound of chattering.

At last the following words were spoken by a solemn, muffled voice, which rang out ever more clearly as it proceeded.

'Unhappy King Sekakis, who scorned the understanding of nature and, blinded by the evil spells of the malignant demon, looked upon the false Teraphim instead of the true spirit!

'At that fateful spot, in Famagusta, concealed in the depths of the earth, lay the talisman, but since you brought about your own ruin, there was no principle that could restore its frozen powers to life. In vain did you sacrifice your daughter, the fair Gamaheh; vain was the despairing love of the thistle Zeherit; but the blood-thirsty Leech Prince, too, was impotent and ineffectual. Even the lubberly spirit Thetel was compelled to abandon his sweet prey, for the half-extinguished idea within you, O King Sekakis, was still mighty enough for you to restore the lost one to the primal element from which she had sprung.

'Mad retailers of nature, why did the poor girl have to fall into your hands when you discovered her in the pollen of that fatal Haarlem tulip! Why did you have to torment her with your loathsome experiments, fancying in your childish conceit that your vile arts could effect that which only the power of the sleeping talisman can accomplish!

'And you, Master Flea, were not privileged to glimpse the secret, since even your clear gaze lacked the power to penetrate the depths of the earth and espy the frozen carbuncle.

'The planets went on their way, their paths crossed in

wondrous ellipses, and their frightful conjunctions brought forth astounding events which remain forever concealed from the ignorant eye of man. Yet no stellar conflict could awaken the carbuncle; for the human heart was not yet born that was to shelter the carbuncle, so that on discerning the highest glories of man's nature it should wake into joyous life—until at last . . .

'The miracle is fulfilled, the moment has come.'

A bright, flickering light flashed past Peregrinus's eyes. Half-waking from his stupor, he was greatly astonished to behold Master Flea. In his microscopic form, but enrobed in the capacious folds of a magnificent gown, and bearing a blazing torch in his front paw, Master Flea was hopping busily around the room and uttering shrill piercing tones.

Mr Peregrinus tried to rouse himself fully from sleep, but suddenly a thousand rays of fiery lightning shot through the room, so that it seemed to be filled by a single glowing ball of fire. Then, however, a mild aromatic smell suffused the fierce fire, which soon smouldered away and turned into gentle moonlight.

Peregrinus found himself standing upon a splendid throne, dressed in the rich garments of an Indian king, with the sparkling diadem on his head and the mystical lotus-flower in his hand instead of a sceptre. The throne was erected in a hall which stretched further than the eye could see, and its thousand pillars were slender cedars rising to the sky.

Among them the fairest roses, along with wondrously fragrant flowers of every kind, lifted their heads from the dark shrubs, as though impelled by thirsty yearning for the pure azure which looked down, as if with loving eyes, through the tangled branches of the cedars.

Peregrinus recognized himself and felt that the carbuncle, recalled to life, was glowing in his own breast.

In the remote background the spirit Thetel was endeavouring to rise into the air, but he proved unable to reach half the height of the cedar trunks, and tumbled down ignominiously to earth.

There the odious Leech Prince was crawling to and fro, squirming disgustingly, and making loathsome attempts alternately to swell up and to elongate himself, groaning as he did so: 'Gamaheh—still mine!'

In the midst of the hall Leuwenhoek and Swammerdamm were sitting on colossal microscopes and pulling miserable and lamentable faces as they reproached each other: 'You see, *that* was the spot in the horoscope whose meaning you couldn't work out. We've lost the talisman for ever!'

Close by the steps of the throne, however, were Dörtje Elwerdink and George Pepusch, who seemed not so much asleep as lying in a profound swoon.

Peregrinus, or—as we may now call him—King Sekakis, threw back the royal robe whose folds covered his chest, and from within him the carbuncle, like fire from heaven, cast its dazzling rays through the spacious hall.

Just as the spirit Thetel was trying to soar aloft once more, he crumbled, with a dull groan, into innumerable colourless flakes, which scattered in the bushes as though pursued by a gale.

The Leech Prince, with a terrible cry of heart-rending lamentation, curled up and vanished into the earth. An angry rumble could be heard, as though the earth were reluctant to receive the hideous and unwelcome fugitive into its bosom. Leuwenhoek and Swammerdamm fell off their microscopes and collapsed in a heap; their fearful moaning and groaning, their terrified gasps, as though they were at death's door, revealed what torments they were undergoing.

But Dörtje Elwerdink and George Pepusch, or, as they should more fittingly be called here, Princess Gamaheh and the thistle Zeherit, awoke from their swoon and knelt before the King, apparently imploring his mercy with sighs of yearning. Their eyes were cast down, however, as though they could not endure the light of the radiant carbuncle.

Peregrinus spoke solemnly: 'The evil demon kneaded you together from vile clay and the feathers lost by a slow-witted, clumsy ostrich, so that as the spirit Thetel you might deceive mankind. Therefore, you empty will-o'-the-wisp, you have been annihilated by the beam of love, and could not help crumbling into nothingness and vacuity.

'And you too, blood-thirsty monster of night, hateful Leech Prince, have had to flee into the bosom of the earth to escape the beam of the glowing carbuncle.

'But you wretched deluded fools, unhappy Swammerdamm, miserable Leuwenhoek, your whole lives were one incessant, unbroken error. You sought to explore nature, but had no inkling of the significance of her innermost being.

'You boldly ventured to pry into her workshop and eavesdrop upon her mysterious workings, fancying that you could with impunity behold the frightful mysteries of those abysses which are forever concealed from man's sight. Your hearts were cold and dead; true love has never awoken you to life; the flowers, the colourful gauze-winged insects, have never spoken sweet words to you. You thought you were observing the lofty and sacred wonders of nature with pious admiration and reverence, but in impiously toiling to discover the most hidden causes of these wonders, you yourselves destroyed that reverence, and the knowledge you sought was but a phantasm by which you were deceived, like inquisitive and impertinent children.

'Fools! for you the carbuncle's beam has no consolation, no hope.'

'Ha, ha! there's still some consolation, still some hope; these old fellows will have an old woman for company; that's love, that's loyalty, that's tenderness. And the old woman is now a queen, right enough, and she'll take her dear little Swammerdamm and her good little Leuwenhoek to her kingdom, and there they'll be beautiful princes, and pull out gold and silver threads and scraps of silk, and do other clever and useful things.'

Thus spoke old Aline, suddenly standing between the microscopists, dressed in extraordinary garments that almost resembled the Queen of Golconda's outfit in the opera. The microscopists meanwhile had shrunk so much that they seemed scarcely six inches tall. The Queen of Golconda took the two little fellows to her bosom, despite their moaning and groaning, and caressed and fondled them like infants, speaking kindly to them in baby-talk. Thereupon the Queen of Golconda laid her pretty dolls in two dainty little cradles carved from the most beautiful ivory, and rocked them to sleep, singing:

> Sleep, my baby, sleep,
> My garden has two sheep,
> A black one and a white one . . .

While this was going on, Princess Gamaheh and the thistle Zeherit were still kneeling on the steps of the throne.

Peregrinus spoke: 'No! The error that drove your lives astray is now dispelled, you loving couple. Come to my breast, beloveds! The carbuncle's beam will enter your hearts, and you will enjoy the bliss of heaven.' With a cry of joyous hope Princess Gamaheh and the thistle Zeherit rose to their feet, and Peregrinus pressed them to his flaming heart.

As soon as he let them go, they fell into each other's arms in exalted rapture. The corpse-like pallor had vanished from their faces, and fresh, youthful life was blooming on their cheeks and shining from their eyes.

Master Flea, who had been standing by the throne all this time like a dainty bodyguard, suddenly assumed his natural appearance, and, with a piercing cry of: 'Old love never fades!', took a flying leap and landed on Dörtje's neck.

But, wonder of wonders, at that very moment Rosie lay on Peregrinus's breast, resplendent in the lofty and indescribable charm of lovely maidenhood, like a heavenly cherub, surrounded by the radiance of the purest love.

The cedar branches rustled, the flowers raised their heads more joyously, glittering birds of Paradise soared through the hall, sweet melodies streamed from the dark blushes, and jubilant rejoicing seemed to echo from the far distance, and a thousand voices joined to fill the air with a hymn of rapturous pleasure, and in love's holy sacrament the supreme bliss of life stirred and blazed up as the pure ethereal fire of heaven!

Mr Peregrinus Tyss had bought a handsome house in the country, just outside the town, and here his marriage was to be celebrated on the same day as that of his friend George Pepusch to little Dörtje Elwerdink.

The kind reader will doubtless dispense me from the obligation of describing the wedding banquet and from recounting in detail all the other events of the festive day.

I willingly give my fair female readers liberty to design the costumes of the two brides in accordance with whatever image happens to be floating before their minds. It must only be observed that Peregrinus and his lovely Rosie displayed cheerful

child-like ease, while George and Dörtje were sunk in thought
and, gazing into each other's eyes, seemed to behold, to feel,
and to think of nothing but themselves.

It was midnight when suddenly the balmy smell of the torch-
thistle with its huge flowers spread through the whole extent
of the garden and the house.

Awaking from sleep, Peregrinus thought he could hear the
deep and sorrowful melodies of hopeless yearning, and a strange
sense of foreboding took possession of him. He felt as though a
friend were tearing himself forcibly away from his breast.

Next morning there was no sign of the second couple, George
Pepusch and Dörtje Elwerdink, and no small surprise was occa-
sioned by the discovery that they had never entered their bridal
chamber.

At that moment the gardener came in, quite beside himself,
exclaiming that he didn't know what to make of it, but a
strange miracle had appeared in the garden. All night long he
had dreamt about a *Cactus grandiflorus* in bloom, and only now
had he learnt why. 'Come and see for yourselves!'

Peregrinus and Rosie went down into the garden. In the
midst of a fine shrubbery bed a lofty torch-thistle had shot up,
but its blossom had withered in the morning beam and was
hanging down. Around this blossom a lilac and yellow striped
tulip was clinging affectionately; it too was dead.

'My foreboding did not deceive me!' cried Peregrinus, his
voice trembling with deep melancholy. 'The carbuncle's beam
that aroused me to supreme life gave you death, you couple
linked by the strange intertwining of a mysterious dissonance
of the dark powers. The mystery is disclosed: the supreme
moment of fulfilled yearning was also the moment of your
death.'

Rosie too seemed to suspect the meaning of the miracle. She
bent down to the poor dead tulip and shed frequent tears.

'You are quite right,' said Master Flea, suddenly sitting on
the torch-thistle in his pleasing microscopic guise, 'yes, you are
quite right, worthy Mr Peregrinus; it is just as you say, and I
have lost my beloved for ever.'

Rosie was at first alarmed by the tiny monster, but Master
Flea looked at her with such intelligent and friendly eyes, and

Peregrinus seemed on such familiar terms with him, that she plucked up courage, looked boldly into his dainty little countenance, and gained more confidence in the curious little creature when Peregrinus whispered to her: 'This is my dear, good Master Flea.'

'My dear Peregrinus,' said Master Flea, very tenderly, 'my dear and lovely mistress, I must now leave you and return to my people, but I shall remain your loyal friend for evermore, and you shall feel my presence in a way that gives you pleasure. Farewell, farewell to you both! I wish you every happiness!'

While saying these words Master Flea resumed his natural appearance and vanished without a trace.

It is said that Master Flea always showed his presence as a guardian spirit in the family of Mr Peregrinus Tyss. He was especially active a year later, when the gracious couple were delighted by the arrival of a little Peregrinus. Master Flea sat by the bed of his lovely mistress and bit the nurse in the nose if she fell asleep; if the invalid's broth were not cooked properly, he would jump in and out of it; and so forth.

It was particularly kind of Master Flea that on Christmas Day he never failed to supply the Tyss progeny with the daintiest little toys, made by the most skilful artists among his people, and thus gave Mr Peregrinus Tyss a pleasant reminder of those fateful Christmas presents which were also the starting-point for the wildest and most wondrous events.

Here the records suddenly break off, and the wondrous tale of Master Flea comes happily to

THE END

MY COUSIN'S CORNER WINDOW

My poor cousin has suffered the same fate as the famous Scarron.* Like him, my cousin has entirely lost the use of his legs owing to an intractable illness, and he needs the help of some stout crutches, and the muscular arm of a surly ex-soldier who acts as a nurse when in the mood, to stagger from his bed to an armchair piled with cushions, and from the armchair to his bed. But there is yet another similarity between my cousin and Scarron, whose special type of humour, deviating from the usual path of French wit, has given him, despite the scantiness of his works, a secure place in French literature. Like Scarron, my cousin is a writer; like Scarron, he is endowed with an especially lively wit, and indulges in remarkably humorous jesting in his own way. To the credit of the German writer, however, let it be noted that he never thought it necessary to spice his little savoury dishes with asafoetida in order to tickle the palates of his German readers, who do not relish such things. He is content with the nobler sort of spice which both delights and invigorates. People enjoy reading what he writes; it is supposed to be good and diverting; I am no judge of such matters. I always used to find pleasure in my cousin's conversation, and it seemed pleasanter to listen to him than to read him. But it is just this unconquerable inclination for writing which has brought the blackest misfortune upon my cousin; the gravest illness could not stop the wheels of his imagination from turning; they continued to work, always bringing forth new things. Thus it was that he would tell me all manner of charming stories, which he had invented in spite of the many and various pains he was enduring. But the path that his thoughts had to follow in order to appear fully formed on paper had been blocked by the evil demon of illness. Whenever my cousin wanted to write something down, not only did his fingers refuse their office, but even his ideas were scattered and dissipated. This plunged my cousin into the blackest melancholy.

'Cousin!' he said to me one day in a tone that alarmed me, 'it's all up with me! I feel like the old painter whose mind was completely unhinged and who spent entire days sitting in front of a framed canvas with a first coat of paint on it, and telling all his visitors about the manifold beauties of the rich and magnificent painting he had just completed. I give it up, the active, creative life that emerges from my mind in distinct forms and links me with the world! My spirit is retiring to its cell!' From that time onwards my cousin refused to see me or anybody else. The surly old ex-soldier would send us away, growling and scolding, like a watch-dog that might well bite.

It is necessary to mention that my cousin lives in a small room with a low ceiling, high above the street. That is the usual custom of writers and poets. What does the low ceiling matter? Imagination soars aloft and builds a high and cheerful dome that rises to the radiant blue sky. Thus the poet's cramped quarters are like the garden that consisted of ten square feet enclosed within four walls: neither broad nor long, but always at an agreeable height. Moreover, my cousin's lodgings are in the most attractive part of our capital city, overlooking the big market square* which is surrounded by magnificent buildings and has the colossal theatre, a work of genius, adorning its centre. The house where my cousin lives stands on a corner, and from the window of a tiny room he can overlook the entire panorama of the splendid square at a single glance.

It happened to be market-day when, forcing my way through the throng of people, I came down the street where my cousin's corner window can be seen from a considerable distance. I was not a little astonished to see in this window the well-known red cap which my cousin used to wear in happier times. Nor was that all! As I came closer, I noticed that my cousin had put on his fine Warsaw dressing-gown and was smoking tobacco in the Turkish pipe he used on Sundays. I waved to him and fluttered my handkerchief; this succeeded in attracting his attention, and he gave me a friendly nod. What hopes! I hurried upstairs with lightning speed. The ex-soldier opened the door; his face, which with its wrinkles and folds normally looked like a wet glove, had been smoothed out by some sunshine into a quite passable physiognomy. He said his master was sitting in the armchair and was available to visitors. The room had been cleaned, and on the screen separating the bed from the rest of the room had been pinned a sheet of paper on which the following words were written in big letters:

Et si male nunc, non olim sic erit.[*]

All this suggested the return of hope, the reawakening of vital energy.

'Why,' called my cousin, as I entered the tiny room, 'here you are at last, cousin; do you know that I have really been longing for you? For although you don't care two pins about my immortal works, I still like you, because you're a cheery soul, and amusable if not exactly amusing.'

I felt the blood rising to my face at this compliment from my outspoken cousin.

'You probably think', went on my cousin, ignoring my reaction, 'that my health is improving, or that I've made a complete recovery. That's anything but true. My legs are disloyal vassals who have refused obedience to the head of their ruler, and want nothing more to do with the rest of my worthy corpse. That's to say, I can't move from the spot, and cart myself to and fro in this wheelchair in the most charming fashion, while my old soldier whistles the most tuneful marches he remembers from his army years. But this window is my comfort; it is here that life in all its colour has been revealed to me anew, and I feel at home with its incessant activity. Come, cousin, look outside!'

I sat down opposite my cousin on a small stool for which there was just room in front of the window. The view was indeed strange and surprising. The entire market seemed like a single mass of people squeezed tightly together, so that one would have thought that an apple thrown into it would never reach the ground. Tiny specks of the most varied colours were gleaming in the sunshine; this gave me the impression of a large bed of tulips being blown hither and thither by the wind, and I had to confess that the view, while certainly very attractive, soon became tiring, and might give over-sensitive people a slight feeling of giddiness, like the not disagreeable delirium one feels at the onset of a dream. I assumed that this accounted for the pleasure that my cousin derived from his corner window, and told him so quite frankly.

My cousin, however, clapped his hands together above his head, and the following conversation developed between us:

MY COUSIN: Cousin, cousin! I now see clearly that you haven't the tiniest spark of literary talent. You lack the first prerequisite for treading in the footsteps of your worthy paralysed cousin: an eye that can really see. The market down there offers you nothing but the sight of a motley, bewildering throng of people animated by meaningless activity. Ho, ho, my friend! I can derive from it the most varied scenery of town life, and my mind, an honest Callot, or a modern Chodowiecki, dashes off a whole series of sketches, some of them very bold in their outlines. Come on, cousin! Let me see if I can't teach you at least the rudiments of the art of seeing. Look directly down into the street—here are my field-glasses—do you see the somewhat strangely dressed person with a large shopping-basket on her arm who is deep in conversation with a brush-maker and seems to be hurriedly settling domestic matters quite unconnected with bodily nourishment?

ME. I've got her. She has a bright lemon-yellow cloth wound round her head like a turban, in the French style, and her face, as well as her whole appearance, shows clearly that she's a Frenchwoman. She's probably a refugee from the last war who has made a pile for herself.

MY COUSIN. Not a bad guess. I'll wager that her husband makes a tidy income from some branch of French industry, so that his wife can fill her shopping-basket with plenty of good things. Now she's plunging into the throng. Cousin, see if you can follow the various twists and turns of her course without losing sight of her. Her yellow head-cloth will be your guide.

ME. Goodness, how that bright yellow dot forces its way through the crowd. Now she's already close to the church, now she's haggling over something at the booths, now she's gone—oh dear, I've lost her!—no, she's popped up at the far end over there, over near the poultry. She's taking hold of a plucked goose. She's feeling it with expert fingers.

MY COUSIN. Good, cousin; you have to focus your attention if you are to see distinctly. But instead of giving you boring lessons in an art which can hardly be learnt, let me draw your attention to all sorts of diverting things which are being revealed before our eyes. Do you see the woman who is making room for herself with two sharp elbows, down there at the corner, although the crowd isn't particularly dense?

ME. What an extraordinary figure: a silken hat whose capricious shapelessness has bidden defiance to every fashion, with coloured feathers waving in the breeze, a short silk jacket, whose colour has returned to the primal nothingness, over it a fairly decent shawl, her yellow calico dress, embroidered with flowers round the edge, reaches to her ankles, bluish-grey stockings, laced boots. Following her, a fine-looking maid with two shopping-baskets, a fish-net, a meal-bag. God help us! What furious glances the person in silk is casting all around, how furiously she forces her way into the thickest clusters of people—how she grabs everything, vegetables, fruit, meat, and so forth; how she looks at everything, feels it, haggles over it, and yet never buys anything.

MY COUSIN. This person never misses a single market-day, and I call her 'the rabid housewife'. I suspect that she must be the daughter of a wealthy townsman, perhaps a well-to-do soap-boiler, and that some minor privy secretary, not without difficulty, gained her hand, and all that appertains thereto. Heaven did not endow her with beauty or grace, but all her neighbours considered her the best home manager of any girl they knew, and she is indeed a good manager: she manages to make her husband's life, from dawn till dusk, such a misery that he doesn't know whether he's standing on his head or his heels, and wishes he were at Jericho. The entire register of which drums and trumpets are capable is constantly in use for purchases, orders, petty commerce, and the manifold needs of the household, and so the privy secretary's domestic life resembles a watch-case in which the watch, having been wound up, perpetually plays a wild symphony composed by the Devil himself. On every fourth market-day or so she is accompanied by a different maid.

'*Sapienti sat*!* Do you see. . . ? But no, no! The group that has just formed deserves to be immortalized by the pencil of a Hogarth.* Just look, cousin, into the third doorway of the theatre!

ME. A couple of old women sitting on low chairs, with all their odds and ends displayed in a fair-sized basket in front of them: one is selling brightly coloured cloths, mere fal-lals, calculated to dazzle stupid people's eyes, the other has a vast store of blue and grey stockings, wool, and so on. They are bending towards each other and whispering in each other's ears. One is enjoying a cup of coffee; the other, completely absorbed in the subject of the conversation, seems to have forgotten about the glass of schnapps which she was about to swallow; indeed, a couple of striking physiognomies! What a demonic smile! What gesticulations with their withered bony arms!

MY COUSIN. These two women always sit together, and although they are selling different things and should therefore have no conflict or commercial rivalry, until today they have always cast hostile glances at each other, and, if I may trust my skill in reading physiognomies, thrown sundry invectives at each other. Oh, look, look, cousin! They are becoming more like bosom friends by the minute! The cloth-seller is giving the stocking-dealer a cup of coffee. What can that signify? I know! A few minutes ago a young girl came up to the basket, attracted by the fal-lals; she was sixteen at most, as beautiful as the day, and her whole appearance and behaviour revealed her moral propriety and her shamefaced poverty. She had her eye on a piece of white cloth with a coloured border, and was perhaps sorely in need of it. She haggled over it, and the old woman used all her mercantile craft, spreading the cloth out and letting the garish colours shine in the sun. They reached an agreement, but when the poor girl took her few coins from the corner of her handkerchief, there was not enough for such an expense. The girl, her cheeks burning and her eyes glistening with tears, made off as quickly as she could, while the old woman gave a mocking laugh as she folded up the cloth and threw it back in her basket. I dare say a few pleasant remarks were uttered. But the other she-devil knows the girl, and was able to serve up the sad story of a family reduced to poverty as a scandalous chronicle of irresponsibility and possibly even crime, to delight the heart of the disappointed vendor. The cup of coffee was doubtless the reward for some coarse and brazen piece of defamation.

ME. It may be, dear cousin, that not one word of all your conjectures is true, but as I look at the old women your vivid description sounds so plausible that I am compelled to believe it, willy-nilly.

MY COUSIN. Before we leave the wall of the theatre, let us cast a glance at the fat, good-humoured woman with cheeks bursting with health who is sitting in Stoic calm and composure on a cane chair with her hands concealed under her white apron; she has spread out in front of her, on white cloths, a vast quantity of brightly polished spoons, knives, and forks, Faience crockery, china plates and dishes of old-fashioned shape, tea-cups, coffee-pots, hosiery, and what not, so that her goods, probably clawed together at petty auctions, form a veritable *Orbis pictus*.* She listens impassively to the offers made by hagglers, unconcerned whether or not they reach an agreement; she strikes a bargain and extends one hand from beneath her apron, simply to receive the money from the purchaser, who is allowed to remove the goods himself. She is a calm, prudent trader who will make her pile. Four weeks ago, all her goods consisted in half-a-dozen or so fine cotton stockings, and the same number of drinking glasses. Her trade increases with every market, and as she never brings a better chair and still keeps her hands concealed under her apron, she evidently possesses a stable character and is not being led into pride and conceit by her good fortune. Now, what put this bizarre notion into my head! I've just imagined a mischievous little imp, like the one who crawls under the pious woman's chair in the engraving by Hogarth,* creeping under this market-woman's chair because he envies her good fortune and maliciously sawing away the legs of her chair. Plop! down she tumbles among her glass and china, and her business is in smithereens. That would be a commercial crash in the most literal sense.

ME. Truly, dear cousin, you have already taught me to see better.

As my gaze roams amid the colourful, surging throng, I keep noticing young girls who wander through the market in the company of neatly dressed cooks carrying large and gleaming shopping-baskets, and haggle over such household necessities as the market affords. The girls' modest attire and respectable bearing proves that they come at least from good middle-class homes. What are they doing in the market?

MY COUSIN. That's easily explained. For some years past it's been customary for even the daughters of higher officials of state to be sent to the market to gain practical experience of that part of housekeeping which concerns the purchase of food.

ME. Indeed, a laudable custom, which must not only be of practical use but inculcate a housewifely state of mind.

MY COUSIN. Do you think so, cousin? I for my part think the opposite. What can be the point of doing one's own shopping, unless to convince oneself of the quality of the goods and the real market prices? There are other ways in which the young housewife can easily learn the qualities, the look, and the characteristics of good vegetables, a good piece of meat, and so on. It doesn't prevent the servant from taking a few pence for herself, since she has no difficulty in arriving at a secret understanding with the vendors; and even if it did, that wouldn't outweigh the disadvantages which can easily arise from a girl's visiting the market. I would never, just to save a few pence, expose my daughter to the danger of mingling with the dregs of the people and hearing a smutty joke or having to put up with some vulgar talk from an abandoned woman or a brutal fellow. And then, when it comes to the speculations of lovelorn, blue-coated youths on horseback, or on foot wearing yellow pea-jackets with black collars, the market is . . . But look, look, cousin! how do you like the girl who is just walking past the pump, accompanied by an elderly cook? Take my field-glasses, cousin!

ME. Ha, what a rare creature, how charming and adorable! But her eyes are modestly downcast, her every step is timorous and uncertain, she clings shyly to her companion, who is clearing a path into the crowd by forcing an assault. I'm following them. There's the cook standing by the baskets of vegetables. She's haggling. The girl, in response to a summons, half averts her eyes and in great haste takes some money out of her purse and hands it over, glad to get away. I can't lose sight of her, thanks to her red shawl. They seem to be searching vainly for something . . . At last, at last, they are lingering with a woman who is offering fine vegetables in dainty baskets. The lovely girl's attention is absorbed by a basket of beautiful cauliflowers. The girl herself chooses a cauliflower and puts it in the cook's basket . . . What, the bold hussy! She takes the cauliflower straight out of the basket, puts it back in the seller's basket, and chooses another, while the violent agitation of her heavy bonneted head indicates that she is showering reproaches on the poor girl, who wanted to make her own decision for the first time.

MY COUSIN. Just imagine that girl's feelings when forced to engage in household tasks which are repugnant to her delicacy. I know the lovely girl; she is the daughter of a Privy Financial Counsellor, a thoroughly natural person devoid of any affectation, truly feminine, and endowed with the infallible judgement and sensitive tact that such women always possess . . . Ho, ho, cousin! that's what I call a happy coincidence. Her antithesis is just coming round the corner. How do you like *this* girl, cousin?

ME. Why, what a slender, dainty figure! Young, stepping lightly, and facing the world with a bold and unabashed look: someone for whom the sun is always shining and the air is always filled with merry music. With what an audacious, carefree air she trips towards the crowd! The maidservant following her with the shopping-basket seems no older than she, and there is a certain cordiality linking the two. The young lady is dressed in very pretty things, her shawl is in the latest fashion. Her hat matches her morning costume, her dress has a tasteful pattern. Everything about her is pretty and decent . . . Oh dear! What do I see? The young lady is wearing white silk shoes. Cast-off dancing-pumps in the market! Indeed, the more I look at this girl, the more I notice something peculiar which I cannot put into words. She certainly seems to be doing her shopping with care and diligence: she always chooses and haggles, she speaks and gesticulates with a vivacity that comes close to excitement; but I have the feeling that she wants to buy something else besides her household needs.

MY COUSIN. Bravo, bravo, cousin! Your eyes are getting sharper, I see. Just look, my dear fellow: despite her modest dress, and leaving aside the lightness and frivolity of everything about her, the fact that she is wearing white silk shoes to market ought to have told you that the young lady belongs to the ballet, or some other branch of the theatre. As for the other things she's looking for, I expect we'll soon find out—yes, right enough! Look up the street, dear cousin, a little to the right, and tell me whom you see on the pavement outside the hotel, where there are not many people about?

ME. I see a tall, slim youth in a short yellow pea-jacket with a black collar and steel buttons. He is wearing a small red cap with silver embroidery, under which his fine dark curls spill forth almost too luxuriantly. The expression of his handsome, pale, thoroughly masculine face is considerably heightened by the little black moustache on his upper lip. He has a brief-case under his arm and is obviously a student on his way to a lecture, but he is standing rooted to the spot, looking fixedly towards the market, and seems to have forgotten the lecture and everything around him.

MY COUSIN. That's right, dear cousin. All his thoughts are directed towards our little *comédienne*. The appointed time has come; he is approaching the big fruit stall, where the most attractive goods are piled up in an appetizing display, and seems to be asking for fruit that is not available at present. No proper lunch can possibly be complete without a fruit dessert, so our little *comédienne* must finish her shopping for the table at the fruit stall. A round apple with ruddy cheeks slips mischievously out of her little fingers! The man in the yellow jacket bends down and picks it up, a dainty little curtsey from the little fairy of the theatre, their conversation is under way. They help and advise each other in the difficult task of choosing oranges, thus consolidating an acquaintance which they have doubtless already formed, and enjoying a delightful rendezvous which is sure to be repeated and varied in countless ways.

ME. Let the son of the Muses flirt and choose oranges, as much
as he pleases; that does not interest me, especially as the
angelic child, the charming daughter of the Privy Counsellor,
has caught my eye again at the corner of the theatre, where
the flower-sellers are offering their wares.

MY COUSIN. I don't like looking at the flowers there, cousin,
and thereby hangs a tale. The vendor who usually displays
the most beautiful array of select carnations, roses, and other
rarer blooms, is a very nice, pretty girl, striving to cultivate
her mind; for whenever she is not occupied by trading, she
diligently reads books whose uniform shows that they belong
to Kralowski's* great literary army, which is victoriously
spreading the light of intellectual culture into the remotest
corners of our capital. A flower-girl who reads books is an
irresistible sight for an author of fiction. It so happened that
long ago, when my way took me past the flowers (they are
displayed for sale on other days besides market-day), I noticed the flower-girl reading and stopped in surprise. She
seemed to be seated in a thick bower of blooming geraniums,
and had her book open on her lap, with her chin propped on
her hand. The hero must have been in deadly danger, or some
other crisis in the plot must have been reached, for the girl's
cheeks were flushed, her lips were quivering, and she seemed
miles away from her surroundings. Cousin, let me quite un-
reservedly confess to you the strange weakness of a literary
man. I was unable to leave the spot, where I shifted nervously
from one foot to the other, wondering what the girl was
reading. This thought absorbed my entire mind. The spirit
of literary vanity awoke and tickled me with the notion that
it might be one of my own works which had transported the
girl into the fantastic world of my dreams. Finally I plucked
up courage, walked over to her, and asked the price of a bunch
of carnations standing in a distant row. While the girl was
fetching the carnations, I said: 'What are you reading, my
pretty child?' and picked up the book which she had hastily
clapped shut. O ye gods! It was indeed one of my works,
namely ****. The girl brought the flowers and told me their
very reasonable price. Flowers? Carnations? At that moment
the girl represented a far more estimable public than the

entire elegant world of our capital. Excited and inflamed by the sweetest feelings an author can have, I asked with feigned indifference how the girl liked the book.

'Well, sir,' replied the girl, 'it's a very funny kind of book. At first it makes your head spin a bit; but then you feel as if you were right in the middle of it.'

To my considerable astonishment the girl recounted the plot of the little fairy-tale quite clearly and distinctly, so that I perceived that she must have read it several times; she repeated that it was a very funny kind of book, and said that at times it had made her laugh heartily, and at other times she had felt like crying; and she advised me, in case I had not yet read the book, to collect it from Mr Kralowski one afternoon, for it was in the afternoons that she changed her books. I now prepared to deliver my master-stroke. With downcast eyes, in a voice that rivalled the honey of Hybla for sweetness, I lisped: 'Here, my angel, is the author of the book which has given you such pleasure, standing in front of you as large as life.'

The girl stared at me, speechless, wide-eyed and open-mouthed. I took this for the expression of extreme admiration, indeed of joyous terror that the sublime genius whose creative power had produced such a work should have appeared so suddenly among the geraniums. As the girl's countenance remained unaltered, I thought: 'Perhaps she simply can't believe that a fortunate coincidence should have brought the celebrated author of **** so close to her.' I tried every possible way of explaining that I was identical with that author, but she seemed petrified, and nothing escaped her lips except 'Hm—oh—well—why . . .'. But why should I spend a long time describing the deep humiliation that I incurred at that moment? Apparently it had never entered the girl's head that the books she read must first have been composed. She had no idea that such things as writers or authors existed, and I verily think that closer enquiry would have elicited from her the pious, child-like belief that God made books grow, like mushrooms.

In a subdued voice I asked once more how much the carnations cost. In the mean time, another obscure notion about the production of books must have formed in the girl's mind; for as I was counting out the money, she asked quite frankly and naïvely whether I made *all* Mr Kralowski's books? Seizing my carnations, I rushed off like lightning.

ME. Cousin, cousin, that's what I call fit punishment for an author's vanity; but while you were telling me your tragic story, I kept my eye fixed on my little darling. Only when she was buying flowers did the impudent demon of the kitchen grant her complete freedom. The surly kitchen governess put the heavy shopping-basket on the ground and devoted herself to the indescribable joy of conversation with three colleagues. At times she crossed her plump arms, at other times, when the external rhetorical expression of her speech seemed to demand it, she placed her arms akimbo; and, contrary to the Bible, her speech was certainly much more than yea and nay. Just look what a magnificent array of flowers the lovely angel has chosen; she has given it to a burly lad to carry. What's this? No, I don't quite like the way she eats cherries from her little basket as she walks along; will the fine cambric cloth which the basket probably contains survive contact with the fruit?

MY COUSIN. An impulsive youthful appetite doesn't bother about the stains made by cherry-juice, which can be dealt with by salt of sorrel or some such well-tried preparation. And it shows a truly child-like absence of affectation that she should indulge herself like that as soon as she has regained her freedom from the tribulations of the wicked market. But I've had my eye for some time now on an extremely puzzling figure: the man standing by the second, more distant pump, beside the cart on which a peasant woman is dispensing plum jam from a large barrel. First of all, dear cousin, do admire the woman's dexterity. Armed with a long wooden spoon, she first deals with the major purchases of quarter-pounds, half-pounds and whole pounds of jam, and then with lightning speed she throws a threepenny dollop to each of the greedy sweet-lovers who are holding out paper bags and sometimes even their fur caps to receive the jam, which they promptly devour with great enjoyment as a superior snack—the people's caviar! As I watch her dispensing the jam so skilfully by brandishing her spoon, I recall hearing in my childhood about a rich peasant's wedding conducted in such splendour that a delicious rice-pudding, coated with a thick crust of cinnamon, sugar, and cloves, was dispensed by means of a threshing-flail. Each of the honoured guests had only to open his mouth cheerfully to receive his portion, and so it was just like the Land of Cockayne. But, cousin, have you got your eye fixed on this man?

ME. Certainly! What sort of person can this strange, extraordinary figure possibly be? A gaunt man, at least six feet tall, and as straight as a ramrod, indeed bending backwards! From under his three-cornered, squashed-looking little hat there sticks out the cockade attached to a bag-wig, which then spreads out and nestles against his back. His grey coat, cut according to the fashions of yesteryear, is buttoned up from top to bottom and clings close to his body, without a single crease, and when he was walking over to the cart I noticed that he was wearing black breeches, black stockings, and immense tin buckles on his shoes. Whatever has he got in the rectangular box which he is carrying so carefully under his left arm? It almost resembles the box that a pedlar carries round his neck.

MY COUSIN. You'll soon find out; just watch him attentively.

ME. He's opening the lid of the box. The sun shines in, radiant reflections . . . The box is lined with metal. He is lifting his hat and making an almost reverent bow to the woman selling plum jam. What an original, expressive face: narrow lips, an aquiline nose, big dark eyes, a high forehead, black hair, his wig dressed *en cœur*, with stiff little curls above his ears. He's giving the box to the woman on the cart; she immediately fills it with plum jam, and hands it back to him with a friendly nod. The man takes his leave with a second bow. He winds his way past a keg of herring. He pulls out a drawer from the box, puts in some salted almonds which he has purchased, and closes it again. A third drawer, I see, is intended for parsley and other vegetables. He now walks to and fro across the market-place with long, dignified strides, until he stops in front of a table richly spread with plucked poultry. Here, as always, he makes several deep bows before beginning to haggle. He talks volubly and at length to the woman, who listens with a particularly friendly expression. He puts the box cautiously down on the ground and seizes two ducks, which he stuffs quite comfortably into the capacious pocket of his coat. Heavens! they're followed by a goose! As for the turkey, he only casts yearning glances at it, but he can't refrain from caressing it with his second and third fingers; he quickly lifts his box, bows to the woman in a most obliging manner, tears himself forcibly away from the tempting object of his desires, and strides away! He is heading straight for the butchers' stands. Is he a cook who has to prepare a banquet? He purchases a haunch of veal and slips it into another of his gigantic pockets. Now he has finished his shopping; he goes up the Charlottenstrasse with such a peculiar air of solemnity that he seems to have been wafted here from some foreign country.

MY COUSIN. I've already spent plenty of time racking my brains over this exotic figure. What do you think, cousin, of my hypothesis? The man is an old drawing-master who has pursued his career, and perhaps still does, in schools of middling quality. Thanks to various industrious enterprises, he has accumulated a lot of money; he is miserly, mistrustful, a hateful cynic, a selfish bachelor; his burnt offerings are reserved for one god—his belly; his sole pleasure is good eating, all alone in his room, of course; he has no servants, but attends to everything himself. On market-days, as you saw, he buys provisions for half the week; he prepares his own food in a little kitchen next door to his miserable room, and since the cook always pleases the master's palate, he devours it with a greedy, perhaps a bestial appetite. You also noticed, dear cousin, the practical skill with which he has turned an old box of paints into a shopping-basket.

ME. That's enough about this disgusting person.

MY COUSIN. Why disgusting? A man who knows the world tells us that 'such odd fish are necessary too',* and he is right, for there can never be enough colour and variety. But if you dislike the man so much, dear cousin, I can propose another hypothesis about what he is and does. Four Frenchmen, all of them Parisians—a language-teacher, a fencing-master, a dancing-master, and a pastry-cook—arrived in Berlin simultaneously as young men, and made a good living, as they could hardly help doing then (that is, towards the end of the last century). From the moment when the carriage brought them together on their journey they formed a close friendship and were familiar cronies. After finishing their work, they spent every evening together, like true old Frenchmen, in lively conversation over a frugal supper. The dancing-master's legs had lost their agility, the fencing-master's arms were enfeebled by age, the language-teacher had lost his pupils to rivals who claimed to know the latest Parisian dialect, and the crafty inventions of the pastry-cook had been surpassed by young culinary artists who had been trained by the most individual gastronomes in Paris.

ME. This invention does credit to your literary talents, dear cousin. For the last few minutes, however, I have been gazing at those lofty white plumes rising from the densest part of the crowd. At last the figure of their owner is emerging, just beside the pump: a tall, slim woman, not at all bad-looking. Her coat of heavy pink silk is brand new. Her hat is in the latest fashion, the veil attached to it is of fine lace, she has white kid gloves. What compelled this elegant lady, who is probably invited to lunch somewhere, to force her way through the throng of the market-place? But what's this? Is she out shopping as well? She is standing still and beckoning to a dirty, ragged old woman, a living image of the miserable dregs of the populace, who is laboriously hobbling after her with a broken shopping-basket in one hand. The well-dressed lady is beckoning at the corner of the theatre, in order to give alms to the blind militiaman who is propped against the wall there. She pulls the glove off her right hand with some effort. Good heavens! a blood-red fist appears with a decidedly masculine appearance. But, without spending much time over her choice, she hastily presses a coin into the blind man's hand, runs into the middle of the Charlottenstrasse, and then adopts the majestic gait of somebody making a promenade. In this manner she saunters up the Charlottenstrasse towards Unter den Linden, paying no further heed to her ragged companion.

MY COUSIN. The old woman has put her basket on the ground in order to have a rest, and you can survey all the elegant lady's purchases at one glance.

ME. They are strange enough, in all conscience. A cabbage, a lot of potatoes, a few apples, a small loaf, some herrings wrapped in paper, a sheep's-milk cheese, not of the most appetizing colour, a sheep's liver, a small bunch of roses, a pair of slippers, a boot-tree. What in the name of goodness . . .

MY COUSIN. Hush, cousin, that's enough about the lady in pink! Take a careful look at the blind man who was given alms by the thoughtless child of corruption. Could there be a more touching image of undeserved human misery and pious resignation to the will of God and fate? Propped against the wall of the theatre, with his wizened, bony hands supported on a staff which he has pushed one pace forward so that the mindless crowd shall not tread on his toes, with his pallid countenance raised and his militia cap pulled down over his eyes, he stands motionless on the same spot from early morning until the market closes.

ME. He is begging, and yet such good provision is made for blind soldiers.

MY COUSIN. You couldn't be more wrong, dear cousin. This poor man is the slave of a woman who sells vegetables and who belongs to the lower class of vegetable-sellers, since the superior class have their goods transported in baskets loaded on carts. Every morning, you see, this blind man arrives laden with baskets full of vegetables, like a beast of burden, almost sinking under his load, and managing with great difficulty to remain upright by using his staff to help him stagger along. When his strength is almost completely exhausted, the big, robust woman whose servant he is (unless she just uses him to bring the produce to market), hardly bothers even to take him by the arm and help him on to his resting-place, the spot he occupies at present. Here she takes the baskets from his back and carries them to her stall herself, and then leaves him standing there without troubling about him in the slightest until the market closes and she loads the baskets, now empty or partially so, on to his back once more.

ME. It is curious that one can always recognize a blind person, even if his eyes are not closed or if there is no other visible defect to betray the absence of eyesight, by the upright posture of the head which is characteristic of the blind; it seems to imply a perpetual effort to discern something in the night which envelops the blind man.

MY COUSIN. For me there is no more moving spectacle than such a blind man who, with his head erect, seems to be gazing into the far distance. Life's sun has set for the poor fellow, but his inner eye is already striving to glimpse the everlasting radiance that lights his way into a hereafter full of comfort, hope, and joy. But I am growing too serious. Every marketday the blind militiaman provides me with a treasure trove of observations. You perceive, dear cousin, how this poor man brings out the generosity of the people of Berlin. Often whole lines of people walk past him, and not one of them fails to give him alms. But what matters is the way in which the alms are handed over. Watch for a while, dear cousin, and tell me what you perceive.

ME. Three or four fine-looking, sturdy maidservants are just coming past; their baskets, piled high with heavy goods, seem almost to be making scars and bruises on their muscular arms; they have good reason to hurry in order to get rid of their burdens, and yet each of them pauses for a moment, hastily puts her hand in her shopping-basket, and, without even looking at the blind man, presses a coin into his hand. This will appear as a necessary and unavoidable expenditure on the budget for market-day. Quite right!

'Here comes a woman whose outfit and whose whole appearance clearly reveal her comfort and prosperity. She stops in front of the invalid, pulls out her purse, but cannot find a coin that seems small enough for the act of charity she intends to perform. She calls to her cook. It turns out that the latter has also run out of small change. She must first ask the vegetable-women for change. At last they have obtained the threepenny bit which is to be given away. She taps the blind man's hand to make sure he knows he is going to receive something. He holds out the palm of his hand: the charitable lady presses the coin into his palm and closes his fist for him so that the magnificent gift shall not get lost.

'Why is the dainty young lady skipping to and fro and gradually coming closer to the blind man? Ha! as she hurries past, she slips a coin into the blind man's hand, so quickly that nobody can have noticed it except me, since I happen to have my glasses focused on her. That was certainly more than a threepenny bit.

'The sleek, well-fed man in the brown coat who is marching along so cheerfully must be a very wealthy townsman. He too stops in front of the blind man and engages him in a lengthy conversation, while blocking other people's way and preventing them from giving the blind man any alms; at long last he draws a fat green purse from his pocket, undoes its buttons, not without difficulty, and rummages in his money so dreadfully that I fancy I can hear it chinking from here. *Parturiunt montes*!* But I am disposed to believe that the noble-hearted friend of humanity, carried away by the sight of misery, deigned to dispense a simple penny. Despite all this, I suspect that on market-days the blind man makes a considerable income, by his own standards, and I'm surprised that he takes everything without the least sign of gratitude; I think I can make out a slight movement of his lips which alone shows that he says something that is presumably thanks—but I perceive even this movement only occasionally.

MY COUSIN. There you have the definite expression of complete and final resignation. What is money to him? He can make no use of it; only in the hands of another person, in whom he must place unreserved trust, does it acquire any value. I may be quite wrong, but I think the woman whose baskets he carries is an abominable shrew who treats the poor fellow badly, even though she probably confiscates all the money he receives. Every time she brings back the baskets she gives the blind man a tongue-lashing, and its gravity depends on how well or badly she has fared in the market. The blind man's pallid face, his half-starved figure, his ragged clothing, are enough to suggest that his situation is an unpleasant one, and an active friend of humanity ought to look into it more closely.

ME. As I survey the entire market-place I notice that the reason why the covered flour-wagons over there look so picturesque is that they afford a resting-place for the eye, around which the colourful throng falls into distinct groups.

MY COUSIN. I know something which is the exact antithesis of the white flour-wagons and the dusty miller's boys and the rosy-cheeked miller-girls, each of them a *bella molinara*.* For I sorely regret the absence of a family of charcoal-burners who used to offer their wares just opposite my window and have now, I hear, been assigned a place on the other side. This family consists of a big, robust man with an expressive face and strongly marked features, vigorous and almost violent in his movements—in short, a faithful copy of the charcoal-burners who appear in novels. Indeed, if I met this man in a lonely forest, I would tremble somewhat, and at such a moment his friendly disposition would please me better than anything else in the world. There is a strange contrast between this man and the second member of his family, a strangely misshapen fellow, scarcely four feet tall, who is extremely comical. You know, dear cousin, that there are some very strangely built people: at the first glance one recognizes them as deformed, and yet on closer inspection one cannot say where the deformity lies.

ME. This reminds me of the naïve remark by a witty soldier who had many dealings with one of these freaks of nature and was annoyed by his inability to explain why the man was so oddly built. 'That man has a hump,' he said, 'but where his hump is, the Devil only knows!'

MY COUSIN. Nature originally intended to make my little charcoal-burner into a gigantic figure about seven feet tall, as is shown by his colossal hands and feet, which are almost the biggest I have ever seen. This little fellow, dressed in a short coat with a high collar and with a funny-looking fur cap on his head, is in a perpetual flurry of movement; he hops and skips to and fro with rather unattractive agility, turning up now here, now there, and he does his best to play the gallant, the ladies' man, the *primo amoroso* of the market-place. He never lets a woman go past, unless she belongs to the upper ranks of society, without skipping after her, and, with inimitable postures, gestures, and grimaces, uttering sweet nothings which, I dare say, suit the taste of the charcoal-

burners. At times he takes his gallantry so far that in conversation with a girl he will slip his arm gently round her waist
and pay homage to her beauty, cap in hand, or offer her his
service as her true knight. It is remarkable that the girls not
only put up with all this but also nod to the little monster
in a friendly manner and seem in general to enjoy his gallan-
tries. The little fellow is unquestionably endowed with a
plentiful dose of natural mother-wit, a decided talent for
clowning, and the energy to put his talent to use. He is the
harlequin, the dashing hero, the life and soul of every party
in the district that includes the forest where he lives; he is
indispensable at every christening, wedding banquet, dance,
or drinking-party; people look forward to his jests, and recall
them mirthfully for a whole year afterwards. The rest of the
family consists, as the children and maids are left at home,
only of two women of robust stature and a dark and surly
appearance, heightened, of course, by the coal-dust lodged in
the wrinkles of their faces. From the tender devotion of a big
Pomeranian, with which the family share every bite of food
they take on market-day, I gather that life in the charcoal-
burners' hut must have all the honest, old-fashioned virtues.
What is more, the little chap possesses gigantic strength, and
therefore his family uses him to deliver sacks of coal to the
customers' houses. I have often seen him being loaded by the
women with as many as ten big baskets, piled on top of one
another on his back, and he skipped off with them as though
unaware of carrying any burden. From behind he looked like
the strangest and most extraordinary figure you could possibly see. Naturally the esteemed figure of the little chap
himself was completely lost to sight: one could see only a
monstrous sack of coals with a pair of feet growing out of it.
It was as though a fabulous animal, a fantastic kind of kan-
garoo, were hopping across the market-place.

ME. Look, cousin, there is a commotion starting over there
beside the church. Two vegetable-women have probably got
into a violent dispute over the vexed question of *meum* and
tuum,* and, with their arms akimbo, seem to be treating each
other to some choice expressions. The crowd is flocking to
them. A dense circle surrounds the two quarrelling women.

Their voices are growing louder and shriller by the minute. They are waving their fists more and more fiercely. They are approaching each other more and more closely. We shall have fisticuffs any moment. The police are clearing a path. What's this? Suddenly I spy a crowd of shiny hats between the two angry women, the old crones instantly manage to quieten the infuriated pair. The dispute is over, without the aid of the police. The women return quietly to their vegetable-baskets and the crowd disperses, having indicated its approval by loud cheers only once or twice, presumably at especially ferocious moments in the dispute.

MY COUSIN. You observe, dear cousin, that during the entire length of time we have been here at the window that was the only quarrel to flare up in the market-place, and that it was dealt with solely by the crowd. Even a more serious and threatening quarrel is commonly curbed by the crowd, which squeezes between the combatants and separates them. Last market-day there was a big, ragged fellow, insolent and savage in his appearance, who was standing between the meat-stalls and the fruit-stalls, and suddenly got into a quarrel with a passing butcher's boy; without more ado he aimed a blow at the boy with the hideous cudgel which he was carrying over his shoulder like a rifle, and would probably have laid the boy out cold if the latter had not adroitly dodged it and leapt into his stall. There he armed himself with a huge butcher's axe and was all ready to attack the big fellow. All the signs pointed to a murderous end which would call the criminal court into play. However, the fruit-sellers, all powerful and well-fed women, felt obliged to enfold the butcher's boy in such loving and tight embraces that he could not move from the spot; he stood there with his weapon raised aloft, like the rugged Pyrrhus* in that rhetorical speech:

> So, as a painted tyrant, Pyrrhus stood,
> And, like a neutral to his will and matter,
> Did nothing.

In the mean time other women, brush-makers, shoe-tree sellers, and so on, had surrounded the big fellow and thus

given the police time to arrive on the scene and seize him;
apparently he was a convict recently released from gaol.

ME. So the populace does indeed have a sense that order must
be maintained? This instinct must have the most salutary
effects for all concerned.

MY COUSIN. In general, dear cousin, my observations on the
market-place have confirmed my opinion that the Berlin
populace has undergone a remarkable change since that unfortunate period when an insolent and overbearing enemy
inundated our country and laboured in vain to suppress the
popular spirit, which soon rebounded with new strength, like
a spring that has been forcibly depressed. In a word: their
behaviour has become more polished; and if you take the
trouble, one sunny summer afternoon, to go to the tents and
watch the groups of people embarking on boats bound for
Moabit,* you will notice even ordinary servant-maids and
day-labourers striving to attain a certain courtesy, which is a
pleasure to behold. The mass of the people has undergone the
same experience as an individual who has seen many new and
unaccustomed things and, along with the principle of *Nil
admirari*, has acquired smoother manners. The common
people of Berlin used to be rough and brutal; a stranger could
scarcely ask his way to a street or a house, or anything else,
without receiving a coarse or mocking reply, or being deliberately misinformed as a joke. There is no longer any such
creature as the Berlin guttersnipe who used to exploit the
slightest occasion, such as somebody's unusual attire or a
ridiculous accident, for the most outrageous and revolting
offences. For these boys beside the gate, selling the cigars
called 'The Jolly Fellow from Hamburg *avec du feu*', these
limbs of Satan who will end their lives in Spandau or Strauss-
berg, or on the scaffold as one of their race did recently, are
quite different from the true Berlin guttersnipe. The latter
was not a vagabond, but usually apprenticed to a master, and,
ridiculous though it sounds, despite all his godlessness and
depravity he did have a certain code of honour, besides being
well supplied with very amusing native wit.

ME. Oh, dear cousin, let me tell you quickly how the biting
wit of the common people put me to shame not long ago. I

was walking out of the Brandenburg Gate and was followed
by carters from Charlottenburg who offered me a lift; one of
them, a boy of sixteen or seventeen at most, took his im-
pudence so far as to grab me by the arm with his dirty fingers.
'Don't touch me, you ruffian' I snapped. 'Why, sir,' answered
the boy calmly, goggling at me with his big blank eyes, 'why
shouldn't I touch you? Aren't you honest?'

MY COUSIN. Ha, ha! That's a real joke, but it comes from the
foul pit of the deepest depravity. The jokes of Berlin fruit-
sellers and such-like used to be famous all the world over,
and were even honoured by being called Shakespearean, although on closer inspection their energy and originality consisted mainly in the shameless impertinence with which they
served up the vilest filth as a savoury dish. The market used
to be the scene of quarrels, beatings-up, deceit, theft, and no
honest woman could venture to do her own shopping without
exposing herself to grievous injury. For not only did the
hawkers wage war on each other and on everybody else, but
some people were expressly intent on stirring up unrest in
order to fish in murky waters, like the riff-raff from every
hole and corner that used to serve in the regiments. You see,
dear cousin, how nowadays, by contrast, the market offers a
delightful picture of prosperity and peaceful manners. I know
that this improvement in the outward decency of our common people is furiously denounced by perfervid zealots* and
super-patriotic ascetics, who think that such polishing di-
vests them of their popular character. I for my part am firmly
and sincerely convinced that a populace that treats both fellow-
countrymen and foreigners, not with rudeness or mocking
contempt, but with polite manners, can never thereby lose
its character. I could cite a most telling example which would
demonstrate the truth of my assertion and put me in very bad
odour with the aforesaid zealots.

All the while, the throng had kept growing thinner and the
market emptier. The vegetable-women packed some of their
baskets on newly arrived carts and carried the rest away themselves; the flour-wagons departed; the garden-women removed
the remaining supply of flowers on large wheelbarrows; the

police showed themselves more active in maintaining the proper order, especially in the line of carts; nor would this order have been disturbed if the occasional schismatic country boy had not taken it into his head to steer boldly across the market-place in order to discover and explore his very own Bering Straits, running boldly through the fruit-stalls and straight towards the door of the Lutheran church. This gave rise to a considerable hubbub and boded ill for the too gifted charioteer.

'This market', said my cousin, 'is still a true picture of ever-changing life. Bustling activity and momentary needs brought the mass of people together; within a few minutes all is deserted, the voices that mingled in a bewildering tumult have died away, and every abandoned spot utters only too audibly the dread message "There *used to be* . . ."'.

A clock struck, the surly ex-soldier entered the room, and, screwing up his face, urged his employer to leave the window and eat before the dishes got cold.

'So you have some appetite, dear cousin?' I asked.

'Oh yes,' replied my cousin with a painful smile, 'you'll soon see.'

The ex-soldier wheeled him into the main room. The dishes were a soup-plate half-full of broth, a soft-boiled egg placed upright in salt, and half a roll.

'A single bite beyond this,' said my cousin in a low and melancholy voice, pressing my hand, 'the slightest scrap of even the most digestible meat, causes me frightful pains, and robs me of all my spirits and of the last spark of good humour that still occasionally tries to glimmer faintly.'

Falling into my cousin's arms and embracing him warmly, I pointed to the sheet of paper attached to the screen beside the bed.

'Yes, cousin!' he exclaimed in a voice that pierced me to the core and filled me with heart-rending sorrow,

'Et si male nunc, non olim sic erit!'

My poor cousin!

EXPLANATORY NOTES

The Golden Pot

2 *Linke's Restaurant*: an open-air restaurant and garden, extremely popular with fashionable circles in Dresden. Kosel's Garden and Anton's Garden were similar establishments.

3 *King in the Twelfth-Night revels*: on Twelfth Night or Epiphany (6 January) it was customary to serve cakes, one of which contained a bean; whoever found a bean in his cake was King for the evening and received mock homage.

duffer: *Kümmeltürke*, a student whose home is in or near the town where he studies. Such a person was looked down upon at a time when German students normally studied at several universities remote from their homes.

4 *The Woman from the Danube: Das Donauweibchen*, an opera by Ferdinand Kauer (1751–1831), first performed in 1799, and based on a very popular Viennese play by Karl Friedrich Hensler (1759–1825).

11 *leeches*: Friedrich Nicolai (1733–1811), a bookseller and writer prominent in the Berlin Enlightenment, seriously claimed, in a lecture published in 1799, to have cured himself of hallucinations by applying leeches to his bottom. Goethe ridiculed him for this in *Faust*, Part I, ll. 4172–5.

Graun: Karl Friedrich Graun (1703–59), a noted composer; on the accession of Friedrich II of Prussia in 1740 he was appointed court conductor.

50 *the Masters of Bhagavadgita*: the *Bhagavadgita* is a didactic poem which forms part of the Sanskrit epic *Mahabharata*; Hoffmann found the name in Friedrich Schlegel's *Über die Sprache und Weisheit der Inder* ('On the Language and Wisdom of the Indians', 1808).

64 *imagined he was a grain of barley*: a case reported by the Swiss doctor Johann Georg Zimmermann in his widely read *Über die Einsamkeit* ('On Solitude', 1784–5).

68 *Cross school*: the Kreuzschule, the leading school in Dresden; some of the boys formed a choir, hence the reference to Italian choruses.

74 *Sunday's Child—Sisters of Prague (Das Sonntagskind, Die Schwestern*

von Prag): two comic operas by Wenzel Müller (1767–1835), conductor of the Leopoldstadt Theatre in Vienna. They were first performed in 1793 and 1794. Hoffmann refers to them admiringly in his dialogue *Der Dichter und der Komponist* ('The Poet and the Composer', 1813).

80 *Gabalis*: see Introduction.

Swedenborg: Emanuel Swedenborg (1688–1772), Swedish philosopher and mystic, who claimed to have visions and converse with spirits.

The Sandman

86 *Franz Moor begged Daniel*: in Act 5, Scene 1 of Schiller's *Die Räuber* ('The Robbers', 1781) the villain, Franz Moor, has a terrible dream about the Last Judgement, and vainly urges his pious old servant Daniel to mock him for it.

88 *Coppelius*: cf. Italian *coppo* 'eye-socket'.

96 *Spalanzani*: the name comes from the famous biologist Lazzaro Spallanzani (1729–99), who helped to explain the physiology of blood circulation in man and animals, and reproduction and respiration in animals and plants.

Cagliostro: Giuseppe Balsamo (1743-95), alias Count Alexander Cagliostro, a notorious impostor who travelled round Europe, especially Italy and France, selling the 'elixir of life' and pretending to foretell the future; he was arrested in Rome in 1789, tried for propagating Freemasonry, and sentenced to life imprisonment.

Chodowiecki: Daniel Chodowiecki (1726–1801), engraver, whose works included many drawings of everyday life in Berlin; hence he is also mentioned in *My Cousin's Corner Window* below.

99 *Battonis Mary Magdalen*: Pompeo Battoni (1708–87) painted a 'Penitent Mary Magdalen' which Hoffmann saw and greatly admired in the gallery at Dresden.

Ruysdael: either Salomon van Ruysdael (1602–70) or his nephew Jacob van Ruysdael (1628–82), Dutch landscape painters.

110 *the legend of the dead bride*: an allusion to Goethe's poem *Die Braut von Korinth* ('The Bride of Corinth', 1798), in which a girl returns from the grave to join her lover.

115 *Sapienti sat*: 'that is enough for a wise person'.

119 *Little Zaches, otherwise Cinnabar*: the review of this story (*Klein Zaches genannt Zinnober*) in the *Heidelbergische Jahrbücher für Litteratur* ('Heidelberg Literary Yearbooks', 1819) maintained that several episodes were not original but taken from other stories; hence Hoffmann's rebuttal.

Callot: see Introduction.

Gozzi: Carlo Gozzi (1722–1806), Venetian dramatist; see Introduction. *Il re de' geni ossia la serva fidele* ('The King of the Spirits or the Faithful Servant-Girl') was first performed in 1765.

121 *Ruspoli Palace*: see Goethe's *Italienische Reise* ('Italian Journey', 1816–17), where we learn that the pavement outside this palace was a favourite meeting-place of elegant Carnival revellers: 'The elegant world takes its seat there, and all the chairs are soon occupied or claimed. The most beautiful women of the middle class, in charming masks and surrounded by their friends, display themselves there to the inquisitive eye of the passer-by. Everyone who comes into the area lingers to survey the pleasing ranks . . .'

Fortunatus's purse: the inexhaustible purse of the hero of a well-known chapbook.

paoli: plural of *paolo*, a small silver coin.

123 *Giulio Romano*: painter and architect (1492–1546), pupil of Raphael and later his chief assistant. The only painter mentioned by name in Shakespeare (*The Winter's Tale*, V, ii).

125 *Argentina Theatre*: Goethe says this theatre specialized in serious opera with interpolated ballets.

Prince Taer: the hero of Gozzi's *Il mostro turchino* ('The Blue Monster', 1764).

128 *'Vien . . . smorfiosella'*: 'Come here, pretty Dorina, don't look so sulky!'

the Church of San Carlo: a baroque church on the Corso, begun in 1612, its façade added in 1690.

Ciarlatano: mountebank selling alleged miracle cures.

130 *sbirri*: policemen.

131 *Cophetua*: a mythical king whose name, along with Prince Cornelio's kingdom, Hoffmann probably took from Shakespeare's *Henry IV Part II*, V. iii. 100–1: 'O base Assyrian knight, what is thy news? | Let King Cophetua know the truth thereof.'

Serendippo: the setting of Gozzi's *Il re cervo* ('The Stag King', 1762).

Queen of Tarot: from Gozzi's *L'augellino belverde* ('The Green Bird', 1765).

136 *Frascati*: a small town about 15 miles south-east of Rome.

vetturino: coachman.

139 *Chamisso*: Adalbert von Chamisso (1781–1838), a German writer of French origin, was one of Hoffmann's cronies in Berlin. He was the author of *Peter Schlemihls wundersame Geschichte* ('The Wonderful Story of Peter Schlemihl', 1814), whose eponymous hero sells his shadow to a man in grey (the Devil) in exchange for Fortunatus's purse. In 1815 Chamisso was appointed botanist to accompany a three-year expedition round the world.

141 *fritteroli*: cooks using oil and fat.

baiocco: small coin.

149 *tabarro*: cloak.

155 *Armida*: a reference to Gluck's opera *Armida* (first produced in 1777), based on the episode from Tasso's epic *Gerusalemme liberata* ('Jerusalem Delivered', 1575) in which the hero Rinaldo falls in love with the sorceress Armida.

156 *Caffè Greco*: in the Via Condotti near the Piazza di Spagna; now a national monument. German expatriates were regular customers from the 1780s onwards.

German artists: the Guild of St Luke (*Lukasbund*), founded in Vienna in 1809 by Friedrich Overbeck (1789-1869) and Franz Pforr (1788–1812), moved to Rome in 1810 and took up their quarters in the disused monastery of Sant' Isidoro. Their aim was to regenerate German religious art, and they became known as the Nazarenes. Their best-known member was Peter Cornelius (1783–1867).

157 *"Ammazzato sia . . . moccolo"*: 'Let anyone be killed who is not carrying a candle' on Shrove Tuesday. Goethe recounts this in his *Italian Journey*.

158 *Urdar*: Hoffmann took the name from the account of Scandinavian mythology in Schubert's *Ansichten der Nachtseite der Naturwissenschaften* ('Views of the Night-Side of the Natural Sciences'), where the name is explained as meaning 'necessity'.

159 *Paris rappee*: coarse snuff.

Memphis: a city of ancient Egypt where many kings are buried.

Ophioch: the name comes from Schubert, who mentions it as the Greek name of a constellation.

160 *Büsching*: Anton Friedrich Büsching (1724–93), author of an important geographical handbook.

163 *Hermod*: the name again comes from Schubert. Hermod was the messenger of the gods in Scandinavian myth.

167 *Edda*: a cycle of Icelandic poems, known as the Elder Edda by contrast to the Prose Edda, and including the Voluspa.

   Somskritt: i.e. Sanskrit, the ancient language of India, once regarded as the ancestor of all other languages, and hence appropriate to the mythical age. Hoffmann learnt about it in Schlegel's *Language and Wisdom of the Indians*, where it is called 'Sonskrito', but here Hoffmann implies that 'Somskritt' is a book.

170 *Sancho*: see Cervantes's *Don Quixote*, Part II, chapter 68: 'Now blessings light on him that first invented this same sleep.'

171 *Mauchardt*: Immanuel David Mauchardt edited the *Allgemeines Repertorium für empirische Psychologie und verwandte Wissenschaften* ('Universal Handbook of Empirical Psychology and Related Sciences'). Volume I includes an essay on 'Loss of Personality in Drunkenness'.

172 *Chiari*: Hoffmann himself connects this figure with Gozzi's antagonist, the dramatist Pietro Chiari (1711–85).

173 *Martellian verses*: the dramatist Pier Jacopo Martello (1665–1727) devised lines modelled on the twelve-syllable Alexandrine but with two additional unstressed syllables. Both Chiari and Gozzi used this verse-form.

   French poet: Nicolas Boileau-Despréaux (1636–1711).

174 *Trissino*: Giangiorgio Trissino (1478–1550) wrote, in *Sofonisba* (1524), the first Italian tragedy based on classical models.

   Speroni: Sperone Speroni (1500–88) followed Trissino in writing the classical tragedy *Canace* (1546).

   "il trotto d'asino dura poco": 'the donkey's trotting does not last long'.

184 *Circe*: an enchantress who turned the companions of Odysseus into swine: see the *Odyssey*, Book 10.

   Arcadia: an area in Greece taken as a model of the ideal rural paradise.

186 *Bergamo*: a town in northern Italy from which several characters

in Gozzi's plays are said to come; hence it suggests a *commedia dell'arte* setting as much as, or more than, a real place.

198 *Typhon*: in Greek mythology, a giant with a hundred heads; here, simply the evil counterpart to Hermod.

199 *the not-self*: parody of Johann Gottlieb Fichte's account in his *Wissenschaftslehre* ('Theory of Science', 1794–6) of how the self ('Ich') posits the not-self ('Nicht-Ich').

209 *liquor anodynus*: a pain-killing liquid.

215 *Gyges's ring*: according to Herodotus, Gyges was a shepherd from Lydia in Asia Minor who made himself invisible by means of a magic ring; with its help he introduced himself to the Queen of Lydia, killed her husband, and became king.

223 *Georg Christoph Lichtenberg*: (1742–99), professor of physics at Göttingen and an outstanding satirist. His essay 'I wish you were on the Blocksberg: A dream like many dreams' (1799) begins with an anecdote about a queen giving birth to two crown princes joined at the buttocks; it mentions the difficulty of designing breeches for them, and the differing inclinations of the two princes, one being active and the other sedentary.

Jean Paul: pseudonym of Johann Paul Friedrich Richter (1763–1825), immensely popular and admired author of humorous and sentimental novels full of word-play and allusion, which owed much to Sterne and were imitated by Carlyle. The reference is to a passage in his *Komischer Anhang zum Titan* ('Comic Supplement to [his novel] *Titan*').

Master Flea

239 *Roman poet*: Horace's *Art of Poetry* advises the epic poet to carry his reader right into the thick of the story.

242 *Blocksberg*: a mountain, more usually called the Brocken, in the Harz in Central Germany, on whose flat summit witches were said to assemble on Walpurgisnacht (30 April).

Queen of Golconda: the opera *Aline, Reine de Golconde* (1803), by Henri Montan Barton (1767–1844), was conducted by Hoffmann in 1808 in Bamberg.

262 *Leeuwenhoek*: Antoni van Leeuwenhoek (1632–1723) developed the microscope and thus was able to observe blood corpuscles for the first time and to establish that micro-organisms (bacteria and

infusoria) were animals.

264 *Sekakis*: this and Gamaheh, Zeherit, Thetel, and Nacrao are names modelled on Persian which Hoffmann took from Peter Friedrich Arpe's *Geschichte der Talismannischen Kunst* ('History of Talismanic Art', 1717).

Famagusta: this and Samarkand are names given to imaginary duchies in the lyrical drama *Die lustigen Musikanten* ('The Merry Musicians', 1804) by Clemens Brentano (1778–1842) which Hoffmann set to music.

267 *solar microscopes*: an improved version developed by John Cuff in 1743.

269 *Pantagruel*: in Book II, chapter 28 of Rabelais's *Gargantua and Pantagruel* Pantagruel picks up a ship laden with spices and attaches it to his belt.

Three Oranges: Gozzi's *L'amore delle tre melarance* ('Love of Three Oranges', 1761).

271 *Bethmann*: the actress Friedrike Bethmann, whom Hoffmann saw as Queen of Golconda in 1807–8.

282 *Swammerdamm*: Jan Swammerdam (1637–80), biologist, particularly known for his study of insects. His main work was the posthumously published *Biblia naturae sive historia insectorum* ('Bible of Nature or History of Insects', 1737–8).

312 *Mariane, Philine, and Mignon*: female characters in Goethe's novel *Wilhelm Meisters Lehrjahre* ('Wilhelm Meister's Apprenticeship', 1795–6).

314 *Jünger's Abduction*: the comedy *Die Entführung* ('The Abduction', 1792) by Johann Friedrich Jünger (1759–97).

Corpus delicti: material evidence that a crime (*delictum*) has been committed.

325 *Philo*: the Greco-Jewish philosopher Philo of Alexandria (1st century AD), author of a lost work called *On the Reason of Animals*. Hoffmann is here indulging in the humorous display of pedantic learning familiar to English readers from Sterne's *Tristram Shandy*. His knowledge was second-hand: the titles are quoted from a German translation of Bayle's *Dictionary*.

Hieronymus Rorarius: these works by him appeared in 1547.

Lipsius: the philosopher Justus Lipsius (1547–1606).

Leibniz: the philosopher and mathematician Gottfried Wilhelm von Leibniz (1646–1716) denied in his *Monadology* (1720) that animals had reasoning powers, but credited them with mental processes analogous to those of reason.

Maimonides: the Jewish philosopher Maimonides (1135–1204) thought that animals possessed will, though not reason.

Gomez Pereira: in a work *On the Immortality of the Soul* (1554), he anticipated Descartes's argument that animals are only a kind of machine.

326 *World Spirit*: this view of dreams comes from Hoffmann's reading of Schubert's *Die Symbolik der Träume* ('The Symbolism of Dreams', 1814).

339 *Rabbi Isaac Ben Harravad*: he lived at the end of the twelfth century. See Bartolocci, *Bibliotheca rabbinica*, iii, 888. [Hoffmann's note.] The story of Isaac Ben Harravad's death is Hoffmann's invention; the rest of the anecdote comes from biographical dictionaries and from a book on vampires by Michael Ranfft, *Tractat von dem Kauen und Schmatzen der Todten in Gräbern, worinnen die wahre Beschaffenheit der Hungarischen Vampyrs und Blutsauger gezeigt* ('Treatise on Chewing and Munching by the Dead in the Grave, wherein is shown the True Nature of Hungarian Vampires and Blood-Drinkers', 1734).

350 *Tsilmenaya, or Tilsemoht*: names of unknown origin, probably invented by Hoffmann.

357 *Ariosto*: the Italian epic poet Ludovico Ariosto (1474–1533), author of *Orlando Furioso* (1516).

360 *Werther's Lotte*: see the episode in Goethe's *Die Leiden des jungen Werther* ('The Sorrows of Young Werther', 1774) in which Werther first meets Lotte distributing bread and butter to her small brothers and sisters.

My Cousin's Corner Window

377 *Scarron*: Paul Scarron (1610–60), French humorist, paralysed for the last twenty years of his life.

378 *market square*: from 1815 on Hoffmann's apartment overlooked the Gendarmenmarkt in Berlin, described here.

379 *Et si male nunc, non olim sic erit*: from Horace, *Odes*, ii. 10: 'Though things are bad now, they will not always be so.'

382 *Sapienti sat*: 'that is enough for a wise person'.

382 *Hogarth*: William Hogarth (1697–1764), draughtsman and painter; Hoffmann knew not only his works but also the commentary on them by Lichtenberg.

383 *Orbis pictus*: title of numerous books which gave information in pictures; the best known was by the Bohemian educationalist Johann Amos Comenius (1592–1670).

engraving by Hogarth: 'Credulity, Superstition, and Fanaticism'.

387 *Kralowski*: owner of a large lending library.

391 *'such odd fish are necessary too'*: Goethe, *Faust*, Part One, l. 3483.

395 *Parturiunt montes*: Horace, *Art of Poetry*: 'The mountains shall be in labour, and there shall be born—a silly mouse.' Translation in D. A. Russell and M. Winterbottom (eds.), *Ancient Literary Criticism* (Oxford, 1972).

396 *bella molinara*: 'miller's beautiful daughter'. Hoffmann knew the opera *La molinara* ('The Miller's Daughter') by Giovanni Paisiello (1740–1816).

397 *meum and tuum*: mine and yours.

398 *Pyrrhus*: see *Hamlet*, II. ii.

399 *Moabit*: district near the centre of Berlin.

400 *perfervid zealots*: an allusion to the extreme patriot Friedrich Ludwig Jahn (1778–1852); see section on *Master Flea* in the Introduction.

Eirik the Red and Other Icelandic Sagas

The German-Jewish Dialogue

The Kalevala

The Poetic Edda

LUDOVICO ARIOSTO   **Orlando Furioso**

GIOVANNI BOCCACCIO   **The Decameron**

GEORG BÜCHNER   **Danton's Death, Leonce and Lena, and Woyzeck**

LUIS VAZ DE CAMÕES   **The Lusiads**

MIGUEL DE CERVANTES   **Don Quixote**
Exemplary Stories

CARLO COLLODI   **The Adventures of Pinocchio**

DANTE ALIGHIERI   **The Divine Comedy**
Vita Nuova

LOPE DE VEGA   **Three Major Plays**

J. W. VON GOETHE   **Elective Affinities**
Erotic Poems
Faust: Part One and Part Two
The Flight to Italy

E. T. A. HOFFMANN   **The Golden Pot and Other Tales**

HENRIK IBSEN   **An Enemy of the People, The Wild Duck, Rosmersholm**
Four Major Plays
Peer Gynt

LEONARDO DA VINCI   **Selections from the Notebooks**

FEDERICO GARCIA LORCA   **Four Major Plays**

MICHELANGELO BUONARROTI   **Life, Letters, and Poetry**

Women's Writing 1778–1838

WILLIAM BECKFORD	**Vathek**
JAMES BOSWELL	**Life of Johnson**
FRANCES BURNEY	**Camilla**
	Cecilia
	Evelina
	The Wanderer
LORD CHESTERFIELD	**Lord Chesterfield's Letters**
JOHN CLELAND	**Memoirs of a Woman of Pleasure**
DANIEL DEFOE	**A Journal of the Plague Year**
	Moll Flanders
	Robinson Crusoe
	Roxana
HENRY FIELDING	**Joseph Andrews** and **Shamela**
	A Journey from This World to the Next and **The Journal of a Voyage to Lisbon**
	Tom Jones
WILLIAM GODWIN	**Caleb Williams**
OLIVER GOLDSMITH	**The Vicar of Wakefield**
MARY HAYS	**Memoirs of Emma Courtney**
ELIZABETH HAYWOOD	**The History of Miss Betsy Thoughtless**
ELIZABETH INCHBALD	**A Simple Story**
SAMUEL JOHNSON	**The History of Rasselas**
	The Major Works
CHARLOTTE LENNOX	**The Female Quixote**
MATTHEW LEWIS	**Journal of a West India Proprietor**
	The Monk
HENRY MACKENZIE	**The Man of Feeling**
ALEXANDER POPE	**Selected Poetry**

The Oxford World's Classics Website

www.worldsclassics.co.uk

- Information about new titles
- Explore the full range of Oxford World's Classics
- Links to other literary sites and the main OUP webpage
- Imaginative competitions, with bookish prizes
- Peruse the Oxford World's Classics Magazine
- Articles by editors
- Extracts from Introductions
- A forum for discussion and feedback on the series
- Special information for teachers and lecturers

www.worldsclassics.co.uk

American Literature

British and Irish Literature

Children's Literature

Classics and Ancient Literature

Colonial Literature

Eastern Literature

European Literature

History

Medieval Literature

Oxford English Drama

Poetry

Philosophy

Politics

Religion

The Oxford Shakespeare

A complete list of Oxford Paperbacks, including Oxford World's Classics, Oxford Shakespeare, Oxford Drama, and Oxford Paperback Reference, is available in the UK from the Academic Division Publicity Department, Oxford University Press, Great Clarendon Street, Oxford OX2 6DP.

In the USA, complete lists are available from the Paperbacks Marketing Manager, Oxford University Press, 198 Madison Avenue, New York, NY 10016.

Oxford Paperbacks are available from all good bookshops. In case of difficulty, customers in the UK can order direct from Oxford University Press Bookshop, Freepost, 116 High Street, Oxford OX1 4BR, enclosing full payment. Please add 10 per cent of published price for postage and packing.